The Early Records of the Town of Dedham, Massachusetts 1636-1659

A Complete Transcript of Book One of the General Records of the Town, Together with the Selectmen's Day Book, Covering a Portion of the Same Period, Being Volume Three of the Printed Records of the Town. Illustrated with Fac-Similes of the Handwriting of Four Town Clerks and of Autographs of Fifty of the Early Settlers

Volume III

Don Gleason Hill

HERITAGE BOOKS
2006

HERITAGE BOOKS
AN IMPRINT OF HERITAGE BOOKS, INC.

Books, CDs, and more—Worldwide

For our listing of thousands of titles see our website
at
www.HeritageBooks.com

A Facsimile Reprint
Published 2006 by
HERITAGE BOOKS, INC.
Publishing Division
65 East Main Street
Westminster, Maryland 21157-5026

Copyright © 1892 Don Gleason Hill

— Publisher's Notice —
In reprints such as this, it is often not possible to remove blemishes from the original. We feel the contents of this book warrant its reissue despite these blemishes and hope you will agree and read it with pleasure.

International Standard Book Number: 978-0-7884-1813-0

To the Memory of

ELEAZER LUSHER,

OF DEDHAM,

For many years chosen to "Keepe the Towne Booke;"
A man of diverse talents, frequently employed
by the General Court in important public
affairs of the Colony, and at the same
time a leader at home in all
matters religious, civil
and military,

This Volume is Respectfully Dedicated.

*MAN was at first a perfect upright Creature,
The lively Image of his Great Creator:
When Adam fell all Men in him Transgress'd,
And since that time they Err, that are the best
The Printer Errs, I Err much like the Rest.
Welcome's that Man, for to complain of me
Whose Self & Works are quite from Error free.*

Nathaniel Ames (Almanack), 1729.

INTRODUCTION.

THE year of the two hundred and fiftieth Anniversary of Dedham, 1886, the Town published its first volume of printed Records, comprising the Births, Marriages, and Deaths, 1635-1845. Two years later it published a second volume, comprising records from the several churches, and inscriptions from the cemeteries, 1638-1845. At the last annual Town meeting the Town made another appropriation towards printing a third volume, to commence with the earliest general records of the Town, by means of which this book is published. It contains the whole of Book One of the Town Records, also, commencing with page 150, is a transcript of the Selectmens' Day Book, a very interesting little book, which has seen hard service, and which has not been so faithfully cared for in the past as the other record books of the Town; by its paging it would appear that at least seven leaves are gone at the beginning and probably a few at the end of the book. In cases where the entries made in the Day Book were found entered in Book One, and printed therefrom, they have not been again reprinted, references only having been made thereto.

September, 3, 1635, the Court ordered a plantation to be settled about two miles above Charles River. *Mass. Col. Rec., Vol.* 1, *page* 156. Preparations for the settlement were soon made, and we have a recorded meeting Aug. 18, 1636, [p. 20]. At the third recorded meeting, Sept. 5, 1636, "all ye names of them wch are admitted into our Society are subscribed" (twenty-two in all) to a petition to the Court for an additional grant of land, and praying that the Town might be distinguished by the name of CONTENTMENT. As a copy of this petition appears at the beginning of Book One, this printed volume begins with that petition. The prayer was granted except in regard to the name, which was called DEDHAM.—*Mass. Col. Rec., Vol.* 1, *p.* 179. At the beginning of the record of the first two meetings, however, the name CONTENTMENT was written and afterwards erased and the word DEDHAM written over it. When Book One was put into its present binding, some of the leaves at the beginning seem to have been put together arbitrarily. As now bound, after the petition and the Court order thereon, are eight orders that might now be called by-laws, passed at different dates, and in the arrangement of the matter for this volume it has been thought better to print the Covenant before these orders, and also to include with these eight orders others now bound into Volume three of the Records, as explained by a note on page 4. The record proper begins on page 20 of this printed book.

These Records are important to the student of early Colonial history. Dedham was particularly fortunate in having at the beginning men who understood the importance of carefully written records. This book contains the Records of four different clerks,—Edward Alleyn, Eleazer Lusher, Michael Powell and Joshua Fisher, and a specimen of the handwriting of each is given. The excellent style of making up the records of the meetings commenced by Alleyn was continued by his successors. The members of the whole "society," as it was called, were interested to know that their conclusions were properly recorded, for the custom was early established of reading at each meeting "that which was agreed upon at the last meeting," and confirming the same. Edward Alleyn was probably the ablest man in the original company, but an important addition was made July, 1637, when twelve new men were admitted, including the first pastor, Rev. John Allin, and Eleazer Lusher, and from that date Eleazer Lusher was an important man in the company. Upon Alleyn's death, 1642, Lusher was chosen as the keeper of the Town Book.

Lusher was a member of the first board of seven men chosen to order the affairs of the Town, May, 1639, and from that date during nearly the whole period covered by this book, and for many years after, he was one of the seven men, selectmen as they are now styled, and for many years he was also chosen to keep the Town Book. The interesting sketch of Major Lusher following this introduction, written by Erastus Worthington, shows what an important man he was in the Colony. Under such skilful hands our records read from the very beginning more like the complete records of a modern corporation than like those of a little company of hardy settlers, struggling to make for themselves a home in the wilderness. Indeed so minute in detail were the records made of their early proceedings that over two hundred large pages are required to print the records of less than a quarter of a century (and this does not include the Register of Births, Marriages and Deaths, or Record of Grants of Land).

In the second volume of the Printed Records, the whole of Book One of the records of the First Church in Dedham was published, containing a minute history of the formation of the Church, written by Rev. John Allin, the first pastor. Mr. Allin's Ms. is quoted in *Felt's Ecclesiastical History of New England*, Vol. 1, *pp.* 374–5, and Rev. Henry M. Dexter, D. D., in his exhaustive work on *Congregationalism*, page 571, says: "One of the best minute descriptions of the methods in use in New England is that of the ordination of Rev. John Allin over the First Church in Dedham, April, 1639." The late Wm. F. Allen, A. M., Professor of History in the University of Wisconsin, wrote the Editor — "It seems to me one of the most valuable documents, as illustrating the religious life of our fathers of the seventeenth century which I have ever read." A rare opportunity is thus offered in these two volumes of printed Records to study the relations of the Town and the Church to each other in the earliest days of the Colony.

INTRODUCTION. vii

This printed volume will also be found interesting to students of family history, especially to such as trace back into the early Dedham families.

It has been repeatedly stated that the period of greatest immigration to the New England Colonies was between 1630 and 1640: that at the latter date there was a population in New England of about twenty-one thousand, and that after 1640 more persons went back from New to old England than came from old England to New. "Yet so thrifty and teeming have been those New Englanders that from that primeval community of twenty-one thousand persons have descended the three and a half million who compose the present population of New England, while of the entire population now spread over the United States, probably every third person can read in the history of the first settlement of New England the history of his own progenitors." — *Tyler's History of American Literature, Vol.* 1, *p.* 94.

An examination of the index to the *Births, Marriages and Deaths, Dedham* [printed] *Records, Vol.* 1, will show that there are very few large families there recorded, the original progenitors of which (having the family surname) are not to be found upon the general Records of Dedham within the period covered by this printed volume.

The transcript of this Volume of Records for the printer has been made by Miss Martha A. Smith, the Assistant Librarian of the Dedham Historical Society, who has performed her work with intelligent skill in reading the ancient manuscript, and with a full appreciation of the importance of accuracy in such work, and who has also assisted the Editor in reading proof.

The fac-similes of autographs, fifty in number, which are found on pages 221-3-5, have been copied with great pains from various sources, from what purported to be original signatures; the one of Ezekiel Holliman was furnished by Edward Field, one of the Record Commissioners of Providence, R. I.; four more were furnished by James Hewins of the Medfield Historical Society, and the rest by Julius H. Tuttle, Assistant Librarian of the Massachusetts Historical Society and Editor of the *Dedham Historical Register*, who has prepared the whole collection for electrotyping, and who has also contributed the index of subjects and in many other ways rendered valuable assistance to the editor. The tail-piece, page 220, was contributed by Archibald I. Lawrence of Dedham, a pen and ink sketch of articles in the Historical Society Library, where the editorial work upon this volume has been done.

Some of the signs used may need explanation, viz:

[*] The asterisk inside brackets is used to indicate that the words included in the brackets were erased in the original Ms.

† The dagger indicates that in the original manuscript there is a check mark, in some instances looking like an erasure, but which was intended to show that the matter had been recorded elsewhere, generally used in regard

to grants of land, though sometimes used where memorandum was made of something subsequently to be done, which when done was checked off.

The words *indented in italics* are from the margin of the original.

[× × ×] Crosses inside brackets are used to indicate that something was omitted because herein previously printed.

[   ] Space within brackets indicates words illegible, and words within brackets doubtful.

c̃. expedic̃on — expedition. ō. Deacō — Deacon.
m̃. com̃on — common. p. par, per, por – pson—person.
ñ. alieñ — alienation. p. pro – pporc̃on — proportion. pp — proper.

In the index of names, if the same name appears several times on the page it is only indexed once, thus differing from the plan adopted in the index of the two previously printed volumes of Dedham Records.

The New England Historical and Genealogical Society, a few years ago, made an effort to bring home to town officials the importance of printing town records, and a few cities and towns have already undertaken this work. See *Third Report on the Custody and Condition of the Public Records*, to the Legislature, 1891, *pp*. 101–3, by the Commissioner on Public Records. The establishment of that office was an important measure and Robert T. Swan, the Commissioner, has done the State an important service, and his reports are among the most valuable public documents issued by the State. Mr. Swan also has urged upon towns the importance of printing their records. I would here express my concurrence with Mr. Swan as to the importance of printing records, and also my confidence of the feasibility of such work, whenever it is undertaken in the right spirit and not simply for pecuniary gain.

The Records of Watertown, one of the most ancient settlements of Massachusetts, are now in the hands of the printer and will soon be published, and the committee in charge thereof can rest assured that their labor of love will be appreciated, and as quite a number of the first settlers of Dedham came here from Watertown, their records will be interesting to many readers of this volume.

With thanks to all who have rendered assistance and encouragement in this work, this Third Volume of Dedham Records is submitted, in the hope that the public will enjoy reading as much as the Town Clerk has enjoyed editing this book of Ancient Records.

Don Gleason Hill
Town Clerk.

DEDHAM, MASS., Dec. 1, 1892.

ELEAZER LUSHER.

By Erastus Worthington.

Among the twelve men who were admitted as townsmen, and who subscribed to the Covenant of the original Company, in Dedham, on the eighteenth of July, 1637, was Eleazer Lusher. Although that list included Mr. John Allin, Mr. Timothy Dalton, Michael Metcalf, Anthony Fisher and others, men of character and influence, who were a distinct accession to the infant society, yet when we consider the long and distinguished service he rendered subsequently, both to the Town and Colony, to Eleazer Lusher must be accorded the highest place. Concerning his English history nothing as yet can be ascertained, although some search has been made. His name was uniformly written without the prefix, which the Puritans were careful to place before the names of those who had received a Master's degree from any of the colleges in the University of Cambridge, England. Though a devout man, and one of the chosen seven who founded the Dedham Church, yet among those who were considered as eligible to the office of pastor, teacher or elder, his name does not appear. These facts, considered in connection with the great aptitude he exhibited for civil and military affairs, lead to the inference that he had not been educated to become a religious teacher. But of his superior capacity and thorough training, the records of the Town and of the General Court furnish conclusive and abundant evidence.

The civil offices in the Town, which Lusher held almost continuously from the time of his arrival to the year of his death, indicate in some degree the extent of the public service he rendered there. From October 28, 1642, not continuously but with few intervals, in all twenty-one years, he held the office of Town Clerk, and for twenty-nine years he was chosen one of the seven men "for the regulating of the planting and prudential affairs of the town," as the Selectmen were first called. The first records of the Town were the work of Edward Alleyn, who came with the original company and they testify to his accuracy and ability. But in the time of Lusher there appear to be greater fulness and completeness in the records, as well as a more systematic arrangement. Undoubtedly Lusher, being one of the seven men, and devoting for some years nearly his whole time to public business, originated, in some instances the substance, as well as the form of the record. A careful study of the ordinances or by-laws printed in the early part of this volume, forty-eight in number,[1] will show a surprising comprehensiveness not only of small matters incidental and necessary to planting a new settlement in the wilderness, but also of things having a broader import and belonging to an advanced civilization. Many of them in form and substance seem more like the laws of the Colony than the by-laws of a town. From internal evidence these ordinances appear to have been adopted at different times, but they are all recorded in Lusher's handwriting, and were no doubt collated and arranged by him, if he did not frame them, as is quite probable. How well his services to the Town were appreciated by the generation that followed after his time and while he was remembered, may be known from a couplet which was then repeated:—

> When Lusher was in office all things went well,
> But how they go since it shames us to tell.[2]

These services of Lusher received a substantial recognition from his townsmen early in his career, in the gift of lands. It was the custom of the settlers, besides making general dividends of lands to each owner of lots in the Town, to grant unappropriated lands as a recompense for public services. Accordingly at a general meeting of the townsmen, held Jan. 2, 1642–3, the following order was passed :

Whereas Eleazer Lusher hath been more than ordinarily employed in public service in Town affairs, to his great damage and loss of time, it was therefore the mind of the Town, declared by vote, that the seven men now to be chosen, should make him some recompense in this division of lands.[3]

It was in the public business of the Colony however, that Lusher found a wider field for the exercise of his peculiar fitness for duties requiring judgment, skill and capacity. From 1640 to 1662, with the exception of a few intervening years, he was chosen a Deputy or Representative from the Town to the General Court. In 1662 he was chosen one of the Court of Assistants

---

[1] *Infra*, p. 4-19. [2] *Worthington's History of Dedham*, p. 50. [3] *Infra*, p. 92.

or Magistrates. This was the higher legislative body of the Colony, and it was also the highest judicial tribunal. To this latter office Lusher was annually chosen up to 1672, the year of his death. The records of the General Court show, that both as Deputy and Assistant he was active and prominent. Besides his attendance upon the regular sessions, after 1650, Capt. Lusher, as he was then called, was quite constantly employed on various special committees and commissions, to which he was appointed by the General Court. A brief enumeration of these trusts will indicate the high degree of confidence which was reposed in him.

In 1650 he was appointed with Capt. Humphrey Atherton to agree with Plymouth Court "concerning the title to land called Shauwamett and Patuxit, and the protection of the English and Indians there, according to our agreement." In the same year, he was one of a committee to settle the boundary line of Watertown and Sudbury. In 1652 he was appointed at the head of a committee to lay out the boundaries of the Indian plantation at Natick. In 1657 he was authorized to act as a Special Commissioner or Magistrate, to hold Courts in Dedham and Medfield. In 1661 he was appointed with "magistratticall" power, to take proceedings against vagabond Quakers at Dedham. In 1662 he was appointed to hold County Courts at Salisbury, Hampton and Dover. In the same year he was appointed as sole commissioner in the place of Capt. Humphrey Atherton deceased, to perfect the work of running the boundary line between the Massachusetts and Plymouth Colonies. In 1663 he was appointed with Maj. Gen. Leverett to settle some differences with Rhode Island, and in 1665 he was sent on a commission to the County of York, to allay some disturbance or "reviling of the government there."

In 1661 he was one of an important committee of twelve leading men of the Colony, of which Mr. Bradstreet was the head, "to consider and debate such matter or thing of public concernment touching our patent, laws and privileges and duty to his Majesty, as they in their wisdom shall judge most expedient, and draw up the result of their apprehensions." This was just after the Restoration of Charles II, when much disquiet existed in the Colony concerning the disposition of the king towards the Charter, which the colonial authorities guarded with jealous care.

In May, 1672, Major William Hathorne and Major Eleazer Lusher were appointed by the General Court "to make diligent inquiry in the several parts of this jurisdiction, concerning anything of moment that have past, and in particular of what hath been collected by Mr. John Winthrop Sen, Mr. Thomas Dudley, Mr. John Wilson Sen, Capt. Edward Johnson or any other, that so matter being prepared, some meete person may be appointed by this Court to put the same into form, so that, after perusal of the same it may be put to press." Though it does not appear that the committee made any formal report, and the General Court took no further action upon the subject until 1679, when a committee was appointed to peruse Hubbard's History of New England with a view to its publication, it has been thought that the materials collected by the committee of 1672 were placed in Hubbard's hands. An interesting letter, written by Maj. Lusher to Governor John Winthrop, Jr., of Connecticut, inquiring concerning the writings of his father, the late Governor Winthrop of Massachusetts, shows that Major Hathorne had left that part of the work to him.[1]

Perhaps the most important and responsible duty which was assigned to Major Lusher by the General Court was that of collating and revising the laws of the Colony, for which he was appointed at the head of a committee, by an order of the General Court passed May 31, 1670. The order is significant of the confidence which was reposed in his capacity for such work.

Whereas there is a great want of law books for the use of the several Courts and inhabitants of this jurisdiction at present, and very few of them that are now extant or complete containing all laws now in force amongst us, it is therefore ordered by this Court, that Major Eleazer Lusher, Capt. Thomas Clarke, Capt. Edward Johnson, Capt. Hopestill Foster, Capt. George Corwin and Capt. Joshua Hubbard, or any four of them, whereof Major Lusher to be one, shall and hereby are appointed to be a committee to peruse all laws now in force, to collect and draw up any literal errors or misplacing of words or sentences therein, or any liberties infringed, and to make a convenient table for the ready finding of all things therein, that so they may be fitted for the press, and the same to present to the next session of this Court, to be further considered of and approved by the Court.[2]

The laws of the Colony at this time were printed for each year, and in 1648 the laws were first collated and were printed in 1649. In 1659 the work of collating and revising the laws was again undertaken, and the edition was published by order of the General Court in 1660. The preface to this edition

---

[1] *Mass. Hist. Coll. 5th Series, Vol.* 1, *p.*417. The letter is dated "Dedham 27. 5. 72."
[2] *Mass. Col. Rec, IV. Part II.* 453.

recites that "the Bookes of Lawes of the first impression, not being to be had for the supply of the Country put us upon a thought of a second." In 1670, as it appears from the language of the order just cited, a similar want had arisen. The committee, of which Major Lusher was the head, made its report at the October session of 1670,[1] when it was very critically considered, and many verbal amendments made, which are printed in the General Court Records. At the May session of 1671, it was ordered that the book of laws be printed with a table and notes of repealed laws. It seems, however, that it was not printed under this order, for a similar order was passed May 15, 1672, and it was printed that year. Its title was:

The General Laws and Liberties of the Massachusetts Colony, Revised & Reprinted by order of the General Court holden at Boston, May 15, 1672. Edward Rawson, Secr. Whosoever resisteth the Power resisteth the ordinances of God and they that resist, receive to themselves damnation. Rom. 13.2 Cambridge. Printed by Samuel Green For John Usher of Boston 1672.

As to what portion of this critical labor was done by Major Lusher no exact information has been obtained, but from his known capacity and his position at the head of the Committee, it may fairly be inferred, that much of it devolved upon him. It was printed in the last year of his life, and it may be regarded as the best memorial of his eminent usefulness in the affairs of the Colony.[2]

Such in outline, were the civil offices held by Major Lusher, and such were the varied and extended civil services he rendered in both Town and Colony. But to all these he superadded a military service in which he attained a high rank, and by his military titles he is best known. In 1648, upon the petition of the town of Dedham, he was appointed Captain of the train band. This office was neither a sinecure nor an empty honor, as the inhabitants were required to assemble for a weekly training.

He was also one of the founders of the Ancient and Honorable Artillery

---

[1] The original report of this Committee, made Sept. 29, 1670, is now among the archives at the State House. It is carefully drawn up in Major Lusher's handwriting, and proposes many verbal and other amendments to existing laws. It is signed by Major Lusher first, and afterwards by the other four members of the Committee.

[2] Copies of the Edition of 1672 are extremely rare. There is one in the State Library and another in the Library of the Boston Athenaeum. A copy was sold with the Library of George Brinley at New York, in March, 1879, for $130, which is in the State Library at Hartford, Conn.

Company, and in 1646 and 1647 was an Ensign and Lieutenant of that corps. Finally he was chosen Major of the Suffolk Regiment, which was the rank and title of its commanding officer. Under a law of the Colony the title of the Commander of a regiment was Sergeant Major, and he was chosen by the County. No record when Major Lusher was chosen to this office has been found, and it is not known how long he served, but he is often referred to in the General Court Records as Major Lusher, and once as the Worshipful Major Lusher.

The services of Major Lusher were recognized by the General Court in two grants of land, one of two hundred and fifty acres in 1659, which were located in Medfield in 1665, and the other, of five hundred acres in 1664, which were located near Concord, in 1666.

The records of Dedham do not furnish complete information concerning the family of Major Lusher. It is certain, however, that he was married when he came to Dedham in 1637, and that his wife came with him. In the history of the formation of the Dedham Church by Mr. Allen[1], it is stated, that among those who were joined to the Church during the winter of 1638, was "the wife of Eleazer Lusher," but her christian name is nowhere given, and there is no record of her death. In the record of deaths in 1638, appears the name of Samuel Lusher "deceased the 30 of the 10 m°."[2] It will be observed that this date is near the time when Mrs. Lusher was admitted to the Church, and in the record of her admission an allusion is made to her afflictions. Connecting this record with the fact, that elsewhere Major Lusher appears to be the sole representative of the name in the Town or Colony, the inference that Samuel was the son of Major Lusher, seems to be reasonable and satisfactory.

But in 1662 Major Lusher was married to a second wife. This appears from the records of Charlestown by the following entry:[3]

"Eleazer Lusher (Capt.) Dedham m. Mary Gwinn Aug. 8 1662."

It further appears that Mary Gwinn was the widow of John Gwinn of Charlestown. Her maiden name is not stated by Wyman, but an examination of her will, discloses that she was the sister of Jonathan Bunker of Charlestown, and of Martha, the wife of John Starr of Boston. These were

---

[1] *Dedham Church Records* (Hill), p. 14.
[2] *Dedham Births, Marriages and Deaths* (Hill), p. 127.
[3] *Genealogies and Estates of Charlestown* (Wyman), pp. 450, 636.

the children of George Bunker of Charlestown, of whom, Savage says, "he owned the summit of that hill of glory bearing his name."[1] George Bunker had a daughter Mary, according to Wyman, so that the identity of Mrs. Mary Lusher, with Mary the daughter of George Bunker, is fully established.[2]

Major Lusher died November 13, 1672, and his wife died on the twenty-sixth of the following January. The wills of both were proved together, Feb. 6, 1672-3, and are now on file in the Suffolk Registry. Major Lusher's will is written in his own clear and uniform handwriting, and is apt and exact in its forms of expression.

In the published Journal of the Rev. William Adams, not then ordained as the second minister of Dedham, but who had received a call and preached there before accepting it, occur these entries made in November 1672:[3]

13. Major Lusher mortuus.   18. Sepultus.
24. Concionem habui funebrem qualem qualem Dedhamiae in
    obitum Majoris Lusher Armigeri.

In January 1672-3, there is this further entry:
Jan. 26. Mrs. Lusher widow of Maj. Lusher Esq. died.

Major Lusher died without children, and no one bearing the surname of Lusher has since been known among us. Indeed the name apparently has become extinct.[4] But as a given name, the name of Lusher has been transmitted since 1685, through successive generations in a branch of the Gay family. In Maj. Lusher's will, it is stated that Lydia Starr, the daughter of Martha, the sister of Mrs. Lusher, had lived in his family from infancy, and she received legacies and lands by the wills of both Major and Mrs. Lusher. Lydia Starr was afterwards married to Nathaniel Gay, and the name of Lusher has been repeated in each generation of their descendants.

Maj. Lusher's house lot was on the easterly side of East street,—"the highway four rod broad"—and the second lot southerly from the present Walnut street. At the time of his death, the following entry was made in the Church book, as it is found in the Century sermon of Mr. Dexter, preached in 1738:[5]

---

[1] *Genealog. Dict. (Savage) Vol. I., p.* 299.
[2] *Dedham Historical Register, Vol. II., pp.* 131, 135.
[3] *Mass. Hist. Coll.* 4th *Series, Vol. I, p.* 18.
[4] *Suffolk Surnames, (N. I. Bowditch) p.* 253.
[5] *Century Discourse,* by Rev. Samuel Dexter, Nov. 23, 1738 (Second Edition), and note, *p.* 26.

Major Eleazer Lusher, a man sound in the faith, of great holiness and heavenly mindedness, who was of the first foundation of this Church, and had been of great use, as in the Commonwealth so in the Church, especially after the death of the Rev. Pastor thereof, Mr. John Allin, departed this life, Nov. 13, 1672.

Capt. Edward Johnson, the author of *Wonder Working Providence*, and who was often associated with Major Lusher in the public business of the Colony, describes him as "one of a nimble and active spirit, strongly affected to the ways of truth;" and again, as "one of the right stamp and pure mettle, a gracious, humble and heavenly minded man."[1]

---

[1] *Wonder Working Providence*, by Capt. Edward Johnson. (Poole's Edit.) *pp.* 110, 191.

NOTE. An article in the *Dedham Historical Register*, Vol. II, p. 93, presents satisfactory evidence that Major Lusher's tomb in the Old Parish Cemetery is now marked by a slab of slate, bearing an inscription with the name of Timothy Dwight.

THE PETICION

1 May it please this Honourd Court to Ratifie vnto your humble petitioners your grante formerly made of a Plantacion aboue the Falls that we may posesse all that Land which is left out of all former grants vpon that side of Charles Riuer. And vpon the other side five miles square. To haue and enjoye all those Lands Meadowes. Woodes and other grounds. together with all the Waters and other benifits what so euer now being or that may be within the Compasse of the afore said Limits to vs with our ascociats and our assignes for euer.

2 To be freed from all Countrey Charges for foure yeares. And millitarye excercises to be onely in our owne Towne except som extraordinary occasion Require it

3 That such distribution or Alottm^{ts} of Lands Meadowes woods &c within our said limits as ar done and pformed by the Grantees their successors or such as shall be deputed there vnto : Shall and may stand for good assureance vnto the seuerall posessors ther of and thier assignes for euer

4 That we may haue Countenance from this Honoured Courte for the well ordering of the Nonage of our scocietie according to the best rule. And to that purpose to assigne vnto vs a Constable that may regard peace and trueth.

5 To distinguish our Towne by the name of Contentment or otherwise what you shall please.

6 And lastly we intreate such other helps as your Wisdoms shall knowe best in favour to grante vnto vs for our well empveing of what we ar thus entrusted withall vnto our pticular but especially vnto the genrall good of this whole weale publike in succeeding times.

Subscribed by all that haue vnder written in Coven^t at [p^{r}s^t]

1636 The 10th of ye 7 Moneth this Peticion was published in a full Genrall Court and granted as followeth : vizt

1 That this Plantacion shall haue 3 yeares Immunitie from publike charges

2 That our Towne shall beare the name of Dedham

3 All the rest of ye Peticion fully granted by a genrall voate. freely and cheerefully with out any exception at all where vpon this short Order was drawen vp and Recorded by ye Secretary Mr Bradstreete

Ordered y^t the Plantacion to be setled aboue Charles Riuer shall haue. 3 yeares. Immunitie from publike Charges. as Concord had. to be accounted from the first of Maye next. and the name of the said Plantacion is to be Dedham.

To inioye all that Land on the Easterly and southerly side of Charles Riuer. not formerly Granted. vnto any Towne or pticular pson. And allso to haue 5 miles square on ye other side of the River

This Draught: or Tract of our Plantacion. being p^rsented vnto the Court Genrall. after publishing of our Peticion. It pleased the said Court. by a full consent. to grante our said Towne of Dedham to extend euery waye according to the same forme there in Delineated. without any contradiction at all made of. or concerning the same. being viewed by the whole Courte.

Dedham, Towne Booke, for the Entering, and Recording, of all such Orders as ar or shall be for the Gouerment there of as followeth,

THE COVENANT

1 We whose names ar here vnto subscribed. doe. in the feare and Reuerence of our Allmightie God, Mutually: and seuerally pmise amongst our selues and each to other to pffesse and practice one trueth according to that most pfect rule. the foundacion where of is Euerlasting Loue :

2 That we shall by all meanes Laboure to keepe of from vs all such. as ar contrarye minded. And receaue onely such vnto vs as be such as may be pbably of one harte, with vs as that we either knowe or may well and truely be informed to walke in a peaceable conuersation with all meekenes of spirit for the edification of each other in the knowledg and faith of the Lord Jesus : And the mutuall encouragm^t vnto all Temporall comforts in all things : seekeing the good of each other out of all which may be deriued true Peace

3. That if at any time difference shall arise betwene pties of our said Towne. that then such ptie and pties shall p^rsently Referre all such difference. vnto som one. 2 or. 3 others of our said societie to be fully accorded and determined. without any further delaye. if it possibly may bee :

4 That euery man that now. or at any time heereafter shall haue Lotts in our said Towne shall paye his share in all such Rates of money. and charges as shall be imposed vpon him Rateably in pportion with other men As allso become freely subiect vnto all such orders and constitutions as shall be necessarielly had or made now or at any time heere after from this daye fore warde. as well for Loueing and comfortable societie in our said Towne as allso for the psperous and thriueing Condicion of our said Fellowshipe

especially respecting the feare of God in which we desire to begine and continue. what so euer we shall by his Loveing fauoure take in hand
5 And for the better manefestation of our true resolution heere in. euery man so receaued: to subscribe heere vnto his name. there by obligeing both himself and his successors after him for euer. as we haue done

Names subscribed to the Couenant as followeth:

Robert: Feke
Edward: Alleyn
Samuell: Morse
Philemon Dalton
John: Dwight
Lambert: Generye
Richard: Euered
Ralph: Shepheard
John: Huggin
Ralph: Wheelock
Thomas Cakebread
Henry: Philips
Timothie Dalton
Thomas Carter
Abraham Shawe
John Coolidge
Nicholas Philips
John: Gaye
John Kingsbery
John Rogers
Francis Austen
Ezekiell Holleman
Joseph Shawe
William: Bearstowe
John: Haward
Thomas: Bartlet
Ferdinandoe Adams
Daniell: Morse
Joseph: Morse
John Ellice
Jonathan Fayerbanke
John: Eaton:
Michaell Metcalfe
John Morse
John Allin
Anthony: Fisher
Thomas: Wight
Eleazer: Lusher
Robert: Hinsdell
John Luson
John: Fisher
Thomas: Fisher

Joseph Kingsberye
John Batchelor
Nathaniell Coaleburne
John: Roper
Martin Philips
Henry Smyth
John: Fraerye
Thomas Hastings
Francis Chickering
Thomas: Alcock
William: Bullard
Jonas Humphery
Edward Kempe
John Hunting
Tymothie Dwight
Henry: Deengaine
Henry Brocke
James: Hering
Nathan Aldus
Edward Richards
Michaell Powell
John Elderkine
Michaell: Bacon
Robert Onion
Samuell Milles
Edward Colver
Thomas Bayes
George Bearstowe
John: Bullard
Thomas: Leader
Joseph Moyes
Jeffery Mingeye
James: Allin
Richard Barber
Thomas: Jordan
Joshua: Fisher
Christopher Smith
John Thurston
Joseph Clarke
Thomas: Eames
Peter Woodward
Thwaits Strickland

John: Guild
Samuell Bulleyne
Robert Gowen
Hugh Stacey
George: Barber
James Jordan
Nathaniell Whiteing
Beniamine Smith
Richard: Ellice
Austen: Kalem
Robert: Ware
Thomas: Fuller
Thomas: Payne
John: Fayerbanke
Henry Glover
Thomas Hering
John Plimption
George Fayerbanke
Tymoth Dwight
Andr: Duein
Joseph Ellice
Ralph Freeman
Joh: Rice
Danll Ponde
John Hovghton
Jonathan Fayerbank Jur:
James Vales
Thomas Metcalfe
Robert Crossman
William Avery
John Aldus
John: Mason
Isaac Bullard
Cornelus Fisher
John Partridge
James Draper
James Thorpe
Samuell Fisher
B Benjamin Bullard
Ellice **W** woode
Thomas Fisher

Number 1[1]   It is Ordered that whosoeuer shall receaue.
Equall Charges and posesse Lands in our Towne of what sorte so euer. either by Grante purchase or Inheritance or any other waye shall beare all equall charges with other men according to his pportion that so publike Charges that concerne the Towne may be borne and defrayed from time to time. according as any shall receaue benefit from the same

2   It is ordered : that all waters as well Riuers as Ponds
Waters free   shall be kept free from being Appriated except such as shall lye wholley encompassed within any one mans pper Lands. that so the said waters may be kept free for the vse of the Inhabitants. in comon for the vse of Fishing or other wise. as occasion may require

3   For as much as due and seasonable apearance at publike
Meeteings   Towne Meeteings ar oft times much neglected to the hin-
apearance   derance of ye seasonable dispatch of publike occasions and the discouragement of such as giue better attendance.   It is for the p^{r}uention there of for the time to com Ordered that who so euer of our Towne. that is admitted a Townesman with vs shall delaye more then halfe an houre after the time of meeteing where of he shall haue had reasoneable notice shall paye for that his neglect one shilling : and for the whole time of meeteing being absent he shall paye two shillings and sixe pence except the reasons of his or thier absence in either of the said cases. be apved of by the company assembled. or in case the pson shall declare the reasons of thier absence vpon reasonable demaund. to the select men they shall haue power to issue the same as to them shall apeare meete and in case of refuseale or neglect of seasoneable and due payment as before said, a distresse shall be taken vpon the goods of the pson so not makeing due payem^t by warrant from the select men for the time being : directed to the Constable : and for the better execution of this order according to the true intent there of : its allso ordered that euery Towneseman shall be called halfe an houre after after the time appointed is com

4.   It is Ordered by Genrall consent : that euery Twelue
Swampe to   Acre Lott shall haue foure acres of swampe granted in the
Lotts   first grante there vnto. besids what may be granted in any deuident of swampe that may afterward be layed out :   And that allso : in like manner euery Eight Acre Lott shall haue the like grante of three acres of swampe layed out as due there vnto

---

[1] The first eight of these orders are now found on a leaf bound into Vol. I, between the Petition and the Covenant, the rest are on leaves now bound at the end of Vol. IV; but similarity of hand-writing and paper, and consecutiveness in numbering make it seem probable that they all belong together, and as they were nearly all passed during the period covered by this printed volume, it has been thought more convenient to print them all together.—[ED.

5. For the p^ruention of damage offences and disturbances
Fences   in Corne Lands or other Lands to be enclosed. It is therfore Ordered. that all Fences in our Towne whether of Rayles or pales or what so euer other manner of fenceing may be alowed of against any high waye or comon Land or other vninclosed grounds. shall be made and mayntayned. to the height of three foote and one halfe. good sufficient and strong. and so carefully kept in that state free from gapps rayles left downe. or slipt out at one. or both ends. or posts broken and loose. or pales broken or vnfastened. from the twentieth daye of ye first Moneth vntill the Twelfth daye of ye eight Month from time to time and from yeare to yeare. without fayle. And whoso euer shall fayle heere in or be neglegent of the pformance heere of according to the true intent. and meaneing of this p^rsent Order as is aboue exp^rssed shall forfiet vnto the Towne and the vse there of such penalties and so to be payed as in the Order for vieweing of fences. is heere after exp^rssed

6 It is Ordered that euery man that hath an whole Lott
Meadow Lotts   shall haue so many Acres of Meadowe. as he hath of vpland. in his first grante for an house Lott. where of part of such such pcells of Meadowe as lyeth adioyneing. to his said Lott shall be granted to him in pt and the remainder shall be made vp else where

7 It is Ordered by generall consent that such as ar. or.
p'cells Townes   shall be admitted Townes men with vs haueing lesse portions
men   of Land then formerly haue bene granted vnto other men shall enioye all p^ruelidges as other Townes men. and beare all charges according to thier pportions. as other men from time to time shall doe

8 It is Ordered that some smale pcels of vpland. that lye
Vpland to mead: adioyning to the seuerall deuisions of Meadowe shall be añexed vnto the same. where it may conueaniently be layed out there vnto without p^riudice of other deuisions after ward to be layed out

9 The question concerning the power of the select men
Select:mens   being pposed in a Genrall Towne Meeteing and being in
power   a full Assembly considered. It was. for the auoideing of all scruples in time to com, by Genrall consent Ordered, that what so euer power all the whole Company of Townesmen them selues so mett togher had before any such Choice was made The very same power is now put into the hands of ye select men now chosen and so to remayne in full force. for the space of one whole yeare from the daye they ar chosen. in all things except in these thre cases. vizt 1 The admitting of men to the p^rvelidg of being Townesmen: 2 the granting of a genrall deuident: 3 the granting of Farmes 1 of 11 mo: 1650

10 For the direction of Wood reeues or such as shall from
Wood reeues   time to time be chosen to that care or office. It is Ordered that all the care and necessary power. for the execution of

all such orders that from time, to time, shall be of force, concerning the ordering. makeing. maintayning and vieweing of fences in our Towne, as allso the due pformance of the orders concerning Ladders. the apveing or disaloweing of them in respect of the sufficiencie. length. and strength. shall be in thier power. and care as allso the supplyeing of the Inhabitants with Timber. for thier vse of building or repayering houses in our Towne. or for makeing or repayering of fences and such like occasions. according to the orders of the Towne in that case pvided and in case of the breach or defect of the orders or any order in any of the cases aforesaid. it shall allso belong to thier office to demand & receaue such penaltie or penalties as by the order or any order in force in each case respectiuely is required. and the same so receaued to keepe in a true bill and that bill to deliuer som time in the Nyenth Moneth from yeare to yeare vnto the select men for the time being or to som one of them. that so they may dispose of the said sumes for the vse of the Towne. or in case of refuseall of payem^t duely made vpon reasoneable demaund vpon any offender as aforesaid. then they shall deliuer the bill of debts thvs refused to be payed in any the cases aforesaid. to the selectmen in the first fitt season. who shall direct a warrant to the Constable. for the due levieing all such penalties for the vse of the Towne

Swine 10 For the p^{r}venting of damage that might com by swine. it is Ordered that who so euer shall finde any swine at libertie abroad in any comon Land high waye or in any mans Land except the owners of the swine after the last daye of the first Month from time to time that is not sufficiently yoaked shall haue heereby power & libertie to put all or any such swine in to the hand of the keeper of the pounde who shall not deliuer them to the owner. but vpon sattisfing the ordinarie fees due for poundage. and when so euer any damage shall be done by swine such indifferent men as shall according to the order of the Courte be chosen to viewe and value the scathe shall haue allso power to aproue or disalowe the yoakes of all such swine as by whome the damage is done and so to settle the damage vpon the owner of the fence or other wise vpon the owner of the swine if they be not sufficiently yoaked as they shall iudge most equall. but if damage be done by swine that ar vnyoaked the damage shall be borne by the owner of the swine without respect to the fence. whether it be good or badd. pvided that if it shall apeare that any swine haueing lost thier yoake and by that meanes ar found vnyoaked such swine shall not be put to the pound except the owner haue first notice there of. and neglect seasonably to yoake them againe. And it is further ordered that all swine shall be kept well & sufficiently Ringed all the yeare thorough & yoaked from the last day of the first moneth to the twelfth of ye eight moneth from yeare to yeare

*Alienatio
to certifie*

11 It is Ordered. that who so euer heere after shall receaue any Lott or other pcell of ground. lyeing within our Towne in waye of Alienation by purchase or by exchange or by any other meanes. shall within one Moneth. after any such act done make the same knowen to the Towne Booke both the quantitie and quallitie to haue the same entered. who so euer shall fayle heerein shall forfiet to the Towne and the vse there of the sume of one shilling for euery Moneth so neglected contrary to the true meaneing this p^{r}sent order and in case such forfieture be not duely payed within 14 dayes after demand i made. by the assignem^t of the select men. then a distresse shall be taken vpon the goodes of any such offender as aforesaid. by warrant from the select men. directed to the Constable for the Levieing there of for the vse of the Towne

Ladders

12 For the p^{r}uention of damage that might arise by fire vpon any house in our Towne. It is Ordered. that euery housholder in our Towne shall forth with pvide and mayntaine one good stronge. and sufficient Ladder. that may be sufficient in all respects for the speedie and safe attayneing of the toppe of the Chimney of his house vpon all occasions which said Laders shall be kept in posession constantly at: against or neere the house or Chimney wher fire is vsually made and for the greater care heere in as in a case of so great concernm^t. It is further Ordered. that who so euer being an housholaer. in our Towne. shall fayle in any the pticulars aforesaide for the space of fourteene dayes together. shall forfiet vnto the Towne and the vse there of the sum of five shillings. for euery such defect to be payed vpon reasoneable demand made. by them to whome the care of the execution of this order belonge and in case of the neglect of such due payement as abouesaide the Constable by warrant from the select men shall Levie the same by distresse. vpon the goods of any. such delinquent. And for the further encouragem^t. that Laders may be duely pvided as aboue saide it is further Ordered. that it shall be in the libertie of euery such householder. to take for the vse aforesaid such Ladder piece or pieces. vpon the Comon Land of the Towne: it being for his owne vse and not to sell as he from tme to time shall stand in need of:

Rate to gather

13 It is Ordered that henceforth. the Constable or any other that shall be deputed. to gather any Rate in our Towne, shall stand charged with the whole sume. in the said Rate. and shall not haue power to abate any man or set of any former debts. but if any shall refuse to paye. they that gather the Rate shall referre them to the select men for the time being. who shall haue power to abate or sett of: as they shall finde to be Just. And allso euery man that is or shall be deputed to gather any Rate in our Towne except the Countrie Rate shall giue Accouut there of to the select men or so many of them as they shall depute there vnto. when they shall require the same: pvided that this account be

called for within three Moneths after the rate be gathered: or ought to be gathered: And if any shall refuse or neglect as before said. to giue accounte of any such rate. being there vnto required. they shall paye for the same. to the vse of the Towne. as the selectmen shall iudge meete. that the case doe require

14 For the direction and Ordering of high way worke. and *High way worke* the p^{r}uention of neglect there in. It is Ordered. that the Surveyors for the time being and thier successors from yeare to yeare. shall apoint and by publike notice. giuen to the Towne. shall declare. sixe dayes for the high way worke: of which sixe euery Inhabitant shall pforme four dayes work according to the surveyors appointment. the last of which sixe dayes shalbe before the 20th of the seauenth Moneth: and who so euer of the fore said Inhabitants shall not haue pformed 4 dayes worke. before the last of the foresaid sixe days be past. being appointed as beforesaid shall compound for that thier neglect. with the select men for the time being. to which end the surveyors shall carefully keepe a true bill yearely. of all such worke as is pformed by euery Inhabitant. in pticular. as is beforesaid which bill they shall deliuer to the selectmen or any one of them. within fourtene dayes after the last of the foresaid sixe dayes be past which bill shall be subscribed by all the surveyors or the major number of them. And for pformance heere of as is aboue exp^{r}ssed it is further Ordered. that such of the Inhabitants aforesaid as shall be found vpon good knowledge. to be then behinde in thier worke. shall forfiet and paye to the vse of the Towne for those thier neglects. as is heereafter exp^{r}ssed: vizt

for ye neglect of one man one Carte: four Bullocks }
for each daye } 6s – 0
for the neglect in the like manner of 1 man 2 bullocks }
and 1 Carte } 4 s
for the neglect of 1 daye worke of one man   2 s

All which said sumes. shall be payed in Merchantible Corne at the currant price except the said psons can compound with ye surveyors to thier sattisfaction. before thier bills be deliuered to the select men as aforesaide. who shall not accept of lesse in this case then eight houres sufficiently empved. in high waye worke. at thier appointment. for one daye: or if they shall put out any pt of the said worke. by the piece or lumpe: they shall not compound with any pson to the damage of the Towne or at lower or easier rates then according to the former penalties pportionably. Allwayes pvided that the surveyors shall call in no other man. nor for more. or fewer dayes. then as they shall receaue in a List from the select men: and in case any vpon demand. by order from the select men shall neglect or refuse to make seasonable payement as is aforesaid then the Constable by warrant from the select men to him directed shall by distresse Leuie the same vpon The goods of the pson or psons so not makeing due payement and deliuer the same to the select men or to whom they shall assigne the same for the vse of the Towne. And it is further Ordered that it shall be in the Libertie and power of the surveyors in any of the sixe dayes. before mentioned. to accept of the helpe of hands in steade of Teames as the occasions of the Towne shall require and they can agree with any Inhabitant

15 For the p^{r}uention of damage that might arise thorough *Fences to viewe* defects in fences it is Ordered that ye Woodreeues shall yearely. som time betwixt the twentieth and the sixe and Twentieth daye of the first Moneth. carefully. and pticularly. viewe. all the Fences in our Towne. that ar in or about all our home Lotts. that lye next any high waye or comon Land. and what defects so euer they shall finde in the said Fences they shall giue p^{r}sent notice there of. to the owner of the fence where in the defect is founde. who shall within foure dayes. after such notice giuen sufficiently make or repayer the same. or else for the neglect there of shall paye to the vse of the Towne. the sume of sixe pence. in currant Countrey paye for euery such defect To which end. the Woodreeues shall demand the same and in case of refusall or neglect of due payement in reasonable time they shall giue a true & pticular Bill forthwith to som one of the select men. who shall pceed in this case according to the order in that case pvided and further allso the said Woodreeues shall keepe a true account of all such forfietures in this case as they or any of them shall receaue vpon demand as aforesaid which sumes: or a true & pfect bill of of the same they shall deliuer to the select men according as in the order in that case is required. And for as much as doubts and questions about settling or pportioning Fences in genrall or pticular: or wante of due mayntayneing or repayering fences in any season of the yeare may arise. it is therfor allso Ordered that the saide Woodreeues. from time. to time vpon notice giuen by any of the psons concerned in any of the cases aforesaid shall in due time. vpon viewe and due consideration of the p^{r}mises resolue settle conclude & determine the same as to themselues or the greater number of them shall apeare most iust and reasonable

16 For the encouragem^t of such as may make discouery of *Mines* any Mine of Mettall or other Mineralls wthin our Towne in any of the Comon Lands there of as allso for the enabling and furnishing of them with such necessary helps and accomadacions as may be necessary in any such worke that may be helpfull for priuate and publike good

It is ordered as followeth granting to all such according as is heere after exp^{r}ssed. We doe giue and grante to euery Inhabitant amongst us. that is admitted a Townesemen and to his heyers and assignes for euer. All such Mine or Mines of any sort of mettall or Minerals what so euer (Jron Mine onely excepted. vntill the date of ye Countries grante be expired). that he or they shall really discouer and finde out by them selues or any waye or meanes by them ₚcured or at thier charge in any pt of our Towne being out of y^e ₚprietie of any man together allso with such conueainecie of Land : to be layed out to them as may be needfull for building pastureing of Cattell or other needfull occasions being such as the said worke shall really require and the place is found capeable of—Allso we doe grante vnto the Grantees aforesaid Libertie to take such sufficient woode timber or stone. as shall be founde needefull for ye emₚvem^t of ye said Mine or Mines so that the said Woode or Tymber be not cutt. within one mile of any house Lott in our Towne now in being. yet reserveing. to the Towne and the vse there of. such Oakeing timber trees as the select men for the time being shall reasonably se cause to marke out: ₚvided all wayes and granted with these condicions vizt. that the said Grantee or Grantees. thier heyers and assignes shall yearely paye. into the Com̅on Treasury of the Towne the Tenth pt of all the ₚffits. which shall cleerely arise of the said Mine or Mines thus granted. after such grantee or grantees: shall haue receaued in againe such charges as they haue formerly disbursed. vpon the said worke. ₚvided allso that. it be one mile from the Towne or vpward. but if it be lesse then so much then they shall paye the eight pt of the cleere ₚffits as beforesaide. And allso that such grantees doe really endeauour the emₚvem^t therof within the space of three yeares next after the discouery thereof is made except the select men see cause to grante longer time And allso further ₚvided that no such grantee aforesaid shall bring in any ptner or purchaser. to haue share in the p^{r}mises. that is no Townesman with vs. so long as any one that is of the Towne. will buye or take of from his hand any such Mine or pt there of. vpon such tearmes as the said stranger will doe. neither shall any such Grante or grantees or purchaser shall at any time bring in amongst vs any such ptner purchaser or constant workeman as is not for his honest and peaceable conuersation aₚved of by the select men. for the time being. wch last condicion if they shall break euery such one shall forfiet his liberty of takeing woode before heere in granted

And for ye p^{r}uenting of such Mistakes or offences as may heereafter arise about the discouery or findeing of such Mines or Minerals or the further emₚvement thereof. we doe further order and declare. that who so euer of our Towne heereafter. being a Towneseman as beforesaid shall first giue notice to two of the select men whereof the keeper of the Booke is to be one of any such Mine as beforesaid. that he hath by any meanes discouered. and so discribe the place. that they may vnderstand that no other hath already giuen notice thereof. then the saide discouerer shall haue the ₚpriety of that so exp^{r}ssed reserued to himselfe the space of sixe Moneths in which time none shall haue libertye to p^{r}uent him while himselfe or his assignes make further ₚfe of what he shall fully finde and emₚve. by vertue of this former grante And further allso if any shall finde one Mine very neere another: that is allready founde out so that ther arise iust question whether it be not another pt of the same. in that no naturall bounde. that must necessarrily disioyne or difference of Mettall resolue the doubt. then it shall be accounted as one & the same Mine allready appriate by the former grante. vnto the former posesser.—And allso if two distinct Mines be founde so neere together. that any question arise concerning the Land timber or woode to accomodate the same according to the former grante and that the ppriators of the said Mines cannot agree there in. it shall then be in the libertye and power of each of the said ppriators or grantees to chuse one indifferent man and the select men to chuse another. in the behalf of the Towne. and the major pt of the men so chosen shall fully end settle and determine the same

Paynes to sattisfie
17 It is Ordered that all such men as shall heere after. by the Select men for the time being. be chosen ordered or deputed: to doe any such seruice as concerne the Towne in genrall shall be reasonably satisfied for thier paynes and time therein. at the charge of the Towne

Disorderly feedeing
18 For the pruention of disorderly feedeing of pprieties as well in Meadowes as in Cornefields: It is Ordered. that euery ppriator what so euer that hold or empve any Land in any Corne fielde in our Towne. shall yearely and euery yeare. take in all his corne. of what sorte so euer it be. out of all such Fields as lye in a comon enclosure together with others before the Twelfth daye of yᵉ eight Moneth. vpon the penaltie in the neglect there of of beareing all the damages what so euer may fall after the daye beforesaide. before which said 12 of yᵉ 8 Month. no man what so euer shall haue libertie to put his cattell of any sorte to feede in any such fielde vpon such penaltie as the Court hath allreadye apointed but after the saide 12 daye of yᵉ 8 Month. it shall be free for all such ppriators to feede in such Fields as wher themselues posesse lands as owners or vpon rente and no man what so euer shall put in his Cattell to feede: in any Field where himselfe is no posessor vpon penaltie of forfieting five shilling for euery such offence: except it be in such time as such cattell ar employed in worke there for any posessor in the same fielde. Neither shall any keeper of any hearde of Cattell what so euer put the heard by him so kept or any pt thereof into any corne Field to keepe them there to feede. though the Corne be all out. vpon penaltie of payeing of five shillings for euery offence against the true meaneing of this order. neither shall he suffer them wittingly or willingly to continue ther if thorough defect of the fence they goe in of themselues vpon the like penaltie as beforesaide or if ther be any damage done by the heard in Corne. the keeper by whose default it is. shall paye the damage. besides the penalties aforesaide. all which penalties shall be payed vnto whom so euer the greater part of the possessors of the field wher the damage is done shall apoint to receaue. the same vpon demande.

12 DEDHAM TOWN RECORDS.

Platt to take 19 It is Ordered: that a Platt shall be taken of the Bounds & Lynes of ye whole Towne, and that it be made Capeable of a distinct Bounde and Platt of euery pprietie of each mans Lands in the Towne

Fire woode 20 For the more orderly felling of firewood for the supplye and vse of each Inhabitant in the Towne, It is Ordered. that it shall henceforth be in the libertie of any man that is admitted a Townesman heere with vs. to fell any such fire woode as he shall for his owne vse stande in neede of. from time to time. all wayes pvided that no Oake trees be felled. but such as ar granted to such psons. according to the order of the Towne. in that case pvided and for euery offence comitted. against the true meaneing. of this p^{r}sent order as is aboue exp^{r}ssed. the offender shall paye to the vse of ye Towne such a penaltie as ye Select men for ye time being. shall adiudge meete. so that no fine exceed five shillings for any one Tree felling

Grants to enter 21 Where as vpon the examination of the Booke of Towne Recorde it apeare that seuerall grantes, made to sundery of ye Inhabitants of ye Towne ar not yet entered or Recorded in any of our Bookes belonging to the Towne in genrall It is therfore in consideration there of Ordered that all such Grantes. where of good euedence may apeere. shall be yet entered. which grants so now entered shall be good and sufficient assureance vnto the Grantee and his heyers for euer

Rayles downe 22 For the p^{r}uention of leaueing downe of Rayles. leaueing gates set or by other meanes stayed or held open. wherby damage haue bene oft times done in seuerall respects. It is therfore Ordered. that who so euer here after. betwixt the twentieth daye of the first Moneth and ye Twelfth daye of ye eight Moneth. from yeare to yeare. shall offend in either of the said cases aboue saide shall for euery such offence that is for takeing & leaueing downe Rayles or any rayle in the Fence of any Field or Lott. wher Corne or other croppe is groweing. shall forfiet to the owner of the Fence the full value of repayering the Fence if neede be. and the sume of sixe pence for euery such offence allthough no scath be done therby and the like sume for leaueing any gate by themselues vnderset or otherwise held open. but if scathe be done thereby he shall allso paye & sattisfie the full value of ye damage to the pson or psons so therby wronged pvided all wayes that the offence be duely pved.

Meadfielde power 23 It is by the Towne Ordered, that all the power, right or p^{r}uelidge of Towne Goverment that hetherto or at p^{r}sent is remayneing in the Towne shipe of Dedham or any thier Trustees or assignes where by they haue or did act. in and on the behalfe of the Towne of Meadfielde shall be heerby wholley and totally Transmitted and deliuered into the hands power and disposeing of the Townshipe of

Meadfielde aforesaid in Genrall and the Select men there of and thier Successors for euer.

Great Playne waye

24 It is Ordered. that the waye leading from the Towne to the Greate playne. shall be taken care of to be made. and kept in due repayerations. from time to time by the Surveyers in and by publike high waye worke:

Deuident

25 It is Ordered. that the Land. now to be layed out in a Genrall deuident shall be first Surveyed: at the Townes charge and deuided vnto the Inhabitants by the rules of persons and estates: each person in the Towne what so euer. being an Inhabitant: shall receaue as much there in as eight pounde Estate:

Purchasd Lands

26 The ppriators of the Purchased Lands haue Joyntly agreed and Ordered for the better Jmpvement there of. that the said Meadowe. be deuided. in to foure parts according to the number of ppriators. in each part and haueing cast Lotts wher each part shall be. the ppriators in the Jland ar to begin next the little Bridge and so measure North warde so much as fall to thier pportion•and the Inhabit vpon the Middle Playne ar to be next to the Iland deuision and the East Street deuision to lye next them of the Middle playne and ye smoothe playne deuisiō is to lye most Northward. And it is agreed. that what is wanting of the said purchased Lands. shall be made vp in vpland wher it may conueaniently be founde for each deuision

Booke keepeing: recompence:

27 For the recompence of such writing as shall from time be done for The Towne in genrall. or otherwise for any the Inhabitants ther of: being such as ought to be pvided for. by order by the Towne It is Ordered that who so euer shall hereafter from time to time be chosen to keepe the Towne Booke and that shall accept therof shall haue for the entering in the Record in our Towne Booke. & the coppie deliuered to the person. whom it shall concerne wherin onely one pcell is exp^{r}ssely bounded by the Abuttm^{ts} there of sixe pence and for euery Coppie wherin more then one pcell is so discribed. he shall haue for the first pcell sixe pence as aforesaid and for each other therein discribed by the Abuttments one penye be they more or fewer these to be payed as beforesaide by the p^{r}sent posessor of the Land so Alienated. And for euery grante made by the Towne he shall haue for the entering & the Coppie there of sixe pence to be payed by the grantee. And the Transcribeing of each of these in each case aboue exp^{r}ssed shall be done according to Court Order in that case pvided. by the said keeper of ye Towne Booke as payed for in the saide recompence. before exp^{r}ssed. without expecting any more. And further: he shall haue for the entering of each Towne order sixe pence to be payed & sattisfied. by the Towne from time to time

DEDHAM TOWN RECORDS.

Rates to asesse & Levie

28 For the setling of one constant. and knowen waye: in the makeing and Levieing of all Towne Rates what so euer. It is Ordered that all Towne Rates as aforesaide. shall be Asessed and Levied vpon the p^{r}sent posessor of houses. Lands. or Cattell. whether owners or hyeres by the yeare or other wise: whether by the yeare or for a longer time

Tymber. 6 Monthes

29 For the p^{r}uenting of the Waste of Timber in our Towne by any Inhabitants ther of that shall haue grante of Timber for thier supplye according to the Order of the Towne. in that case $p$vided It is Ordered that whosoeuer of y^e Inhabitants. aforesaid. that shall haue grante of Timber for his supply in what he standeth in need of. for any vse in the Towne & not to sell: being such as he or they haue not of thier owne Lands formerly granted them or thier p^{r}decessors: and shall let the said Tymber or any pt therof Lye vnem$p$ved. more then the space of sixe monthes after the same is felled. shall forfiet all the same timber so left wholley into the hands of y^e Towne. to be disposed of by the Wood reeues from time to time by new grante at thier discretion $p$vided allwayes that this shall not p^{r}iudice or hinder any speciall grante made: or to be made. to any pson in $p$ticular: of longer libertie

Canooes

30 For as much as diuers men that haue Canooes for thier necessary vse and occasions haue complayned of great wronge done to them. by seuerall psons in takeing awaye thier said Canooes: wthout thier Leaue or knowledge. which haue bene much to the trouble and damage of ye saide owners: therfore in consideration and for ye p^{r}uention thereof It is Ordered: that if any pson w^{t}soeuer after the daye of the publication heereof shall Remoue or take awaye any Canooe or Canooes. wthin our Towne from the place wher the owner or his Assignes haue left or fastened the same. from time to time. without Leaue or consent from the owner thereof first had or attayned. shall for euery such offence. Forfiet to the owner thereof or to his Assignes: the sume of one shilling. or if the said Canooe be so taken awaye or Remoued that the owner or his Asignes be disappointed of the vse therof. the space of one whole daye or more. then the person or persons that did remoue the same. shall paye to the owner thereof or his assignes double the damage. w^{t}soeuer may be made appeere. that was susteyned therby. to be recouered in both cases. by Legall $p$ceedings. as other debts in case the same be not payed quietly otherwise

Wayes to cleere

31 It is Ordered. that if any pson wthin our Towne w^{t}so euer shall after the publication heere of. Encumber. Interupt. or Anoye. any high way or drawen waye in y^e Town or in the woods. by felling any Tree or Trees crosse or into any such waye either by ye Body or Topp or any pt thereof and doe not forth wth before he or they dept from the same. fully and sufficiently take the same awaye. and cleere

the waye. he shall paye and sattisfie. for euery such Tree so felled. to ye Anoyeance of any such waye as afore saide. the sume of Twoo shillings. to him or them that shall first giue notice thereof. to ye Select men of our Towne for ye time being or to any twoo of them. And if ye pson that haue so felled the saide Trees shall not vpon demaund of the said Twoo shillings p tree. by the Informer forth with remoue the said tree or trees as before saide. then the saide pson so felling those Trees: shall for euery weeke that they lye vncleered out of the waye. paye to the Towne and the vse there of: Five shillings p tree into ye hand of the Constable for the time being.

     32 At a genrall meeteing of the Inhabitants of the Towne
Select mens dyet: 1651 It was ordered. that the Select mens dyet expended at thier Town Meeteings shall be payed for at the charge of the Towne. from time to time heereafter;

     33 At a genrall meeteing of the Inhabitants of the Towne
Schoole 20£ 1651 It was ordered that Twentie pounds p Ann: at the least shall be the settled recompence of the Schoole master for the space of seuen yeares next ensueing;

     34 At a generall meeteing of the Inhabitants of the Towne
Dp^t payed 1651 It was ordered. that all such men as shall heere after be chosen by our Towne according to Lawe and shall pforme the seruice of deputies at the generall Court from time to time. shall be payed for that thier seruice ·at the charge of the Towne. the sume and manner there of is left to the select men now to be chosen to determine

     35 Whereas it apeare vpon experience that such fire woode
Fire woode as hath bene hetherto alowed to be made vse of. as in Comon Libertie to each of our Inhabitants is now much spent and there for. for the more conueanient supplye of the Towne. more libertie is founde necessary. and that allso·such care be taken to p^rserue such Oake trees as at p^rsent or heere after ar like to be vsefull Timber. for the supplye of building. Fencing &c:

It is therefor Ordered that it shall be henceforth in the Libertie of euery Inhabitant in our Towne from time. to time. to fell take and carrye awaye. any such fire woode of the Comon Lande of the Towne as he or they shall neede for his or thier owne burning. from time to time pvided allwayes that the same be such Trees onely: as by reason of the Rottennes crookednes or other defect ar vnfitt for Timber: but if any man shall fell any such oake tree or young oake stande or plante as in a Reasoneable ap^rhension or judgement may apeare by this order is truely jntended to be p^rserued: as not being burnt at the bottom or stubb or very crooked or defectiue as afore saide euery such offender shall Forfiet for euery tree so felled contrarey to the true jntent of this order the sume of 2^s: 6^d: except such pson haue leaue from the Towne regularly the offence to be judged by the woodreeues the forfiet or penaltie to be payed the one halfe to the Informer and the other halfe to the

Towne any order or clause or pvisoe: in any order to the contrary heeretofore made is heere by repealed

pvided allso that if any Inhabitant shall fell firewood and suffer it to lye vncutt or vnset vp 14 dayes after the same is felled. it shall then be in the Libertie of any Inhabitant of our Towne to take the same and carry the same awaye for his owne vse;

Booke to subscribe:
36 It is Ordered. that all such Inhabitants in our Towne from time to time as doe not subscribe thier names to our Towne Booke of Orders. and therby declare his engagem^t to be subiect to the gouerm^t of our Towne and beare pportionable Charges therein: &c: according to the Couenant where vnto we haue generally subscribed: shall be heereby debarred all libertie of cutting firewood or hearding or putting cattell in any of the comon Lands of our Towne except such as shall by Inheritance posesse any one house Lott allready builte whose p^{r}decessors haue formerly subscribed as aforesaide.

pvided that the Libertie and power of the Towne exp^{r}ssed in the second Article of the Couenant be not p^{r}iudiced therby but remayne in full force.

pvided allso that it shall be in the power and Libertie of the Select men for the time being. to alowe and grante libertie to any Inhabitant to make vse of the Comon p^{r}uelidges before exp^{r}ssed vntill he may haue an optunitie to subscribe and is by the Towne admitted there vnto;

Dp^t paye what & how
37 For as much as it was comitted to the select men by the last genrall meeteing of our Towne to settle & determine the recompence that should be allowed to the deputies of our Towne. It is therfore ordered that euery man that shall henceforth be chosen orderly to be a deputie in the behalfe of our Towne and shall so attend the seruice of the Genrall Courte. that the Towne be not occasioned thorough his defect to chuse another. shall haue for that his seruice for that yeare he is so chosen allowed & payed to him or his Assignes the summe of Three pounds out of the Towne Rate

Schoole m^r pay: how raised
38 For the raiseing of the 20£ pann for the Scile m^r recompence: agreed vpon the last generall Towne Meeteing. It is ordered 1 that all such Inhabitants in our Towne as haue Male Children or seruants in thier Families betwixt the years of 4 and 14 yeares of age shall paye for each such to the Schoole m^r for the time being or to his vse at his Asignm^t in Towne in Currant payem^t the sume of 5^s p ann. 2 that whatsoeuer these sumes shall fall short of the foresaid sume of 20£ shall be Raised by waye of Rateing vpon Estates according to the vsuall manner. 3 that these sumes shall be payed in twoo equall parts and pportions for the space of Seauen yeares next ensueing the first daye of January Anno 1651: each half part to be payed at the end of each halfe yeare from time to time

DEDHAM TOWN RECORDS. 17

Fences to repayer: 39 Whereas the Generall Court hath Ordered that the Select men of each Town within this Iurisdiction. shall make such Orders within thier seuerall Townes Respectiuely concerning the due and seasoneable repayering of Fences within thier seuerall Limits. It is therfore accordingly ordered that all Fences within our Towne as well Generall as pticular and pticionall that ar heereafter to be made or Repayered by newe postes. shall be made sufficient to the height of Foure foote. except such Fences as ar. or shall be made of stones. which shall be allowed sufficient at the height of Three foote and one halfe. and that all psons what so euer that shall neglect or refuse the due repayering or makeing the Fences belonging to them according to Lawe. pportion pticular agreement or composition after the time allready p^rfixed Order: 15: and after due warning giuen by the woodreeues as in the foresaid Order is required: shall paye for euery such seuerall defect in his or thier Fence so neglected to be repayered. as aboue said. the sume of Five shillings: and for euery daye so neglected after that time he or they so neglecting shall paye the penaltie of 2^s & 6^d vntill those defects be sufficiently Repayered: All these penalties shall be Levied according to the manner all readye ordered. in the Order before named: and allso disposed of for the vse of the Towne as is ther required. And further the psons so neglecting shall be Lyeable to paye all damages that may arise in any pt of the time that any pt of the Fence aforesaid shall want due reparations

And further: whereas: Fenceing Timber begin to be scarce in seuerall pts of our Towne and in regard thereof as well as of other reasons considerable. It is Ordered. that all Fences that ar. or shall be made about enclosed Lands that Lye at a mile distance or vpward from any house within the p^rcinct of our Towneshipe. shall be alowed to be made of 3 Rayles pvided it be made to the height of 4 Foote as a fore said to p^ruent damage by horses & otherwise

Swine to Ringe 40 Whereas ther is much complaint of great damage done by Swine: being not kept sufficiently Ringed notwithstanding the order already pvided in that case: It is for the p^ruention therfore Ordered: that for time to come all swine of what sorte so euer. after they come to the age of Two monthes shall be kept sufficiently yoaked: continually according to the former order: in that case pvided and vpon the same penaltie therein exp^rssed. And further all swine that being aboue the age afore saide shall be founde. not sufficiently ringed. the owner shall forfiet for euery such swine or pigge sixe pence the one halfe to him that shall giue information thereof to som select man and the other halfe to the vse of the Towne. And for the more full and due execution heereof to effect: It is allso further Ordered: that if any pson shall neglect sufficiently to Ringe his or thier swine after due notice there of then that owner of such swine shall forfiet sixe pence for euery day so neglected to be payed as aforesaid. and if any offender heere in shall neglect or refuse to make due payem^t as afore saide then vpon complaint to the select men at any of thier meetings. they shall by warrant to the Constable directed leuie the same: 14: of 11 mo 1655:

Voates for Townesmen 41 It is ordered at a generall Towne meeteing that all Voates that shall henceforth be giuen for the accptance of psons to be Townesmen shall be giuen in by kernels of wheate. and Indian Corne: the wheat to be vnderstood to be for the affirmatiue and the Indian corne for the negatiue. 1 of. 11. 1655

Inmates 42 This is to giue publike notice that we the Select men vpon consideration of that charge and trust committed to vs by the Court: Title order Townships: Sect 4: doe there heerby declare. that though we haue bene willing to coniue at some and be slowe in our actings in this case hetherto: yet now we Resolue and accordingly publish and by vertue of the fore recited Lawe Order that no man (being a single man) shall liue out of seruice or sojourn in any place or Familie within this Towne or be Inmate (either single man or others without the consent and allowance of the Select men for the time being: and from time to time: vpon the forfieture of the penall sume of Twentie shillings for euery such offence continued for the space of one whole month: ye 14 of 11 mo 1655

Townsemen remoued 43 Whereas seuerall men that haue bene admitted to the p^{r}uelidge of being Townesmen with vs and therby to such rights & p^{r}uelidges and enjoym^{ts} as are anexed there vnto and yet remoue themselues and thier Families out of our Towne. It is therefore Ordered that all such psons as are allready Admitted as before saide or shall heereafter be admitted. and that haue or shall heereafter so remoue themselues and thier Families and remaine and dwell out of our Towne the space and time of one whole yeare: all and euery such pson and psons shall therby loose all the p^{r}uelidge of being or being reputed Townesmen: and all the freedoms rights and benefits ariseing from his or thier admission and if after warde any such pson or psons returne & dwell in our Towne and shall desire to renewe the forsaid p^{r}uelidge it shall be in the Libertie of the Towne in any of thier Generall meeteings to accept or refuse as they shall se cause. ye 17 of ye 10 mo. 1656:

Swine to be ringed all the year 44 For the better exsecution of thos orders formerly made about Swine that thay be suffitiently yoaked and Ringed accordinge to the orders of the towne Richerd Elice is deputed to take care of the east street and midle plaine so fare as the mettinge hovse to see the orders duely exsequted and for his paines therin the former penalties imposed vpon the owners of such swine as are not suffitiently yoaked and Ringed are to bee recauied by the said Richard for his owne vse: and vpon his neglect of his trust in not exsequtinge the towne orders he shall forfitt for every such ofence to the towne one shillinge.

And the like trust and charge in every respect that we haue commetted to Richard Elice we doe commett to John Bacon for the rest of the Towne he to recaiue the like feews for his paynes and pay the like penalties for his neglect this power to remaine in thes mens hands till other be chosin in ther rome: Dated 14: 11 m⁰ 1656

Power of viewars of Fences about remot filds
45 Conceringe the orderinge of fences about remot fillds Itt is Ordered that the viewars of fencis about the remote filds are invested with the same power concerninge Fencis about such filds: as thay are appointed vnto; that the woodrciues haue by the Towne order and to actt in all respects accordingly.

Killin of Blakbirds &c
46 Itt beinge found by much exsperience. that much Damage is done by blackbirds espetially in Indian Corne both in the Springtime and afterward and att this time more then ordanarie and no effectuall course haue ben takin for the subduinge of them which same other townes haue done and by ther exsperience haue found it much for ther advantage as also for the destroying crowes Jayes Chirie birds which also doe much harme

Itt is therfore Ordered that henceforth who soever shall kill in our Towne any of the blackbirds shall haue ninepence a dozin & for the other birds a peny a bird provided thay bringe the heads of all such birds as thay kill to sume one of the Selectmen who is to keep account of the heads so brought and the persons that bringe them that so thay may haue there pay out in a Towne rate which shall be levied vpon the arable land in the Towne

This order to stand in force till the Selectmen see case to alter it.

Dry Cattell restrayned
47 In consideration of the anoyance and trouble that haue bene somtimes formerly to seuerall of the home heardes and heardsmen by reason of drye Cattell goeing at liberty without a keeper. It is therefore Ordered. that if any Inhabitant of this Towne shall suffer any of thier dry Cattell (working oxen onely excepted) to goe at home at libertie so as any of the home heards shall be pʳjudiced by them or any of them then euery such Inhabitant shall paye to the owners of the heard so pʳjudiced the summe of five shillings for euery beast so goeing at liberty: 25 of 12 mo: 1658:

For the meting howse lader
48 Whear as it doe apeare the Towne lader that do belonge to the meeting howse and haue beene mad oncapable of sarvic in respecte of breaking and loosing ovt the staues which tend to the damage of the Towne: it is theirfore ordered: that whosoeuer shall remove or cavse to be removed the aforesayd lader excpt in cause: of fire vpon sume hovse shall forfit to the vse of the Towne for every such ofence: the sume of five shilings: 9 10 mo 1661

DEDHAM
[*Contentment]   The 18 August 1636 being ye 6: month
Assembled whose names are heervnd^r written vizt Edward Alleyn, Abraham Shawe, Samuell Morse, Phillemon Dolton, John Dwite, Richard Eu^{r}ard, Rafe Shepheard, John Coolidge, Thomas Hastings, Nicholas Phillips, John Kingsbery, John Gaye, John Rogers, Francis Austen, Daniell Morse, Joseph Morse, John Huggen, John Ellis
    And with one accord agreed vpon these conclusions followeing vizt
        1 Wheras all men that are admitted into our society doe
Informacon   First of all Coven^t by subscribeing their names to keepe of
discou^{r}ed from vs all such as shall not be fownd fitting. For wch Cause
it is necessary that every man in our sayd assembly shold give Informacon what he knoweth concerneing any man that is soe p^{r}sented vnto vs to be enterteyned. But for as much as some soe doeing & the same after becomeing discou^{r}ed by some false brother vnto the sayd ptie (& that padventure also wth some misconstruction) [   ] much emulacon may arise & faithfull pceedings [   ] For ye p^{r}vention wherof we doe order That wh [   ] of our society shall soe doe, & therof vpon good Te[   ] be evicted. He shall then henceforth be excluded [   ] Assemblyes as a Covenant breaker & as a man not [   ] to be admitted into society of such as seeke peace & ensue it. And in case of noe humiliacon for satisfaction be made then such a fyne to be set vpon him as at the next meeting after shalbe thought fitting.
        2 That ther shall not any waters wthin the compas of our
waters   s[   ] Towne become Imppriate vnto any pticuler man: but shall Rest free for the Comon benefit of the wholl Towne For matter of Fishing.
        3 That noe man whoe is in Covenant tyed vnto any other
Servants pson for service for any tyme or Tearme shalbe admitted vnto vs to Receive any Lott vntill the sayd tearme or tyme shalbe fully expired: And good testemony then given vnto vs of the same.
    Set out & measured by Thomas Bartlet Lotts for seu^{r}all men as followeth vizt.
    For Samuell Morse   12. Acres.   For Raffe Shepheard   12. Acres.
    For Philleman Dalton 12. Acres.   For Lambert Genere   12. Acres.
    For Daniell Morse   12. Acres.   For Nicholas Phillips 12. Acres.
    For Joseph Morse   12. Acres.
all these confirmed at this meeting & are Abuttalled as by the pticulers in foll: appeth
        1. Set out and measured for Abraham Shawe 12: Acres
Abr: Shawe Also graunted vnto him all that medowe wch lyeth betweene the 2: Riu^{r}s & his Lott soe farre as his Lott extendeth west-

---

* The asterisk within the brackets indicates that the words enclosed therewith were erased in the original text.

DEDHAM TOWN RECORDS. 21

ward & Southward to haue & possesse the same to him & his Assignes for ever

Graunted vnto Edward Alleyn & his Assignes for ever All that pcell of land & Medowe wch lyeth betweene the Riv^{rs} toward the East & the wood towards the West And abutteth vpon the woody hill towards the North & vpon the Cliffe of the Smooth playne towards the South And to haue soe much [   ] wood vpon tbe sayd playne as may [   ] beyonde the Cliffe [   ] wher it may be [   ] make a ditch & a bridge vpon the same through [   ] a Fence to pte ye land soe graunted from the sayd playne. Allwayes pvided John Gaye to haue his Lott   by shall haue some Medowe pcell of the same. And also that he or they maye heerafter Conferre an other Lott out of the same vnto some other Freind such an one as our society may appve of. And moreover ther is graunted soe much of ye woods as may be necessary for 3: Lotts, the sayd Edward Alleyn to haue soe much therof as shalbe fi [   ] at the discretion of Abraham Shaw Samuell Morse or Phileman Dalton, to be anexed vnto the sayd land soe graunted to him & his assignes for euer.

2 That every man that hath an wholl Lott shall haue [   ]
Medowe   Acres of medowe as he hath of vpland in his first graunt an house Lott, & [   ] pte of such medowe as adioyneth [   ] such Lot shalbe possessed by ye same man & what fales shorte is to be supplyed els wher:

DEDHAM
[*Contentm^t]   1636 The 29th of ye 6^t: Month. called August
Assembled whose names are vnderwritten vizt Rob^{te} Feke, Edward Alleyn, Abraham Shawe, Samuell Morse, Philemon Dalton, John Dwite, Lambert Genere, John Kingsbery, John Coolege, R[   ] Shepheard, John Gaye, Nicholas Phillips, Thomas Hastings, Frances Austen, Ezechiell Holliman, John Rogers, Joseph Shawe, Willm Bearstow

And wth one accord agreed vpon these conclusions following vizt
1 Ordered that m^r Robte Fekes shall haue the same
Robte Fekes   pportion of grownd for house lot y^t others haue had assigned vnto them: And y^t he shall for a Fearme haue wth in twoe [   ] of his seate, soe much vpland & medowe as shalbe sufficient, in good Judgem^t & he him selfe shall loveingly accept of.

2 Ordered y^t single men shall henceforth haue Eight Acres
8: accre Lotts   for an house lott and noe more for y^{er} first sitting downe, & soe much medowe grownd thervnto. Resolucon y^t as their [Families] increase they [   ] inlargem^t as shalbe thought fitting & soe neer vnto t[   ] former Lott as conveniently may be pformed. And allso [   ] is ordered y^t they shall haue ech of them An acre and an halfe of

swampe to be cleered in maner & forme & cumpas of such tymes as Form^{r}ly is limited vnto ye two acre Lotts.

That ye next meeting shalbe vpon ye second day of ye next week at ye 6^t: houre in ye morneing at John Gayes house.

Dedham   The 5th of ye 7: Month   Called Septemb^r. 1636.
Assembled whose names are vnderwritten vizt. Edward Alleyn, Abraham Shawe, Samuell Morse, Phileman Dalton, Ezechiell Holliman, John Kingsbery, John Dwite, John Coolidge, Richard Eu^{r}ed, John Haward, Lambert Genere, Nicholas Phillips, Rafe Shepherd, John Gaye, Thomas Bartlet, Francis Austen, John Rogers, Joseph Shawe, Willm Bearestow.

Peticon   All these being assembled subcribed their names vnto a peticon vnto y^e gen^{r}all Courte for confirmacon of [   ]
[Graunt] to be comp^{r}hended [   ] our towne whatsoeu^r is left from all form^r grañts on that side of Charles R .:. /|\ & 5 miles square vpon the other side of y^e sayd Riu^r wth certeyne privileges of exemtion from cuntry charges for 4. yeares &c.

Edw. Alleyn   Confirmed vnto Edward Alleyn that litle Iland wth y^e 2 drowned Iletts before graunted at y^e first meeting to him & his assignes forever.

Ordered y^t y^e next Fair day eu^{r}y man of our society shall meet at ye foule [   ] & assist to mend ye same and soe many as can to bring whelbarrowes

note y^t after ye assembly was disolved: m^r Robte Feke came and subscribed his name vnto ye sayd peticon.

And Thomas Hastings & John Huggin did the like at Boston. soe y^t all ye names of them wch are admitted into our society are subscribed thervnto.

The Coppy of wch peticon is in ye beginning of this Booke as also of ye Court order vpon ye same.

Dedham   [   ] month   Called September
Assembled whose names are vnderwritten vizt
Edward Alleyn, Abraham Shawe, Samuell Morse, Philemon Dalton, John Kingsbery, Lambert Genere, Richard Eu^{r}ard. John Coolidge, Thomas Hastings, John Gaye, John Haward, Thomas Bartlet, John Rogers, Daniell Morse

Confirmacon   After thanksgiving made vnto God for our good successe at ye Courte Gen^{r}all, before specefied By virtue of w^{ch} [   ]
soe made vnto vs: we doe est [   ] confirme all y^t was ordered & done by vs before this daye [   ] distinctly Red & well weyed accordingly.

DEDHAM TOWN RECORDS. 23

Collector	1 Samuell Morse chosen Collector for money to be [ ] & payd out according to such seu^{r}all occasions as shall [arise] of & conc^{r}neing our sayd Towne: And to give account therof at what tyme or tymes soeu^r, the same shall be Requiered of him accordingly.
Money	Ordered y^t eu^{r}y man shall p^{r}sently paye into ye Collectors hands according to his pportion of Lott. vizt for eu^{r}y 12.[ ] lot 18.^{d} & for eu^{r}y 8. acre Lott 12^d towards expen [ ] made at ye last Court, buying of Bookes, & [ ] of Bridge [ ] ou^r the litle Riu^r.
Swamp mended	3 Samuell Morse & Phileman Dalton vnd^{r}takeing to mend y^e [ ] betwen Watertowne & Mr Haynes his farme. it is ordered That eu^{r}y man of our societye shall pforme one dayes worke in the same, or otherwise to paye vnto ye sayd vnd^{r}takers [ ] sum of 2^s: 6^d: towards ye same worke. wch is to be begon [ ] vpon ye 4th day of ye next weeke.

4 A note Received from y^v Wo^{rpll} John Winthrop deputy Go [ ] in Recomendacon of his servant Henry Kingsbery y^e [ ] to sit [ ] wth vs: was Reade, And his Request condecended vnto only Respited vntill ye expiracon of ye tyme of his s [ ] wch is next not to violate our order formerly [ ] in that behalfe.

25 [November]

Assembled whose names are vnderwritten vizt Robte Feeke, Edward Alleyn, Abraham Shawe, Samuell Morse, Phileman Dalton, Ezechiell Holliman, John Dwite, Lambert Genere, John Haward, John Coolidge, Raffe Shepheard, Thomas Bartlett, Thomas Hastings, John Huggens

For as much as the Court Generall was pleased to depute m^r Danforth, m^r Alcocke & m^r Alleyn, to set out ye bownds of Roxebery & such Farmes as lye neer vnto our Towne of Dedham we thinke Fitting to give ayde thervnto by Thomas Bartlet, whome we assigne to assist m^r Alleyn therin; And also we assigne Daniel Morse to attend m^r Danforth in pformance of the sayd busines if he shall Requier ye same.

Wheras our Towne of Dedham being far Remote from other Townes soe that it is Requesite we shold enioye what number of people we may for our better saffety from danger : as also for other compforts depending thervpon. Wherfore we doe nowe by a generall consent order that all those wch haue or shall heerafter Receive Lott in our sayd towne: shall before the First daye of November next become Inhabitant within our sayd Towne to impve their sayd Lotts & soe shall ther constantly Remayne dwelling in their [ ] or such their heyers or assignes as shalbe appved of. And that for the space of Seaven yeares to come next after the First day of the third month next, comonly called May daye next ensueing this p^rsent daye—Except those wch are Covenanted wth other Congregaçons wch we doe order & enioyne to come & setle as above sayd wth in Sixe monthes after a Church wth officers shalbe gathered in our sayd towne & ther Inhabiting. pvided that all such pties shall in ye meane tyme make all necessary p^rparaçon by building &c: as may be Fitting thervnto.

And yf any pson or psons haveing Lott shall not pforme heerin according to the true meaneing hereof: That all such graunte or graunts made vnto any such ptie or pties shall become voyde as yf the same had never ben. And the same Lott or Lotts wth all the appurtenances shall Returne vnto the sayd Towne to be disposed of otherwise at our pleasure vnto such as will & shall become Inhitants wth vs.

For as much as vpon good consid^raçon we have Form^rly ordered y^t noe man shalbe admitted to haue Lott wth vs vnleast he First subscribeth both to pay equall share of Charges wth other men of the same pportion of grownd & submitt vnto all such orders & constituçons made or to be made conc^rneing our sayd towne: as also y^t he shalbe a man appved of by the wholl Company: wch we doe desier faithfully to maynetayne & keep vnviolated wth our best indeavoure.

Against Alienacons   Wherfore we doe nowe Further order that noe pson soe admitted & haveing Lott wth vs shall at any tyme heerafter alienate bargen sell set over or assigne the sayd Lott or any pcell thervnto belonging: vnto any other pson w^t soeu^r (not being of our society) for the tearme of one wholl yeare or more except it be vnto such as the Maior pte of our sayd wholl Company shall appve of & the same to be Recorded in the towne booke. That onely such may still be Re[   ] vnto vs, as are desiered by our first graunts. Soe y^t yf any shall soe doe contrary vnto our true meeneing heerin specefyed: the sayd Lott & lotts or pcell therof soe alienated or set over shall become voyd from ye sayd Grantees and assignes, as wholly as yf they had never possessed the same. And shall Returne vnto our sayd Towne, as free to be granted vnto any other as ever it was. Provided allwayes that what cost hath really ben bestowed vpon the same, shalbe allowed vnto the sayd pties offending, to be valewed by three vnd^rstanding men. Provided also y^t this order shall not extend vnto ye case of death: Soe that it shall & may be lawefull for any ptye soe of Lott possessed to bequeath the same by will vnto whom he shall please. And also every heyer at comon lawe after death may enter vpon ye same & possesse it as his Inheritance anything heerin to the contrary notw^th-standing.

Moreover it is further pvided and agreed vpon that th p^rsent order shall stand in Force as abovesayd For the Space & tearme of Seaven yeares next to come & [   ]longer w^thout confirmaçon of the same to be heerafter made for longer tyme:

Dedham The 31 December 1636

Assembled whose names are heervnder written vizt Robte Feke, Edward Alleyn, Abraham Shawe, Samuell Morse, John Kingsbery, Phileman Dolton, John Dwite, John Hayward, John Coolidge, Richard Evered, John Gaye, Thomas Bartlet, Thomas Hastings, Willm Berstowe, John Huggens.

First y^t wch was agreed vpon the last assembly was Read and confirmed.

Wheras Nicholas Phillips hath felled c^{r}teyne trees wth out his Lott wth out licence contrary to an order made in that behalfe. Therfore he is fyned to pay vnto ye Collecto^r for the vse of the Towne Sixe pence for every tree soe felled.

And for y^t Ezechiell Holliman hath felled one greate Timber tree for clapboard wth out his owne Lott contrary to an order made in that behalfe, therfore he is fined to pay vnto the Collector for ye vse of ye Towne the sum̃ of Ten shillings.

And the sayd Ezechiell is to paye in like manner for every lesser tree soe felled contrary vnto the sayd order the sum̃ of sixe pence for a fyne as aforesayd.

The sayd Ezechiell Holliman is moreover Fyned the sum̃ of Fifteene shillings to be payd vnto ye Collector For that y^t he hath covered his house wth Clapboard contrary vnto an order mad in that behalfe.

Clapbord Wheras c^{r}teyne of our Company are gone up to inhabite this winter at our Towne of Dedham, & y^t other materialls are not well to be had for the [   ] closeing in of their houses in such a season, wch thing being well taken into consideracõn : we doe therfore give liberty only for every such inhabitant abouesayd to make vse of Clapboard to any pte of his house for his p^{r}sent necessety from this p^{r}sent daye vntill the first daye of the third month next called May daye And not afterward y^t soe the order in that behalfe made may stand still in force & effect to all intents and purposes for wch it was soe made accordingly

Repealed
Timber tres
[* Ordered by gen^{r}all consent y^t yf any man henceforth from this day shall fell any Tree of sixe Inches thicknes in the Carfe or of any scantling aboue sixe Inches in any place wthin our sayd Towne, save only wthin his owne Lott wth out licence of such as are or shalbe deputed thervnto Contrary vnto an order form^{r}ly made in that behalfe. Shall for every such tree soe felled wth out licence Forfitt the sum̃ of Twenty shillings of English money to be p^{r}sently payd vnto our Collector for the tyme being to the vse & benefit of our sayd wholl Towne accordingly.]

[*It is ordered by gen^{r}all concent y^t yf any man from henceforth shall fell any tree lesse then Sixe inches in thicknes at the carfe, wthin ye distance of

---

* Erased by line drawn through in the original.

DEDHAM TOWN RECORDS.

One myle from the place wher the Meeting house is assigned to stand in onr sayd Towne except in his owne Lott: shall for eu^{r}y such tree soe felled Forfet the sum of twelve pence of English money to be p^{r}sently payd vnto our Collector the tyme being to the vse & benefitt of our wholl towne: y^t soe noe waest may be made in any grownds wch might become any mans Lott heerafter to his p^{r}uidise or hindrance wch we desier carefully to p^{r}vent.]

Swampe Wheras it is ordered form^{r}ly y^t eu^{r}y man shall haue a c^{r}teyne pportion of Swampe wch he is to cleer of vnd^{r}growne stuffe:
Pyne trees as by ye order appeth: And it nowe vpon viewe appeth y^t c^{r}teyn places of the sayd Swampe have many good Pyne trees groweing & other places fewe or none: Therfore we doe agree & order that eu^{r}y Lott of twelue acres may ther take Three Pynes, & eu^{r}y Eight acre Lott twoe pynes for their p^{r}sent vse. And the same to be well viewed: y^t soe eu^{r}y man may haue an equall pportion soe neere as may be of the same soe viewed: To be taken before or after ye acres be measured at their pleasure vnto whomesoeu^r ye same shall fall.

A pposicon made for somewhat to be done conc^{r}neing the 30 Acres of purchased Lands, but the same is to be considered against the next meeteing wch is to be for y^t purpose vpon the 6th day of the next weeke at the house of John Haward at 8. of ye Clocke in ye Morneing

Dedham   The 28. January being ye 11th month 1636
Assembled whose names are heere vnderwritten vizt. Robte Feke, Edward Alleyn, Abraham Shawe, Samuell Morse, John Kingsbery, Phileman Dolton, Ezechiell Holliman, John Haward, John Dwite, John Coolige, John Gaye, Joseph Shawe, Thomas Hastings, Francis Austen, Willm Bearstowe, John Huggens

First y^t wch was agreed vpon at our last assembly was nowe Read & confirmed

Purchased   Wheras ther was form^{r}ly by ye gen^{r}all Court graunted vnto
Landes   m^r Samuell Dudly 300. acres of medowe & vpland: which sayd 300 acres Samuell Morse; Phileman Dalton; John Dwite and Lambert Genere did for Twenty pownds lately purchase from the sayd m^r Dudly for the furtherance of a plantacon to be aboue ye Falls. And for that our Towne nowe named Dedham is seated neer vnto the sayd purchased lands: We are Willing to give vnto ye said purchasers the sum of Twenty pownds more for their advantage in buying ye same. Vnto wch Samuell Morse, Phyleman Dalton & John Dwite being nowe p^{r}sent have assented & accepted of. Wherfore it is nowe by gen^{r}all consent ordered that ye first 30. Lotts allredy graunted out shall paye Thirteene shillings & foure pence p Lott vpon ye Thirtith daye of this Month into the hands of Samuell Morse Phileman Dalton & John Dwite or to one of them for satisfaction of the first Twenty pownds.

DEDHAM TOWN RECORDS.   27

And further it is ordered that a c^rteyne quantety of y^t medowe wch lyeth next vnto ye litle River shall become a somer pasture for milch Cowes: And eu^ry man that payeth 13: 4^d as aforesayd shall haue the free depasturing of Twoe Cowes vpon ye p^rmises. And the aforesayd purchasers shall haue the depasturing of three Cowes thervpon forever because they haue soe loveingly Resigned the same vnto our sayd Towne. And in case y^t any man shall fayle in paym^t of the sayd money vpon ye sayd 30. daye of this month shall forfet his depasturing of Cowes aforesayd for ever. Except Raffe Shepheard for twoe lotts, Lambert Genere John Ellis, Richard Everard, John Rogers, & Robte Whitmore being absent: Which are vndertaken for by Ezechiell Holliman & Phileman Dolton nowe p^rsent And yf any of the sayd pties shall not pforme paym^t of the sayd 13. 4^d. accordingly w^thin ye space of one month: It is ordered that such pty fayleing shall forfet ye sayd benefit of his depasturing: And the same shall belong wholly vnto the sayd vndertakers as their pp Right for ever.

Moreover it is ordered that ye other Twenty pownds shalbe payd by other Thirty lotts next to be graunted vizt Thirteene shillings & four pence p lot as every man shalbe admitted, to make vp Sixtye Lotts in all. And eu^ry man soe paying 13. 4^d shall haue the like benefit of depasturing of Twoe Cowes as ye form^r 30 lotts had. And yf it shall happen y^t soe many lotts be not granted w^thin ye Cumpas of one yeare from this daye That then, all we y^t are allredy admitted shall make good to ye sayd pties whatsoeu^r is wanting of the sayd last 20: £ & haue vnto ourselves & assignes ye sayd depasturing forever.

Jo: Coolidge   It is agreed y^t John Coolidge (in consideracon of his laying downe of some Right he had in ye sayd purchased 300. acres) Is Released of y^t Iniunction for coming to inhabit w^thin 6. monthes as appeth by an order made ye 14 November last.

Ez: Holliman   Allso y^t Ezechiell Holliman is Remitted all his Fynes form^rly seased in consideracon of some moneyes disbursed by him for ye benefit of our Towne.

Dedham   The 21 February being ye 12. Month 1636 Assembled whose names are herevnder written Edward Alleyn, Abraham Shawe, Samuell Morse, Philemon Dalton, Ezechiell Holliman, John Kingsbery, John Dwite, John Haward, John Coolidge, Thomas Bartlet, Thomas Hastings, Francis Austen, John Huggens

First y^t wch was agreed vpon at our last assembly was nowe Reade & confirmed.

Ab: Shawe Wheras Abraham Shawe is Resolved to erect a Cornemill
Myll in our towne of Dedham, we doe grante vnto him Free liberty soe to doe. And for that purpose we haue nowe assigned Edward Alleyn Samuell Morse Ezechiell Holliman

Thomas Bartlet & Nicholas Phillips, or any 4: or 3. of them to accompany him & his workmen to fynd out a convenient place And viewe what Fitting [timber] is about y^t place soe fownd for y^t purpose: As also to order everything conc^{r}neing ye pfecting of ye same.

N. Phillips   Remitted vnto Nicholas Phillips all his fynes in consideraĉon of his charges in enterteynm^{ts} form^{r}ly & diu^{r}sely made.

Set out by Abraham Shawe & Samuell Morse pcell of ye wood amongst the Rocks vnto Edward Alleyn &c according to a graunt made vnto him y^e [18:] of ye 6: month to haue straight vp vnto ye m^{r}ked tree, & to haue ye same distance throughout adioyneing to ye graunted p^{r}mises vnto ye Riuer accordingly. Done in the p^{r}sents of Raffe Shepheard & many others &c The same to beginne at the Southermost lyne of the sayd 2 Lotts soe set out & measured by Tho: Bartlet & soe alongst amongst ye sayd Rocks vnto ye River the aforesayd distance throughout.

Dedham   The 23th of ye first Month called March
1636–7   The First Assembly in Dedham by whose names are vnderwritten vizt Edward Alleyn, Abraham Shawe, Samuell Morse, Phileman Dalton, Joseph Shawe, Ezechiell Holliman, Lambert Genere, Nicholas Phillips, Raffe Shepheard, John Gaye, Francis Austen, Willm Berstowe, John Rogers, Daniell Morse, John Huggens

   1   First y^t wch was agreed vpon ye last assembly was Read & confirmed.

   2   Jonathan Fearebanke being p^{r}sented by John Dwite was accepted & subscribed.

S: Morse   3   Graunted to Samuell Morse y^t necke of medowe lying next vnto ye medowes graunted vnto Edward Alleyn towards the North to have it for a medowe Lott: And yf it pveth by measure to be more or lesse then 12: Acres to be Reckoned vnto him accordingly. Also graunted vnto him. All y^t vpland wch lyeth betweene ye Rocks & ye sayd Medowe, to begiñe at ye Northermost end of those lands graunted vnto Edw: Alleyn & to extend soe farre as the sayd nowe graunted medowe extendeth towards ye North.

Hogsyeard   4   Ordered y^t in ye greate Iland vnd^r ye Rocke shall a yard be paled in for Swyne, the pale to be cut 6: foote, a single Rayle 12: Foote longe. ye posts mortised, pales to be bownd to ye Rayles wth poles & withes: wch Lambert Genere hath vnd^{r}taken to doe at 2^s. 4^d p Rod, & to build a sufficient sheåd to lodge the Swyne into the bargayne. to be payed by those of our towne y^t doe put any Swyne therinto Sam: Morse, Jonath: Fearebanke, & Willm Bearestowe or any twoe of them are to assigne the Tymber for it.

Ab. Shawe Myll   5   Wheras ther hath ben made some pposiĉons by Abraham Shawe for ye erecting of a Corne Mill in our Towne. We doe now grante vnto ye sayd Abraham Sixty Acres of Land to belong vnto ye sayd Mill soe erected pvided allwayes y^t the same be a Water Mill, els not. We order also y^t eu^ry man y^t hath lott wth vs, shall assist to breng the Milstones from Watertowne Mill by land vnto ye boateing place neer m^r Haynes his farme. It is alsoe further graunted vnto ye sayd Abraham y^t the sayd grownd & mill soe to be builte shalbe at his owne disposeing in case of sale or other alienaĉon at his pleasure. Saveing y^t our Towne shall haue ye first Refusall of it, at such a price as an other man wold Realy give for any such alienaĉon accordingly.

Edw: Alleyn

6 Granted vnto Edward Alleyn two Acres vpon the Smoth playne to lye Right before & next vnto his Iland for his better accomodaĉon in building & inhabiting his sayd Iland.

Ph: Dalton
L: Genere
Ra: Shepherd
Jos: Morse

7 Granted vnto Philemon Dalton, Lambert Genere, Raffe Shepheard & Joseph Morse, one pcell of Medowe as it lyeth vpon ye River, betwene ye barren hills & ye sayd Riu^r: in consideraĉon of their paynes taken in first discou^ry of the North side of our Towne.

S: Morse
Ed: Alleyn

Towne.

8 Granted vnto Samuell Morse & Edward Alleyn one smale pcell of medowe lying next above & neere vnto ye form^r medowe soe granted & as ye same doth: in consideraĉon of their like paynes taken in discou^ry of y^t side of our

Smale tres
Swampe

9 Wheras vpon ye 31. December last it was ordered to Restrayne trees of vnd^r 6: inches in ye carfe for being felled w^thin a myle distant from our Meeting house intended. It is nowe by vs p^rsent ordered y^t it be Restrayned vnto vpland grownd only: soe y^t all Swampes soe long as they are not lotted out, are Free for such trees to be taken only for necessary vses, wch also may further ye cleering of Swamps wch is much to be desiered.

1637   The 25th Aprill being ye 2^d Month   1637

Dedham   Assembled whose names are vnderwritten vizt Edward Alleyn, Abraham Shawe, Samuell Morse, Philemon Dalton, John Kingsbery, John Dwite, John Haward, Lambert Genere, Raffe Shepheard, Nicholas Phillipps, John Gaye, Frances Austen, Jonathan Farebancke, Daniell Morse, Willm Bearestowe, John Rogers, John Huggens.

1 First y^t wch was agreed vpon the last assembly was Read & confirmed

Th: Carter

2 Mr Thomas Carter p^rsented by Philemon Dalton was p^rsented accepted & subscribed.

Seriante

3 Ordered y^t the watches & wards shalbe carefully set & kept & all other things done & pformed according to ye order of [   ] in ye best manner we may be able. And to that purpose Daniell Morse Chosen Seriant at Armes to order the same vntill we haue other supply.

*Fr: Austen
tefyed.*

4 Wheras Frances Austen made knowne vnto vs y^t his Lott ɡveth very defective & soe Refering himselfe vnto ye company. It was Resolved by vs y^t it shold afterward be Rec-tefyed.

Clapbord

5 Wheras Lambert Genere haueing ɡvided Clapbord for his house, but hindred laying the same both by sicknes as also by some imploym^{ts} for our generall good. In wch Respect at his Request liberty was [   ] graunted vnto him for laying ye same vntill ye first of June next the form^r order to ye contrary not wth standing.

*Absence fro
meeteings*

Wheras meetings haue ben agreed vpon & tymes apoynted accordingly, it hath often happened y^t by ye slacknes of many their comeing, others haue by long attendance waested much tyme to their greate damage. It is nowe for p^{r}vention therof agreed & ordered that whoesoever shall haue Received notice of such a meeteing & shall absent himselfe one halfe houer after ye beateing of the drume shall forfet twelve pence. And yf any shall wholly absent himselfe shall forfet the sum of Three shillings & Fower pence. except ther be some greate occasions to the contrary & ye same to be allowed of accordingly in eyther of ye sayd cases.

Dedham   The 11.th of ye Third Month comonly called Maye.
1637   Assembled whose names are vnderwritten vizt. Edward Alleyn, Abraham Shawe, Samuell Morse, Philemon Dalton, John Dwite, Lambert Genere, Nicholas Phillips, Joseph Shawe, Raffe Shepheard, John Gaye, Jonathan Farebanke, Daniell Morse, Willm Bearestowe, Joseph Morse, Francis Austen, John Rogers.

1 That wch was agreed vpon ye last meeting was Read & confirmed.

Cakebread.

2 Wheras Thomas Cakebread of Watertowne hath diu^{r}sely manifested his desier to come and have Lot wth vs. It is agreed y^t vpon good consideracon of his knoweledge in Marshiall afayers & in other cases he may become an vsefull man in our Towne. Therfore Abraham Shawe Clarke of our trayned band Daniell Morse Sariant, & Philemon Dalton are apoynted to treate wth him conc^{r}neing such ɡposicons as may be thought Fitting conc^{r}neing the same his enterteynem^t

3 Edward Alleyn, & Abraham Shawe appoynted to attend the next court both for defence conc^{r}neing Watertowns ɡposicons against the North side of our Towne : as also for other businesses ther to be pformed. And also that they may choose other of our society to assist them yf yf occasion serve & all at a comon Charge.

Swampe

4 Wheras vpon good viewe taken of ye Swampes next ye Towne they are fownd to be soe greate y^t ye form^r ɡportion allotted to men will not be neere sufficient to cleere them wherfore we doe nowe by a gen^{r}all consent order that soe many as haue 12:

acre lotts may haue 4 acres for their 2: acres form^{r}ly granted, & those 8 acre lotts may haue 3. acres of Swampe yf they please, otherwise not. Provided allwayes that [   ] the fourth pte of y^t w^{ch} [   ] man doth accept of shalbe cleered eu^{r}y yeare in manner and forme according to ye first order Ordering also y^t whosoever shalbe fownd defective shall for eu^{r}y defaulte soe made forfett ye price of an Ewe kid then to be [   ] valewed and payd vnto ye collector for benefit of ye wholl towne. It is to be the [   ] valewe of an Ewe kid of Eight weekes old when ye defect is soe fownd.

Agreed to take swampe according to y^{is} order

	Acres		Acres		Acres
Ed: Alleyn	4	La: Gen^{r}e	4	Da: Morse	4
Ab: Shawe	4	Ra: Shepherd	4	Jo: Morse	4
Sa: Morse	4	Ni: Phillipps	4	Wm: Berstowe	3
Ph: Dalton	4	Jo: Gay	4	Jon: Farebanke	4
Jo: Dwite	4	Jos: Shawe	3	Fr: Austen	4

Jo: Rogers refuse. 58

Ab: Shawe
5 Graunted vnto Abraham Shawe one litle hill of grownd as it lyeth incompased wth Swampe aboue the Easterly side of ye litle Riu^r, in consideraĉon of some care & paynes taken of & conc^{r}ning our Townes busines. pvided that he take 4: acres of Swamp to him selfe & his soñ Joseph 3. acres all to adjoine vnto ye said litle hill, and cleer ye same accordingly.

Ph: Dalton
John Dwite
6 Agreed y^t Phileman Dalton shall haue his 4: acres of Swampe to lye next aboue m^r Shawe & John Dwite his 4 acres next above Phil: Dalton.

Hoggs
7 Ordered y^t strangers hoggs may be enterteyned to be kept amongst ours in the Iland, yf they paye [   ] shillings p yeare for ech heade or Swyne. wherof 18^d is to be payd at the entrance & the rest before the Swyne be taken awaye.

Jo: Eaton
8 Thomas Hastings laying downe his lott vnto our society John Eaton is enterteyned into ye same & subscribed.

9 Wheras ye evill disposiĉon of ye Natiues hath caused vs of late to vnd^{r}goe very much watching & wardings &c wherby much expence of municõn &c hath ben amongst vs to our greate Charge & detrim^t besids our tyme expended & the samelike still to continewe. wherfore we doe by gen^{r}all concent order y^t eu^{r}y man that henceforth shalbe admitted vnto vs shall p^{r}sently paye vnto our Collector Ten shillings of English money to be imployed for municõn &c for gen^{r}all defence of our Towne y^t all men [in some] ₚportion beare charge accordingly.

Dedham The 14th of ye 5th month coṁonly called July 1637 1637 Assembled whose names are vnd^{r}written vizt. Thomas Carter, Edward Alleyn, Abraham Shawe, Samuell Morse, John Kingsbery, John Haward,

Phileman Dalton, John Dwite, John Coolidge, Nicholas Phillips, John Gaye, Raffe Shepherd, Joseph Shawe, Jonat: Farebanke, Frances Austen, Daniell Morse, John Rogers, Wm Bearstowe.
That wch was agreed vpon ye last meeting is confirmed.
Ralph Wheelocke Thomas Cakebread & Henry Phillipps admitted whoe subscribed accordingly.

Dedham The 18th of ye 5th month comonly called July 16&7
1637 Assembled whose names are vnderwritten
Thomas Carter, Edw: Alleyn, Abra: Shawe, Sam: Morse, Phil: Dalton, John Dwite, Lambert Genere, Nicho: Phillips, John Gaye, Raffe Shepheard, Joseph Shawe, Jonath: Faerbanke, Frances Austen, Daniell Morse, John Rogers, Willm Bearestowe.
1 That wch was agreed vpon ye last meeting is confirmed.

2 Ezechiell Holliman Requireing concent of our society to
Ez: Hollimans turne over his Lott, as also y^t wch he purchased of Raffe
alienacon to Jno Shepheard vnto John Kingsbery & Joseph his brother it is
& Jos: Kings- condescended soe to doe. pvided y^t the sayd Joseph subscribe
bery vnto our Covenant accordingly

3 Vpon some agitacon conc^{r}neing m^r Daltons Joyneing wth
m^r Dalton vs It is consented vnto, vpon ye manifestacon of his Resolucon to sit downe wth vs in a Civell condicon wthout further expectacons pvided y^t y^t he brengeth c^{r}tifficate from ye magestrats.

4 Mr John Allen wth diu^{r}se others being ppownded to sit
m^r Jno Allin downe wth vs onely in the same condicon. they are accepted soe to doe pvided y^t they breng c^{r}tifficate from ye magestrates according to the order of Courte as they ought to doe.

5 It is agreed conc^{r}neing Clapboarding of houses y^t it
Clapboard shalbe at liberty vntill midsomer day next. not wth standing ye order wch is afterward to stand in force from y^t day forward

Ferdinando Adam, Michaell Metcalfe, m^r John Allen, An-
Admitted thony Fisher, Tho: Wight, Eleasor Lusher, Robte Hinsdall, John Luson, John Fisher, Thomas Fisher, m^r Timothy Dalton & John Morse. pduceing c^{r}tifficates from ye Magestrates subscribed vnto our Covenants accordingly.

Dedham The 11th of ye 6: Month comonly called August
1637 Assembled whose names are vnderwritten, vizt m^r Tymothy Dalton, Ralph Wheelocke, Edw: Alleyn, Abra: Shawe, Sam: Morse, John Haward, Mich: Metcalfe, Ferd: Adam, Ant^o: Fisher, Eleas: Lusher, Lam: Genere, Nich: Phillips, Jonat: Farebanke, Raffe Shepheard, Tho: Wight, John Luson,

Tho: Fisher, Fra: Austen, John Morse, Dan: Morse. Jos: Morse, Willm Bearstowe, Henry Phillips.

That wch was agreed vpon ye last meeteing was Read and Confirmed.

1 Imp^r wheras Certeyne Lotts haue long lyne wast vpon the names of John Ellis & John Coolidge wth out any imploym^t. It is ordered y^t yf they doe not wth in 6. dayes set on to build & impve the sayd lotts as is Requesite. That then the sayd Lotts shalbe at liberty to be disposed of vnto some other men. And they to haue Lotts layd out for them whensoeu^r they will set on to impve ye same as they ought to doe. And the very like for that lott wch John Dwite hath layd out for a freind in grateficacon.

m^r Prudden
2 It is ordered y^t yf m^r Peter Prudden wth 15. more of his Company shall please to come vnto vs, they shall haue enterteynem^t & Lotts accordingly to be layd out for them. brenging c^{r}tifficate from ye magestrats as is Requiered.

2: acre Lotts
3 Wheras ther are about 16: acres of land Remayne lying at the Southermost corner of the mydle playne as yet vnlotted out. It is ordered y^t it shalbe layd out into 2: acre lotts to set houses vpon: And their Swampe lotts shall adioyne thervnto. yf ther it may be had. And further shall haue layd out for them vnto ech 2: acre Lott 12: or 14: acres of grownd according vnto ye neernes or goodnes of the same: to be ether vpon the Wigwam playne or els vpon the Eastermost playne beyond Robte Hinsdalles, And to y^t purpose we doe order that noe more houselotts shalbe layd out vpon the sayd East playne.

p'celling of Lotts to be recompensed
4 Moreover yf any man shalbe willing to depte wth any pcell of his Lott for ye accomodateing of any to be ent^r-teyned for their habitacons. We doe order y^t such shall haue layd out for them in Recompence vpon ye wigwam playne or vpon the Eastmost playne or some other place of y^t distance as shalbe agreed vpon for eu^{r}y acre soe depted wth: One acre & an halfe: or yf further convenient distance shall haue twoe acres for eu^{r}y acre soe depted wth And such as accept of such pcells shall haue them made vp compleat Lotts after such like pportions.

R. Shepherd gratef: Lott Alienated
5 It is consented that Nic^o: Phillipps may purchase of Joseph Kingsbery y^t Lott wch form^{r}ly was graunted vnto Raffe Shepheard for a grateficacon: to dispose vnto some other man

Enterteynm^t. Jo: Roper Jo: Bacheler Ma: Phillips
6 Graunted y^t John Bacheler, & John Roper may haue Lotts wth vs. Also ye like to Marten Phillips vnto whom Nic^o: Phillips pmiseth pt of his lott to set an house vpon pvided that they breng c^{r}tifficates & subscribe vnto o^r coven^{ts} accordingly.

Nat: Colborne to   7   It is consented that Nathaniell Colborne may haue
Ph: Dalton   Philemon Daltons grateficaĉon Lott, brenging c^{r}tifficate &
grateficacon Lott subscribeing accordingly.

                 8   It is ordered y^t eu^{r}y man y^t hath not done his dayes
N: towne   worke at Newtowne Swampe shall meete ther vpon the third
Swampe   day of the second weeke followeing this to mend the same &
                 other places.

                 9   Ordered y^t ther shalbe 2: Rods broade p^{r}sently cutt
Pond head   downe & cleered for an high waye in the Swampe at the
                 heade of the pond vnto the [   ] of the Wigwame playne.
And Nicholas Phillips vnd^{r}taking ye same It is ordered that our Collector shall make payment therfore.

                 10   It is ordered y^t a dilligent & a carefull Respect shalbe
High wayes   had for ye laying out of all high wayes y^t may be conceived
                 Fitting & to be well m^{r}ked & dooled, & the bredthes seu^{r}ally
Recorded. And for y^t we may not foresee all that afterward may be fownd fitting in that behalfe. We therfore as carefull of the compforte of succeeding tymes doe order that it may be lawefull at any tyme heerafter for our society or some of them y^t may be deputed for such busines, to take & laye out in or through any mans lott: a sufficient Cartewaye, horseway, or Footewaye for ye vse of all men or some pticuler mans accomodations. Allwayes p̱vided that care be had to doe the same wth as litle p^{r}iudice vnto ye owner as may be. And y^t such full Recompence shalbe made vnto ye sayd possessor as may be vnto his satisfaction by some other pcell of grownd in our sayd Towne to be therfore valewably (as shalbe adiudged) given vnto him: both for ye grownd itselfe & the conveniency therof, as also for the fenceing of ye same in all Respects: yf ye same be to be done by the possessor or otherwise by our Towne accordingly.

                 11   It is agreed y^t Jeffery Myngey shall haue a c^{r}teyne pcell
Jeff: Mingay   of grownd given him to build vpon & to imploye as may be
                 sufficiently convenient for his subsistance.

                 12   It is condescended that m^r Wheelock may lay out some
R: Clarke   pte of his Lott vnto Rowland Clarke to build an house vpon
G: Bearestowe   & y^t our Towne shall conferre vpon him some more grownd
                 for an addiĉon thervnto. And the like to Willm Bearstowe
for his brother George Bearstowe.

                 13   It is by a gen^{r}all consent agreed y^t Henry Smith shall
H. Smith   haue ye next Lott y^t is graunted out in our Towne.

                 14   For as much as our pportion of allottm^{ts} that we haue
Noe more   form^{r}ly Resolved vpon are nowe fully compleate according
enterteynem^t   to o^r Intendem^{ts} We doe nowe therfore fully agree by a
                 gen^{r}all consent that noe more Lotts shalbe graunted out
vntill a further viewe be made what accomodaĉon may be fownd, for comp-

fortable enterteynem^t of others. In the meane tyme those whoe haue given [on] their names desiering to haue Lotts wth vs shall haue a negatiue Answer given them. for y^t we haue as many as we conceive can yet be enterteyned.

Bridge   15 Mr Dalton, m^r Shawe, Samuell Morse, & Jonathan Farebanke Chosen to viewe, & estimate the Making of a Caunsey & bridge ou^r the litle River: That wth expediōon somewhat may be done for effecting of the same.

Robte Fekes farme   Wheras it was ordered y^t m^r Robte Fcke shold haue an house Lott as others haue & also y^t he shold haue for a farme wth in 2: myles soe much vpland & medowe as shalbe sufficient & he accept of. Soe it is nowe y^t he hath accepted of 12: Acres for an house Lott lying by ye Rocks towards the East And 150 acres at ye backe of ye Rocks towards ye west. And one pcell of Medowe lying beneath the same towards ye North next Charles Riu^r as it lyeth by the sayd Riu^r buttelled & bownded betweene a litle brook & c^{r}teyne Rocks: As also to haue 12. Acres of Medowe to be Layd out els wher as other men haue. pvided allwayes y^t what portion shall at any tyme fall vnto him by other devisions in ye Towne: the same shalbe layd out to adioyne vnto the sayd 150: acres as is Required.

Jno. Kingsbery   Layd out For John Kingsbery in y^t greate Iland about 9. acres more or lesse as it lyeth betweene the medowe & hill towards the South of ye Rocks towards the North & abutteth vpon ye Claypitts towards the West & ye swampe towards the East: together wth a c^{r}teyne Corner of grownd lying at ye West syd of ye Claypitts. As also One pcell of Rocky grownd as it lyeth betweene pte of his sayd Lot & the Riu^r towards the South to make vp his full Lott soe estimated.

Dedham   The 28th of ye 9th Month.
1637   Assembled whose names are vnderwritten

John Allen, Tymothy Dalton, Thomas Carter, Raffe Whelocke, Edw: Alleyn, Abr: Shawe, Sa: Morse, John Kingsbery, Mich: Metcalfe, Ant^o: Fisher, John Luson, John Haword, John Bacheler, Joseph Kingsbery, Phileman Dalton, John Dwite, Tho: Wighte, Nich: Phillipps, John Gaye, Raffe Shepheard, Jon: Farebancke, Jos: Shawe, John Eaton, Fra: Austen, John Morse, Daniell Morse, Jos: Morse, John Rogers, Henry Phillipps, Eleaser Lusher, Robte Hinsdall, John Roper, Marten Phillippes.

That wch was agreed vpon the last meeteing was Reade & Confirmed.

m^r Prudden   1 Wheras m^r Prudden wth 13. more of his Company at our last meeting had liberty given to come & haue Lotts in our Towne yf they soe pleased: But not haueing since vnd^{r}stood anything of their acceptance: we nowe hould ourselves noe longer to stand engaged vnto them therin.

Measurer Comittees

2 For as much as Tho: Bartelet hath not attended vnto ye Measuring out of our Lotts, wherby our Towne is much p^riudised. we wholly discharge him of that Imploym^t vntill he shall come & inhabit wth vs. And we make Choyce of Eleaser Lusher to pforme the same busines & to haue the like wages. And doe give him liberty to make choyce from tyme to tyme of whom he shall please to assist him: And for ye better effecting of all such businesses, we doe make choyce of m^r Tymothy Dalton Edw: Alleyn & Abraham Shawe Comittees, y^t they or any twoe of them shall direct such measurings or setting out of all such lands as are or shalbe graunted as is necessary accordingly.

Swampe Pynes

3 We order y^t eu^ry mans Swamp not yet layd out shalbe done wth all expedic̄on. And therfore we also order y^t noe more Pynes be felled any wher w^thout the pticuler assignem^t of ye aforesayd Comittees or twoe of them. Only those pynes y^t before this daye are felled vpon other mens Lotts shall stand good vnto the fellers, yf they take them both stock & toppe awaye cleer before the first daye of the third Month next, els not, & then moreover yf he taketh awaye pte and not all, he shall forfet twenty shillings vnto the Towne. And also pvided that such feller shall pmit him vpon whose Lott such tres weare felled, to take in like mañer soe many such trees vpon his owne swampe at any tyme afterward when he shall please after ye same be layd out, the sayd Pynes to be ther assigned by 2: of ye aforenamed Comittees.

Trees to be Assigned

4 We doe order y^t eu^ry Inhabitante in our Towne y^t hath not Pynes Clapbord trees, or other Tymber convenient for their vse: may have it assigned vnto them for supply of their appent wants by our sayd Com̄itties or twoe of them. Every mans ppriety allwayes Reserved.

Highwayes

5 We doe order y^t all highwayes p^rsently needfull shall wth expedic̄on be orderly set out by our Measurer, & twoe of ye sayd Comittees, wth the assistance of some of the neighbours, wch the sayd high wayes are adiacent vnto. And the same to be well m^rked & dooled wth lastinge dooles.

400 Planke

6 Ordered y^t 400: planke shalbe forth wth sawne & layd for a passage over the litle River. Mr Dalton vnd^rtaking to sawe the same w^thin one month we order y^t our Collector shall pay him for the same. And John Dwite shalbe alowed for shulveing ye Snowe

Bridge

7 John Kingsbery & John Hayward appoynted to order ye makeing of a foote bridge over the greate River over against m^r Carters lott At a Com̄on Charge.

DEDHAM TOWN RECORDS. 37

Canooe

8 It is agreed that whoesoeu^r shall Really intend to make a Cañooe for his pp vse may haue one Pyne assigned vnto him by twoe of our sayd Comitties (not haueing of his owne sufficient y^{er}vnto. Provided that he doth finish ye same Cañooe wthin thirty dayes after ye same be felled vpon ye penalty of 20^s. fyne as Form^{r}ly in case of Tymber disordered felled.

H: Smith

9 Henry Smith is accepted to haue a lott according to our former pmise, subscribeing his name vnto our Covenant, paying Chaiges & brenging certifficate.

Ed: Coluer

10 Ordered that Edward Colver wheelwright shall haue twoe Acres layd out for ye p^{r}sent for imploym^t in his trade & after to haue an addicon els wher as shalbe fownd needfull. In the meane tyme to haue free liberty of taking Timber for his trade every mans ppriety Reserved.

Hoggs Parke

11 It is Agreed y^t soe many as will Joyne together to fence in a pcell of grownd for ye keeping of Swyne shall haue soe much set out vnto them in some convenient place for y^t purpose: And y^t the same shalbe in equall pportion pp vnto them for ever. Provided y^t every mans pportion of Fenceing alike be pfected before the 15th day of ye second Month next & those y^t doe beginne and not pfect ye same soe vnd^{r}taken shall loose their labour & the Rest may finish ye same imediatly after ye same daye & possesse ye same. Also it is agreed y^t those wch doe not Joyne nowe, may at any tyme after haue assigned vnto them grownd in ye like pportion for y^t purpose to adioyne vnto the former or in some other place.

Fenses

12 It is agreed y^t all fences agaynst high wayes next every mans Lott shalbe made before ye last of ye second month next sufficient in ye Iudgem^t of 4: men to be Choesen thervnto. And the same to Iudge of every damage y^t shall arise by any such defect ether in makeing or maynteyneing ye same to be p^{r}sently made good by him y^t is the ocasion therof.

Joh: Dwite

13 Wheras John Dwite haueing his grateficacon Lott layd out next vnto Elea: Lusher he is contented the Towne shall make vse of the same otherwise yf they please. Provided that he may haue one other Lot layd out els wher when he shall p^{r}sent a frend y^t ye Towne shall accept of for ye same. John Fraery & Robte Willms are ppownded conc^{r}neing the sayd Lott but not p^{r}sent.

R: Shep:
6: acres

14 John Eaton manifesting himselfe to be willing to laye downe vnto ye Towne ether his Lott in ye Iland or that sixe acres in ye playne wch he purchased of Raffe Shepheard, & wch of these to doe he hath taken 6. weeks liberty to give his Resolucon.

Dedham The First of ye 11th Month

1637 Assembled whose names are herevnder written

Mr John Allen, m^r Tymothy Dalton, m^r Raffe Wheelocke, Edw: Alleyn, Abr: Shawe, Sam: Morse, John Haward, Mich: Metcalfe, Ant°: Fisher, John Luson, Tho: Fisher, Phil: Dalton, Joseph Kingsbery, John Dwite, Lambert Genere, Nich: Phillips, John Gaye, Raffe Shepheard, Joseph Shawe, Jon: Farebanke, Tho: Wighte, Eleaser Lusher, Robte Hinsdale, John Morse, Daniell Morse, Jos: Morse, John Rogers, John Huggens, Willm Bearestowe, Henry Phillipps, Ferd: Adam, John Roper, Marten Phillips, Henry Smith, Fra: Austen.

That wch was agreed vpon ye last meeteing was nowe Reade & confirmed.

Smiths Lott — Vpon a motion made by Ant° Fisher It is condescended that Josua Fisher may enter vpon the Smithes Lott & ther fitt himselfe ye building & otherwise for to doe some worke of y^t trade for ye Towne in the behalfe of his Father wch is expected this next somer. Provided y^t yf he cometh not in such a tyme as may be conceived fitting by our sayd society Then the sayd Josua shall leave ye sayd Lott & ye Towne to be at liberty to put in another Smith: aloweing vnto the sayd Josua his wholl Charges vpon the same to be alowed by 2: Judicious men.

Meetinghouse — Michaell Metcalfe, John Luson, Ant°: Fisher & Jos: Kingsbery Choesen to contriue the Fabricke of a Meetinghouse to be in length 36 Foote & 20: foote in bredth, & betweene the vpp & nether sell in ye studds 12: foote, the same to be girte and to order men to worke vpon the same in all workes as they are seu^rally apted accordingly. As also to pportion the same workes & wages equally in all cases. And they are alowed to take Pynes for ye same house for board vpon ye wigwame playne or vpon ye entry goeing vnto the same. And are alowed to take Oakes vpon y^t grownd betweene Raffe Shepheards Lott & the Swampe westward

Timber — Ordered y^t considering ye p^rsent deepe Snowe If any man shall lend Timber neer the same shall haue as much layd vpon his Lott by the Towne afterward when they shall Requier the same.

Ph: Dalton — Wheras Phileman Dalton hath consented to laye out 2. Acres of the west end of his Lott vnto Rowland Clarke to build an house vpon. It is ordered that Phileman Dalton shall haue soe much layd out vnto him in some other place wth advantage according to the order form^rly made in y^t behalfe.

DEDHAM TOWN RECORDS. 39

The 18: of ye 11th Month: 1637

Our weekely meeting appoynted for other occasions falling to be at Joseph Kingsberies became altogether spent in agitacon conc^rning the meeteinghouse wher these conclusions weare agreed vpon & soe ordered y^t they shold be added vnto ye busines of the form^r meeting, most of the same men being also nowe p^rsent

Meetinghouse   First it is agreed y^t ther shalbe alowed vnto such as doe fell Pynes of 2: Foote over at ye carfe sixe pence, & for Oake of the same thicknes Eight pence: And for greater & smaler after ye same Rate.

Thomas Wight, John Dwight, Nicholas Phillipps, John Eaton haue vndertaken to fell all at the same Rates.

And agree y^t yf any tree split by the default of the feller he shall loose ye felling.

Crosse cutting every 2: foote over to be alowed sixe pence & soe eu^ry scantling after y^t Rate.

Samuell Morse, Phileman Dalton, Ferd: Adam, Raffe Shepheard haue vndertaken to pforme the same.

To allowe for digging of Pitts 12: foote in length 4½. foote broad [and] 5: foote deepe [2^s]. 6^d

John Morse vnd^rtaketh to pforme the same, & hath liberty to take what helpe he pleaseth.

To alowe for saweing Pyne board 5^s & for spliting 6^s p Cent^m And for ye breaking Carfe of 2. foote deepe 3^d p foote Running measure.

Carpenters to haue for makeing of pitholls 12^d ye payer

Those 4. men appoynted to order ye worke shall appoynt wages for getting Tymber to ye pitts & other such necessary busines.

R: Shep: 6: acres Wheras John Eaton hath Relinqueshed vnto our Towne
to m^r J: Allen those 6: acres wch he purchased of Raffe Shepheard. Provided y^t the Towne doe satisfye Ra: Shepheard & doe discharge him of ye sayd bargen. And y^t nowe m^r John Allen vndertaking to satisfye the sayd bargen, We doe wth a gen^rall cosent condescend thervnto: And y^t he may confer ye same vpon one or 2: freinds afterward for house scituacons we aloweing vnto such his sayd freinds. Lotts els wher as is Requesite in y^t behalfe.

Dedham   The 20th of ye Last Month: 1637

1637 Assembled whose names are heerevnder written vizt Mr John Allen, m^r Tho: Carter, m^r Tim: Dalton, m^r Raffe: Whellocke, Edw: Alleyn, Abr: Shawe, Sam: Morse, John Haward, Phi: Dalton, Jos: Kingsberye, John Dwite, John Coolidge, Lam: Genere, Nic: Phillipps, Mich: Metcalfe, Ant^o: Fisher, Tho: Wight, Elea: Lusher, Tho: Fisher, John Luson, Robte Hinsdall, John Gaye, Ra: Shepherd, Jos: Shawe, Jon: Farebanke, John Eaton, Daniell Morse, Jos: Morse, Ferdi: Adam, John Rogers, John Huggens, Will: Bearestowe, Rich: Eu^{r}ed, Hen: Phillippes, John Morse, John Bacheler, Nat: Colberne, John Roper, Mar: Phillipps, Hen: Smith, Tho: Hastings, John Frary, Robte Williams.

That wch was agreed vpon ye last meeting was Read & confirmed.

J: Frary
John Frary [*& Robte Willms] enterteyned to haue y^t Lott wch John Dwyte layde downe vnto ye Towne wth all ye benefits y^r vnto ye same to be belonging [*to devide ye same betwixt them selues as they agre, we pmising at all tymes to give them further accomodacons according to y^t they shall seu^{r}ally need in their Imploym^{ts} & as ye towne can well afoarde vnto them]

Th: Hasting
errors in Lotts Rectefyed
Thomas Hastings enterteyned agayne & subscribed. Fcr y^t some men suppose y^t their Lotts layd out are not full measure according to their graunt: We doe nowe order y^t yf any man soe conceiveing conc^{r}ning his owne Lott maye haue the same measured agayne, & whatsoeu^r shall therin be wanting shall haue it made good wher it may most convenient be. Provided y^t such pson agreeth wth the measurer for his paynes therin & twoe of our Comittees to to viewe & Rectefy ye same: And also pvided y^t none shall in such case medle wth any other mans lott or other grownds at all the pty him selfe Resting satisfyed

supply for defects in Lotts
Wheras diu^{r}se men haveing Lotts in ye smooth playne falling shorte of Twelve acres in their lyne: ther is set out vnto them by our measurer & our Comittees soe much amongst ye Rocks as was adiudged fitt to make vp the valewe of 12 acres according to their seu^{r}all wants, as by the Abuttalls & bownds m^{r}ked out appeth. All wch we alowe of: And nowe order y^t all others shalbe supplyed in ye like case yf neede Requireth: And all to be exactly Recorded in our Towne booke accordingly That w^t grownd is granted vnto every man may in quantety or quallety be made good vnto them

L. Generes pte of 300 acres
For as much as ther hath ben often & much agitacon wth Lambert Genere conc^{r}neing ye purchase of his Eight pte of the 300. acres, but noe convenient agreem^t ariseing out of ye same. we doe nowe Relinquish vnto ye sayd Lambert all

DEDHAM TOWN RECORDS. 41

pposicons formerly made conc^{r}neing ye same, soe y^t it may henceforth Remayne vnto himselfe wth out any more treateing wth him to any other purpose.

And for y^t ye Reckonings conc^{r}neing ye sayd purchased *to p'fect ye Acc°:* Lands are not as yet pfected: we doe make choyce of m^r *of 300 acres* John Allen, m^r Tymothy Dalton, m^r Wheelocke, Edw: Alleyn, Abr: Shawe, Ant°: Fisher, & Elea: Lusher, to pfect ye same wherby such as we yet stand engaged vnto may haue satisfaction made vnto them forthwth

At the Request of m^r Dudly desierous to confer vpon m^r *m^r Greene* Greene 100: Acres of his gift land & desiering the towne to confer vpon him soe much grownd fit for a seate of an house as nere ye same as may be : we condescend to doe it, only Respit vntill we can take viewe wher it may be & then give him knowledge accordingly

Swampes Wheras ye depth of the snowe & hardnes of ye weather hath ben such y^t mens Swampes could not be measured out, much lesse could cleer them in pte as ye form^r order did enioyne Wherfore we nowe by gnerall consent agree y^t liberty Resteth vnto every man for ye pformance of y^t first pte vntill May day next come 12: monthes except some just cause may appe to ye contrary. ye penalty notwth standing soe that y^t & ye second fourth pte be both fully cleered before ye sayd first daye of Maye vpon ye penalty therin specefyed. pvided y^t those 2: fourth pts of ech mans Swampe wch is next the Towne be soe first cleered.

That ye feild wch is agreed to be fenced vpon ye East side of *East feild for* ye litle Riu^r may haue Tymber assigned by twoe of our Com- *Fenceing* itties for the side fences wch may not conveniently be had vpon ye side Lotts Provided y^t care be had, to take it only vpon such places as are likely to continewe waest: as also y^t the best Tymber be not waested for ye vse of fenceing.

Dedham The 6th of ye 2^d Month

1638 Assembled whose names are herevnder written

m^r John Allen, m^r Tho: Carter, m^r Tym: Dalton, m^r Rafe Whelocke, Edw: Alleyn, Abra: Shawe, Sam: Morse, John: Kingsbery, Phi: Dalton, Jos: Kingsberye, John Dwite, Lamb Genere, Nic°: Phillips, Raffe Shepherd, Jon: Farebanke, Jo: Eaton, Fra: Austen, Dan: Morse, Jos: Morse, Jo: Gaye, Jo: Huggens, Hen: Phillips, Mich: Metcalfe, Ferd: Adam, Ant°: Fisher, Elea: Lusher, Joh: Luson, Tho: Fisher, Nat: Colborne, Joh: Roper, Mar: Phillips, Henry Smith, John Fraryе

That wch was agreed vpon ye last meeting was Reade & confirmed. somewhat being altered Robte Willms not comeing vnto vs.

Tho: Alcocke[1]   It is condescended y^t Thomas Allcocke shall haue sixe acres of vpland & sixe acres Medowe yf he shall vpon his viewe accept of the same, not being nowe p^{r}sent

Fra: Chickering   Francis Chickering accepted vnto Tho: Cakebreads Lott yf they agre for y^e [cost] done ther. Otherwise to haue accomodaĉon els wher as ye Towne can aford, yf he like ye same vpon his viewe.

Jon: Humfry   Jonas Humfry accepted to haue a lott, yf he shall accept of y Lott wch the Towne can lay out for him vpon his viewe of ye same betwene this & soon after planting tyme.

Buriall place   Joseph Kingsbery & Nic^o: Phillips laying downe ech a pcell of grownd for a buriall place, are to haue good alowance of grownd in some other place for ye same. As also y^e [sayd] Nicholas for a pcell of grownd layd downe by him at the Keye.

Tho: Bayes   Thomas Bayes accepted to haue a convenient pcell of grownd layd out for him wher it may be fownd fitting for him to subsist by in his calleing.

Je: Allen   Jeames Allin accepted to haue sixe acres layd out for him in y^t corner by Jeffery Myngey yf ther it may [be] fownd fitt

m^r Carter   It is consented y^t m^r Carter maye haue pte of y^t hill in the Iland form^{r}ly layd out vnto John Kingsbery. And the sayd John to haue for satisfaction other grownd Layd out vnto him by 2: of our Comittees accordingly

---

[1] Fac-simile of the original grant, showing handwriting and autograph of Edward Alleyn.

DEDHAM TOWN RECORDS. 43

Lesse portions
Townsmen

It is by gen^{r}all consent ordered y^t such as are or shalbe taken into our Towne haueing lesse portions of Land then form^{r}ly graunted vnto other men shall· enioy all priviliges, as other Townesmen, & beare all charges according to their proportions as others doe.

Swyne

Ordered by gen^{r}all consent y^t all scathes done: by any Swyne shalbe be satisfyed by ye owner thereof: In mañer following. The First Scath shalbe satisfyed to the full valewe. The Second scath done by the same Swyne shalbe satisfyed to the full doble valewe of ye damage done by them. The third scath shalbe satisfyed by paying 3. tymes soe much the damage then done doth amount vnto. being done by ye same Swyne. And y^t all the sayd damages are to be payd vnto ye Towne, To be valewed by 3: Indifferent neighbours accordingly. This p^{r}sent order is to begine to be in force ye 8th day of y^{ls} month before wch tyme eu^{r}y man is to m^{r}ke his owne Swyne.

Further it is ordered conc^{r}ning Swyne y^t yf any man whose Swyne have done scath shall Refuse to satisfy vnto ye Towne what is soe adiudged wthin one month after demand made. The Towne shall haue power to cease vpon ye Swyne for full satisfaction as aforesayd. wherfore yf any man haueing Scath done shall conceale ye Swyne & not discover whose they weare: himselfe or any of his Famely knoweing ye same shall Receive noe satisfaction for such scath done. And yf he hath Received ye same. he shall Repaye it backe agayne yf it be pved y^t he or his knewe the Swyne.

A survey
of Lands

Wheras it is Required by ye Court y^t a booke shold be made of all ye graunts of Lands done in Townes & other matters necessary & the same to be deliu^{r}ed into ye Court & a Coppy therof to be kept in Towne & y^t Coppyes may be deliu^{r}ed vnto ye possessors according to their seu^{r}all Entryes at such Rates as the Court hath ordered in y^t behalfe. For wch purpose we haue desiered Edward Alleyn to take survey of all lands layd out & To drawe notes & a Booke therof accordingly. We doe therfore wth gen^{r}all consent order y^t for his care & paynes in ye sayd busines every Lott shall paye vnto him twoe shillings. And y^t for his assistance he may take what neighbours he shall please to further him in ye same for ye pfecting of ye sayd booke.

Dedham   The 30th of ye 3^d Month 1638.

1638 Assembled whose names are herevnder written

m^r John Allen, m^r Tim: Dalton, m^r Tho: Carter, m^r Rafe Whelocke, Edw: Alleyn, Abr: Shawe, Sam: Morse, John Kingsbery, Mic: Metcalfe, Ant^o Fisher, John Luson, Tho: Fisher, John Frarye, John Haward, Phi: Dalton, John Dwite, Lam: Genere, Jos: Kingsbery, Nic^o: Phillipps, John Gaye, Ra: Shepherd, Jon: Farebanke, John Eaton, Dan: Morse, Jos: Morse, Fra:

Chickeringe, Tho: Wighte, Elea: Lusher, Robte Hinsdale, John Morse, John
Bacheler, John Rogers, John Huggens, Hen: Phillips, Nat: Colberne, John
Roper, Mart. Phillips, Hen:.Smith, Tho: Baye.
  That wch was agreed vpon ye last meeteing was Reade and Confirmed.

Medowe
  Ordered y^t m^r Tymothy Dalton, Edw: Alleyn, Abr: Shawe,
Tho: Wight, Sam: Morse, John Haward & Jon: Farebanke
shall measure out those pcells of Medowe wch adioyne to
mens Lotts. And to measure out soe much medowe in seu^{r}all pcells as is allotted vnto eu^{r}y man according to their graunts made vnto them. As
also for soe many men more as may be thought fitting to be afterward enterteyned vnto vs. And this being done then to haue a
meeting to determine the same, yf by any meanes it possibly may be
pformed. otherwise to comit ye same vnto y^e [Society] by Lot to be resolved
yf then it may be soe adiudged fitting

Smale p'cells of vpland to Medowes
  Also it is agreed y^t some smale pcells of vpland adioyneing
ye severall devisions of medowe shalbe anexed vnto ye same
wher it may be conveniently layd to the same wth out
p^{r}iudice vnto other devisions of vpland afterward to be layd
out.

Plowe grownd
  Further it is agreed y^t the aforesayd men shall set out some
plowe grownd for such men as may make vse of ye same in
some shorte tyme convenient.

  It is agreed by a gen^{r}all consent y^t Mr John Oliuer shalbe pcured to
measure out the aforesayd medowes yf it may be

Courte
  Mr Timothy Dalton & Edw: Alleyn appoynted to attend the
next gen^{r}all Court for such busines as ther may befall conc^{r}neing our Towne.

Meetinghouse Rate
  Agreed y^t a Rate shalbe made of & for all charges conc^{r}neing ye meeting house according to those Lands in pportion
wch eu^{r}y man nowe hath graunted vnto him. And apoynted
to make sayd Rate are Ant^o: Fisher, Joseph Kingsbery, Mic: Metcalfe, Jo:
Luson, Edw: Alleyn, John Kingsbery, Samuell Morse.

:20:
:17:
  Ordered by ye maior pte y^t ye Mettinghouse shalbe sett vp
in ye place wher it nowe lyeth, or vpon some pte of ye waest
grownd neer thervnto, as it was left for y^t purpose.

 Dedham The 6th of ye 5: Month 1638

 1638 Assembled whose names are vnder written

  Mr John Allen, m^r Tim: Dalton, m^r Tho: Carter, m^r Rafe Whelock,
Edw: Alleyn, Abra: Shawe, Sam: Morse, John Kingsbery, Mich: Metcalfe,
Ant^o: Fisher, Mar: Phillips, Phi: Dalton, Jos: Kingsbery, Jo: Dwite, Jo:
Luson, Tho: Wight, Ele: Lusher, Tho: Fisher, Lam: Genere, Nic^o: Phillips,

Jo: Gaye, Ra: Shepherd, Jo: Bacheler, Jo: Frarye, Jos: Shawe, Jona: Farebanke, Jos: Morse, Joh: Rogers, Jo: Huggens, Jo: Ellis, Hen: Phillips, Ferd: Adame, Robt Hinsdell, Nat: Colberne, Tho: Baye, Hen: Smith.

Wm Bullard
Jn⁰ Bnllard

Willm Bullard & John Bullard accepted of the Towne to haue pte of those Lands formerly graunted vnto Edw: Alleyn wth some convenient adiĉon of vpland to be anexed for their inlargem^t as it lyeth adioyneing vnto ye p^{r}mises accordingly.

Clapbord

The Clapboarding of houses set at liberty vnto all men from this tyme forward.

Meetinghouse

It is condescended for loveing satisfaction vnto some neighbours on ye East side of ye litle Riu^r y^t ye Meetinghouse shall stand vpon ye End of Jos: Kingsberies Lott, not wth standing ye order made ye last meetinge. And therwth it is ordered y^t satisfaction shalbe made vnto ye sayd Joseph in some other Lande for y^t acre of grownd he hath [yeilded] to set ye Meetinghouse vpon.

Portions neere

It is ordered y^t The Towne shall Indeavour by all meanes to contrive for ye accom̄odateing such as haue Lotts farre distant from ye Meeteinghouse wth some portions of grownd to set houses vpon neerer.

Jn⁰: Allen

And thervpon it is condescended y^t m^r John Allen may possesse y^t pte of Rafe Shepheards lot soe purchased vnto himselfe in all or in pte at his pleasure for his neerer accom̄odaĉon to ye meetinghouse.

Dedham   The 28th of ye 5th Month 1638

1638   Assembled whose names are vnder written.

m^r John Allen, m^r Tim: Dalton, m^r Raffe Whelocke, Edw: Alleyn, Abra: Shawe, Sam: Morse, Mich: Metcalfe, Ant⁰: Fisher, Phi: Dalton, Jos: Kingsbery, Jn⁰: Luson, Jn⁰: Dwite, Tho: Wight, Elea: Lusher, Tho: Fisher, Jn⁰: Frarye, Lam: Genere, Nic⁰ Phillips, Raf: Shepheard, Jn⁰ Gaye, Jon: Farebanke, Fra: Austen, Dan: Morse, Jos: Morse, Ferd: Adam, Hen: Smith, Jn⁰: Rogers, Jn⁰: Huggens, Willm Bearstowe, Hen: Phillips, Jn⁰: Morse, Nath: Colberne, Jn⁰: Roper, Tho: Baye.

This meeting was only for ye distribution of Medowes & pformed as foloweth vizt.

Medowe

Assigned vnto Jn⁰ Dwite 6 a^{crs}: 2: 23: poles of medowe as it is measured out lying between the Riu^r & the Hill in pte of his owne Lott: And 6: acres at the lower end of the greate medowe next ye River in pte of his grateficaĉon Lott.

Assigned vnto m^r Timo: Dalton 6: acres of medowe as it was measured out lying beneth streame betwene the Riu^r & the hill. And also 6: acres more lying next ye same betwene the end of ye sayd hill & ye River northwest. And alsoe graunted vnto him all y^t hill y^t lyeth betwen ye sayd Medowes to runne wth a streight lyne over ye sayd hill from one corner vnto ye other of ye sayd medowes.

Assigned vnto m^r John Allin 12 a^{cs}: 1: 8: pole of medowe as it lyeth next ye River aboue [stream]

Assigned vnto Sam: Morse 8 a^{cres}: 1:—of medowe as it lyeth betwene m^r Jno: [Allin] & John Bachelers medowe vpon condičon y^t Dan: Morse shall haue y^t medowe form[^{r}ly] graunted vnto him.

Thomas Fisher 8 a^{cr}: 1:—of medowe as it lyeth next Jno: Dwite betwene ye River & the Hilles.

Anthony Fisher—7 a^{cr} :—: 20^{po}. as it lyeth next Tho: Fisher.

Thomas Wight—6 a^{cr} :—:— medowe as it lyeth next Ant^o: Fisher.

John Luson 6 a^{crs} :—: 30^{po} of medowe as it lyeth next Tho: Wight besides 3. rods broade through ye same being 22. p^o: broade is 66. p^o. in all for an high way.

John Fisher—6 a^{cr}: 1: 8^{po}. of Medowe as it lyeth next John Luson besi des ye high waye 3. rods broade lying betweene ye Riu^r & ye same.

Raffe Shepheard, Lambert Genere, Jos: Kingsbery Jos: Shawe, & Nat: Colberne are assigned to take ye 16 a^{cr}: 3: 12^{po}: lying downe streame next aboue y^e [pond] & devide ye same betwixt them to make vp ther halfe Lotts. Raffe Shepherd to have ye over plus towards satisfaction of y^t he pted wth at home.

Assigned y^t Dan: Morse shall haue soe much of ye next medowe to y^t was form^{r}ly graunted vnto his Father, to make it vp 6: acres wth y^t acre & halfe at home.

Ordered y^t those wch Inhabit on ye East side of ye litle River shall haue for y^r Medowe next beneth ye greate pond. Eleaser Lusher to haue ye first 8: acres, 1. Roode. & 22: p^o to be reckoned vnto him for 6. acres

Robte Hinsdall 6:—:—: besides ye hill
John Frary 6:—:—: besides ye hill
Fred: Adam 6:—:—: besides ye vpland
Mich: Metcalfe 6:—:—
Jon: Farebancke 6:—: 5

Jo: Rogers
Wm Bearestowe   6:—:—
Fra: Chickering   6:—:20   these 18 a^{cr}:—: 20^{po} is to be Devided amongst those sayd 5: men according to their pportions to make vp their halfe Lotts.
Tho: Hastings   6:—:—
The Smiths Lot

John Dwite   6:—:— being pt of his grateficačon Lott as above specefyed.
Joh: Huggens   6:—:—& 96: pole allowed for ye waest Grownd.
Jos: Morse   6:—:—& 96: pole allowed for ye waest grownd.

DEDHAM TOWN RECORDS. 47

Joh: Morse	6:—:—
Rich: Euered	6:—:—
Joh: Colidge	6:—:30
Jo: Roper	6:—:20
H: Smith	6:—:—
. . . . . .	6:—:—

Ordered by gen{'r}all consent y{'t} those w{'ch} haue not stover enough for y{'e} catle they nowe possesse, shalbe supplyed by y{'e} appoyntm{'t} of our 3: Comittees or one of them. And then others to be supplyed as may be conveniently. pvided y{'t} those w{'ch} nowe haue y{'e} worst shalbe in y{'e} next devision Recompenced accordingly in a Just and an orderly waye.

The 13{'th}: of y{'e} month

Blacke Smith   Most of our Towne assembled in y{'e} Morneing to take order about a Blacke Smith to be enterteyned. It was agreed by diu{'r}se men to lay downe c{'r}teyne moneyes to buy coles to further y{'e} same. amounting vnto 3£: 11: 8. as by y{'e} pticulers in a note herevnto anexed. the same money to be wrought out by y{'e} Smith for y{'e} sayd seu{'r}all men when he shalbe thervnto Required

m{'r} Carter   That m{'r} Carter is to haue soe much of Medowe to be p{'r}sently layd out for him as may make vp y{'t} he nowe hath to be 12: Acres.

Swyne   Abraham Shawe, Samuell Morse, & John Kingsbery assigned to viewe scares done by Swyne.

Dedham   The 28: of y{'e} 6: Month Comonly Called August
1638   Assembled whose names are vnderwritten.

m{'r} John Allen, m{'r} Timo: Dalton, m{'r} Tho: Carter, m{'r} Raffe Whelocke, Edw: Alleyn, Abra: Shawe, Sam: Morse, Mich: Metcalfe, Ant{'o}: Fisher, Jn{'o}: Luson, Jn{'o}: Haward, Phil: Dalton, Jn{'o} Dwite, Lam: Genere, Nic{'o}: Phillips, Raffe Shepheard, Jon: Farebanke, Jn{'o} Eaton, Fra: Austen, Jn{'o}: Rogers, Rich: Euered, Jn{'o}: Frary, Eleas{'r} Lusher, Robte Hinsdall, Ferd: Adam, Jn{'o} Roper, Mart: Phillips, Hen: Smith, Fra: Chickering, Willm Bullard, Tho: Baye.

That w{'ch} was agreed vpon y{'e} last meeting was Read & Confirmed

Ed: Kempe   It was agreed y{'t} Edw: Kempe Blacksmith shalbe enterteyned vnto the Smiths lott, to haue y{'e} one halfe of y{'e} same as it was form{'r}ly layd out together also w{'th} one halfe of all y{'e} dependances thervnto belonging & certificate pduced.

Ti: Dwite   Timothy Dwite enterteyned vnto his brother Jn{'o}: his gratificacon Lott to haue halfe an acre for situacon of his house next y{'e} hether end of y{'t} grownd w{'ch} the wheelwrite had, & y{'e} Rest to be at the East end of his brothers Lott. His sertifficate pduced.

Jno: Hunting   John Hunting enterteyned to purchase John Coolidge his Lott & c^rtifficate pduced.

H: Deengayne   Mr Henry Deengayne enterteyned vnto 3 acres purchased of Abr: Shawe & to haue an Eight acre Lot layd out for him some distance from ye towne wth other benefitts of our Towne accordingly.

Henry Brocke   Henry Brocke enterteyned to purchase Joseph Shawe his Lott & c^rtifficate pduced accordingly.

m^r Phillips   Agreed by gen^rall consent [   ] shalbe by all good meanes indeavor to obteyne m^r Phillips to come vnto vs, for our further compfort in what God may be pleased to call him vnto. Mr John Allen m^r Dalton m^r Carter m^r Whelocke & Edw: Alleyne assigned to treat wth him to ye same purpose.

Jo: Moyse
Tho: Leder
   Joseph Moyse Joyner——Weeden brickstrieker, Rich Yongs John Folger, & Tho: Leader ppownded to further consideraĉon.

Meetinghouse   John Haward & Nic^o. Phillips chosen to mowe gather vp and breng home thatch for ye Meetinghouse, & to take such assistance vnto them at ye Townes charge as may be convenient for ye expediĉon therof: together wth all mañer of other Materialls for ye same: & to put it out to thatching.

Dedham   The 21th of ye 7th month.

1638   Assembled whose names are vnderwritten

Mr John Allen, m^r Timo: Dalton, m^r Tho: Carter, m^r Ra: Whelock, Edw: Alleyn, Sam: Morse, John Kingsbery, Jno: Haward, Phi: Dalton, Jno Dwite, Nic^o Phillips, Hen: Brocke, Jona: Farebanke, Jno Eaton, Dan: Morse, Jno Rogers, Jno Huggens, Wm Bearstowe, Hen: Phillipps, Ant^o: Fisher, Tho: Wight, Jno Luson, Jno Bacheler, Mart: Phillips, Jno Frary, Willm Bullard, Edw: Kempe, Jno Gaye, Fra: Chickering

men licenced   Phil: Dalton & John Haward chosen to enquier of men Received into our Towne according vnto a warrant Received for that purpose whether men be licenced by ye state to sit downe in y^r Jurisdiction.

Char: Riu^r   Jno Rogers and Jno Farebanke appoynted to goe vpon ye discou^ry of Charles Riu^r wth such men as shall by ye Courts appoyntm^t call them ye 2^d day of ye next weeke.

Jo: Moyse
Tho: Leder
   Joseph Moyse Joyner & Tho: Leder form^rly ppownded to be considered are nowe accepted to haue ech of them 4: acres of Grownd vpon ye wigwam playne. And ——Weeden brickstrieker to haue 6 acres in ye same playne yf he please to accept of ye same & sit downe wth vs.

DEDHAM TOWN RECORDS. 49

Boates   Wheras diu^{r}se abuses conc^{r}neing ye taking of other mens botes & Canooes wth out licence of ye Owner, to ye danger of many differences amongst vs wch we desier to rectify according to a Court order. [Now therfore] ordering y^t whosoeu^r shall hereafter take any boate [contrary to the] peace wth out Licence of ye owner shall for taking any such boate to vse as aforesayd, forfet Ten shillings. And for eu^{r}y Canooe [soe taken] shall forfet Five shillings vnto ye owner or owners therof. And yf any shall faile to levye ye sayd sum or sums soe forfetted of ye ptye offending wth in Thre monthes then ye sayd forfetts to be levyed by our Collector for the vse of our Towne.

Caunsey   John Dwite & Jonathan Farebanke chosen to be head workemen for the Caunsye at ye litle River. And are to Judge of ye valewe of eu^{r}y mans dayly worke ther done & keep Just account of ye same.

Mr Feeke   Mr Robte Feke by m^r Jno Allen manifesting his willingnes to Resigne y^t wholl lott form^{r}ly graunted vnto him vnto ye Townes furth^r disposeing. the towne alloweing him such Charges as he hath ben at conc^{r}neing ye same. & also pvided y^t he shall haue an other Lott layd out for him when he shall come to Inhabit wth vs —all wch we condescend vnto.

Ab: Shawe   Abraham Shawe selleth vnto Mich^{ll}: Metcalfe & John Frary. All his Swamp conteyning Fower acres wth all the appurtenances thervnto belonging as it lyeth neer vnto the house Lotts of ye sayd Mic^{ll} & John in our sayd towne of Dedham as by his bill dated ye 10th: of Octob^r 1638.

Dedham   The 23th of Nouember. 1638
1638   Assembled whose names are vnder written vizt.

Mr John Allen, Mr Timo: Dalton, Mr Tho: Carter, M^r Ra: Whelocke, Edw: Alleyn, Sam: Morse, John Kingsbery, John Haward, Phi: Dalton, Jos: Kingsbery, John Dwite, John Hunting, Lamb: Genere, Will: Bullard, Tim: Dwite, Nic^o: Phillips, Rafe Shepard, Henry Brocke, Jo: Eaton, Dan: Morse, Jos: Morse, Jno Rogers, Jno Huggens, Jno Ellis, Ric: Eu^{r}ed, Hen: Phillips, Mic: Metcalfe, Ant^o: Fisher, Edw: Kempe, Jos: Moys, Tho: Wight, Elea: Lusher, Robte Hinsdell, Jno: Luson, Jno Bacheler, Nat: Colberne, Jno: Roper, Mar: Phillips, Hen: Smith, Jno: Frary, Tho: Bayes, Jef: Mingey, Jea: Allen, Tho: Leder

That wch was agreed vpon ye 2. last meetings was Read & confirmed

Meetinghouse Wheras Tho: Fisher whoe vnd^{r}tooke ye Meetinghouse dieth before it was finished. It is agreed by gen^{r}all consent y^t John Roper, Tho: Bayes, & Jos: Kingsbery, shall estimate what was left vndone of ye agrem^t made wth him: as also other worke done by others interniscuously wth ye finishing therof wthin ye sayd house to be soe distinguished y^t ye Towne may beare ye one & ye wedowe beare ye other accordingly.

Clay Pitts — John Kingsbery hath liberty to exchange a Ditch roome at ye south side of ye Clay pitts for soe much on y^e

Mr Feke — Mr Robte Feke pffering to laye downe his wholl estate in our Towne, vpon condi̅co̅n y^t ther be payd vnto him ye sum̅ of Twenty Markes of English Money when ye sayd Lott & farm form^rly granted vnto him shalbe disposed of vnto others by our Towne, wch is agreed by gen^rall consent to be pformed accordingly.

Tho: Bayes — Thomas Bayes to haue y^t 6: acres more or lesse at it lyeth by ye Smith wth 3: acres of medowe, wher it may afterward be layd out for him wthout farther expecta̅co̅n otherwise then what ye towne may freely bestowe vpon him yf they se cause.

John Ellis — John Ellis to haue y^t 7: acres wch John Hayward layeth downe giveing vnto ye sayd John Haward satisfaction for y^t Cost he hath ben at vpon ye same.

Giles Fuller *Tho: Ward* — Granted vnto Giles Fuller & Thomas Ward to haue ech of them 3: acres to impve & possesse for their owne vse & benefit soe long as they shall Remayne in towne pvided allwayes that they build none house vpon the same wthout further licence of ye towne. And also y^t yf they or ether of them shall depte ye towne, shall laye his pte downe to ye townes vse being alowed for such cost as hath ben bestowed vpon ye same wth out alienating any pte of ye same vnto any other wth out ye townes consent.

Nic^o: Phillips — Granted vnto Nicholas Phillips that hill & pcell of grownd wch lyeth betweene ye high waye & Jonas Humfry wth y^t smale pcell of Medowe ther vnto adioyneing as it Rangeth against ye South side of ye sayd hill.

Tho: Bartlet — Thomas Bartlet laying downe all his Right in ye towne vnto John Kingsbery for 22^s wherof 13: 4^d is for ye purchase medowes wch he is to possesse & the Rest to be payd him by ye Towne, & soe ye Lott to Fall.

Hogsparke — Wheras ther was an order made ye 28th of ye 9th month 1637 for the erecting of an hoggs Parke by such as wold Joyne in ye same in some place to be set out for y^t purpose, And others afterward ye like as by y^t order appeth. And for y^t ye same was not begon̅e by Reason of ye hard wynter Falling soe fast vpon vs. nowe therfor we doe order y^t ye same may be done in ye same mañer as Form^rly is specefyed for y^t purpose by soe many as please to Joyne in ye same.

Edward Richards shomaker . . . . Trumble Cowp. & Richard Barber ppownded to considera̅co̅n against ye next meeting.

DEDHAM TOWN RECORDS. 51

for 20£: Joseph Shawe selleth vnto Henry Brocke his Lott wth all ye Rights thervnto belonging: And also his pte of the purchased medowe therto belonging as appereth by a note vnder his hand dated ye 8th: September 1638.

for 8£ Abraham Shawe selleth vnto Ferdinando Adam one portion of Grownd called an hill or Iland as it lyeth to his home lott It sideth betweene ye Swampe of Henry Brock once Jos: Shawes & y^t Swampe y^t once was Abr: Shawes nowe belonging to Mich^{ll} Metcalfe & John Frary together wth all ye woods wayes and Rights belonging to ye sayd Iland. As appeth by his bill dated ye second day of November 1638.

Dedham The 25th of ye 1. month. Comonly Called March.

1639 Assembled whose names are vnderwritten vizt

Mr John Allin, m^r Timo: Dalton, m^r Tho: Carter, m^r Rafe Whelocke, Edw: Alleyn, Sam: Morse, John Kingsbery, Phi: Dalton, Jos: Kingsbery, John Dwite, John Hunting, Lam: Genere, Nic^o: Phillips, Henry Brocke, John Luson, Eleaser Lusher, Robte Hinsdall, John Frary, Jona: Farebanke, John Eaton, John Bacheler, Dan: Morse, John Morse, John Rogers, John Huggens, Ric: Euered, Hen: Phillips, Raffe Shepheard, Mich: Metcalfe, Fer: Adam, Tho: Wighte, Nat: Colberne, Jno: Roper, Mar: Phillips, Henry Smith, Fran: Chickering, Willm Bullard, John Bullard, Edw: Kempe, Timo: Dwite, Tho: Ledor, John Gaye.

That wch was agreed vpon the last meeting was Read & Confirmed

wed: Fisher [*Agreed y^t Forty shillings shalbe allowed vnto ye wedowe of Tho: Fisher toward y^t bargayne y^t he tooke in building ye Meetinghouse, wch o^r towne is to make good vnto her.]

Fenseditch ¹Ordered y^t a Ditch shalbe made at a Comon Charge through purchased medowe vnto ye East brooke. y^t may both be a pticon fence in ye same: as also may serue for a Course vnto a water mill: yf it shalbe fownd fitting to set a mill vpon ye sayd brooke by ye Judgem^t of a workeman for y^t purpose.

Mill Ordered y^t yf any man or men will vnd^rtake & erect a water Cornemill shall haue given vnto him soe much grownd as was form^rly granted vnto Abraham Shawe for y^t same end & purpose wth such other benefitts & privelidges as he shold haue had in all Respects accordingly. provided y^t ye sayd Mill doth grinde Corne before ye First of ye tenth month as it is Intended.

Smale Lots Wheras it was ordered form^rly y^t those men y^t come vnto vs since ye Pequit warrs shold pay vnto our Towne ten shillings p Lott for y^t those y^t weare heer had expended much y^t

---

¹ Origin of Mother Brook. [ED.

waye. It is nowe agreed by gen^rall consent y^t all those y^t are come vnto vs & sit downe vpon lesser portions then halfe Lotts shall paye nothing towards or conc^rneing ye same.

Swine Ordered for Swyne y^t in case of scath done ther shalbe doble damages payd by ye owner of ye Swyne vnto ye ptie grieved And yf they agree not betweene y^mselves: Then ye sayd scath is to be valewed by Thre Indifferent men, And satisfaction to be made for every scath soe often as it is done wth in one month after ye damages be soe adiudged.

This order is to take effect ye first daye of ye next month And also it is ordered y^t eu^ry Swyne shalbe Earem^rked. And yf any Swyne aboue twoe monthes old be at any tyme fownd vnm^rked as aforesayd : shalbe forfeted to be seased by any man of our towne for ye vse & benefit of our Towne accordingly.

Goates Also It is ordered for Goates in like manner as it is abouesayd conc^rning Swyne in all Cases & Respects whatsoeu^r.

Debts
Rates Edward Alleyn John Kingsbery John Luson & John Dwite are deputed to take in all ye bills of such debts as are due from the Towne vnto any man. And they shall make a Rate for to satisfy all such debts & other Charges: as are p^rsently necessary to be defrayed in or conc^rneing our Towne.

Deputies
for Laying
out Lands &c Edward Alleyn, John Luson & Eleazer Lusher are deputed to laye out grownds, appoynt tymber, and to pforme & doe all other businesses as weare form^rly comitted vnto m^r Dalton & Edw: Alleyn, & Abrah: Shawe, ye sayd Abraham being dead & m^r Dalton Removeing from vs. they or any twoe of them to pforme any such acts accordingly.

John Pope John Pope enterteyned vnto a twelue acre Lott, pvided y^t he subscribeth to our orders & assureth vs of comeing to inhabit wth vs before.

R: Barber Richard Barber enterteyned to haue Fower Acres of grownd wth vs, as a townesman.

Survaye Wheras it was Form^rly desiered y^t Edw: Alleyn shold according to a Court order make a Survey of all our Lands both graunted & alienated in our Towne. We doe nowe by gen^rall consent Ratify ye same: Also ordering y^t he shall haue for ye same soe doeing vizt

For every houselot graunted out Twoe shillings.

For every pcell of 12: acres & vnder further graunted Twelve pence.

And for all pcells aboue 12: acres after that Rate according to ye quantetyes soe graunted.

And for ye Alienaāon of eu^ry pcell sixe pence.

All to be payd from tyme to tyme by ye seu^rall possessors thereof
And for eu^rr other thing y^t is necessary to be incerted into ye sayd survey as a Record for our Towne to be payd by ye same as shalbe Judged Fit according to his paynes taken therein. Wherof ye Court Requireth a transcript by order aforesayd.

Dedham   The 17th: of ye 3: Month. Comonly called Maye.

1639   Assembled whose names are vnderwritten

m^r John Allin, m^r Tim: Dalton, m^r Tho: Carter, m^r Rafe Whelocke, Edw: Alleyn, Sam: Morse, John Kingsbery, Phi: Dalton, Jos: Kingsbery, John Dwite, Lam: Gen^re, Nic^o: Phillips, Rafe Shepheard, John Huntinge, Hen: Brocke, Jon: Farebanke, John Eaton, Dan: Morse, John Huggens, Ferd: Adam, Mich: Metcalfe, Ant^o: Fisher, Tho: Wight, Ele: Lusher, Robte Hinsdell, John Luson, Daniell Fisher, John Morse, John Bacheler, Nath: Colberne, John Roper, Marten Phillips, Hen: Smith, John Frarye, Fra: Chickering, Willm Bullard, Edw: Kempe, Tho: Ledor

That wch was agreed vpon ye last meeting was Red & confirmed.

Rate   Ordered by gen^rall consent y^t ye Rate shalbe made vpon eu^ry mans [   ] Lands according to ye acres y^t are graunted vnto them. And y^t all Catle shalbe Rated according to their somer feede And when ye Rate is made & money demanded for ye same, eu^ry man shall make payment therof w^thin one month after demand soe made therof. And for defect therof it is agreed by vote y^t it shalbe Lawefull for ye Collector to take distresse vpon ye goods of such ptie or pties as shalbe defectiue after ye month soe limited be expired And shall make sale of such distresse taken for satisfaction of ye sayd Rate.

Metinghouse rate   Also it is agreed by gen^rall consent y^t yf any man shalbe defectiue in payment to ye meetinghouse Rate after ye first daye of ye next month ye Collector shall take distresse in like maner for satisfying ye same, [& Charges] therof in arrere

7 men for towne affayres   Wheras itt hath ben fownd [by long experience] y^t ye gen^rall meeting of soe many men in one [   ] of ye Comon affayres therof, haue waested much tyme to noe smale damage & busines [is] therby nothing furthered. It is therfore nowe agreed by gen^rall consent, y^t these 7 men heervnd^r named we doe make choice of & give them full power to contrive execute & pforme all ye busines & affayres of this our wholl towne: to continewe vnto ye First of ye tenth Month next.

Edw: Alleyn, John Kingsbery, John Luson, Elea: Lusher, John Dwite, Robte Hinsdall, John Bacheler

54   DEDHAM TOWN RECORDS.

Lot forfated
Wheras Thomas Hastings hath sould vnto Edward Richards all y^t his Lott Formerly graunted vnto him wth out Cosent of ye Towne & Contrary vnto an order made ye 14th September 1636 wherby ye sayd Lot is become forfated vnto ye Towne: The same is Referred vnto ye aforesayd Seaven Comittees Chosen for ye Towne afayres to be ordered as they shall thinke fitting.

Alienacon for 4½ £
Lambert Genere selleth to John Kingsbery his ptable Medowe graunted to him Joyntly wth other men for service done vnto ye towne in ye begining therof: his pte being twoe Acres more or lesse as it lyeth by Philemon Dalton & trendeth vpon ye Riu^r: to haue & possesse vnto him & to his heyers & Assignes forever as appeth by a note vnd^r his hand & seale dated the Fifteenth of the 4th Month comonly called June 1639.

The 21th: of ye 4th Month 1639

All ye towne being called together about setting out mens potions of Medowe. it was concluded as Followeth vizt

medowes p'fected
That those men whose names are heervnder written by ye Free Choyce of ye wholl Towne, shall appoynt & order vnto eu^{r}y man his pcell of Medowe wch is yet vnlayed out. vnto whose order ye Townsmen gen^{r}ally pffesse y^t they will firmely stand fully satisfyed wth out Complayneing or disquiet howesoeu^r the sayd men shall order their sayd pcells of Medowe. And further that these men shall haue full satisfation for ther labor & tyme expended therin. m^r Edw: Alleyn, John Haward, Fra: Chickerin, Tho: Wight, Robt: Hinsdell.

And Further it is also ordered & Appoynted that Eleaser Lusher shall [   ] out & measure [   ] sayd pcells. wth the [helpe and assistance] of the aboue named men.

Dedham   The 26th of ye 4th: Month. 1639

Assembled whose names are vnder written deputed for ordering of towne affayers

Edward Alleyn, John Kingsbery, John Luson, Eleaser Lusher, John Dwite, Robte Hynsdell.

That wch was agreed vpon ye last meetings was Red & confirmed.

Alienacons to be certefyed
Ordered y^t whosoeu^r shall heerafter Receive any Lott or other pcell of grownd lying wth in our towne in way of Alienacon, by purchase or by exchange or by any other meanes shall wth in one Month after any such acte done make the same knowne both ye quantety & qualety therof vnto ye towne booke to haue ye same entred vpon ye penalty of Ten shillings for eu^{r}y

month soe neglected to be forfated & payd vnto ye towne. And y^t such forfet being made & not payd vnto ye Collector wth in 14: dayes after demand made therof, then a distresse to be taken & sale made therof for satisfaction of ye same.

m^r J^no Allin   Graunted vnto m^r John Allin Pastor y^t smale pcell of vpland & Medowe wch lyeth betwene ye sayd m^r Allin & m^r Tho: Carter: vpon Condicon y^t he shall give vnto Joseph Kingsbery full satisfaction for y^t pcell of grownd wch the Towne had of ye sayd Joseph for a scate for ye Meetinghouse accordingly

Edw: Alleynes engagem^t for 20 m^r kes   Wheras m^r Robte Feke hath form^rly agreed wth our Towne to Relinquish both his Lott & Farme vpon condicon y^t our Towne shall paye vnto him Twenty marks of English money, at such tyme as ye sayd Lott & Farme shalbe graunted out vnto some other man or otherwise disposed of by our sayd towne. And in ye meane tyme the sayd Robte Requiring some one man to stand ingaged for ye true pformance therof in his tyme limited, & he nominated Edw: Alleyn for ye same. Wherfore we doe nowe order y^t the sayd Lott & Farme shall both stand firme in estate vnto ye sayd Edward Alleyn & his Assignes for to secure y^t his ingagement conc^rneing ye same vntill ye sayd twenty Marks be fully satisfyed accordingly.

Lotts to be builte   Ordered y^t whoesoeu^r shall heerafter haue any Lott graunted vnto him in our towne shall enter & build vpon the same w^thin twoe months after ye sayd graunte soe made: wherby it may well appe y^t he both Really prepareth & intendeth to inhabite ye same. otherwise ye sayd graunt to become vtterly voyde vnto such as fayle in ye pformance therof: Except vpon some weighty cause ther be speciall licence graunted further to limit ye same.

Lott seased   Wheras Thomas Hastings hath made sale of his Lott contrary to an order made form^rly in y^t behalfe wherby it is become forfett vnto the Towne. It is nowe ordered y^t the sayd Lott shalbe seased vpon And Remayne in ye hands of ye Towne vntill the sayd Tho: Hastings be spoaken wth conc^rneing ye same, & then disposed of as ther shalbe Just cause.

Sam: Morse   Graunted vnto Samuell Morse twoe acres & one halfe more or lesse as it lyeth by his medowe in ye greate Iland.

2. house Lotts not to be possessed   Ordered y^t noe man shall heerafter possesse twoe house Lotts or more then one at one & ye same tyme for any longer tyme then 6: monthes after ye daye of his purchase or atteyneing vnto ye same by any other meanes whatsoeue^r wth out speciall licence had of ye Towne, or of such as are deputed for ye ordering of Towne affayers. pvided allwayes y^t this Restraint shall not extend vnto Estates by Marryage, Inheritance or other gifts or graunts in case of ye death of any testator

Dedham The 19th of ye 5th Month 1639. July

After ye lector ye 7 men appoynted for towne busines staying to conclude y^t wch we had form^{r}ly consulted of, agreed as Followeth vizt

Wheras m^r John Allin the nowe pastor of our Congregaçon hath for much tyme past taken greate paynes both in exerciseing his gifts amongst vs: & carefull in attending his sayd office since it pleased the Lord to call him thervnto. As also hath ben at much expences in his dilligent & faithfull p̱moteing ye good both of Church & Com̃on wealth amongst vs ye wholl tyme he hath ben wth vs. Which we acknoweledge we are bownd to shewe ourselves thankfull for: by takeing care for that convenient meanes of Imploym^t & Impvem^t of his stocke for his more compfortable subsistance in ye aforesayd office whervnto he is soe called. In wch Respect we doe nowe graunte vnto ye sayd m^r John Allin our p^{r}sent Pastor, & to his assignes for ever Thirty Acres of Medowe lying beyond ye Rocks Westward: to begine at ye North Corner of ye sayd medowe & soe on both sides of ye brooke to measure ye sayd medowe Southward vnto ye portion of 30: Acres compleate. Also we doe graunte vnto m^r John Allin our sayd Pastor & to his assignes for ever One hundred & twentye Acres of Vpland: next adioyneing vnto the sayd Medowe as may be most convenient to be anexed vnto the same: And to be measured out in tyme convenient accordingly as he shall Require ye same to be done. And also for his more peaceable & compfortable subsistence in ye aforesayd office, we doe further graunt y^t ye sayd Medowe & vpland shalbe Free from payment of all Charges in or conc^{r}neing our towne during ye tyme y^t ye sayd m^r John Allin shall Remayne in office amongst vs, & imploy ye same himselfe or by some other to his vse & noe longer.

Nicholas Phillips alienateth & graunteth vnto m^r John Allin Pastor & to his heyers & assignes for ever both his dwelling house & y^t wholl portion of Land wher it stands conteyneing by account 12: acres more or lesse as it lyeth betweene the Land of Joseph Kingsbery towards ye East & Lambert Genere towards the west and abutteth vpon Charles Riu^r towards ye North & ye Swampe towards ye South—together wth twoe acres of Swampe as it lyeth at the South end of ye p^{r}mises. And also all his Right & Clayme vnto Fower acres of Medowe, wch are yet to be layde out by the towne as pte of his 12: acres graunted vnto him accordingly as by his bill of sale vnd^r his hand & seale bearing date the First of August 1639 appeth.

John Huggen selleth vnto Jeames Herring all y^t his Lott of twelve acres & house builte vpon ye same wth twelve acres of Medowe & 4: acres of Swampe together alsoe wth all towne Rights priviliges & other inlargem^{ts} whatsoever belonging to ye sayd 12. acre Lot as by their bills Joyntly subscribed appeth.

Dedham   The 7th of ye 6:th Month   Called August.

Assembled whose names vnderwritten deputed for ordering of Towne Affayres.

Edw: Alleyn, John Kingsbery, John Luson, Eleaser Lusher, John Dwite, John Bacheler

That wch was agreed vpon ye last meeting was Read & Confirmed.

Ric: Barber   Graunted vnto Richard Barber that pcell of grownd wch lyeth betweene The Burying place & Henry Smith to be made vp Fower Acres wth pte of ye Swampe ther.

Edw: Colu^r   Wheras ther was Formerly graunted vnto Edward Colver a smale pcell of grownd by ye Comon Medowe vpon ye East side of ye litle River & ye same pveing p^riudicall for ye towne & not very comodious for ye sayd Edward wherfore he Relinquishing his interest therin & layeing ye same downe to ye towne We graunte vnto him in liewe therof twoe acres more or lesse as it lyeth by ye River pond vpon viewe to be made by the Comittees & soe measured out accordingly pvided y^t yf he desier to put of ye sayd peece he shall lay ye same downe to ye towne agayne.

pownd   John Kingsbery & Eleaser Lusher vndertakeing to sett vp a pownd before ye next quarter Courte: we doe order y^t they shalbe fully payde for ye same by the Towne wth as much as conveniently may be.

Comittees   Wheras Edw: Alleyn, John Luson, & Eleaser Lusher are Appoynted to laye out lands graunted & to pforme other busi-
wayes &c^r   nes for ye towne &c^r We doe for Farther explicacon of ye same trust comitted vnto them Nowe order y^t they or any twoe of them shall haue power to set out wayes wher neede Requireth according to a former order & alsoe to make Recompence for ye same according to ye same order to the full satisfaction of all pties conc^rneing ye same. And also to order all wood & tymber & grasse. And to pforme all other such things for ye good of our towne not Repugnant vnto orders then in being as is necessary thervnto.

Edw: Alleyn   For as much as Edw: Alleyn standeth ingaged vnto m^r Robte Feke of Watertowne for ye paym^t of 13£: 6: 8^d & ye sayd Lott
grasse   & farme ingaged vnto ye sayd Edward for his securetye conc^rning ye sayd Ingagem^t. It is consented y^t ye sayd Edw: Alleyn shall or may haue ye pp vse & benefitt of all the grasse vpon the p^rmises during ye wholl tyme of ye sayd Ingagem^t.

Tim: Dwite   Wheras ther was graunted vnto Timothy Dwite halfe an acre of grownd by ye Comon Medowe to set an house vpon: wch becoming p^riudicall to ye Comon good: wherfore he laying downe ye same agayne vnto ye towne. we doe nowe graunte vnto him in liewe therof y^t smale pcell of Medowe y^t lyeth betwene the high waye & ye litle Riu^r as it Rangeth wth ye North side of John Dwites Lot accordingly.

Dedham
1639

Raffe Shepheard selleth vnto m^r John Allin his heyers and Assignes for ever the one halfe of his twelue acres of vpland lying betweene other halfe of ye sayd Raffe Shepheards twelve acres towards the East & ye Waest towards ye west & Abut. teth vpon ye Swampe towards ye South & ye Medowes next Charles River towards ye North together wth all clayme or interest wch he had or might haue had in ye Swampe or medowe at ether end For wch he acknowledge himselfe by ye sayd m^r Allin & ye towne of Dedham to be fully satisfyed—as by his bill dated the 21th of ye 6th month appeth.

½ £

John Rogers selleth vnto Michaell Metcalfe Thre acres of Medowe more or lesse as it lyeth betwene Willm Bearstow towards ye North & Jonathan Farebanke towards ye South & Abutts vpon Charles Riu^r towards ye East & ye waest Medowe towards ye West With all ye pffits thervnto belonging as appeth by his Deede dated the 21th of ye 6th month comonly called August 1639

Novem 22 1639 Granted to ye worpfu^{ll} Mr Israell Stoughton & to his hiers for euer. one pcell of Land: as it lyeth next vnto the bounds betwixt Dorchester & Dedham & adioyning vnto the Farme of ye said m^r Stoughton for the enlargement therof as followeth.

At the corner of the said bounds of Dedham vpon ye Lowe playne the line ther being fourty & sixe Rodd the lyne lying at the head of the said pcell south east & North west: the said pcell to Runn towards the south west vpon a square half a Mile & from ye North west Corner of ye said square to runne vpon a line vnto ye Tenn Rodd turne in the bounds betwixt Dorchester & Dedham.

For & in consideration wherof the said Mr Stoughton condecendeth to pay vnto ye said Town of Dedham yearly & euery year the sum of Fourty shillings in Currant paye in two seuerall equall sums. vizt: the first paye to be made vpon the first daye of June next ensueing & ye other paye to be mad the first of Decemb^r following: in full sattisfaction for all charges w^t so euer may or might be demanded in regard of charges concerning either ye Town ye Church or ye Comon wealth: vpon ye p^{r}mises: & in case y^t payment be not yearly made as before said it shall be lawefull for ye said Town to make a Reenter vpon ye p^{r}mises if that the said Israell or his sucessors shall refuse to make payment as is aboue said

And further the said Mr Stoughton in consideration of ye p^{r}mises doth grant vnto the said Town of Dedham one smale pcell of Land together wth one litle pcell of meadow as it now lyeth within a Rayled neck of Land adioyning to Naponcet Riuer vpon the North side therof next beneath the mill. to haue & to posesse vnto the said Town & thier sucessors for euer: pvided allwayes that it be empued to the vse of ye said Town in genrall or other wise if the said Town shall alienat the same mor then three years together: either directly or indirectly contrary to the true intent of the said Mr Stoughton. then it shall be lawefull for the said Israell Stoughton or his sucessors to Reenter the p^{r}mises

Dedham   The 28th September 1639
Assembled whose names are vnder written
Edward Alleyn, John Kingsberye, John Luson, Eleaser Lusher, John Bacheler, Robte Hinsdell.
That wch was agreed vpon ye last meeting was Red and confirmed.

Tho: Ledor   Graunted vnto Thomas Ledor Fower acres of land to be layd out by ye purchased medowe For y^t his 4. Acres vpon ye wigwam playne pveth not answerable to expectačon.

m^r Dalton   Mr Timothy Dalton desiering liberty to sell his Lott vnto ...... Parkes It is condescended y^t he may soe doe.

m^r Stoughton   Wheras ye Wor^{pll} m^r Israell Stoughton of Dorchester hath diverse tymes manifested his desier of haueing a graunt from our towne of some inlargem^t of grownd next vnto his farme to be anexed vnto the same vpon fayer pposičons to that purpose. vpon wch well weying many argum^{ts} to move vs thervnto: We doe graunt vnto ye sayd m^r Stoughton to Ruñe from ye ptičon stake Northward by Dorchester bownds 46: Rod & from thence westward halfe a myle vpon a lyne palell wth y^t our bownds next his farme & from thence westward halfe a myle more to meete our bownds in a poynt. the condičons to be agreed vpon afterward.

It is agreed by gen^{r}all consent y^t ye sayd Mr Stoughton shalbe treated wth conc^{r}ning a pcell of grownd & tymber for our towne to build a warehouse neer Dorchester mill.

Jeffery Mingey selleth vnto Frauncis Chickering all y^t his Lott as it lyeth betweene ye Swamp towards ye East & ye wedowe Fisher towards ye west And abutts vpon ye sayd Swamp towards ye North & Jeames Allin towards ye South wth all ye Rights p^{r}viliges & other benefitts thervnto belonging to haue & possesse ye same to him & his assignes for ever as by his deede bearing date the 18. of ye 8:th mo^n 1639.

Dedham   The 18th October 1639
Assembled whose names are vnderwritten:
Edward Alleyn, John Kingsbery, John Luson, John Bacheler, John Dwite, Eleaser Lusher, Robte Hinsdell.
That wch was agreed vpon ye last meeting was Read and Confirmed.

DEDHAM TOWN RECORDS.

m^r Stoughton It is agreed y^t m^r Stoughton shalbe treated wth conc^rneing y^t pcell of Land graunted vnto him ye last meeting, & ye condicōns therof & y^t a pcell of land to build a storehouse vpon & other conveniences at Dorchester Mill for ye benefit of our Towne to be included amongst those condicōns And y^t Edw: Alleyn, John Kingsbery & John Dwite are deputed to viewe ye Conveniency therof: & to drawe all things to some heade towards a Conclusion.

m^r Deengayne Ordered y^t Mr Henry Deengaynes Lott shalbe p^rsently measured out.

Tho: Jordan It is Consented y^t Thomas Jordane may buy of Fra: Chickering y^t Sixe acres wch he purchased of Jeffery Myngey wth the house built vpon ye same.

wolues Ordered y^t whoesoever of our Towne shall kill a wolfe wthin or neer our Towne shall haue payd vnto him Ten shillings to be Raysed vpon the heade of eu^ry beast y^t is kept wthin our sayd Towne.

Trees felled disorderly Wheras Willm Bearestowe & Willm Hudson haue felled many trees in our Towne neer vnto m^r Stoughtons Farme Contrary to an order made in y^t behalfe. It is agreed that they shalbe heard speake the second daye of ye next weeke what they can saye for themselues & then all of vs to goe ye next daye, & viewe what is done, & to take such order then as ye Case shall Require.

Transcripte Mr Raffe Wheelocke & John Kingsbery deputed to Joyne wth m^r Edw: Alleyn in pvseing ye transescript of ye Survay of the Lands graunted in our Towne wch is to be deliu^red into ye Courte. And to subscribe their names thervnto as ye Court order Requireth.

Dedham The 1. of November 1639

Assembled whose names are vnder written vizt

Edw: Alleyn, John Kingsbery, John Luson, John Dwite, John Bacheler, Robte Hinsdell.

That wch was agreed vpon ye last meeting was Reade & Confirmed.

Bridge The towne being Requested to staye it was ppownded conc^rning ye Foote bridge y^t was form^rly agreed to be set at m^r Carters Lott whether nowe they weare willing to haue ye same set at John Eatons Lott, wch was by ye maior pte agreed to haue it ther set.

Tho: Wighte Ordered y^t Thomas Wight may take Fower Foote of ye Waest grownd all alongst the East End of his Lott to make a ditch ther for a Fence at the same End of his sayd lott

DEDHAM TOWN RECORDS. 61

Tho: Jordane   Graunted vnto Thomas Jordan One Acre of Swamp to be layd out next his owne grownd.

Tho: Hastings   Thomas Hastings apping to answer in his Case, and he acknowldging his fault in making sale of his Lott wth out consent of ye Towne Freely submitted vnto ye sensure of ye Towne to stand to what they shall determyne in ye same. And for y^t he (liveing at Watertowne) was misinformed y^t ye purchaser was accepted form^{r}ly for a townesman, soe y^t his faulte apped to vs to be Rather of mistake then of any willingnes. Wherfore we thinke fitting to Remitt ye wholl penalty y^t was Fallen vpon ye Lott by ye same fault Comitted.

Dedham   The 15th November 1639 being ye 9th Month

1639   Assembled whose names are vnderwritten

Edw: Alleyn, John Kingsbery, John Luson, John Bacheler, Eleazer Lusher, Robte Hinsdell

That wch was agreed vpon ye last meeting was Reade and Confirmed

Boston Bownds   John Luson & John Haward are apoynted to Assist Edw: Alleyn in setting out ye bownds betweene Boston and Dedham whoe is to meete m^r John Oliu^r ye second Daye of ye next weeke to pforme ye same.

m^r Stoughton   Edward Alleyn, John Kingsbery Eleaser Lusher & Jno Bacheler are assigned to set out the grownd graunted vnto m^r Stoughton & to conclude all other busines betweene him & our Towne vpon ye 5th daye of ye next weeke.

Edw: Richards   And y^t they or some of them to Joyne wth John Luson in gieveing estate vnto Edw: Richards of y^t Lott he bought of Tho: Hastings, pvided y^t he subscribe his name vnto ye Towne booke before.

Dedham   The 29.th November 1639 being ye 9th Month

Assembled whose names are vnder written

Edw: Alleyn, John Kingsbery, John Luson, John Bacheler, Robte Hinsdell.

That wch was agreed vpon ye last meeting was Reade & Confirmed.

Robte Mason   Robte Mason Requesting liberty to purchase Joseph Shawe & John Shawe their Lott wch was given them by their Fathers last will & testam^t: he was pmitted soe to doe. And alsoe Lambert Genere his Eight pte of ye purchased 300: Acres of Medowe & vpland.

Powell   Michael Powell pmitted to purchase m^r Daltons Lott in case y^t —— Parkes doth not buye ye same according to former licence given vnto him soe to doe.

Wheras by an order ye 18th October last it was agreed y^t Wm Bearstowe & Wm Hudson shold be heard speake for themselues & y^n all of vs shold goe viewe what they had done in disord^{r}ly felling of trees: And they being heard, & ye trees by ye greatest number of vs soe viewed: And fynding ye same disorderly done in a greate measure: yet seeing ye same was done by misvnd^{r}standing of some things & ye men pore & confessing their faulte. It is ordered y^t they shall loose only their labor & soe ye Rayles & posts wth ye Resedue of ye trees whatsoeu^r soe felled shall Rest in ye power of ye towne to be otherwise disposed of for ye best benefitt of ye towne accordingly.

Dedham   The 31th of ye 10th Month 1639   Called December

Wheras ye wholl towne weare warned to meete together this Daye to make Choyce of newe men for ye Ordering of the Towne affayers according vnto a Courte Order in that behalfe. The greatest pte of ye Inhabiting townesmen being assembled accordingly made Choyce as Followeth vizt

Mr Raffe Whelocke, John Kingsbery, John Luson, John Bacheler, John Haward, Eleaser Lusher, John Dwite, Robt Hinsdell

Extent of power   Wheras ye question was ppownded in ye Full assembly (to avoyd all scruples heerafter) howe farre ye power of these men thus Chosen shold extend in ordering towne Affayers.

It was answered & thervpon gen^{r}ally concluded that whatsoeu^r power all ye wholl Company of Townsmen themselues soe met together had before any such Choyce was nowe made: The very same power is nowe put into the same mens hands nowe Chosen to Remayne in full Force for one wholl yeare from this p^{r}sent daye.

Fynes   Wheras Willm Bearestowe & Willm Hudson haue disorderly felled many trees, for wch it was ordered Considering their pou^{r}ty y^t they shold only satisfy their forfett by loesing their labor done vpon the sayd trees as by the sayd order appeth. And nowe they further peticõning & acknowledging their fault & pleading pou^{r}ty in ye p^{r}sents of the wholl assembly, the same men for towne affayers being agayne Chosen & twoe more added vnto them: the most wherof being nowe p^{r}sent & well waying the p^{r}mises doe in the p^{r}sence of the wholl assembly Remit vnto them all the Rayle & posts agayne. Provided y^t they paye vnto the towne ech of them Ten shillings when they shall Receive their first paye of m^r Stoughton.

Provided further & it is ordered y^t yf any pson shall heerafter offend in any kinde in ye breach of ye same order, & y^t ye sayd pties soe heerafter offending shall Instance in this pticuler example, & therby pleade to haue any mittigaċon: It is nowe ordered that noe mittigaċon shalbe vnto any such pties for such offence but shall paye ye wholl penalty due to ye towne from such offenders by y^t afforesayd order in y^t case made ye 31th of ye 10th month 1636

Dedham The 3 of ye 12th Month called February.

1639 Assembled whose Names are vnderwritten

Mr Ralph Whelocke, John Kingsbery, John Luson, John Dwite, John Haward, John Bacheler, Eleaser Lusher, Robte Hinsdell.

That wch was agreed vpon ye last meeting was Read & Confirmed.

Apoyntm^t *of trees*
Wheras men haue ben form^rly deputed amongst other businesses to set out & Appoynt trees for eu^ry mans necessety as appeth by an order made ye 28th of ye Nynth Month 1637.

And ye same men not Recompenced form^rly for such their paynes in any kynd whatsoeu^r. We therfore as Justice Requireth Doe nowe order y^t whoesoeu^r shall haue a tree of 12 Inches thicke at ye Carfe appoynted vnto him shall paye 2^d vnto ye sayd Comittees for eu^ry such tree vnto 18: Inches thicke, & from 18: Inches to 24. Inches, 4^d: And from 24. Inches vpward vnto any scantling 6^d. And all trees lesse then 12. Inches to be Reckoned 3. for 2. or 2: or 3: or more for one as may be thought fitting. And soe y^t eu^ry tree be m^rked by one of ye sayd Comittees & one of ye other Concent thervnto.

Provided allwayes y^t eu^ry of ye sayd trees be felled wthin 30. dayes after the m^rkeing, or els ye same appoyntm^t to be voyd & ye same to be appoynted vnto any other mans occasion. And y^t satisfaction be made for ye appoyntm^t before y^t any of ye same tymber be taken away wch is limited to be wthin 6. monthes after ye m^rkeing therof otherwise any other man may take & possesse ye same & eu^ry pte of ye sayd trees after ye sayd 6. monthes paying the appoynters what is due vnto them. Also pvided y^t it maye in some sorte well appe y^t such as Requier any trees: haue not of their owne such trees as are sufficient for y^t purpose & vse for wch ye same are soe Required That only such as haue apparent neede may be supplyed according to y^t former order as aforesayd.

Jno Farebanke *Ceeder*
Graunted that John Farebanke maye haue one Ceder tree set out vnto him to dispose of wher he will: In consid^raċon of some speciall service y^t he hath done for ye towne: And not y^t this shold be a president for others to obteyne the like wth out some speciall cause guiding thervnto.

Dedham   The 26th of ye 12th Month Called February
1639   Assembled whose names are vnderwritten
   mr Ralph Wheelocke, John Kingsbery, John Haward, John Dwite, John Bacheler, Eleaser Lusher, Robte Hinsdell

Ladders
Ordered yt every pson Inhabiting our Towne that possesseth an house wherin a fyer is kept shall before the first Day of the third Month next pvide a strong & sufficient ladder wherby the toppe of the Chimny maye conveniently be atteyned vnto in case of Danger vpon ye penalty of Five shillings to be forfet & payd to ye towne for Defect of ye same.

And every such pson shall continue to keepe such a ladder as aforesayd in his owne possession neere vnto his sayd house to be in Redines at all tymes: And yt every pson yt shall fayle in ye pformans heerof Contrary to our true intent & meeneing heerin, shall forfett the like sume of Five shillings for every tyme yt he shalbe fownd Defectiue therin for ye space of Fourteene Dayes after ye aforesayd first Daye of ye third Month next. And also it is ordered that every pson yt shall heerafter build or possesse any other house wthin our towne then nowe is in being shall wthin thirty Dayes after ye fyer is made in ye Chimny therof pvide keepe & maynteyne such a ladder in all cases & Condicons as aforesayd vpon the penalty of ye like sume of five shillings to be payd to ye towne for every defect yt shalbe fownd for ye space of foureteene dayes together from tyme to tyme after ye sayd daye.

And for ye certeyne pformance of this thing according to our true intent heerein as a matter of much consequence as often we haue cause to take notice of considering ye losse & dangers yt haue appered vnto vs: we therfore further order that noe such ladder or ladders shalbe allowed to be sufficient wthout the appbacon of such men as the towne shall from tyme to tyme appoynt to take good viewe of ye same. And for wante of ye paymts of such forfetts soe made a distresse to be taken accordingly.

Collector
John Kingsbery is Choesen Collector for one wholl tyme vizt vntill the first Daye of the Eleaventh month next.

Rate
It is ordered by genrall consent yt the Rate for towne Charges that is nowe to be made shalbe Raysed according to ye estate of every man in our towne as in our best Judgmts it maye visibly appe vnto vs.

Dedham   The 23th of ye First Month 1639
Assembled whose names are vnderwritten
   Mr Ralph Wheelocke, John Kingsbery, John Luson, John Haward, John Dwite, John Bacheler, Eleazer Lusher, Robte Hinsdell.
   That wch was agreed vpon ye last meeting was Read & confirmed In ye prsence of ye inhabitants.

Swyne

For as much as it is well app^rhended y^t it wold produce greate benefit vnto our towne y^t Swine might goe at liberty considering y^t we haue an abowndence of waest grownd amongst the Rocks and els wheare fit for y^t purpose: but for this p^rsent yeare cañot be well accomplished by fenceing. Wherfore we doe order that all grownd y^t shalbe planted after ye first of the Second month wch shalbe in ye yeare 1641 shalbe well and sufficiently Fenced agaynst Swyne that are well yoaked & Ringed (as heerafter is specefyed) both agaynst high wayes & alsoe next vnto any other waest or vnplanted grownds & the owner shall soe constantly maynteyne ye same fence to be appved to be sufficient by such men as the towne shall depute to viewe ye same in all tymes convenient accordingly. And whoesoeu^r shall not make his fence sufficient before the abouesayd Daye to all intents & purposes as aforesayd shall forfet Sixe pence for every Rod not soe done. And that eu^ry pson not makeing & maynetyneing his fence sufficient as aforesayd for ye space of Foure dayes after the sayd First of the Second Month shall Forfet Sixe pence for every Rod or gappe soe often as any pte of such fence be fownd vnsufficient the like space of foure dayes from tyme to tyme accordingly. pvided allwayes y^t in ye meane tyme of ye same Defect he shall beare all damages y^t doe fall out by ye same.

To wch purpose we doe nowe order that ever Swyne that shalbe put out at liberty shalbe well & sufficiently Ringed & also shalbe strongly yoaked. Viz^t That every yoake soe put on shalbe halfe soe long as the Swyne is: to measure from the nostrills vnto the Tayle. And that the Keyes therof shalbe as long aboue the crossing, as is the space betweene the Eye & the end of the nostrills. And yf any Swyne shalbe fownd wth out such Rings or yoake as aforesayd the owner therof shall forfet Sixe pence for every daye that it shall soe Remayne after the sayd owner or putter out of ye same Swyne shall haue knoweledge therof—& shall paye all Damages that shall happen by the same.

Jos: Fisher

Josua Fisher allowed to purchase pte of ye wedowe Fishers Lott.

Floerditch

It is Condescended y^t every pson maye at his pleasure make a Floare Ditch in the high waye next his Lott for Fenceing the same soe y^t he doth not exceede Eighteene Inches in depth. pvided allwayes that every waye be mayneteyned in its full bredth notw^thstanding such banke soe Raysed & made & w^thout ye same banke accordingly.

Wheras we haue much Desiered that some Recompence shold haue ben made for much care & paynes that Certeyne men haue long vnd^rgone in setting out Tymber vnto such of our Towne as vpon their neede haue Required the same: that they might haue still continued that service for the good of the Towne. But nothing as yet falling in convenient or sutable to that purpose It is therfore thought fit to disburthen them by deputing some others to y^t care & paynes in their Roomes.

Woodreeus   Wherfore it is nowe ordered that Michell Metcalfe Fraunces Chickering & Willm Bullard—shall heerafter set out & appoynt such tymber trees vnto such of our Towne as shall haue neede therof by not haveing of their owne according to such orders formerly made, or Rules y^t nowe or heereafter shalbe given vnto them. Viz^t That they haue not of their owne fit for y^t purpose for wch they Require the same—As y^t order made the 28th of ye 9th month 1637 Intendenth. And y^t one of the sayd appoynters doth marke every one of the sayd trees & another consent thervnto. Also that yf the trees soe appoynted be not felled wthin 30. dayes, then the appoyntm^t to be voyde & the same maye be appoynted for an other y^t hath neede of such And the trees felled or whatsoever is left of them at the end of 6. monthes after the appoynting therof shall be in the hand of the Town agayne to be disposed by them as they shall iudg conueanient and it shall hencforth be in the liberty of no man to take the same except by a new grant from ye Town or such as shall be deputed therto

Dedham   The 30th of ye first Month 1640   Called March

Assembled whose names are vnderwritten

m^r Ralph Whelocke, John Kingsbeiy, John Luson, John Bacheler, John Haward, Robte Hinsdell

That wch was agreed vpon ye last meeting was Reade and Confirmed

gath^r rate   John Kingsbery & John Bacheler Deputed to gather the Rate.

Measurer   Daniell Fisher Chosen to be our measurer: only Reserveing the Medowes & Swampes wch shold haue ben done the last yeare to be pfected by Eleaser Lusher.

fynd wayes   Anthony Fisher, Tho: Wight, John Dwite, Francis Chickering, m^r——Powell Fardinando Adam Willm Bullard & George Bearestowe, Deputed to fynd out the high wayes betweene Dedham & other townes according to the Court order.

Ant^o: Fisher, & Tho: Wight for Watertowne waye John Dwite, & George Bearstowe, & ye Rest to agree & Joyne wth them for all ye other wayes.

Storehouse   Edward Kempes house appoynted to be ye storehouse for lost goods according to the Courte order.

Register   Edward Alleyn gent Deputed to Register Birth, Burialls & marriages in our towne, & make transcript therof to ye Court according to ye order of Courte.

DEDHAM TOWN RECORDS. 67

	Wheras by an order made the 11th of ye 6: Month 1637. y^t
Highwayes	high wayes might be layd out through any mans grownd &
Recompenced	Recompence in land to be given for ye same &c^r.

It is nowe ordered y^t all such pcells of grownd as haue ben or heerafter shalbe soe taken out of any mans Lot for the sayd purpose, & Recompenced wth other grownd according to ye sayd order: All ye sayd Recompenceing grownd soe allowed ether for ye grownd soe taken or for any fenceing to be done by ye ptye (yf any such be) shall become & Remayne forever, as aptinate & pcell of ye sayd Lott & soe to be Reckoncd wthout further Charges, then y^t wch shold otherwise be imposed vpon ye same Lott, yf nothing had ben taken from it or added vnto ye same.

Dedham   The 17. Aprill being ye 2^d: Month.

1640   Assembled whose names are vnderwritten.

m^r Ralfe Wheelocke, John Luson, John Dwite, John Bacheler, John Haward, Robte Hinsdell

That wch was agreed vpon ye last meeting was Reade and Confirmed.

Xofer Smith   That Christofer Smith shalbe Received to the 5: acres y^t form^rly was graunted to Jonas Humfrey, wth that litle pcell of Meedowe thervnto adioyneing, payeing vnto ye sayd Jonas such pportion of Charges as ye same will amount vnto.

Measure p'cells   Edward Alleyn gent is Requested to measure out such pcells as are allredye graunted what he can, wth assistance of some
p'fect Lotts   of ye neere neighbours vntill a measurer be established.

John Luson being Requested also to assist what he maye in pfecting of Lotts.

fences p'portion   Edward Alleyn gent John Kingsbery, & Nathan Aldus are Deputed to pportion Fences, & to Regard ye same from tyme to tyme to be kept sufficient.

High wayes   And y^t high wayes be set & kept sufficient.

And y^t Ladders be made & kept sufficient according to order
Ladders   in y^t case pvided.

Dedham   The 6:th of ye 3^d: Month called Maye.

1640   Assembled whose names are vnderwritten

m^r Ralph Wheelock, John Kingsbery, John Haward, John Luson, John Bacheler, Eleaser Lusher, Robte Hinsdell, In p^rsens of our Pastor.

That wch was agreed vpon ye last meeting was Read & Confirmed.

A farme   Graunted vnto Edward Alleyn gent & to his assignes forever Thre hundred acres of vpland, & Fiftye Acres of Medowe grownd All to lye in or aboute that place called Bogastowe or not farre of from thence, wher the sayd Edward shall make Choyce before any other doe make entrance therabouts of any lands whatsoeu^r.

Dedham   The 26th of ye 3: Month Called Maye
1640   Assembled whose names are vnderwritten

m^r Ralfe Wheelocke, John Kingsbery, John Luson, John Bacheler, John Haward, Eleaser Lusher, Robte Hinsdell

That wch was agreed vpon ye last meeting was Read & Confirmed.

m^r Cooke
m^r Smith
m^r Bacon

It was by Inhabitants appoynted such are deputed to order Towne affayres, & others also being Called together for advice therin. Vpon deliberaĉon & good consideraĉon assented vnto & agreed vpon that the Towne of Dedham shall enterteyne m^r Samuell Cooke together wth his estate And also m^r Smith & m^r Bacon all from Ireland & afford to them such accomodaĉons of vpland & medowe as their estates shall Requier, & as ye Towne wthout Reall p^{r}iudice to ye sayd Towne can afforde wth all such accomodaĉons as their or any of their estates may competently Requier & Impve And y^t the same pvision of medowe & vpland shall principally lye in or about y^t place of medowe Comonly called Bogastowe medowe. Together also wth such other vpland or house places or such other pcell or pcells as maye be sutable to ye sayd psons, & ye p^{r}sent condiĉon of ye sayd towne, wch sayd pcells shall lye in ye sayd towne as may be most conveniently fownd for ye same vse of building vpon.

Dedham   The 23th: of ye 4th: Month called June.
1640   Assembled whose names are vnder written

m^r Ralfe Wheelocke, John Kingsbery, John Luson, John Haward, John Dwite, John Bacheler, Elea: Lusher, Robte Hinsdell

That wch was agreed vpon the last meeting was Reade & Confirmed.

Jno Kingsbery

That smale pcell of vpland adioyneing to the 2. acre medowe of John Kingsbery is Confirmed vnto him to belong vnto the same.

H: Wilson
S: Bullen

Graunted vnto Henry Wilson & Samuell Bullen to haue that pcell of Land wch lyeth in ye Corner beneeth & next vnto m^r DeEnganes Lott to be Devided betwixt them. Memorandum y^t Henry Wilson is content to lay downe this grant so he may be puided for els where:

Jno Farebacke

Graunted to John Farebanke 6. acres at ye east end of his Fath^{rs} Lott.

M: Metcalfe   Graunted y^t Michaell Metcalfe maye haue y^t pte of swampe y^t lyeth next vnto y^t Lott he purchased of John Morse.

mrs Smith
mris Bacon
Wheras m^{ris}: Smith & m^r Bacon being lately arived heer from Ireland. haue ben in our towne & not only well app̱ved of, but also gen^{r}ally desiered y^t they might inhabitte wth vs: And howesoeu^r their housbands are not yet come, yet liberty is graunted vnto them to purchase in our towne for an habitac̃on: And such other accom̃odac̃ons both of vpland & medowes to be given vnto them as their stocks and estates shall Requier as appeth by a former order conc^{r}neing ye same.

m^r S: Cooke
Graunted vnto m^r Samuell Cooke all y^t 12. acre Lott y^t was Form^{r}ly graunted vnto m^r Robte Feke wth the 12. acres of Medowe thervnto belongeing to haue vnto him & his assignes for ever.

Dedham The 6th of ye 5th Month called July.

1640 Assembled whose names are vnder written

m^r Ralfe Wheelocke, John Kingsbery, John Luson, John Haward, John Bacheler, John Dwite, Eleaser Lusher, Robte Hinsdell

That wch was agreed vpon ye last meeting was Reade & Confirmed.

m^r S: Cooke
Wheras ther is graunted vnto Samuell Cooke gent that twelue acre Lott wch late was Robte Feks gent wth ye apurtenances And y^t other lands are to be conferred vpon him for further Imp̱vem^t of his Stocke neer home besides that wch lyeth farre of. We therfore nowe for that purpose Doe further graunte vnto ye sayd m^r Samuell Cooke also. All that farme form^{r}ly graunted vnto the afore named m^r Robte Feke Conteyneing one hundred & fifty acres at ye backe of ye Rocks, lying Downe vnto Charles Riu^r; And one pcell of Medowe lying by the same vnto ye sayd Riu^r: as more at large is specefyed by an order made the 11th of ye 7th month 1637

Discharging y^t 20: m^{r}kes wch was to be payd vnto the sayd Robte vpon his Resigneing of ye sayd Lot & farme vnto ye towne for Charges he had expended vpon & aboute ye same. The sayd Farme to be set out in tyme Convenient by m^r Ralph Wheelocke Jno Kingsbery John Luson Robte Hinsdell & Eleaser Lusher or any 4: of them.

Jno: Luson
Tho: Wight
Swampe
John Luson and Thomas Wight are ordered to haue that Swampe as it lyeth at ye west End of their Lotts to be devided betwixte them as they are agreed, for their twoe acre Swampe enioyned them to haue by the first graunte, to be cleered, as other men in ye like case.

Ro: Hinsdell Graunted vnto Robte Hinsdell one pcell of vpland lying vpon the backside of his Furthest pcell of medowe & betwixte the sayd medowe & one pcell of Course medowe lying on the other side therof. wch sayd pcell of vpland shalbe further viewed by m^r Ralph Wheelocke, John Haward & John Dwite or any twoe of them whoe shall fully Determyne ye extent & bownds therof according as to them shall appe Convenient.

m^r Wheelocke Graunted vnto m^r Ralph Wheelocke one pcell of y^t Deade Swampe lying in the Rocks wch pcell of Swampe shall be taken in aloweance for twoe acres of his Swampe Due to him vpon ye towne order pvided for ye Disposeing of Swampes. W^ch sayd pcell shalbe further viewed by m^r Edward Alleyn & John Luson & by them to be limited & bownded as they shall see most convenient.

J^no Haward Graunted to John Haward one pcell of vpland to be anexed vnto a pcell of medowe late by him purchased of John Ellis wch pcell shalbe viewed, by m^r Wheelocke, John Kingsbery & John Dwite, & Robte Hinsdell & by them limited & bownded as they shall see fitt or any twoe of them.

Dedham   The 27th of ye 5th Month called July:
1640   Assembled whose names are vnder written

Mr Ralph Wheelocke, John Kingsberye, John Luson, John Dwite, John Haward, John Bacheler, Eleaser Lusher.

That wch was agreed vpon ye last meeting was Read & confirmed.

J^no Haward et als Ordered y^t all those portions of Medowe wch adioyne vnto that pcell of vpland that John Haward adioyneth vnto as is menconed in an order ye last meeting: shall haue portions wth ye sayd John Haward of ye sayd vpland to be conveniently devided by those men appoynted to pforme ye same to ye aforesayd John Haward as in ye aforesayd order is specefyed accordingly.

S. Morse
J^no: Dwite
Fr: Chickering
Ordered y^t Samuell Morse John Dwite & Fra: Chickering shall haue such a portion of land beyond ye East brooke for to Depasture their workeing Cattle to them & their heyres for ever to be set out by Edward Alleyn Mich^ll Metcalfe John Kingsbery Eleaser Lusher & J^no Haward before ye first of October next—or ye maior pte of them.

Dedham   The 28th of ye 7th Month. Called Septemb^r.
1640   Assembled whose names are vnderwritten

m^r Ralph Wheelocke, John Luson, John Haward, John Bacheler, Eleazer Lusher.

That wch was agreed vpon the last meeting was Read & confirmed.

DEDHAM TOWN RECORDS. 71

Viewe defects John Dwite & Robte Hinsdell Deputed to measure Frauncis Chickerings Lot y^t was Frauncis Austens, & viewe ye Defects of ye same. And licence given him to keepe ye same in his hands for Sixe monthes from this Daye, yf he cañot other wayes Dispose of ye same before that tyme, according to a former order.

P: Woodward Licence graunted to Peeter Woodward to purchase in our towne & soe become a Townes man: Provided y^t he subscribeth his name to ye Towne orders in ye booke.

Tho: Eames Graunted to Thomas Eames that pcell of grownd form^{r}ly graunted to Henry Wilson & Samuell Bullen next vnto m^r Deengaynes Lott in the greate Iland pvided that he subscribeth to ye towne orders.

H. Wilson Wheras Edward Alleyn hath given vnto Henry Wilson a smale pcell of land to sett an house vpon beyond ye Lott of Willm Bullard towards the North. We doe graunt vnto the sayd Henry Wilson more Sixe acres for planting grownd to lye beyond the other portion of ye sayd Edward that lyeth beyond Vine brooke to be set out by ye sayd Edward, m^r Wheelocke John Luson & John Kingsbery or any 3. of them.

Jos: Clarke Wheras Edward Alleyn hath graunted vnto Joseph Clarke one acre of land next Vine Brooke towards ye North for setting an house vpon: We Doe graunt vnto ye sayd Joseph one acre of land to adioyne thervnto for to make vp an house Lott. And more we doe graunt vnto ye sayd Joseph Clarke Sixe Acres of planting grownd, to ly beyond Vine Brooke to be set out by ye aforesayd men y^t are appoynted to pforme for Henry Wilson pvided y^t he subscribe to ye towne orders.

m^r Whelockes Recompence Wheras m^r Ralph Wheelocke hath form^{r}ly graunted vnto Joseph Clarke twoe acres to plante vpon we doe nowe graunte in Recompence therof Foure acres of grownd to lye beyond Vine brooke, & to be set out by 3 of the aforesayd men.

Dedham The 22th of October being ye 8th Month.

1640 Assembled whose names are vnderwritten

m^r Ralph Wheelocke, John Kingsberye, John Haward, John Luson, Eleazer Lusher, John Bacheler, Robt Hinsdell

Samuell Morse & John Dwite are Deputed to see ye Carte bridge, ye Caunsey & ye High waye from the sayd bridge vnto Robte Hinsdells house mended by the Townsmen & also a Foote bridge made over Milbrooke.

Pastors Farme Mr Wheelocke, John Luson, & Robte Hinsdell are appoynted to set out for m^r Allin our Pastor one hundred & twentye Acres of vpland form^{r}ly graunted vnto him for a Farme.

Dedham The 27th October being ye 8th Month.
1640 Assembled whose names are vnder written

mr Ralph Wheelocke, John Kingsbery, John Dwite, John Haward, Eleazer Lusher, John Bacheler, Robte Hinsdell.

That wch was agreed vpon ye 2. last meetings was Reade and Confirmed.

mr Lower Ordered yt mr John Allin our Pastor hath liberty to purchase Land in our towne for mr —— Lower of —— & the sayd mr Allin haueing nowe soe done, ther is graunted vnto him for ye sayd Mr Lower Twenty acres of planting grownd by his owne farme in Exchange for Five acres more or lesse once pcell of Raffe Shepherds lott as it lyeth wthin ye Towne vpon ye south side of the high Streete & west side of ye sayd Lott, the same 5. acres to Remayne in the townes hands for their occasions.

Generes vpland Ordered yt John Dwite & Eleazer Lusher shall assist Robert Hinsdell in setting out & measuring Lambert Genere his purchased vpland & the waye therby; & also to measure out the Lotts of Jno. & Timothy Dwite, Edw: Richards & ye 2. lotts of Frances Chickering to haue them Rectefyed.

John Kingsbery & John Dwite depteing ye Rest pceeded as Foll. vizt.

An: Fishers 15. acres R: Wheelocke Jno Luson Th: Wight Graunted vnto Anto: Fisher Fifteene acres of planting grownd to lye vpon ye Southeast side of mr Allin our Pastor his farme to be set out by mr Wheelocke Tho: Wight & Robte Hinsdell. Also Graunted vnto mr Ralph Wheelocke John Luson; & Thomas Wight, to each of them Fifteene acres all to lye neer about our Pastors Farme & to be sett out & measured by ye aboue named men accordingly.

S: Bullen Th: Strickland Graunted to Samuell Bullen & Thwaits Strickland to each of them Sixe acres of planting grownd to lye adioyning to Anto. Fishers 15: acres & to be set out & measured by the abouesayd mr Wheelocke, Jno Luson & Tho: Wight accordingly.

Dedham The 28th of ye 9th Month Called November
1640 Assembled whose names are vnderwritten

mr Ralph Wheelocke, John Kingsberye, John Luson, John Dwite, John Haward, John Bacheler, Robte Hinsdell.

Footebridge Wheras Willm Bullard & John Eaton had taken the Footebridge over Charles Riur to make & set vp ye same, the sayd Willm to haue Fifty shillings & the sayd John to haue Forty shillings for effecting ye same. But for as much as ye the sayd worke pves to be more then they or we did Expect Therfore we doe nowe vpon good informaçon of the same order yt the sayd Willm Bullard shall haue Thre pownds

& Ten shillings & John Eaton Thre & Fifty shillings for ye pfecting of ye sayd Bridge for their full satisfaction as is thought Fitting.

Hugh Stacye Graunted vnto Hugh Stacye twoe Acres as it lyeth between the trayning place towards the North & the Lotts of Edward Alleyn gent, Anto: Fisher & Tho: Wight towards ye South ye Residue of that smale pcell of Swampe to be pte of ye sayd 2: Acres soe graunted. Allwayes pvided y^t he Relinquish that pcell form^rly graunted him in ye greate Iland And also y^t yf at any tyme heerafter he shall Resolue to Depte wth these 2: acres nowe soe graunted or any pte of ye same, he shall pmit the towne to haue the same agayne at such a price as 2: or 3. Indifferent men shall adiudge ye same to be worth yf they agree not betwixt them selues accordingly.

[¹   [   ] of vpland fit
          [   ] granted to Robert
          [   ] pcell of meddow to be layd
     [   ] to lay out y^t [   ] of Robt Hinsdell
     [   ] pcell of vpland lying at the lower
     [   ] waye & the swamp lyeing there against
     [   ] 2 acres of land to be layd out where [it] shall
     [   ] playne vpon the great Iland which 2 acres
     [   ] for halfe an acre of broken ground that he
     [   ] Thomas Payne to further the Brickill :]

[¹ [   ] grant was form^rly made to Hugh Stacy of a pcell of
   [   ] pt of the ground formerly appoynted to ly for the training
   [   ] he same being so granted that if the sd Hugh should pte
   [   ] same the Towne should haue the first refusall vpon the
   [   ] of 2 or 3 Indifferent men the sd Hugh being now to part
   [   ] with the towne & the sd Hugh hath nominated and chosen m^r
   [   ]w: Alleyn & Samuell Morse to set such a value vpon the same
   [   ]s they shall se to be indifferent & in case they agree not they haue power to chose a 3^d man to be vmpier therein :]

[¹ [   ] is Ordered that m^r Edw: Alleyn: Jno Kingsbury & Jno Luson or any 2 [   ] them shall treate with Michael Bacon about satisfaction for a [   ]igh way through his Lott vpon the smoth playne leading to the place where the bridge is entended to be built. & also they are [   ] to view the sd way : & if they se cause to vary or alter it to some other pt of the sd pcell or Lott they haue power so to do. Also to [tender] such satisfaction for the sd high way and the fencing thereof as they shall se cause & to setle the same as they shall se cause : If they can :]

---

[1] The three paragraphs enclosed in brackets are all that can be deciphered of a fragment of a leaf bound at the end of Vol. I., but evidently out of its proper place.

74 DEDHAM TOWN RECORDS.

Jon: Humfry   Wheras Jonas Humphry had form^{rly} a twelue acre Lott graunted vnto him, wch afterward he Relinquished agayne vnto ye towne, & to haue his Charges Disbursed vpon ye same Repayd vnto him, wher fore it is nowe ordered that Xofer Smith whoe hath pte of ye sayd Lott wth Twoe Cowes depasturing vpon ye Comon medowe purchased & therfore to paye vnto ye sayd Jonas 24^s: 10^d And the towne to paye the Rest being 24^s. the wholl some being—2£: 8: 10^d.

John Dwits gratificacon   Graunted to John Dwite Twelue acres of planting grownd to make up his grateficaōon Lott, pvided y^t he taketh ye same adioyneing vnto m^r Stoughtons Rayles, & y^t he come not vpon the East playn wch yf he Refuseth then ther is graunted vnto ye sayd John Nyne Acres at the End of ye home Lotts soe y^t he extend not vnto the sayd playne.

Dedham   The 2^d: of ye 10th Month Called December
1640   Assembled whose names are vnder written

m^r Ralph Wheelocke, John Dwite, John Luson, Eleazer Lusher, John Bacheler, Robte Hinsdell.

Bricke   John Kingsbery, John Haward, & John Bacheler or any twoe of them are deputed to search for Bricke earth & pvide a place necessary to burne bricke vpon, & also to appoynt wood sufficient for ye same & all this in ye greate Iland wher conveniently they maye be had to the satisfaction of the Brickmaker Thomas Eames. And also ye sayd men deputed maye laye him out y^t litle pcell of medowe adioyneing to his home Lott, yf they shall thinke meete soe to doe. And moreover to give satisfaction to Tho: Allcocke for any damage he maye susteyne in digging or carying of the Bricke earth or any other waye concerneing ye Bricke.

Geo: Barber   George Barber is accepted for a Townes man & hath liberty to purchase wher he maye; condiconally that he subscribes to the Towne booke.

Je: Jorden   Graunte vnto Jeames Jordan Sixe acres of grownd to lye next beyond Jeames Allins Lott vpon the side of the Swampe as Jeames Allin doth.

Pe: Woodward   Graunted vnto Peter Woodward Twelue acres of land to lye next vnto y^t land last graunted vnto John Dwite to make vp his grateficaōon lott or neere therabouts. Eleazer Lusher appoynted to assist ye measurer herin.

Assist   Mr Wheelocke & John Luson are appoynted to assist the measurer to Laye out Jeames Jordans Lott or ether of them.

DEDHAM TOWN RECORDS. 75

Dedham   The 23th: December being ye 10th Month
1640   Assembled whose names are vnderwritten
   m^r Ralph Wheelocke, John Kingsberye, John Luson, John Haward, Eleazer Lusher, John Dwite, John Bacheler, Robte Hinsdell.
   That wch was agreed vpon ye 2. last meetings was Reade & Confirmed
              Graunted to Samuell Bullen Foure acres of grownd vpon the
S: Bullen   East adioyneing vnto m^r DeEngaynes Lott yf it may be con-
              veniently ther had in ye Judgem^t of those y^t are men Deputed
to set out ye same Viz^t Jno: Kingsbery & John Haward. pvided y^t he Relin-
quish ye 6: acres formerly graunted vnto him els wheare.
              Graunted vnto Robte Gowen Sixe acres to haue ye same
R: Gowen   Layd out neere vnto John Dwites newe graunte

              Edward Alleyn & Eleazer Lusher are Deputed to assist Jno
Bricke   Kingsbery & the other form^{rly} Deputed to fynd & sett out
              Bricke Earth, & all other necessaryes conc^rneing makeing of
Bricke &c^r according to a former order made in y^t behalfe.

The 29 day of the 10th Month: 1640:
Assembled those whose names are vnder written:
   Mr John Alleyn Pasto^r, Eld^r Huntinge, Sam Morse, Mich Metcalfe, Nathan Aldhouse, m^r Ralph Wheelocke, John Dwight, Fr: Chickringe, Robt Mason, Tho: Wight, Johnathan Fairbanke, Jno Bullard, Jno Frary, Robt Hinsdell, Joseph Kingsbury, Jno Gaye, Dan: Morse, Ric Euerard, Jno Morse, Jno Ellis, Jno Eaton, Hen Phillips, Ric Barber, Willm Bullard, Jno Batcheler, Ed Richards, Jno Roper, Jno Haward, Dan: Fisher, Jos Fisher, Twaits Strick-land, Robt Gowen, Jos Morse, Eli Lusher, Tim: Dwight, John Luson :——:
                      It is ordered that he that shalbe chosen hereafter to keepe
Recompence for   the booke: shall in recompence of his paynes haue for euery
Keeping the   grant entring six pence to be payd to him by the grantee:
Booke   And for entring euery Towne order six pence to be payd him
                      by the Collecter.
   Eliazer Lusher is Chosen to keepe the Towne booke for this next yeare & to act in all causes as one of the 7 men: Chosen to Joyne with him M^r Ed Alleyn Sam Morse Tho Wight Nathan Aldhouse Michael Metcalfe & Franc Chickringe: who are chosen to act in behalfe of ye Towne for one whole yeare next ensuinge haueing the same power put into their hands y^t their p^rdesessors haue had.
              John Kingsbury Willm Bullard & Robt Hinsdell chosen
Surveyers   Surveyers for ye high wayes for the next yeare.

January 12: 1640

Assembled: M^r Ed Alleyn, Sam: Morse, Mich Metcalfe, Tho Wight, Nathan Aldus, Franc Chickring & Eliazer Lusher

Measurer to be paid   Whereas by reason of ye weight & difficulty y^t is found in publike busynes & ye many discouragments that fall vpon them that are imployed therein: it is therfore ordered that whosoeuer hereafter shall haue any grant of Lands whatsoeuer within o^r sd Towne & shall not within ten dayes after the same is layd out & measured satisfie the measurer & keep of the booke: that his grant shall be voide & fully in ye hand of ye Towne to be disposed of as they shall se conuenient.

Fences   It is ordered y^t these men whose names are vnderwritten shall take care for the next yeare followinge: for the due pportion & sufficiency of fences & the due extent of high wayes & to se y^t ladders be puided acording to the order in y^t case puided

Mr Edw: Alleyn }
Tho Wight   } for ye smoth playne:

Sam Morse   }
Nathan Aldus   } for ye midle playne

John Kingsbury }
John Hayward, } for ye Iland.

John Dwite   }
Eliazer Lusher } for East Streete

Austen Kalem is chosen measurer for to pforme all such worke as belongs to the measurer for or within our Towne:

Fac-simile of original grant. showing hand-writing and signature of Eleazer Lusher.

DEDHAM TOWN RECORDS. 77

February
16: 1640

Fences

Assembled m^r Edw Alleyn, Tho Wight, Nathan Aldus, Sam^{ll} Morse, Fran Chickering, Mich Metcalfe, and Eli Lusher

It is ordered y^t all fences y^t are made of Rayles or pales shalbe made vp to the heigth of four foote either against high wayes or comon grounds or pticuler mens fences on their deuisions: and such fences as ar made by dytching shall be left to the Judgment of those men formerly deputed.

Jno Hayward

It is ordered y^t m^r Edw Alleyn and John Kingsbury shall haue power to satisfy John Hayward in respect of any real defect y^t may appeare to be in the laying out of his house lot: or that may fall therevnto by laying out of a high way thereby: & in case John Haward shall so desire he may haue liberty to chuse any 2 other men to joyne with them which four men shall haue full power to determine the sd case dependinge betwene the sd Jo Hayward & the towne in respect of the defects aforesaid.

February
22: 1640

Assembled Mr Edw Alleyn: Sam Morse: Na Aldus: Tho Wight: Mi Metcalfe: Fran: Chickering & Eli Lusher.

Whereas vpon good consideration & rule of Court in was ordered y^t no grants of any lands what so euer should be made to any manner of pson y^t was engaged to any pson by way of seruice or any such relation & was not frely at his owne disposinge yet forasmuch as it is now supposed y^t some young men y^t haue grants of lands formerly made to them would be willing to yeld themselues to seruice if their grants might remayne good to themselues

Seruants

It is now ordered that any such psons y^t haue any such grants made to them may yet notwithstanding yeld themselues to ye seruice of any pson within our towne & yet their grants shall remaine good to themselues their heyres or assignes: any order formerly made to the contrary notwithstanding: puided allways y^t ye sd grantees shall pay such charges as shall rateably be imposed vpon the sd lands.

m^r Sam: Cooke

Granted to Mr Samuell Cooke gent: one pcell of woodland as it now lyeth betwene one pcell of the like land formerly granted to M^r Ed Alleyn & ye way as it is now drawne toward the Meddowes:

Mr Ralph Wheelocke Jo Luson & Thomas Wight are appoynted to assist the measurer in laying out thereof adjoyning Estward vpon the lot of Henry Wilson & Joseph Clarke which is to be first layd out:

March: 16: 1640:

 Assembled Mr Edw Alleyn, Sam Morse, Na Aldus, Tho Wight, Mich Metcalfe, Fran: Chickering, & Eli Lusher.

Twaits
Strickland
 Granted to Twaits Strickland 3 acres & a halfe of land lying at the hethermost end of the South playne to be layd out to him by the men y^t shalbe deputed therevnto: it is to be layd out vpon the East side of the high way as it is now drawne.

A: Fisher
 Granted to Anthony Fisher 6 ackres of plowing land to be layd out accordinge to the discresion of men deputed therevnto it is to be layd out next Twaits Stricklands land on the South playne: heading vpon the high way toward y^t west & ye Swamp toward the East allwayes guided y^t he lay downe the former grant made to him of land neere m^r John Allins farme:

m^r J^no Allin
 Granted to Mr John Allin Pastour 9 acres of plowing ground vpon ye south playne in exchang for satisfaction for y^t land that he layd downe to Joseph Kingsbury vpon the midle playne: being to be layd out to him by men deputed therevnto: to lye next the land of Anthony Fisher: & in the same manner: Alwayes guided y^t he laye downe y^t land that was granted formerly to him for ye same end.

H: Chickering
 Granted to Henry Chickeringe 6 acres of plowing land on the south playne: to lye next to that pcell granted to Mr John Allin Pastour to be layd out by some men deputed therevnto:

 Tho Wight } are deputed to assist & direct the measurer in ye laying out
 Eli Lusher } of these former pcells according to the grants.

high wayes
 It is ordered that who so euer hereafter shall annoy any high way or drawen way wth the bodies or tops of trees which they felling shall suffer to lye more then 4 dayes after the fall thereof euery such offender shall forfeit for euery tree so annoying the said wayes the some of 5 shillings to be payd to the Collecter of our Towne within ten dayes after he shall demand the same & who so euer shall suffer any such annoyance to be made by any tree which he hath allready felled & shall not within [14] dayes after the publication hereof remoue the same annoyance shall also forfeit the like penalty to be payd as aforesaid.

repealed
meetings
 [*It is ordered y^t vpon euery 2^d: 4th day of euery month there shalbe constantly a meeting of the 7 men to order Towne affaires: either at the Meeting house: or some place nere: that so any pson that hath any busines with them may haue recourse at time & place aforesaid.]

May 12 1641

Assembled: Mr Edw Alleyn, Tho Wight, Na Aldus, Sam Morse, Eli Lusher, Mich Metcalfe.

Jn° Hunting
N: Colbourne
H: Smith

Whereas there was formerly granted to seuerall men diuers planting lotts vpon the Eastermost playne & now vpon farther experience diuers of those lotts are not found fit for y^t vse there is therefore now granted vnto John Huntinge Eld^r & Nathaniell Colbourne and to Henery Smith to haue one planting lott nere or vpon the southermost playne: the lott of Henry Smith to lye nere the lot of ye sd Jn° Hunting & Nath Colbourne to be layd out to them by the Towne. Alwayes puided y^t they shall lay downe their rights in those lots vpon ye East playne formerly layd out to them or their predesesors: Each of these planting lots shall conteyne 12 acres of land mo^r or lese as it shalbe layd out to them by m^r Ralph Wheelocke Henery Chickering Thomas Wight & Eliazer Lusher:

July 14th 1641

Assembled: Mr Edw Alleyn, Thomas Wight, Nath Aldus, Sam^ll Morse, Michael Metcalfe, Franc Chickering, & Eli Lusher.

Towne bounds

It is ordered y^t Willm Bearestowe Daniell Fisher John Ellis Nathaniell Colbourne Tim Dwight & Thomas Jorden shall asist m^r Jn° Oliuer measurer in laying out the bounds of this Towne compleate who together with Mr Edward Alleyn are appoynted to pforme the same 4 of these men are required to asist herein together ye one halfe of ye time other 4 to doe the like the other halfe thereoff:

Jn° Guile

Michael Metcalfe Robert Hinsdell & Eliazer Lusher are appoynted & enabled with power to lay out and determine the extent of John Guyles Lott which he bought of John Roper according as by their discresion they shall judge to be equall and satisfactory.

wayes to Mill

It is Ordered y^t Francis Chickeringe John Dwight Johnathan Fairbanke or any 3 of them shall search out appoynt determine and lay out a Cart way to our Water Mill for a common leading way where euer they or any 3 of them shall by their discresion judg most conuenient for the Towne as also such foote pathes as may most conueniently be found nighest & best pasable or y^t may be made passable: and also the sd men or any 3 of them shall haue power to make such satisfaction to any that shall haue damage as by their discresion they shall judg equall and as the Towne in other the like cases doth giue.

Jn° Kingsbury

Granted to John Kingsbury certaine land for an enlargment by his swampe for a pasture to stay his Bullocks:

Jn⁰ Hayward

Granted to John Hayward also a pcell of land to stay his working Bullocks both these parcells now granted are to be layd out and fully determined at ye appoyntment & by the direction of Mr Edw Alleyn John Bacheler and John Eaton: these are to be pformed wthin 3 monthes after ye date hereof

Jn⁰ Bacheler

Granted to Jn⁰ Batcheler one smale pcell of land nere the clay pitts on the Iland: to be layd out by the direction of Mr Edw Alleyn: John Kingsbury & John Eaton: who are also to lay out the high way leading from the clay pits to the common nere John Haywards

Sept 15 1641

Assembled Mr Edw Alleyn: Sam^{ll} Morse, Michael Metcalfe, Thomas Wight, Nathan Aldus and Eliazer Lusher

Tho Wight:

Granted to Jn⁰ Luson & Tho Wight one pcell of vpland being a smale playne lying vpon the top of a hill: nere or about the south playne to be equally deuided betwene them: allwayes prouided y^t ye land so layd out to them exceed not ye measure of twelue acres: Henery Chickering Mr Ralph Wheelocke are deputed to asist & direct the measurer in laying out this grant:

Low: playne

Granted vnto John Dwight Francis Chickeringe Eliazer Lusher Johnathan Fairbanke Michael Powell Peter Woodward Michael Metcalfe & John Frary that percell of the Low playne (nere Mr Stoughtons farme) that belongs to this Towne to be deuided amongst themselues as they or the major part of them shall agree to be layd out by themselues or by whome soeuer they shall apoynt or imploy therein.

Octob^r 25 1641

Assembled: Mr Edw Alleyn: Sam^{ll} Morse Francis Chickering Thomas Wight & Eliazer Lusher

North Meddow

For as much as certaine meddow formerly layd out to certaine men of our Towne as is now taken away by the measuringe of the grant made formerly to the farmes & being there is a certaine quantitie of Meddow nere Oake hill yet vndisposed of it is therefore now promised that the sd pcell of Meddow shall not be granted to any man vntill these men be first Considered & prouided for:

Novemb^r 11 1641

Assembled: Sam^{ll} Morse Nathan Aldus Thomas Wight Fra: Chickering El Lusher

Tho: Eames

It is Ordered y^t wheras Tho Eames hath made improuement vpon a pcell of the townes land for making Bricks the Towne doth hereby promise y^t he shall haue liberty still so to Doe

DEDHAM TOWN RECORDS. 81

& farther y^t if the Towne shall se cause to take the sd pcell from him they shall not so doe but vpon paying such satisfaction to the sd Thomas or his heyres as shalbe then thought fit by two or 3 Indifferent workemen chosen by the towne & ye sd Thomas Eames or his heyres:

H: Aldridge   Henery Aldridge is entertained vpon two acres of Tho Eames his lott Tho Eames is therfore granted to haue so much layd to his lott out of ye wast thereby as shall make ye remainder two acres & also to haue two acres layd out vpon ye plowing playne vpon the Iland in satisfaction for ye 2 acres y^t he pted withall to Hen: Aldridge.

Bullocke pasture   Whereas there was form^{r}ly granted certaine land for a pasture for working Cattle vnto Samuell Morse, John Dwight & Francis Chickeringe: to be layd out next Dorchester Bounds It is now Ordered y^t [*m^r Edw Alleyn] Jo Kingsbury John Haward: & Mich Metcalfe or any 3 of them shall haue full power to lay out the same according to the said grant at their discresions Antho: Fisher seni Nath Coaleburne ar ioyned to the other 3 men befor named any 3 of wch 5 haue power to settle this grant.

Decemb^r 8th 1641

Assembled Mr Edw Alleyn: Nathan Aldus Tho Wight Sam^{ll} Morse Eli Lusher Francis Chickerey & Michael Metcalfe.

Collector   Mr Ralph Wheelocke Michael Metcalfe & Nathan Aldus are hereby deputed to take the accounts of John Kingsbury Collector within ten next after the date hereoff:

m^r Wheelocke   Whereas there was form^{r}ly a grant made to m^r Ralph Wheelocke of 4 acres of land to be layd out beyond vine brooke & now vpon further view it is questionable whether the sd pcell wilbe found fit for his vse or not It is therefore now Ordered that J^{no} Kingsbury Tho: Wight & J^{no} Bacheler shall assist the measurer & direct the sd 4 acres by their discresion either in ye foresd place or on the North side of Charles Riuer as they shall judg most fit and conuenient.

South playne   Whereas diuers psons haue had form^{r}ly certaine pcells of land granted them vpon the south playne & being now about to fence in the same & being willing if it may be to spare timber & labour which is hopefull to be done by makeing fences through the swamp the towne therefore in consideration hereof doth hereby giue liberty to those psons that haue lands in the aforesd place to make vse of such vnderwood & rayles as they shall need in the swampe & to make such fences from their sd pcells to the pond called the great pond as may be sufficient for their vse. The swamp that they shall so enclose shall yet remaine in ye hands of the towne notwithstanding to dispose of as they shall se cause

Swampe

Granted vnto Tho Eames Mr Henery Deengaine John Ellis and Austen Kalem: to each of them 2 acres of swampe lyinge in ye end of the swampe next the meddow in the great Iland & to Samuell Bullein 2 acres of swampe lying on the north End of the sd Iland next the meddow there:

Decemb 28: 1641

Assembled Mr Edw Alleyn Sam^{ll} Morse Michael Metcalfe Na: Aldus: Fra: Chickering: Tho: Wight and Eli: Lusher.

m^r Edw: Alleyn

Whereas by vertue of an order in such cases ɡuided by ye towne there haueing appeared an vnauoydable necesitie of a high way through ye house lott of Mr Edw: Alleyn: the Towne haueing taken parcell of the sd lott for the vse of the towne for a high way according to ye aforesaid order: wherby also the sd m^r Edw Alleyn is occasioned to stand charged with the makeing & maintaining of such fences vpon both sides of the sd way through his Lott as may be sufficient to secure the sd Lott: the Towne doth therefore in consideration of the premisses grant to the sd m^r Alleyn: such land in our Towne for satisfaction as shall by our Comittees (together with m^r Alleyn) herevnder named be thought equall and just & both pties agree vpon according to the form^r order the sd land to be layd out vpon the north side of Charles Riu^r ouer against or neere the fearme formerly granted to m^r Sam^{ll} [Cooke]

Mr Ralph Wheelocke, John Kingsbury Thomas Wight or any 2 of them are comittees for ye pformance hereof

Fra: Chickering Edw: Richards

Whereas there hath bin cleare proofe made y^t the house lotts of Francis Chickering & Edward Richards are defectiue & also that Jno Dwight wants halfe a Lott which remaines yet due to him.

It is therefore Ordered y^t whereas the aforesd psons haue nominated & chosen John Kingsbury & the Towne hath on & in behalfe of themselues hath chosen [   ] Lusher for to view setle & determine satisfaction for each of the [   ] as followeth: viz: for John Dwight on the swamp playne for Francis Chickering on the wigwam playne for Ed Richards [   ] against the East end of the lotts in ye est streete & in case the Comittees shall not agree they shall haue power ioyntly to chose whome [   ] shall please as vmpier to determine the same or any of the sd satisfactions: or in case y^t in any of [   ] places there shall not be found ground fit or sufficient [   ] liberty & power to make satisfaction els where.

DEDHAM TOWN RECORDS. 83

Dedham   The 22th of ye 12th Month calld Fabvry
1641 Assembled whose names are vnd'written.

M^r: Edward Alleyn: Nathan Alldus: Sam^{ll} Morse: Henry Chickring: John Dwite: Thomas Wight: Fra: Chickring.

That wch was agreed vpon ye last meeting was read & confirmed

Henry Smyth his house being lately burnte & looseing his Corne therby Requesteth 2 piñes for board to gayne Corne wth at ye Baye to wch it is condescended:

Ord^rd that ye note of debts shalbe deliu^red to ye Collector that he may gather w^t can be gotten wth expedicō for defraying of Charges necessary:

Graunted vnto John Eld^rkin 3 acres of Land vpon ye East side of the Milbrooke, next to ye Millpond:

Nathan Aldus & John Dwite, appoynted to Joyne wth ye measurer in setting out of ye same speedely:

The 28th of ye 12th Month

Assembled whose names are vnd^rwritten: Fra: Chickring Mr Edw: Alleyn, Nathan Aldus, Sam^{ll}: Morse, Henery Chickring, John Dwite, Thomas Wight.

John Roper, being destitute of Corne, craveth licence to make sale of some board wch he hath ready sawne, for [   ] out of Towne: It is graunted soe to doe, and to take more Timb^r by ye wood Reeves to ye quantety of 1000 boards for ye same purpose:

John Fairbanke, desireth ye like for a smale quantety to ye same purpose, and graunted him:

Dan:^{ll} Morse desireth Cead^{rs} for boad for ye same case, to be set out by ye Wood Reeves: If he hath not of his owne:

Iland Playne   Ordered y^t Mr Edward Alleyn, Sam:^{ll} Morse & Nathan Aldus. shall wth ye measurer set out the playne in ye great Iland vnto such men as are named in a note Giueing vnto o^r sayd comittees full power to hold or to Alter any of ye sayd quantetys to more or lesse acres as in their descretions they shall see fitt, according to ye quantety of ye whole, that they shall ther finde: The portions y^t ought to adioyne to ye Medowes first to be set out by them: And y^t ye sayd comittees shall apoint a good pt of ye small yong trees at ye corner next ye pond for ye Comon fence if they se [   ] to doe & apoynt ye same.

Dedham   The 1th of ye first Month: called March:
1641 Assembled whose names are vnd^r written:

Mr Edw: Alleyn, Nathan Aldus, Sam^{ll} Morse, Henery Chickring, Thomas Wight, Jno Dwite: Fra: Chickring:

That wch was agreed vpon ye last meeting was read & confirmed:

John Bullard hath lib^{r}ty to mowe y^t pcell of Meddowe that is ye comon Clay pitt, next to Ant^o: Fishers for this yeare:

Fences Vpon complaynt by Henery: Chickring as a greevance concerning a fence not made, whereby he hath sustayned much Damage, Wee appoint Mr Edw: Alleyn: Jno: Kingsb^{r}y and Eleazar Lusher to viewe & pportion ye same fence by whome to be made & mayntained & all other fences in ye same field:

Wayes The sayd men or 2 of them, to viewe & set out & ord^r all high wayes & necessary footpathes in all ye Towne, y^t all may be recorded, And to appoint, Gates, Barres, or stiles wth necessary stepps to be made by ye owners of ye fence for ye comfortable passage ou^r ye same, wth Corne, Meale, or other burthens &c: accordingly:

Kemp Francis Chickring, Eleazar Lusher, are appoynted to viewe Edward Kemps lott, as hee requesteth.

Graunted to Eld^r Hunting one slipe of Land adioyning to his Lott towards ye South: vpon ye South playne in quatety about halfe an acre, to be set out by Henery Chickring and Tho: Wight:

H Phillips Whereas form^{r}ly Philemon Dolton being possesed of a 12 Acre Lott, did graunt 2 Acres of ye same vnto Rowland Clarke to haue it recompenced: as by a Towne ord^r appeth and after selleth the same Lott, to Nic^o Phillips who sells ye same also to Henery Phillps who now requireth satisfation for ye same 2 Acrs It is ordered y^t Henery Chickring & Tho: Wight shall set out soe much as shall satisfy him for ye sayd 2 Acres vpon ye South Playne next vnto Nathani: Colborne, if ther it may be had.

Fences Whereas many Fences in o^r Towne are neglected by Gaps in ye same, Barrs left downe, & otherwise insufficient, that mens Corne nowe sowne & p^{r}sently to be sowne; In the field cannot be in saffety, as it ought to be: It is therefore now ordered y^t eu^{r}y man haueing any defects in his fences as aboue sayd; shall repayer & make ye same sufficient before ye 20th day of this p^{r}sent month, and constantly maynetayne ye same sufficient vpon those penulties imposed by former orders, made concerning sufficiency of fences, for ye saffety of Corne accordingly: And men deputed to take care as aboue in their seu^{r}all limitts, & may alsoe be called els where to assist in difficult cases, Are vizt

Jno: Kingsbery } for ye Iland.
Jno: Hayward,

Jno: Dwite } for East Streete
Eleazar Lusher

Sam^{ll} Morse } for midle playne
Nathan Aldus

Mr Edw: Alleyn } for ye smoth playn:
HeneryChickring

And ye same men to take care of Ladders according to form^r orders in y^t behalfe.

DEDHAM TOWN RECORDS.   85

Dedham   The 4th of ye 2d Month Called Aprill.

1642   Assembled whose names are vnder written vizt

Mr Edw: Alleyn, Henry Chickering, Nathan Aldus, Fran: Chickering, Sam: Morse, John Dwite.

Swine: For as much as ther hath ben many Comp^t Conserneing Swyne of much Damage done the last yeare by them notwth standing the strict order form^rly made for to p^rvent such inconveniences as many men haue vndergone by reason of the neglect of Execuçon of the aforesayd order made the 23: of the first month 1639. Admitting then more then an wholl yeares warneing for pviding Fences agaynst ye same. All Swine being to be yoaked & Ringed as by the order appeth: wch nowe we inioyne to be sevearly Executed & the penalties therof. And therfore doe further order that whoesoever of our towne from henceforth shall see any Swyne vnyoaked or vnringed & not in the grownd of its owner, nor followed wth a keep neer p^rsent contrary to ye aforesayd order shall give spedy knoweledge to the owner therof: or shall put the same Swine into the pownde to be Regulated vpon the penalty of 6^d forfated for every Swyne, & every tyme soe seen as is meete y^t care may be had of eu^ry mans saffety: And the same to be leavyed by distresse for ye vse of the towne accordingly wth out any delaye.

Dedham   The 6th of ye 3: Month. Called Maye

1642   Assembled whose names are vnderwritten

M^r: Edw: Alleyn, Henry Chickering, Tho: Wighte, Nathan Aldus, Fran: Chickering, Sam: Morse, John Dwite.

H: Phillips Henry Chickering & Tho: Wight form^rly deputed to set out a pcell of Land for satisfaction of Hen: Phillips for 2 acres form^rly graunted vnto Rowland Clarke by Philemon Dalton wch the towne pmised to make good vnto ye sayd Lott wch the sayd Henry nowe possesseth. They Returneing answer of their pformance & of his acceptance therof vpon the South playne: wch we also appve of both for ye sayd 2: acres & also for his Interest in the waye layd through his Lott towards the house of Dan Morse accordingly.

Graunted to Sam: Morse; Daniel Morse & to Rich: Ellis ech of them to haue a pcell of vpland In ye greate Iland wthin ye lyne ther what may be conveniently ther had at ye discretion of those men deputed to lay out ye same.

Survey of Wheras some yeares since it was by gen^rall Court directed
Lands y^t a gen^rall survaye of all graunts & alienaçons of lands & houses Done in our towne shold be made & Record therof kept & the same transcribed to the sayd Court. Whervpon Edward Alleyn gent was Requested to pforme the same as appeth by a towne

order made ye 28 of March 1639 vpon wch he making a begining therin and transcribed ye same to the Courte aforesayd for that tyme But by Reason of many things Remayneing vnpfect: pceedings in the same weare Iterupted vntill this p^rsent: wch we well apprehend not to be saffe for our posterety nor answering ye Courts Comand. Whervpon we agayne Requesting the sayd Edw: Alleyn to make pceeding in ye same. To wch he is Content to make Indeavour therin: we pmiseing that all lands graunted & Alienated shalbe made pfect And y^t he shall haue ye same Alowance form^rly ordered And may take his Kindman John Newton for to assist him in writeing of & Concerneing ye same And further yf the sayd Jno Newton shall ingrosse what was form^rly Transcribed in a booke for ye Towne he shall haue Convenient aloweance for his paynes therin.

 Dedham The 10th of ye 5th Month Called Julye
 1642 Assembled whose names are vnderwritten

 Mr Edw: Alleyn, Henry Chickering, Nathan Aldus, Sam: Morse, Fran: Chickering, John Dwite, Tho: Wighte.

W. Bearstowe Willm Bearestowe complayneing of his 8: acre house lott: it was viewed & fownd to be very Defectiue in the one halfe of the same by a multitude of Stones. Wherfore we order & graunte vnto the sayd Willm Eight acres of vpland betweene the Corners of the greate Naponset Swampe about Southwest from our Towne. To be layd out by men hereafter named.

John: Hayward Wheras ther was an high waye beneath John Haywards Lott The same is fownd inconvenient in diverse Respects. Therfore we doe order y^t an high waye in steade of the aforesayd high waye shalbe layd out 2. Rods broade through the South end of the Swampe of ye sayd John Hayward next vnto John Bachelers Swampe. & the Former waye to be possessed by ye sayd John Hayward in liewe of y^s p^rsent waye.

Jno Hunting
Jno Fairbanke
Jno Frary
 Wheras John Hunting our Elder, Jonathan Farebanke & John Frary had each of them appoynted to haue 6: acres of medowe for their second Devision to make vp 12: acres to their Lotts But by Reason of some Interuption arising by Challenge made of the same medowe to belonge vnto some of the Farmes &c Wherfore we thinkeing it not fitting to hold them in suspence any longer. Doe therfore nowe order & graunte vnto ye sayd three men above named to haue ech of them Sixe acres in ye medowe neere vnto the South side of Ballpate hill to be measured out vnto them seu^rally by our

Measurer & others appoynted thervnto heervnder named for their full satisfaction to make vp the 12: acres of medowe due vnto them
Francis Chickering
John Dwite
Tho: Wighte

pvided that they Relinquist the abouesayd graunts form^{r}ly made vnto them.

Jno Ellis   For as much as John Ellis is in ye same Condicõn as the aboue named men, for 2: acres appoynted him in ye sayd Challenged medowes &c^r We therfore nowe graute vnto him twoe acres of medowe at Ballpate hill to lye next vnto the afore named mens medowe to be measured out by the aboue deputed men. pvided that he Relinquisheth the former 2: acres soe apoynted vnto him.

Swampe   John Dwite & Francis Chickering form^{r}ly deputed to set out the Smale pcells of Swampe next the North East Corn^r of ye Wigwam playne to the adioyneing inhabitants. Edward Alleyn is Chosen to Joyne wth them to assist in the same soe graunted vnto them.

T Wight   Graunted vnto Thomas Wight Eight acres of Land vpon ye hill & vally thervpon neere vnto South medowe. The hill being Form^{r}ly graunted vnto the sayd Thomas & John Luson, whoe nowe both of them doe Relinquish ye former graunt made vnto them. And the aforesayd Thomas Requesting an inlargem^t it is granted vnto him to Ruñe to ye Swampe at ye North end of the same hill vpon his form^r lyne.

E Richards   Edward Richards for defect in his house Lott hath graunted nowe vnto him the other pte of ye hill & vally by the East side of Tho: Wight: Conteyneing 8 acres more or lesse to Ruñe also to the Swampe as ye sayd Thomas doth at ye North end of the sayd Hill.

R: Gowen   Graunted vnto Robte Gowen Sixe acres of vpland neere vnto the South medowe & nexte vnto the West side of Thomas Wight ther: pvided y^t he Relinquish all other graunts made vnto him form^{r}ly.

Ben Smith   Graunted vnto Beniamyne Smith Sixe acres of vpland neere vnto the South medowe to adioyne vnto Robert Gowen yf ther it maye be had.

G Barber   Graunted vnto George Barber Sixe acres of vpland nere vnto the South Medowe & next vnto Ben: Smith yf ther it maye be had.

J Fisher   Graunted vnto Josua Fisher Sixe acres of vpland nere vnto the South Medowe & nexte vnto George Barber yf ther it may be had.

Mr Wheelocke, Hen: Chickering, John Luson, Deputed to assist & direct the measurer in laying out all the form^r graunted pcells And yf they fynd that ther the severall pcells can not be layd out in that order wch is described then we give them or any twoe of the sayd thre soe named full power to order & laye out ther or therabouts what is soe graunted according to their discretions soe neere as they can to make a feild of them together, or otherwise as they may best contriue.

Jno Thurston   Graunted to John Thurston all y^t pcell of Land wch lyeth betweene Jeames Jordan, & the high waye leading vnto ye South playne, & also soe much of the Swampe adioyneing vnto ye p^{r}mises next towards ye south playne as may be thought fitt & carye a fence on that side conveniently streight. Allwayes Reserved vnto ye towne a Carte waye from the aforsayd high waye by the bottome of ye p^{r}mises vnto the Corner betwene ye 2. Swamps wher Tymber hath ben gotten.

Henry Chickering & Tho: Wight to set out ye same & E Alleyn to Joyne wth them in ye same doeing.

Graunted to Henry Chickering all those pcells of Course medowe Conteyneing Sixe acres more or lesse as they lye aboue y^t pcell of medowe form^{r}ly graunted vnto m^r Phillips. To be set out by ———

Graunted y^t Jno Ellis may haue 2. Ceader trees to make board & sell ye same out of towne to atteyne vnto appell.

Eli Lusher   Whereas the Towne according to their vsuall Custome did make Choise of Mr Edward Alleyn gent to keepe the Towne booke and to act in towne afaires with the other 6 men then chosen: And for as much as it hath pleased god to take away the sd Mr Alleyn by death the towne being assembled the 28th of October 1642 did nominate & by their voate chuse & appoynt Eleazer Lusher to succeed in the place & trust in which the sd Mr Alleyn was interressed to sd Eli Lusher so to stand in y^t seruice trust & power vntill y^t terme be accomplished whereunto m^r Alleyn aforsd was deputed

[¹Md: That whereas the town hath formerly according to thier vsuall Custom as allso according to the order of Court in y^t Case puided mad Choice of 7 men for the regulating of the planting & prudentiall affayers of the Town and to that end hath allso mad Choice of Edward Alleyn: gent: to keepe the Town Book and to ayd the other 6 men in the former seruice as may by that act of the Town recorded mor playnely appear and that for as much as it hath pleased God to take away by death the said m^r Edward Alleyn: the town in consideration of the p^{r}mises being mett together vpon the 28 day of October 1642 did

---

[1] A leaf fastened at the beginning of Vol. I., of the original Records. On the reverse of the leaf is the following note:

M^d. This leaf was found in John Bullard, Esq.'s Garret, Sept. 5, 1850.

J. H. Cobb, Town Clerk.

[ED.]

nõminat and by thier voate chuse & appoint Eleazer Lusher to succeed in the place & trust wherin the said Mr Alleyn was by that foresaid Choice of the Town interressed: the said Eleazer Lusher so to stand in that seruice trust & power vntill that tearme be accomplished whervnto m^r Alleyn aforesd was so deputed.

[signatures]

together wth other the inhabbitants of the town then assembled.]

Nouember 4: 1642:

Assembled: whose names are vnder written

Henery Chickering, Samuell: Morse, Nathan Aldus, John Dwight, Thomas Wight, Eliazer Lusher.

J^no Gaye: Wheras John Gaye hath parted with some of his house lott for a high way for the vse of the Towne as also hath bin at charge in fencing against the sd high way which according to order of the Towne ought to be satisfied for: It is therefore ordered that the sd J^no Gaye shall haue satisfaction tendered to him by the men here vnder named which satisfaction shalbe in land in or vpon a certaine smale playne lyinge southwest from Mr Cookes farme & nere the same: it is to be directed and assigned to him by & at the discression of Henery Chickeringe & Thomas Wight

J^no Gaye Granted vnto John Gaye 3 acres of vpland to lye adioyninge to to the aforesd grant to be layd out to him by the direction of the men assigned to lay out the former grant:

Jos Fisher Granted to Josuah Fisher 6 acres of vpland to be layd out to him vpon the foresaid playne nere m^r Cookes farme

Ben Smith Granted vnto Beniamen Smith 6 acres of vpland to be layd out to him on the foresaid playne

prouided that these 2 last grantees lay downe all other right by former grants of land vpon or neare the south hill.

These grants are to be layd out by the direction and assignm^t of the men form^rly deputed to direct John Gayes grant.

Dan: Fisher Granted vnto Daniell Fisher 6 acres of vpland to be layd out vpon the foresd playne at the direction of those men form^rly deputed to lay out the former grants there.

Nouemb^r 19 1642

Assembled those whose names are vnderwritten

Henry Chickering, Sam^{ll} Morse, Nathan Aldus, Franc: Chickeringe, Thomas Wight, John Dwight, Eliazer Lusher.

Timber Wheras there was an order vpon good consideration made for the orderly improuement of timber vpon the common ground of the towne wherein timber for sale out of towne or for any that are not admitted townesmen is restrayned. Yet now vpon good reason moueing therunto it is ordered that the 7 men which are chosen for ye ordering of towne affaires shall vpon the request of any Inhabitant of ye Towne being made in a publique towne meetinge, haue power to depute some one or more of themselues to assigne vnto them such supply of timber from the towne as shall by ye sd 7 men be judged conuenient:

Nouember 25 1642

Assembled those whose names are vnderwritten

Henry Chickering, Sam^{ll} Morse, Nathan Aldus, Tho: Wight, John Dwight, Eliazer Lusher.

Wheras Anthony Fisher hath purchased 4 acres or vpland of Mr Ralph Wheelocke which was granted the sd Mr Wheelocke in recompence for his depting with 2 acres of his home lott: according to an order of the towne in y^t case puided & ye sd Anthony hath declared his desire to haue it layd out to him

A: Fisher There is therefore granted to the sd Anthony Fisher 4 acres of vpland to be layd out to him or his assignes by the men form^{r}ly deputed to lay out the grants vpon that playne which sd pcell shalbe layd out vpon the Northerly side of the pcell which is layd out vnto Daniell Fisher & next therevnto: allwayes puided that he shall lay downe all right or clayme to any grants form^{r}ly made to him for satisfaction of this his purchace & y^t he take this foresd pcell in full contentment for the same:

Jos: Kingsbury Wheras Joseph Kingsbury haueing formerly receiued some damage in regard of his accomodation of meddow & other things of that nature as also y^t he offers to lay downe 2 acres of his meddow nere or against the Comon meddow allready layd out to him There is therefore in consideration of the premisses granted to the sd Joseph Kingsbury 2 acres of meddow being part of a pcell of meddow nere to the hill called bald pate hill: southerly from the parcell of meddow formerly Layd out to Eld^r Huntinge: Allwayes puided that it being layd out according to the grant he take it for full satisfaction for all the sd prejudice or cause of complaynt & lay downe the 2 acres aforesd.

John Dwight & Francis Chickeringe are deputed to direct in laying out this grant:

R: *Weares*   Robert Weares is Admitted to the purchace of Thomas Eames his house lott and 3 acres of land.

T: *Fuller*   Thomas Fuller is admitted to the purchace of Martin Phillips his Lott:

December 30 1642

Assembled: whose names are vnder written

Henery Chickeringe, Nathan Aldus, Thomas Wight, Fran: Chickering, & Eliazer Lusher.

W: *Bullard*   Granted vnto William Bullard 4 acres of vpland to be layd out vpon the playne where John Gaye Daniell Fisher and other of their neighbours haue grants of land form^{r}ly made to them.

Granted to John Bullard 3 acres ½ of vpland to be layd out to him vpon the same playne where Willm Bullard hath his grant.

Henry Chickering & Thomas Wight are deputed to direct in the laying out these 2 parcells

Whereas the Towne hath formerly granted a pcell of land called South hill to be deuided vnto Thomas Wight Robert Gowinge Edward Richards & Georg Barber & for as much as a smale pcell lying nere thereunto falleth conueniently within the compase of the most fit place of setting their fence there is therefore granted to the sd grantees formerly named liberty to take in the sd smale pcell of vpland within their fence: to haue it to themselues & their heyres for euer: this grant to be appoynted & directed by the discresion of John Luson & Henry Chickeringe

Whereas there hath bin formerly a grant of a certaine pcell of the low playne nere Mr Stoughtons rayles made to diuers of ye Inhabitants of east streete as by the sd grant more playnely doth appeare and for as much as the sd pcell cannot conuenient be fenced in without liberty of enclosing some of the waest land of the towne: There is therefore granted to the posessors of the aforesd pcell of the Low playne so much of the common ground of the towne as may most nesesarily be needfull for the directing of their fence about the former grant.

The said addition of land to ly common to the sd grantees and their heyres for euer

The place where the sd fence shall stand according to the intent of this grant shall be appoynted & directed at and by the discression of Nathan Aldus & Henry Phillips.

Dedham   The 2 day of ye 11th Month called January:
1642   Assembled those whose names are vnderwritten

Mr Jno Allin Mr Ralph Wheelocke Hen: Chickeringe John Lewson Anthony Fisher John Gay Thomas Wight: Daniell Fisher John Thurston Willm Bullard John Bullard John Hayward: John Bacheler John Eaton Austen Kalem Thomas Payne Sam^{ll} Bullein: Chris: Smith Tho Allcocke: Henry Aldridge Joseph Kingsbury Robt Mason Eld Jo Huntinge Nath: Colbourne Hen: Phillips Nathan Aldus Daniell Morse John Morse Hen: Smith: John Roper Georg Barber: Tho: Leader Lambert Genere: Tim Dwight Jno Dwight Edw Kempe Tho: Bayes Edw: Richards: Francis Chickering Willm Bearestowe Johnathan Fairbanke Mich Powell Mich Metcalfe John Frary Eli Lusher Robte Hinsdell Petter Woodward Richard Euerard John Guile: Georg Bearestowe Nathaniell Whiteinge:

Whereas it was the desire of the Inhabitants of this Towne that there should be a suruey taken of all such lands nere our towne: as were fit for improuem^t with the plough & that the 7 men then to be Chosen should dispose of them by a generall diuident by those generall rules then ppounded & agreed on: viz: the number of psons is on considerable rule in deuision: yet not ye only rule and it was concluded y^t seruants should be referred to mens estates. 2: According to mens estates: 3 According to mens Ranke & Quallitie and desert and vsefullnes either in Church or Comon Weale: 4 that men of vsefull trades & may haue materialls to improue the same be encouraged by haue land as nere home as may be conuenient and that husbandmen that haue abilities to improue more then others be considered in this deuision

Also it was with an vnanimous consent concluded that some portion of land in this entended deuision should be set a part for publique vse: viz for the Towne the Church & A fre Schoole viz: 40 acres at the least or 60 acres at the most.

Also that some land should be deuided to those lotts in o^r towne that are without present Inhabitants: & y^t more should be reserued in the Townes hand to bestowe vpon them as the Towne shall thinke good.

Also it was Concluded that those that haue allready had free grants of Land besides their house lotts those fre grants shall be accounted as part of their diuident which they are now to receiue.

And wheras Eliazer Lusher hath bin more then ordinarily imployed in publique seruice in Towne affaires to his great damage & lose of time it was therefore the mind of the Towne declared by voate that the 7 men now to be chosen should make him some recompence in this deuision of lands.

And it was the desire & request of the Towne: that our Reuerend Pastour & o^r Reuerend Elder: and John Kingsbury should aduise with the 7 men in this deuision of lands

Michael Powell is Chosen to keepe the Towne booke for this yeare next ensuing: and to Write the Record & Transcript: and to act in all Towne affaires as one of the 7 men: & there is Chosen to Joyne with him Henery Chickering: John Dwight, Thomas Wight, Eliazer Lusher: Francis Chickering and Peter Woodward: who haue the same power that their predecesors haue had to order the planting & prudentiall affaires of the Towne & to dispose of lands by a generall diuident.

John Hayward is Chosen Collector for the Towne for this next yeare.

Thomas Wight
Nathaniell Colborne } are chosen Wood reues for this next yeare.
Henry Phillips

John Eaton
Edward Kempe } are chosen Surueyo^{rs} for ye high wayes for this next yea^r
Daniel Fisher

John Newton,
Robert Crosman } are Admitted Townsmen.
Henry Glouer

Also it was ordered at this generall meeting that what grants of land haue bin formerly made and are not yet layd out that they shalbe layd out that Justice may be first satisfied.

The 18 day of 11 Month 1642

Assembled: Henery Chickeringe John Dwight Thomas Wight Eliazer Lusher: Fra: Chickering Peter Woodward and Michael Powell.

It is Ordered that John Dwight Francis Chickering & Michael Powell shall haue power to lay out swampe formerly granted to the Inhabitants of the East streete: as they shall se conuenient according to an order in that case prouided

The 30th of the 11 Month 1642

Assembled: Hen: Chickering Jno Dwight Tho: Wight Eli Lusher Fra: Chickering Peter Woodward & Mich Powell

G: *Bearstow* — Granted to Georg Bearstowe a pcell or pcells of Swampe to be layd out to his eight acre Lott proportionable to other like lotts according to a former grant to them to be layd out by John Dwight Francis Chickering & Mich Powell

E *Richard Ellis* — Granted to Richard Ellis 6 acres of vpland lying westward of Joseph Morses Meddowe on ye South side of Charles Riuer.

D. *Morse* — Granted to Daniell Morse a pcell of vpland lying nere the sd 6 acres granted to Rich Ellis: so it exceed not the quantitie of 6 acres: prouided that these 2 grantees relinquish their former grants of land vpon the Iland

Jos: Morse
his meaddow.

Mr Ralph Wheelocke Thomas Wight & Willm Bullard are deputed to lay out these 2 former grants: and a parcell of land formerly granted to Joseph Morse there: adjoyning to

Rate

Mr Ralph Wheelocke Jno Hayward & Nathan Aldus & Eliazer Lusher are deputed to make a Rate for charges about ye meting house and other charges annexed thereuntoe.

The 6 of the 12 month 1642

Assembled Henery Chickering Eli Lusher Fra: Chickering Thomas Wight John Dwight Peter Woodward & Michael Powell

Whereas Mr Edward Alleyn was deputed to write the record of the Towne & the transcript & to imploy mr John Newton his kinsman in the worke the Towne promising to giue him satisfaction therefore We haue now agreed with mr Jno Newton for & in the behalfe of mr Edward Alleyn & himselfe and doe allow him for writing allready done 23^s 4^d and for the purchace of ye booke of Record for the vse of the Towne 6^s 8^d & for another paper booke & 5 orders due to mr Alleyn for entring them 3^s 6^d

Eliazer Lusher hath liberty granted him to purchace that grant of land which the Towne hath formerly made & conferred vpon Gyles Fuller and Thomas Ward lying vpon the wigwam playne & farther that the Towne doth hereby declare that if the sd Eliazer shall so purchace the same that then they doe hereby confirme & allow the same for a good & sufficient assurance of y^t parcell of sixe acres formerly posessed by the sd Thomas & Gyles vnto the sd Eliazer Lusher & his heyres for euer

Granted to these 5 Lots hereafter named 2 acres of land to each lott vpon the great playne. viz to Fardinando Adams Lot: to James Herrings lot to Francis Austens lot to Robt Masons lot & to —— Shepherds lot

It is ordered that the remainder of Jno Elderkins grant shalbe layd out to the purchacers of it vpon the great playne.

And that 30 acres formerly promised to mr Timothy Dalton shall be layd out to Michael Powell 10 acres of it vpon the great playne and part of it vpon the north end of the wigwam playne & the rest of it nere mr Parkers cr mr Tings farme where the sd Michael please.

Granted to the Towne of Dedham for euer 40 acres of vpland fit for improuement wth the plough: part vpon a smale playne betwene the great playne & Charles Riuer: and the rest where it may conueniently be found: yet with this resolution that if it may conueniently be found to add more thervnto:

Granted to these psons whose names are vnder written of vpland ground fit for improuement with the plough as followeth

DEDHAM TOWN RECORDS. 95

To: John Kingsbury:	4 acres	——— 13
To: John Hayward:	4 acres	3 roodes
To: Jn⁰ Batcheler:	2 acres:	1 roode 37
To: Mich Bacon	4 acres	3½ roodes: 5
To Tho: Alcocke	1 acre	3 roodes: 38
To Robte Weare:	———	3 roodes. 51
To Tho: Payne:	1 acre	2 roodes. 34
To Austin Kalem	1 acre	2 roodes 50
To Jn⁰ Ellis	2 acres	——— 31
To Jn⁰ Eaton:	5 acres	——— 26
To Tho Eames	1 acre	1 roode 48
To m^r Sam Cooke	8 acres	2 roodes 39
To Willm Bullard	2 acres	——— 49
To Jn⁰ Bullard	0 acre:	
John Gaye:	3 acres	3 roodes 36
Thomas Wight	3 acres	3 roodes 4
Anthony Fisher	4 acres	——— 42
Twaits Strickland	———	3 roodes 32
Henery Chickering:	8 acres	1 roode 53
John Thurston:	4 acres	2 roodes 15
Elizabeth Fisher	3 acres	1 roode 59
Robert Gowen:	———	3 roodes: 28
Thomas Jorden:	2 acres:	2 roodes 7
James Jorden:	1 acre	3 roodes 20
James Allin:	4 acres	0 ——— 43
John Newton } Edward Alleyn }	4 acres	1 roode 12
Edward Culuer	3 acres	1 roode 24
Robte Mason	6 acres	2 roodes 40
M^r Jn⁰ Allin: pasto^r:	23: acres	——— 58
Joseph Kingsbury:	4 acres	2 roodes 27
Henry Brocke	5 acres	2 roodes 41
Nathaniell Colbourne	4 acres	3 roodes 55
Henry Phillips	3 acres	2 roodes 14
Nathan Aldus	6 acres	2 roodes 45
Samuell Morse	6 acres	3 roodes 16
John Morse	4 acres	2 roodes 60
Joseph Morse	4 acres	——— 61
Richard Ellis	———	3 roodes 25
John Hunting Eld^r	14 acres:	3 roodes 6
John Roper	5 acres	1 roode
Henry Smith	4 acres	2 roodes 54
Richard Barber	1 acre	2 roodes 11

Lambert Genery:	7 acres	—	52
Thomas Ledor	3 acres	3 roodes	56
Timothy Dwight	2 acres	1 roode	57
John Dwight	11 acres	—	22
Nathaniell Whiteing	1 acre	2 roodes	9
Edward Kempe	3 acres	1 roode	
Thomas Bayes	2 acres	2 roodes	35
Edward Richards	4 acres:	3 roodes	29
Francis Chickering	14 acres	1 roode	21
Willm Bearstow	8 acres	1 roode	19
Georg Bearstow	1 acre	2 roodes	47
Johnathan Fairbanke	2 acres	2 roodes	
John Fairbanke	3 acres	—	23
Michael Powell	4 acres	1 roode	30
Michael Metcalf	9 acres	—	17
Henry Wilson	1 acre	2 roodes	44
John Frary	4 acres	2 roodes	2
Eliazer Lusher	13 acres	2 roodes	33
Peter Woodward	4 acres	1 roode	49
Richard Euerard	7 acres	2 roodes	1
John Guyle	—	3 roodes	10
Fardinando Adams	2 acres	3	
James Herringe	2 acres	8	
Samuell Bullein			
61 Daniell Morse:		18	

Michael Powell is deputed to Register the Births, Burialls and Mariages in o^r Towne: according to the Order of Court in y^t case prouided.

The 22 day of the 12 month called February 1642

Assembled: Henery Chickering Eliazer Lusher: Fran: Chickeringe Thomas: Wight: : John Dwight: Michael Powell

Christopher Smith hath liberty granted him to take such trees in the high way neare his house lott for fencing his house lott: as may supply his present necesitie.

Mr Henry Deengaine is contented to haue his 8 acres of Meaddow formerly granted to him 4 acres of it in Rosemary meddow & the other 4 acres nere his house lott on the Iland Jno Kingsbury & M Powell deputed to lay it out

John Bacheler John Eaton and Austin Kalem are deputed to lay out land formerly granted to John Haward: according to ye grant made to him

Granted to Edward Culuer one smale pcell of vpland & swampe: nere his house lott: to be layd out by Henry Chickering & Thomas Wight.

Granted to Austin Kalem 2 acres of meddow lately layd downe by Joseph Kingsbury: on the east side of the Iland

Granted to John Plimpton 2 acres of vpland vpon ye Iland: or more if it shalbe thought fit to be layd out by Na: Aldus Sam^{ll} Morse and Michael Powell.

Crosman Granted to Robert Crosman 2 acres of vpland lying on the Iland playne if it may conueniently be found to be layd out by those formerly deputed to lay out Jno Plimptons grant.

Mr Wheelocke Henry Chickeringe William Bullard and Michael Powell are are deputed to lay out land formerly granted to Mr Ralph Wheelocke according to the grant:

These men whose names are vnder written are deputed to view setle & proportion fences to looke to the due extent of high wayes and that ladders be puided according to the order in that case prouided.

Peter Woodward
Edward Richards } for the East streete.

Daniell Morse
Nath Colbourne } for the midle playne

John Luson
Willm Bullard } for the smoth playne

John Kingsbury
Austin Kalem } for the Iland

The 6 day of the 1 month cald March: 1643

Assembled Henery Chickering Thomas Wight Peter Woodward Eliazer Lusher Fran: Chickering Michael Powell

Jno Kingsbury John Bacheler John Eaton and Austin Kalem are deputed to lay out land vpon the Iland granted to John Kingsbury for a pasture to stay his Bullocks, according to the grant

Michael Powell is deputed to joyne with Samuell Morse & Nathan Aldus to finish the grants on the Iland playne

Hen: Glouer Granted to Henry Glouer 3 acres of vpland nere John Guyles lott on the Easterly playne: vpon this condition y^t he shall expect no more land from the Towne by virtue of this grant & that he set his hand to the booke.

Robert Hinsdell & Peter Woodward are deputed to lay out this grant according to their discression.

The 2 day of the 3 Month: 1643

Assembled: Henry Chickering Thomas Wight John Dwight Fran Chickering Peter Woodward Michael Powell

Jnº Haward — Granted to John Haward 4 acres 3 roodes of vpland vpon the Iland: nere his house lott as it is marked & dooled out allready

E Kempe — Granted to Edward Kemp in satisfaction for his defect in his house lott: 2 acres 3 roodes: in pt vpon the norwest end of the Low playne & the rest of it vpon the swamp playne: and three acres one roode vpon the sd swamp playne vpon free grant: John Dwight & Peter Woodward ar to asist the measurer in laying out this graunt

Jos: Kent — Josuah Kent is admitted Townsman & hath libertie to purchace Edward Culuers Lott: wth a resolution to confer more land vpon him as the towne shall see fittinge

T: Eames — Thomas Eames hath a parcell of land granted as an addition to his Lott which was formerly reserued for a high way to the swampe

Jnº Roper — Granted to John Roper 5 acres 1 roode of land vpon Westhill next Jnº Bullards Lott. Jnº Luson & Will Bullard are deputed to asist the measurer in laying it out

It is ordered that Thomas Payne and all that are enclosed by the sd fence in the Iland nere the Brick Kill: shall digg a dytch from the Creeke allready diged to the vpland to fence their corne & medowe: & if the Towne hereafter shall se cause to dig a Creeke to come vp wth a boate from the riuer to the brick kill the Towne shall make the sd parties y^t dig the dich such satisfaction as shall by Indifferent me be Judged that ye sd dich shall farther the digging the Creeke

The 3 of Octob^r 1643

Assembled: Eli Lusher Tho: Wight Franc: Chickering Peter Woodward: Michael Powell:

Crosman — Granted to Robert Croseman four acres of vpland on the East end of the great playne next the Lot of Richard Everard if it may conueniently there be had.

Jos: Fisher — Granted to Josuah Fisher a parcell of vpland on the great playne betwene Land layd out to m^r John Allin and certaine other lots layd out on the Northest of the sd playne

The 18 of the 10 month: 1643

Assembled Henery Chickeringe: John Dwight Tho: Wight Francis Chickeringe Peter Woodward: Mich Powell

Jos: Morse — Granted to Joseph Morse three acres of vpland vpon the great playne next his Lot already layd out there: which land is granted him to make him satisfaction for want of measure in his meadow.

DEDHAM TOWN RECORDS. 99

A Kalem Granted to Austen Kalem ten acres of vpland vpon the great playne to be layd out next the fore said lot granted to Joseph Morse: which land is granted to make him full satisfaction for his house Lot & some mistake about his diuident

Henry Chickeringe is deputed to asist the measurer in laying out these two parcells

Granted to Austen Kalem a smale parcell of vpland nere his meadow vpon ye Iland to be layd out by Jno Kingsbury & John Dwight

J: Thurston Granted to John Thurston a smale parcell of meadow be- twene Mr Cookes farme & the Wigwam to be layd out by Tho Wight & Willm Bullard

N: Colbourne Granted to Nathaniell Colbourne two acres of medow in a meadow lyinge southward of bald pate meadow adioyninge to ye meadow formerly granted to Joseph Kingsbury: Jno Dwight & Franc Chickeringe are deputed to asist ye measurer in laying out this grant:: which land is granted to make vp his meadow 12 acres

J: Clarke Granted to Joseph Clarke a smale parcell of vpland adioyn- inge to his sixe acre lot

T: Dwight Granted to Timothy Dwight four acres of Land to be layd out on ye great playne next the Land granted to Austen Kalem: Hen: Chickering is deputed to assist in laying out this graunt:

J. Luson Wheras John Luson & Thomas Wight haue fenced in a par-
T. Wight cell of Meadow of eight acres: which meadow is yet in ye hands of the Towne it is ordered that the sd Jno Luson & Tho: Wight shall haue the benifit of the sd meadow: till the sd charg of fencing be payd: viz: that they shall pay 12^d an acre for it for ye yeare last past: & two shillings an acre for time to come till they are fully satisfyed

Wheras there is a parcell of meadow in the hands of the towne in Rocke meadow which lyeth within the fence now to be set vp there: it is ordered that Tho: Wight fencing in the sd pcell of meadow w^{th}in the generall fence: shall haue the benifit of the sd meadow: for the two yeares next ensuinge:

The 27th of the 10th month 1643

Assembled: Hen: Chickering: John Dwight: Tho: Wight: Eli: Lusher Peter Woodward: Francis Chickeringe: Mich Powell

H: Chickeringe Granted to Henry Chickeringe four acres of land vpon the great playne to be layd out next the 4 acres granted to Tim: Dwight which land is granted partly to make him satisfac- tion: for some mistake & want of his due pportion in his Lot already layd out on ye sd playne

Wheras the high way already layd out through the house Lot of Josuah Fisher is found to be too strait being but two rod wide and he is contented to lay downe so much of his sd house Lot as may enlarg the high way to be three rods wide: in Consideration thereof the towne doth grant him a parcell of land to be. added to his sixe acre Lot vpon west hill: as it shalbe layd out & determined by Henry Chickeringe and Thomas Wight:

Jos: Kent   Granted to Josuah Kent a smale pcell of land lying betwene the Land of Mr John Allin past^r: and John Luson in Rocke feild: And also there is granted more to him sixe acres of vpland where it may be found conueinent: these two pcells of land to be layd out by John Luson and Thomas Wight where they shall thinke meete

John Bullard granteth to William Bullard & to his heyres or assignes for euer a conuenient Cart way for càrts & Catle through his planting lot downe to the meadowes of the sd William adioyninge therevnto:

    The first day of the 11 month 1643
Assembled those whose names are vnder written

Mr Jno Allin: Jno Hunting Mr Ralph Wheelocke Willm Bullard Jno Bullard, Dan: Fisher, Jno Luson: Tho Wight: Hen Chickeringe Jno Thurston Jos: Fisher Jam: Jorden: Edward Coluer Jno Newton Robt Mason: Rich: Barber Geo. Barber Jos Morse Jno Morse Dan: Morse Jos Kingsbury Hen: Brocke: Nath Aldus Nathanell Colbourne Hen: Phillips Jno Bacheler: Jno Eaton: Tho Alcocke Jno Haward Austin Kalem: Chris Smith: Mich Bacon: Jno Ellis Tim: Dwight Jno Dwight Edw Kemp: Franc. Chickering Michael Powell Jno Frarey Eli Lusher Robt Hinsdell: Peter Woodward Richard Euerard.

Michael Powell[1]: is Chosen to keepe the Towne Booke for the yeare next ensuing & to write the Record & Transcript: and to act in all towne affaires as one of the seauen men: And there is Chosen to Joyne with him John Dwight John Haward Nathan Aldus William Bullard Peter Woodward & Timothy Dwight: Who are to act in the planting prudentiall affaires of the Towne & haue the same power that their predecessors haue had: excepting the deuiding of land by a generall diuident

John Kingsbury: Robert Hinsdell & Daniell Fisher are Chosen Surueyers for the high wayes for the next yeare

Henry Phillips & Nathaniell Colbourne: are chosen Wood reeues.

---

[1] Fac-simile of Record, to show handwriting of Michael Powell.

Wheras it hath bin the Costome of this Towne to Chusse a Collector: It is now ordered that the Constables for the time being shall performe that office of Collector

Wheras the Purchast Meadow & land in our towne hath bin hetherto vnimproued and litle or no profit hath risen to the purchacers of it It is now ordred that John Kingsbury & Samuell Morse shall ioyne with the 7 men now Chosen to cleare out mens proprieties therein: And to contriue some way how it may be improued: and to returne what they haue don in it to the towne by the first of the 1 month next

The 8 of the 11 month 1643

Assembled Nathan Aldus: Jn° Haward: Jn° Dwight Peter Woodward: Willm Bullard: Tim: Dwight and Michael Powell

Thomas Herring is admitted a Townsman

[1]Whereas Mr Edw Alleyn Jn° Luson & Jn° Kingsbury were deputed to treat with Michael Bacon concerning the high way through his Lot: & to tender him satisfaction: & wheras it hath pleased god to take away Mr Alleyn by death: It is now ordered that John Haward shall ioyne with Jn° Luson & Jn° Kingsbury to acomplish the sd worke spedily:

Fences Wheras there is an order formerly made that some men should be deputed yearely to proportion & looke to fences & to the extent of high wayes: & y^t Ladders be puided according to that order And wheras many men whose lots lay in a generall feild & so enclosed by a generall fence, now come to fence their lots in pticuler: wherby some difference may arise concerning what quantitie of fence euery man shall make that shall so fence in his lott in pticuler It is now ordred that the men hereafter named shall view & pportion fences: & looke to the extent of high wayes & that Ladders be puided according to that order And farther that they shall haue power to setle & determine what quantitie of fencing euery man shall make & mayntaine that from a generall feild shall fence in his lot in pticuler

these men are chosen for the whole towne

John Kingsbury: Eli: Lusher Tho: Wight & Nath: Colbourne

The 20th of the 12 month 1643

Assembled: Nath: Aldus Jn° Haward: Jn° Dwight: Willm Bullard: Pet: Woodward & Mich: Powell

South playne There is libertie granted to the possesors of land in the south playne to run their fence where it may be most conuenient for the shorting of the sd fence betwene the sd

---

[1] See last paragraph in brackets on page 73.

playne & John Thurstons Land: and what quantitie of land they shall so enclose betwene the high way & the Swamp shall yet remaine in the townes hand

M^r J: Allin   Mr Jno Allin Past^r hath libertie granted to take in some vpland for the conueniencie of his fence in Rock meadow: prouided y^t he leaue out so much of the land belonging to his farme there in some other place

Also there is granted to him a parcell of land nere the great playne vpon exchange for so much layd downe out of his farme nere rock meadow: this to be viewed by Jno Haward & Mich Powell & they are to asist the measurer in laying it out

Hen: Chickering & Tho: Wight haue libertie granted to take in some vpland for ye conueniency of their fence in Rocke Meadow

Willm Bullard & Mi: Powell deputed to view it: and also Certaine pcells of Meadow granted to Hen: Chickering: nere thereto

Jno Bullard hath Libtie granted to mow one load of hay in a meadow nere Rosemary Meadow

The 17th of the 3 month 1644

Assembled: Nath: Aldus John: Dwight Willm Bullard Tim: Dwight Michael Powell

Millitary Company   Granted to the military Company of this towne and to their succesors for euer: a pcell of land cont. two acres more as it lyeth on on the west^rly end of the trayning ground to be layd out by the sd Company:

R: Crosman   Granted to Robert Crosman a parcell of swamp lyeing betwene his land in old mill feild and Charles Riuer so far as his lot ranges against the riuer

T: Jorden   Granted to Thomas Jorden a parcell of vpland lyeing betwene the south playne and ye swampe & land granted to John Thurston as it shall be thought conuenient by Henry Chickeringe Thomas Wight and Michael Powell

The 29 of the 8 month 1644

Assembled: Nath: Aldus John: Haward: Joh: Dwight Willm Bullard Tim: Dwight: Mich Powell

Cart Bridge   Wheras Michael Bacon hath parted with some of his plantinge Lot on the South side of Charles River for a common high way viz from the Trayning ground to the Cart Bridge ouer Charles Riu^r three Rods broad and may be ocasioned more charge of fencing thereby the Towne doth grant vnto him for full satisfaction for the same and it is fully assented vnto on both sides as followeth That the sd Michael shall haue & enioy to him & his assignes for euer all that parcell of vpland ye remainder of a ten acree lot vpon the Iland and a parcell of meadow: lying on the east side of it Also a pcell of vpland as it lyeth from ye sd ten acre lot downe to Charles Riuer: Reseruing for the vse of the towne for euer a high way three Rods broad throw all the sd two pcells of vpland where the Towne shall think most conuenient: Always guided y^t the sd Michael shall haue all the wood & timber: growinge or y^t shall grow vpon the sd high way

And it is agreed betwene them y^t if the towne shall se cause to desire a fence to be set vp to fence ye high way from ye land of Michael Bacon: in his planting feild abouesd the sd Michael is to prouide ye fencing stuffe ready & ye towne is to be at the Charg of the Carrage of it & ye sd Michael is to set it vp at his owne prop charge and to maintaine it at his owne Charge for euer And in the meane while he is to prouide a gate or gates to secure his corne & to maintaine them

This grant aforesd is in full satisfaction for his land or fencinge or for any trees y^t hereto fore haue bin felled vpon any of the premyses

The sd Michael Bacon is to enioy the sd land wth out paying any Rates for it for euer

M: Metcalfe   Granted vnto Michael Metcalfe senio^r: one acre of land vpon the North end of the wigwam playne

J. Farbank   Granted to Jonathan Fairbanke two acres of land nere ye same place

Granted to John Dwight a smale pcell of land about half an acre lying at the south end of his Lot vpon the great playne

J Clarke
H. Wilson   Granted to Joseph Clarke and Hen: Wilson to each three acres of vpland lying in West feild next John Ropers Lot: to be layd out by Tho: Wight & Willm Bullard

Whiteinge   Granted to Nathaniell Whiteinge an enlargm^t of land adjoyning to his house Lot at ye mill as it shalbe thought fit by Pet Woodward & Michael Powell:

Crosman   Granted to Robert Crosman two acres of land next his land in old mill feild: to be layd out by Jno Kingsbury and Willm Bullard: which sd land is granted in satisfaction for two acres of land layd downe by him vpon the Iland playne

J Eaton   Granted to John Eaton a smal pcell of vpland lying betwene his land vpon the Iland playne & ye swamp of Sam^{ll} Bullen: to make the line strait betwene them. John Haward is deputed to set it out

John Kingsbury Eli: Lusher Jno Dwight & Tho Wight are deputed to lay out a high way from ye Iland to the great playne.

The 6 of the 10 month 1644

Assemb: Jn° Dwight Pet: Woodward Nath: Aldus Mich Powell

Whereas Tho: Leader hath felled Pynes contrary to an order in y^t case it is therefore ordered that he shall pay vnto the Towne one hundred & a half of good pine board to be deliuered at ye meeting house ye next springe

Granted to Peter Woodward 6 acres more or lesse of vpland lying at the south end of Robt Hinsdells Land westward of Charles riuer:which is granted in exchange of 6 acres: granted him nere m^r Stoughtons rayles: Jn° Haward & Willm Bullard deputed to lay it out

Henry Aldridge is amerced 2^s for felling hoope poles contrary to order

Granted to Eld^r Hunting seaddar & pine for 2000 board

The 16th of the 10 month 1644

Assembled: John Haward John Dwight Nath Aldus Willm Bullard & Mich Powell

Granted vnto Austen Kalem certaine small pcells of Meadow lying beyond the great playne so they exceed not the quantitie of 4 acres: to be layd out by John Haward & Michael Powell

'Granted to Franc: Chickering a small parcell of vpland lying on the south end of his lot on the great playne

Wheras there was notice giuen to all that possesed land on the great playne to meete to consider some orderly way of fencing it: the sd land holders comitting the care of it to vs & we consideringe y^t those y^t haue equall benifit should be at an equall charge according to euery mans pportion it Is therfore Ordred that that fencinge stuffe that growes next the east side & all other sides shall be felled & imployed by those y^t posesse land next y^t there may be as litle charge in cariag of it as may be: & for as much as some may be necesitated to goe farther of then others: it is therfore ordered y^t euery man shall beare his due proportion in Cariag of the sd fencing stuffe.

& ye next second day euery shall haue libertie to fell stuffe for the sd fence

1644 At a meeting the first day of the Eleuenth Month

Assembled those whose names are vnder written
with other the Inhabitants of this Towne:

M^r Jn° Allin past^r Jn° Huntinge, Eld^r: Hen: Chickering Tho Wight Jn° Thu[   ] Anthony Fisher Jos Fisher Dan: Fisher Jn° Luson: m^r Ralph Wheeloc[   ] Jn° Gaye: Willm Bullard Jn° Bullard Robt Crosman Hen Wilson Jn° N[   ] Edw: Coluer Hen Smith: Nath Colborne: Nath: Aldus Hen Phillip[   ] Sam^{ll} Morse: Dan Morse Jn° Morse: Jos Kingsbury Jn° Dwite Lamb: G[   ] Edw Kemp: Edw Richards Tho Leader Geo Bearstowe: Jonath Fairba[   ] Mich Powell Mich Metcalfe: Juno^r Jn° Metcalfe

Jn⁰ Frary: Eli: Lusher: R[   ] Hinsdell: Pet Woodward: Jn⁰ Guyle Rich Euered Robt Gowinge &ᶜᵉ:

The sd Inhabitants takeing into Consideration the great necesitie of prouiding some meanes for the Education of the youth in oʳ sd Towne did with an vnaninous consent declare by voate their willingnes to promote that worke promising to put too their hands to prouide maintenance for a Free Schoole in our said Towne

And farther did resolue & consent testefying it by voate to rayse the some of Twenty pounds p annu: towards the maintaining of a Schoole mʳ to keep a free Schoole in our sd Towne

And also did resolue & consent to betrust the sd 20£ p annu: & certaine lands in oʳ Towne formerly set a part for publique vse: into the hand of Feofees to be presently Chosen by themselues to imploy the sd 20£ and the land aforesd to be improued for the vse of the said Schoole: that as the profits shall arise from yᵉ sd land euery man may be proportionably abated of his some of the sd 20£ aforesaid freely to be giuen to yᵉ vse aforesaid And yᵗ yᵉ said Feofees shall haue power to make a Rate for the nesesary charg of improuing the sd land: they giueing account thereof to the Towne or to those whome they should depute

John Hunting Eldʳ Eliazer Lusher Francis Chickeringe John Dwight & Michael Powell are Chosen Feofees and betrusted in the behalfe of the Schoole as afore said

Michael Powell is Chosen to keepe the Towne Booke and to be one of the 7 men for the year next ensuing this is also Chosen Eliazer Lusher Francis Chickeringe: John Haward Robert Hinsdell: Joseph Kingsbury and Henry Phillips which haue yᵉ same power comitted vnto them that the 7 men heretofore haue had

Peter Woodward John Gaye Daniell Morse	} Chosen Surueyers for yᵉ yeare ensuinge
Henry Phillips Nathaniell Colbourne	} are Chosen Woodreeues
Samuell Judsun Robert Onyon Samuell Mills Ralph Daye	} are admitted Townsmen

The 13th of yᵉ 11 month 1644

Assembled: John Haward Eliazer Lusher Robt Hensdell Jos: Kingsbury Hen: Phillips & Michael Powell

John Haward Robert Hensdell & Joseph Kingsbury are deputed to view a high way desired in yᵉ Iland & to treat wᵗʰ the men whome it concernes about it: & to returne answere to the 7 men

106   DEDHAM TOWN RECORDS.

Wheres Nathan Aldus was formerly promised some meadow in Consideration of wood felled vpon his land in the Iland: It is now farther promised y^t when meadowes are disposed of he shalbe considered:

Henry Aldridge & Samuell Bullen are pmised to be considered for some vpland & meadow & John Eaton for some meadow as soone as may be conuenient

Eli. Lusher: chosen by Josua Fisher & Mich Powell deputed by ye towne to setle ye bounds of Josua Fishers lot amongst ye rocks which he purchaced of Eliz Fisher: & to dispose of certaine parcells of Swamp nere Tho Jordens Lot as thay shall se meete

Tho: Eames hath granted vnto him a small parcell of vpland vpon the Iland: vpon Condition y^t he build a house vpon it betwene this & the first of ye 3 month next: John Haward & Hen: Phillips are deputed to set it out:

Tho: Eames hath grantd to him the wood growing vpon a pcell of Swamp: cont. 4 acres more or lesse as it lyeth Northward of the Land granted to m^r Grene: which grant is granted him for so long as he shall burne bricks at ye kill nere therevntoo & no longer

Robert Hensdell & Michael Powell deputed to assist the measurer to lay out Swamp:

Mich Powell is deputed to view a pcell of vpland which Joseph Clarke desireth to haue to shorten his fence nere his meadow & to returne answere to the 7 men.

John Dwight Hen Phillips & Joshua Fisher are deputed to determine where the Fence shalbe set about ye great playne

[¹A Record declareing the pportion of Fence that is about the Great playne wherin is exp^{r}ssed how much fence euery ppriator ther is to make & mayntayne for euer as allso the order & place wher the said fence lye in the pticular pcells: being pportioned to 2 Rodd & 12 foote to each Acre: being done & pformed by the ppryators or the major pt of them in pt & the remaynder setled by such men as wer deputed therto. begining at the end Fence at the south east corner & so pceeding toward the west & coming round about vntill it com to the same place wher it began

	Rodd:	½	Foote				
Rich: Euered	23	0	2	Joh: Kingsbery	6	0	13
Joh: Fraery	18	0	0	Hen Phillips	4	0	14
Ferd: Adam	4	0	15	Sam: Morse	10	0	12
Tho: Wight	15	½	0	Mich: Metcalf	11	½	0
Mich: Bacon	5	0	15	Dan: Morse	4	0	3
Eld^r Hunting	25	½	0	Will Bearstoe	14	0	7
Nath Coaleburn	9	0	13	Ralph Daye	5	0	12
Christo Smith	3	0	7	Fra: Chickering	25	0	8
Joh: Newton	7	0	3	Edw: Kempe	7	0	1

¹That which is enclosed in brackets is from a leaf bound at the end of Volume 1.

Name				Name			
Joh: Dwight	27	0	7	Nath Coaleburn	8	0	0
Rich Ellice	6	0	13	Hen: Smith	8	0	0
Joh: Eaton	9	0	4	Hen: Chickering	22	0	0
Josep Kingsbery	6	0	10	Mr Allen	12	0	0
Edw Richards	12	0	14	Robt: Wares	6	0	0
Mr Powell	22	0	10	Pet: Woodward	9	0	0
Joh: Ellice	5	½	0	Will Bullard	4	0	0
Elea: Lusher	30	0	5	Nath Aldus	12	0	0
Tho: Payne	5	0	6	Hen: Willson	2	0	0
Tho: Wight	24	0	3	Joh: Kingsbery	5	0	12
Joh: Batchelor	15	0	10	Anth: Fisher	9	0	5
Mr Cooke	29	½	0	Hen: Brock	12	0	0
[end] fence end heere				Robt Mason	28	0	0
Joh: Eaton	8	0	0	Mr Allen	75	0	11
Eleaz Lusher	8	0	0	side fence begin			
Edw Kemp	7	0	4	Ferdina: Adams	6	0	3
Joh Ellice	3	0	6	Antho: Fisher	9	0	5
Mich: Bacon	15	0	12	Hen: Brock	6	0	4
Tho: Wight	14	0	9	Joh Kingsbery	7	0	9
Joh: Dwight	30	0	5	Hen Willson	3	0	0
Sam Judson	9	0	0	Robt Wares	4	0	0
Christo: Smith	4	0	0	Nath Aldus	8	½	0
Josep Kingsbery	8	0	6	Willm Bullard	4	0	0
end Fence begin				Nath Coaleburn	15	0	5
Joh: Bacon	23	0	0	Eld^r Hunting	20	0	0
Aust Kalem	28	0	12	Hen Chickering	9	0	4
Josep: Morse	41	0	6	Hen Smith	7	0	1
Elizab: Fisher	10	0	6	Mich Metcalf	12	0	12
Mr Allen	47	0	4	Lamb: Genry	2	0	0
Tymo Dwight	7	0	4	Dan: Morse	16	0	0
Joh Dwight	12	0	0	Fran: Chickering	11	0	0

m^d that Joh Kingsbery & Franc: Chickering ar apointed to make and mayntayne for euer the gate at the North East end of the great playne for wch ther is to each of them abated 5 rodd of fence wch did belong to them mor then in this pportion is setled vpon them

Allso Lambert Genery is to make & mayntaine for euer a gate at the north west end of the playne for and in stead of that fence belonging to the pcell last granted to him: besids that 2 rodd set formerly thervpon

concluded by voate that this settlement as is aboue exp^{r}ssed shall stand firme except any materiall & aparent errour may apeare wch shall be rectified

and allso that wheras som men haue not so much Fence settled vpon them as thier land according to this pportion should beare: it is agreed that they shall buy them them selues free of that fence for euer at the price of 3^s the Rodd: and that the price that shall arise from thence shall be employed for the paym^t of such debts as ar due to any men for publike charge or worke about the said playne allways pvided that w^t can be found to be iust to be payed from any pticulars pson be gathered & to be payed toward the said charges. & the residue left to be accounted for to the company or thier assignes]

The 4 of ye 12 month 1644

Assembled Eli Lusher Franc Chickeringe Jno Haward Jos Kingsbury Hen Phillips Robert Hensdell and Michael Powell

The Inhabitants of this towne declared their mind by voate y^t the remainder of ye Training ground be improued by ye Feofees for ye vse of the Fre Schole in the sd towne and that the Swamp to be layd out to ye Inhabitants of ye Smoth playn ye Iland & the midle playne be disposed of acording to mens grants & Scituations: those y^t liue farthest of to haue y^s Swamp that lyeth nearest

And y^t the pcell of woodland now to be deuided be proportioned according to the number of persons & mens estates

Granted to the Feofees for ye free Schoole in Dedham for the vse of the sd Schoole a percell of the Training ground so much as shalbe set out to them by the Towne which said pcell is granted from this present day vnto the last day of the Eight month which shalbe in ye yeare 1650

Hen: Chickeringe Eli Lusher & Hen Phillips deputed to set out the sd parcell of land aboue said

Whereas it appeares that Anthony Fisher Daniell Fisher Thomas Wight & John Luson are wanting in full measure of their Meadow in their 6 acres of the last deuision: there is now granted vnto them so much as it shall appeare they want in measure In a meadow nere Rosemary meadow where it shalbe found conuenient by John Haward & Michael Powell who are deputed to asist the measurer in laying it out

Robert Crosman hath libertie granted him to build an house vpon a small pcell of land he purchaced of Hen: Brocke nere the meeting house notwithstanding a former order to the Contrary

Samuell Judson hath granted him 4 acres of land vpon the Iland playne nere Tho. Eames last grant: Sam^{ll} Morse Nath: Aldus & M: Powell are to asist in laying it out

Granted to Nathan Aldus: libertie to mowe the grase in a parcell of Meadow lying Southward of Richard Euereds meadow in Rosemary Meadow: for the next yeare And being there hath bin some meadow promised him hereto fore vpon some considerations: therefore if it shall appeare that the said parcell of meadow be not formerly granted to any body: We doe now grant vnto the said Nathan the said pcell for euer if it exceed not two acres: or if it doe we grant him 2 acres of it which is in full satisfaction for all former promises of medow

 Samuell Bullen hath granted to him 2 acres of land vpon the great playne at the end of Joseph Morses Lott

 Wheras John Morse his Meadow ye 6 acres of the second deuision proues very bad in consideration whereof the towne doth grant vnto him two acres of meadow: in Liew of 2 acres of the said 6 acres which he is content to lay downe to the towne: which said 2 acres the towne doth grant him in a mead͞ow Called Rosemary Meadow next below the meadow formerly granted to m^r Samuell Cooke: John Kingsbury & Anthony Fisher are deputed to asist y^e measurer in layinge it out.

Lots	Woodlands granted to diuers men as followeth	
1	Joshua Fisher	5 acres
2	Tho: Eames	1 acre & a half & half a rood
3	Joseph Clarke	3 acres 3 roodes
4	James Jordon	1 acres 1 roode
5	John Newton	5 acres & a halfe
6	Tho Wight	8 acres 20 rod
7	Tho Leader	3 acres $\frac{1}{2}$ & half a roode
8	Nath Whiteinge	4 acres 60 rod
9	Joseph Kingsbury	6 acres & $\frac{1}{2}$ & $\frac{1}{2}$ roode
10	Mr Sam^{ll} Cooke	6 acres $\frac{1}{2}$ & 20 rod
11	John Roper	4 acres
12	Hen: Wilson	3 acres
13	John Dwight	9 acres & a halfe
14	Ben: Smith	1 acre $\frac{1}{2}$
15	Rich Euered	6 acres 3 roods
16	Hen: Aldridge	3 acres
17	Rich Ellice	1 acre 20 rod
18	Mich Powell	7 acres 20 rod
19	Tim Dwight	3 acres
20	Hen Brocke	5 acres
21	Tho: Alcocke	3 acres 3 roods 20 rod
22	Mich Bacon	7 acres 1 roode
23	Austin Kilham	6 acres 60 rod
24	John Ellice	2 acres & a halfe
25	Mr John Allin	14 acres 20 rod
26	m^r Hen Deengaine	1 acre 1 roode
27	Willm Bullard	6 acres 20 rod
28	Mich Metcalf $senio^r$	8 acres 20 rod

29	Daniell Fisher	4 acres 60 rod
30	Sam^{ll} Morse	3 acres 3 roodes
31	Robt: Gowinge	1 acre ½
32	John Luson	5 acres 1 roode
33	John Kingsbury	8 acres 20 rod
34	Pet: Woodward	5 acres ½
35	Geo: Bearstowe	1 acre ½
36	John Bacheler	7 acres
37	John Morse	4 acres 3 roods ½
38	Eli: Lusher	5 acres ½
39	Eliz Fisher	2 acres 3 roods ½
40	Robt: Hensdell	5 acres 3 roods
41	Hen: Smith	4 acres ½
42	John Eaton	7 acres
43	Willm Bearstowe	3 acres
44	Robt Onyon	1 acres 1 roode
45	John Fairbanke	2 acres ½
46	Tho Fuller	2 acres 30 rod
47	Twaits Strickland	1 acre
48	John Thurston	4 acres 3 roods
49	Mich Metcalf Juno^r	2 acres 1 rod
50	Lamb: Genere	5 acres ½
51	Franc: Chickeringe	12 acres
52	John Plimption	1 acre ½
53	John Gaye	5 acres 3 roods ½
54	Jonath Fairbanke	6 acres 1 rood
55	Edw. Coluer	2 acres ½ & ½ a rood
56	Hen Chickering	7 acres 3 roods ½
57	John Bullard	3 acres ½ & ½ rood
58	John Guild	1 acre
59	Edw: Richards	5 acres
60	Robt Ware	1 acre 3 roods
61	Jos: Morse	4 acres ½
62	Tho Jorden	2 acres 20 rod
63	John Frary	7 acres 1 rood
64	Ant: Fisher	8 acres ½ & ½ rood
65	Edw: Kempe	3 acres ½
66	John Haward	8 acres 20 rod
67	Dan: Morse	6 acres
68	m^r Wheelocke	7 acres
69	Hen Glouer	1 acre
70	Fard: Adams	2 acres
71	Chris: Smith	1 acre ½ & ½ rood

72	Robt. Crosman	1 acre
73	Nath: Colbourne	5 acres 3 roods
74	Nath Aldus	5 acres ½ & ½ rood
75	Sam^{ll} Bullen	2 acres ½
76	Tho Payne	3 acres 1 rood
77	Geo: Barber	3 acres
78	Jam: Allin	3 acres ½
79	Tho Bayes	2 acres ½ 20 rod
80	John Hunting Eld^r	7 acres 20 rod
81	Hen: Phillips	3 acres ½
82	Tho Herringe	2 acres 3 roods
83	Robt: Mason	5 acres:

At a meetinge ye first day of the 11 month 1645
Assembled the Inhabitants of this towne

Chosen to act in Towne affaires for the yeare next followinge Henry Chickeringe: Eliazer Lusher John Haward John Dwight Anthony Fisher Edward Richards and Michael Powell: who is chosen to keepe ye towne Booke for the yeare followinge

The propriators of the purchast meadow & vpland haue ioyntly asented for ye better improuement of the same that the said meadow be deuided into 4 parts according to the number of propriators in each part: & haue cast lots: where each part shall be: & the propriators in the Iland are to begin next the litle Bridge: & so measure northward so much as falls to their proportion: & the midle playne is to be next: the East streete next: & the Smoth playne most northwards: & it is agreed y^t what is wantinge of the said purchace land shalbe made vp in vpland where it may be found conuenient for each deuision:

3: 12 month 1645

Rate — It is ordred y^t henceforth the Cunstable or any other y^t shalbe deputed to gather a rate in our towne: shall stand charged with the whole some in the said rate & shall not haue power to abate any man or set off any former debts: but if any shall refuse to pay: they y^t gather ye said rate shall refer them to the 7 men for ye tyme beinge who shall haue power to abate or set of as they se fitt: And also euery man deputed to collect any rate in o^r Towne shall giue account of the said rate to the 7 men or to those whome they shall depute when they shall require it after ye said rate is appoynted to be gathered: & if any such shall neclect or refuse to giue account of any rate being therevnto required shall pay to the vse of the towne as the 7 men shall thinke meete ρvided allwayes that such accounts be called for wthin 3 moneths after such Rate be to be gathered

Samuell Milles hath granted to him a pcell of vpland next the land granted to Joseph Clarke & Henry Wilson nere Westfeild if it may there be found conuenient so it exceed not 3 acres Tho Wight & Willm Bullard deputed to asist in laying it out when they haue layd out ye land formerly granted there

Sam^{ll} Milles hath libtie to cut 400 lengthes of hoope poles on the common: & is to pay 2^s to the towne

Granted to Edward Coluer a small pcell of land nere his house as it shalbe layd out by Eli: Lusher: vpon condition that if he shall depart ye towne it shall returne into ye townes dispose againe as formerly

[1] This grant is confirmed to Ralph Daye and his hiers for euer

It is Ordred that for this p^rsent yea^r euery man both those y^t haue Carts & laborers shall worke 4 dayes in ye high wayes when & where the surueyors shall appoynt & that ye surueyors shall haue no power to dispence wth any man for lesse tyme. but if any shall refuse or neglect those said 4 dayes worke he shalbe refered to the seauen men to doe in the case as they shall se fitt:

The 7 of the 10 month 1646

Assembled Hen: Chickring Eli: Lusher Ant: Fisher John Dwight John Haward Edw: Richards & Mich Powell

John Dwight and Peter Woodward deputed to treat with Georg Bearstoe about a parcell of his house lot to dig clay in: & with Jonathan Fairbanke about a way therunto:: & to tender satisfaction to them for ye same: & to make a full agrement as they shall se meete

The 10 mo: 26. 1646

Assembled Henry Chickering: Joh: Dwight Antho: Fisher Ed: Richards & Eleazer Lusher

Eleazer Lusher is requested to take care of ye Town Booke & to enter therin what is to be recorded. in the absence of m^r Powell

George Bearstow *Claye ground* Georg Bearstow granteth to the Town of Dedham. that pcell of his house Lott that lyeth at ye west end therof: wher Clay is accustomed to be digged: vizt: from the Little Riuer or Creeke at the end of his said Lott all the breadth therof so farr East ward as Clay is to be found. together wth sufficient space for a Convenient Cart passage from ye said pcell to the Streete which waye or Cart passage shall lye next the South side Lyne of his said Lott which foresaid pcell is & shall remaine free to the Inhabitants of ye said Town of Ded-

---

[1] This line seems to have been added later, being in a different hand-writing.

ham: to digge & carry a way Claye wth Free Egresse & Regresse with w^t so euer Carts. Teames. or w^t so euer else shall be necessary for ye Casting or carying a way of Clay as afore said so long as the said Inhabitants shall & will find & make vse of clay in the said pcell & afterward to remayne to the free & peaceable posession of ye said George & his hiers for euer pvided allways y^t the said Inhabitants doe make & mayntaine such a fence as shall be requesite in the south Lyne of the said Lott or pcell therof from that place wher a ditch is began to be made vnto the little Riuer or Creeke befor specified

 For & in consideration wherof the Town of Dedham aforesaid granteth to ye said George Bearstow & to his hiers for euer 4 acres of Swampe together wth all woode & Timber. ther vpon. either standing or felled. wch swampe is to be apointed or set out to the said George at the discretion of John Dwight & Peter Woodward

	Deputed to laye out that pcell of Land neer adioyning to the
great	great Playne: for the pasturing of Cattell in time of worke
Playne	ther according to a former grante Antho: Fisher: Joh Dwight
	Tho Wight: Austen Kalem Edward Richards

 Alowed to Ralph Daye. for beating the Drum̄ at the meetinghouse for the time past 20^s. to be payd in Ceader board at 4^s p. cent

 11 month. 1 day   At a genrall Meeting of the Whole Town.
  1646   assembled

 Mr Joh Allen. Pastor, Henry Chickering, Joh Kingsbery, Antho: Fisher, Joh: Luson, Mich Metcalf. seni, Jonath: Fayerbanke, Joh Dwight, Fran: Chickering, Sam: Morse, Nath Aldus, Elea: Lusher, Tho: Wight, m^r Ralph Wheelock, Willm Bullard, Joh Gaye, Eld^r Joh Hunting, Joseph Kingsbery, Nath: Coalburn, Robt Hinsdell, Timo. Dwight, Pet: Woodward, Joh: Fraery: Rich: Euered, Ed: Kempe, Tho Leader, Ed: Richards, Robt Mason, Dan. Fisher, Hen: Phillips, Josh: Fisher, Lam: Chinery, Joh Fayerbank, Rich: Ellice, Joh: Hayward, Joh Plimpton, Christo: Smith, Geor: Barber, Hen: Smith, Josep: Morse, Robt Gowen, Joh Thurston, Tho: Jordan, Josh: Kent, Joh: Bullard, Josep: Clark, Hen: Wilson, Thw: Strickland, Ben: Smith, Robt Onion, Sam: Mills, Dan: Morse, Geor: Bearstoe, Joh: Batchelor, Mich Bacon, Robt Crossman, Joh: Eaton, Tho. Payne, Tho: Fuller, Joh Moyse, Sam: Judson, Robt Weare, Sam: Bulleyn, Austen Kalem, Jam: Allen, Joh: Ellice, Mich. Metcalf, Ralph Daye, Joh Guilde, Robt Fuller

 It was taken into consideration by the Inhabitants aboue named that the Meeting house being yet vnfinished was not a supplye to the congregation & therfor by joynt consent: It is now ordered that the said Meeting house shall be forthwith Compleatly Finished wth as much expedition as may be. And that the Charge therof shall be raised by a Rate. which Rate shall be asessed vpon Estats onely. and shall be distinct from the former Rate mad for the building of that new pt therof. not respecting the same but shall be for the Compleat finishing therof in what sum̄ so euer the former Rate fall short.

Eleazer Lusher is Chosen to keepe the Town Booke for the year following & to act in the affayres of ye Town equall with the other 6 men now to be chosen

Henry Chickering: Joh Dwight: Tho Wight Fra: Chickering Joh Kingsberye: Antho. Fisher ar Chosen to act in Town affayers for ye ensueing year haueing the same power thier p^{r}decessors had.

Eleazer Lusher is Chosen to attend at the Shire Town concerning ye Country Rate: according to order of Court.

Jonath: Fayerbank
Sam: Morse   ar Chosen surveyers for the ensueing yeare
Joh Eaton

Willm Bullard
Peter Woodward   ar Chosen Woodreeues

Ordered that the way leading to the Great Playne shall be taken care of to be made & kept in repayer by ye surveyers for the time being from year to year

Lambert Genry hath liberty to sell his Land beyond ye mill Creeke to ———— Tyler of Roxberye

Ordered that all Meadowe that is known in our Town fitt for emprouement shall in ye first fitt optunitie be surveyed. & the quantitie ther of taken & answer returned to the Town in a genrall Meeting. that so it may be layed out in pticular pprietyes

Ordered that the one halfe of that yearly Rent of 40^s p an̄n̄ that arise from the Land of our Town in m^{rs} Stoughtons hand. for all the time past: shall be allowed to the Church & the vse ther of

John Kingsbery. John Dwight. Eleazer Lusher. & George Barber: ar deputed to view the Swampe on the south side of the Middle Playne. as allso the vpland on both sids of the said swampe as it may be in fittness for a Cart waye ther. & to treat with ye ppriators on both sids. & to return answer to the Town in genrall

Richard Wheeler and John Farington ar admitted Townsemen.

Graunted to Richard Wheeler & John Farington 2 acres of vpland to be layd out at the discretion Peter Woodward Robt Hinsdell & Richard Euered. beyond the house Lott of the said Richard Euered. & betwixt the high way & ye Swampe ther

The case depending betwixt the Town: Joseph Kingsbery Joshua Fisher: & Lambert Chinnery concerning a waye is referred to the determination of

     Mr Ralph Wheelock   Chosen by the Town
     Michaell Metcalfe   by Jos. Fisher

DEDHAM TOWN RECORDS. 115

    ¹(John Dwight perhaps Kingsburys man)
    John Fraery   by La: Chinnery
    John Gaye   by ioynt consent of all ye pties
Eleazer Lusher is Chosen to keepe the Regester & drawe the transcript according to order of Court

11 Mon: 8:
1646   Assembled
Hen Chickering. Joh Kingsbery Antho: Fisher Fran Chickering: Tho Wight: Joh Dwight & Elea Lusher

Meetinghouse seats   Agreed wth Joh·Thurston to make the seats in ye Meetinghouse: all that shall be placed in the new house & on the East side of the midle Alley in the old house—he to finde all the worke about them. carriag excepted. and to haue timber for that vse of the Towne. & to receaue of ye Town for the said worke 13£ 10^s: to be payed 5£ in Ceader boarde at 4^s p cent. 20^s in Indian Corn at 3^s p bushell. the rest in wheat at 4^s p bushell. all to be deliuered in Town.

    M^d that ye 5 men: vizt: Mr Ralph Wheelock. Michall Metcalfe: Joh Dwight Joh: Fraery·& Joh Gaye: being indifferently & Mutually chosen by the Town. Joseph Kingsbury: Lambert Chinery. & Joshua Fisher doe order & determin that the high waye lying betwixt Joseph Kingsbury & Joshua Fisher. Leading down to ye Landing place. shall lye as it did befor and as it was first layed out by m^r Edward Alleyn & Abraham Shawe. and to ye end that all former grieuances may be forgotten & future may be p^{r}uented. the abouesaid Lambert Chinery doth freely & voluntariely pmise to set vp & mayntayne for euer fifteen rodds of sufficient Fence. In like maner as before said Joshua Fisher. pmise to set vp & mayntayn for euer fiue Rodd of ye like sufficient fence. wch 5 rodd of fencing stuffe Joseph Kingsbery is to fetch from ye place wher it is p^{r}pared. & lay it wher it is to be set vp. that is to saye. at ye vpper end of ye high waye betwixt Joseph Kingsbery his Lott & the high waye against the house of Joshua Fisher Allso Lambert Chinery is to set vp his 15 rodd adioyning to ye said Joshua Fishers. wch 20 rodd is to be set vp befor ye first daye of ye 2 month. this agreem^t made ye 11 of ye 11 month 1646

    mr Ralph Wheelock   Joseph: Kingsbery
    Mich Metcalf   Lambert Chinery
    Joh. Fraery   Joshua Fisher
    Joh. Dwight
    Joh. Gaye

---

¹ Interlined in another hand.

11 mo 13
1646   Assembled: Joh. Kingsbery: Hen Chickering Tho Wight Antho Fisher Joh Dwight. Fra Chickering & Eleazer Lusher

The Accounts of that pt of ye Meetinghouse Rate that was comitted to Peter Woodward ar taken in

Joh Kingsbery. Fran Chickering Tho: Wight Joshua Fisher ar deputed to take in ye bills of mens Rateable estats

3 mo 17   1647

Assembled Hen. Chickering: John Kingsbery: Antho Fisher Jo: Dwight. Francis Chickering: Tho Wight & Eleazer Lusher

Daniell Fisher granteth to the Town & to the vse ther of for euer. the greater pt of the ponde neer his house together wth 2 smale pcells of vpland adioyning therto on the east and west sids ther of. reseruing to himself and to his hiers for euer all the trees groweing vpon the said pcels of vpland

For and in consideration wherof. the Town granteth to the said Daniell and his hiers for euer such a pcell of vpland as may be equall sattisfaction for the same wch said pcell for satisfaction. shall be layed out for him or his hiers when the said Daniell shall find such a pcell as the Town and he shall think conueanient or else when som other Land granted by the Town shall be layed out and if it shall so fall out that the town & the said Daniell or his hiers cannot then agree in the p^{r}mises the case shall be determined by 2 indifferent men being mutually chosen by both pties. in whose arbitrement both pties pmise to stand satisfied.

10 mo 29

1647   Assembled: Joh. Kingsbery: Antho. Fisher: Jo. Dwight Tho Wight. Francis Chickering. and El: Lusher.

Surveyers   Ordered that Sam: Morse Jonath Fayerbanke and Joh: Eaton or any 2 of them. being formerly Chosen Surveyers for the year 1647 ar heerby enabled and authorised to call in such of the Inhabitants of this town as ar yet behind in thier high way worke. to pforme the same. at such time and place. as the said men shall apoint or compound with them to thier satisfaction

Wheras by long experience it apeare. that diuers of the Inhabitants of the Town. haue bene found slack in the pformance of thier high way worke. to the great discouragement of the surveyours as allso of such as ar more forward therin. and the neglect of the due reparations of the wayes in our Town. it is therfor ordered that the surveyers for the time being. shall yearely apoint 6 dayes for the high waye worke. of which 6 dayes euery inhabitant shall pform 4 dayes worke. according to the surveyers appointment the last of wch six dayes shall be befor the 20th of the 7th month called September.

and whosoeuer of the said Inhabitants shall not haue pformed 4 dayes worke befor the last of the 6 dayes be past. so appointed by the surveyors. shall compound for that his neglect wth the selectmen for the time being. to wch end the surveyors shall. from year. to year. bring a true bill of the worke of each pticular Inhabitant vnto the said select men. wthin fourteen dayes after the last of the sixe dayes afore said.

Tho Wight — Granted to Thomas Wight and his hiers for euer one pcell of Swampe conteyning by estemation twoo Acres or vpward. as it lyeth devided from the like pcell of John Luson & abuteth vpon the same toward the North. & vpon one pcell of the vpland of the said Tho: Wight. & vpon the Comon ground of the Town. on all other sids.

Joh Luson — Granted to John Luson & to his hiers for euer. one pcell of Swampe

Joh Batchelor — Granted to John Batchelor and his hiers for euer. one smale pcell of vpland being pt of the Comon ground Lying at the south end of pt of his house Lott: wch pcell he desired to set a barne vpon. this to be layd out to him by John Kingsbery & Fra: Chickering.

11 Mo: 3   At a genrall Meeting of the Inhabitants
1647   11 mo: called January 3 1647

Fences height — Wheras by former order. all Fences made of Rayles or pales wer appointed to be mad sufficient. to the height of 4 foote: yet vpon experience it is now found that lesse then so much is sufficient. It is now therfor Ordered by genrall consent that all Fences w^t so euer being made of pales or Rayles or to be heerafter made shall be made & maynteyned sufficient to the height of 3 foote and an halfe: and shall be allowed of at that height as sufficient in respect of height

Ladders — Wheras we find vpon experience: the vsefullnes of maynteyning Ladders at and against euery dwelling house. according to an Order in that case pvided. It is therfor now ordered by genrall consent that such of the Inhabitants of our Town as shall be heere after from year to year Chosen to the care office. & trust of Woodreeues. shall from time to time take care of the due & full execution of that order concerning Ladders. aforesaid. and allso shall take care of the sufficiency of Fences wth in our Town. according to such orders in our Town as are allready made. or shall heerafter be found needfull to be made therin.

7 men Chosen — Eleazer Lusher is Chosen to keepe the Town Booke ⎫
Joh: Kingsbery: Fra: Chickering: Tymo: Dwight Joh: ⎬
Dwight: Tho: Wight: Will Bullard ar all Joyntly. by ⎭
genrall consent. Chosen: to order the prudentiall affayers of our Town for the yeare next ensueing.

Surveyours: Peter Woodward ⎫ for the year next ensueing. to whose
　　　　　　Nath: Coalburn　⎬ care the breache in the Riuer is left
　　　　　　Joh: Kingsbery　 ⎭ to be repayered.
Wood reeues: Joh. Gaye:　　　Joh. Eaton　　⎫ for the yeare next
　　　　　　　Josep: Kingsbery:　Jonath: Fayerbanke ⎭　ensueing

Joh: Gaye　　　Granted to Joh: Gay a high waye. to his Madowe adioyning vpon the west side of Charles Riuer. wch said waye is layd out thorough one pcell of the vpland of Daniell Morse. by Tho Wight and Saml Morse. being thervnto deputed by the Town

12 mo: 8　Assembled

1647　Joh: Kingsbery: Tho: Wight: Joh: Dwight: Fra: Chickering: Willm Bullard: Tymo: Dwight & El. Lusher.

Fences　　　Wheras we finde by experience. that many Fences in our
to viewe　　Towne ar oft found very defectiue. and an occasion of much damage and offence. notwithstanding. all the former orders in that case pvided. it is therfor now ordered. that for the p^ruenting of such inconueaniencies in time to com. that those men that ar yearely deputed to the care & trust of viewing Fences. shall yearelie som time betwixt the tenth and eighteenth daye: of the first moneth viewe all the Fences. in our Town. in or about all our home Lotts that lye next any high waye or Comon ground. and w^t deffects so euer they shall find. in the said Fences. they shall giue present notice therof to the owner of the fence wherin the defect is found who shall wth in seuen dayes. after such warning sufficiently make or repayer the same or else for default therof. shall paye to the vse of the Town into the Constables hand. the sum of sixe pence in currant Countreye paye for euery such defect to wch end the said viewers of fences shall giue the constable notice therof pticularlye: who shall be charged wth the said penaltye. to Leuye the same or else to paye the same out of his own purse. and the said viewers of Fences shall keepe a true bill of all such penalties or forfietures. so made wch bill at the end of thier year they shall deliuer to the select men for the time being. who by those bills. shall call the Constables to account. for all such forfieturs. the former order wherby viewers of fences ar required to attend that worke wⁿ so euer they ar called therto. is still in force

Ladder　　　For the encouragement of all that ar not yet pvided of sufficient Lad-
pieces　　　ders required by the order of the Town. in that case appointed it is now further ordered that it shall be in the libertye of euery Townesman to take a piece for a Ladder or for Ladders sufficient for his own vse, in any pt of the comon ground of our Town so that it be not sell to any man w^tso euer

12 mo 8 1647

Assemb: John Kingsbery: Joh. Dwight: Tho: Wight: Fra: Chickering: Willm Bullard: Tym: Dwight & El. Lusher

Mynes   For as much as we know our selues bound to wait vpon God in a dilligent vse of all meanes wch he affoards vs. for the carrying on of his worke amongst vs. so far by his blessing began: and allso for our own subsistance and support. And seing allso that amongst other things wth which God blessed his people Israell. he exp^{r}sseth diuers Mettalls for thier encouragment Dut. 8. 9 & 33. 25: And seing that allreadye amongst our selues plentye of Iron and som Leade is discouered. it appeare to vs. that he hath afforded vs allso a Land furnished wth such blessings. And further allso considering the barrennes of a great pt of our Town. doth both giue vs in pticular hopes therof. and allso p^{r}sseth vs to seeke out all meanes of our support

In consideration wherof. we haue thought it our dutie to giue such encouragm^t as we iudge meete to all that doe at any time endeauour the discouery of any mettalls. or other Minerals. amongst vs. and for the better empuement of such an helpe for the Comon good of all our Town. we doe make this grant following

We doe giue and Grant to euery Inhabitant amongt vs. that is admitted a Townesman. and to his hiers & assignes for euer All such Mine or Mines of any sort of Mettall or other Mineralls w^t so euer. (Iron mine onely excepted vntill the date of the Countreys grant be expired). that he or they shall really discouer and find out by them selues or any way or meanes. by them pcured. or at thier Charge. in any pt of our Towne. being out of the ppriety of any man together allso wth such conueniencie of Land. to be layd out to them. as may be needfull for building. pasturing of Cattell. or other needfull occasions being such as the said worke shall really require. and the place is founde capeable of. Allso we doe further grant vnto the Grantees afore said Liberty to take such sufficient woode. Tymber. or stones as shall be found needfull for the empvem^t of ye sd mine or mines. so that the sd wood or timber be not cutt wthin one myle of any house Lott in our Town now in being. yet. reserveing to the Town. and the vse therof. such oakeing timber trees as the select men, for the time being. shall reasonably se cause to marke out

pvided allwayes. & Granted wth these condicions. vizt that the sd grantee. or grantees. thier hiers and assignes. shall yearely paye into the Comon treasury of ye Town. the Tenth pt of all such pffitts as shall cleerely arise of the sd mine or mines thus Granted. after such grantee or grantees shall haue receaued in agayne. such charges as they haue formerly disbursed vpon the sd worke pvided that it be one mile from the Town or vpward: but if it be lesse then one mile from any house lott now in being. then they shall paye the eight pt of the cleere proffits as be fore said: And allso that such grantees.

doe really endeauour the empvem^t therof w^{th}in the space of 3 yeares next after such discouery is made except the select men se cause to grant longer time

pvided allso that no such grantee aforesaid shall bring in any ptner. or purchaser to haue share in the p^rmises. that is no Townesman wth vs. so long as any one that is of the Town will buye. or take of his hand any such mine or pt therof. vpon such tearmes as the sd stranger will really doe.

pvided allso further. that no such grantee. or purchaser shall at any time bring in amongst vs any such ptner. purchaser, or Constant workeman. as is not for his honest & peaceable conuersation. apved of by the select men for the time being. wch last condicion if they shall breake. euery such one shall forfiet his liberty of takeing woode. before heere in granted.

And for the p^ruenting of such mistakes. or offences. as may heere after arise. about the discouery or finding of such Mines or Minerals. or the further empvem^t therof. we doe further order & declare. that who so euer of our Towne. heereafter. being a Townesman as before sd. shall first giue notice to 2 of the select men. for the time being. wherof the keeper of the booke is to be one of any such mine as before sd. that he hath by any meanes discouered. & so discribe the place. as they may vnderstand that no other hath allready giuen notice therof. then the sd discouerer. shall haue the pprietie of that so exp^rssed. reserved to himself the space of sixe monthes. in wch time none shall haue libertie to p^ruent him. while himself or his assignes. make further pfe. of w^t he shall fully finde & empue by vertue of this former grante

And further allso. if any shall. discouer a mine. very neere another that is allready found out. so that ther is iust question. whether it be not another pt of the same. in that no naturall bound. that must necessariely disioyne. or difference of Mettall. resolue the doubt. then it shall be accounted as one. & the same Mine. and all ready apppriate. by the former grant. to the former posessor

And allso if 2 seuerall & distinct Mines be found so neere together that any question arise. concerning the Land. Timber or wood. to accomadate the same. according to the former grant and that the ppriators of the sd Mines cannot therin agree it shall then be in the libertie & power of each of the sd ppriators. or grantees: to chuse one indifferent man & the select men to chuse another in the behalf of the Town & the major pt of the men so chosen shall fully. determin & end the sd case.

this order for Fences was entrd befor

Wheras vpon experience we finde that many Fences in our Town. ar oft found very deffectiue. and an occasion of much dammage. and offence. notw^{th}standing all the former orders in that Case pvided. it is therfor. further ordered. that for the p^ruenting further inconueaniences. those men that ar yearely deputed to the viewing of Fences. shall euery yeare: som time betwixt the 10th. daye. & the 18th daye of the first moneth view all the fences of our home Lotts. wthin our Town. that lye next any high waye or Comon ground. & w^t deffects so euer they shall find therin they shall giue notice therof to the owner of the fence. forthwith. who shall wthin 7 dayes after such warning is giuen. sufficiently make or repayer the same or else shall paye. to the vse of town. into the Constables hand. the sume of six pence. in Currant Countrey paye. for euery such defect. not amended as beforsd to wch end the sd viewers of fences shall giue the Constable notice therof. who shall be charged wth the sd penaltie. to leuye the same. or else to paye the same out of his own purse. & the sd viewers of Fences shall keepe a true bill of all such penalties or forfietures. so made. wch bill at the end of thier yeare they shall deliuer to the select men for the time being who by those bills shall call the Constables to account. for all such forfietures. the former order wherin viewers of Fences. ar required to goe to view any Fence when they ar therto called. remayne allso in full force

5 mo 7: after Lectur
Assem: Joh Kingsbery: Tho Wight: Fra Chickering: El: Lusher.

Wheras Thomas Jordan hath layed down to the vse of the Town for a high waye some pt of his home Lott. ther is. in recompence. & full satisfaction for the same & all things concerning it. Granted to the sd Thomas & his hiers for euer. 4 acres of Meadowe. to be layed out to him. in som one of the neerest pcells of Bogerstow meadowe. at the direction of Tho: Wight

7 mo 4 Assemb. Joh Kingsbery: Joh Dwight: Tho Wight: Willm Bullard: Tymo Dwight: Fra Chickeringe. & Elea: Lusher.

Granted to the trayned Company of this Town. & the officers therof. & to thier successors for euer. the free vse. of all that pcell of Land. Comonly called the Trayning ground. allways pvided that the sd trayned Company. or the officers ther of. shall not at any time heere after appriate the sd pcell. or any pt therof. or empve the same to any other vse. then for the vse of publike excercise of the sd Company. wthout the Consent of the select men of the Town. for the time being first attayned: neither shall it be in the libertie or power of the select men heerafter at any time to dispose of the sd pcell or any pt therof. in any Case: wthout the Consent of the sd trayned Company. & the officers ther of. first had. & manefest

Lamb:
Genery
Granted to Lambert Genery and to his heirs for euer that pcell of Land lying on the great playne, that is hetherto vndisposed of. conteyning 3 or 4 acres mor or lesse. as it lyeth next beyond that pcell formerly granted to Mr Cooke not yet layed out. & westward from the same all ways pvided that the sd Lambert lay down all clayme. title. or right to 6 acres formerly granted to him in that place called the planting field

8 mo 19.   Assemb: Joh: Kingsbery Joh Dwight. Tho Wight & Elea: Lusher.

wolues   Wheras woolues are now of late becom greatly noysom to our Cattell. to the great p^riudice & damag of the Town. it is therfor ordered. for the better encouragm^t of any that shall heereafter bring the head of any wolf. & publikely p^rsent the same at the meetinghouse. shall for his paynes in killing that wolfe haue payed to him by the hands of the Constable tenn shillings in Countrey paye. besids that ten shillings due to him from the Countrey. and shall allso haue such asistance from the Town. for the attayning of that tenn shillings from the Countrey. as the Case shall necessarilye require. allways pvided that it be made apeer that the sd woolf be killed w^thin our towne

9 mo 20   Assemb. Joh Kingsbery: Joh Dwight: Tho Wight: Fra Chickering: Willm Bullard: Tymo Dwight & Elea: Lusher.

Foras much as it apear. that notw^thstanding. the order formerly made for the directing the Inhabitants & surveyors: in the high way worke. and that the surveyors haue allso attended. the trust comitted to them. yet diuers of the Inhabitants of the Town. haue neglected that seruice of high way worke. to the damage of the Town the discouragem^t of the surveyors & euill example to others: It is therfore ordered. that such of the said Inhabitants. as ar at this p^rsent time behind in thier high waye worke aforesd. shall paye for those thier neglects for euery daye. 2^s. vnto the Constable for the vse of the Town. in Merchantible Corne at the Currant price. except the sd psons can compound wth the surveyors. for the time being. to thier satisfaction. who shall not accept of lesse then 8 houres for one day worke. sufficiently empved. in the high way work at thier apointm^t. or if the surueyors shall put out any pt of high way worke by the piece or lumpe. they shall not compound wth any pson to the damage of the Town. or at a more easie way then as beforesd. allwayes pvided that the surveyors shall not call any to doe thier worke for thier neglect but such & for so many dayes. as they shall receaue in a List. from ye select men. from which they shall not haue liberty to vary. but by the consent of the select men vpon further information: And for the neglect of Teames they ar allso heerby enioyned. to paye to the Constable for euery days neglect of 4 bullocks. one man & a cart. 6:^s. For the dayes neglect of 2 bullocks one man: & a cart. 4^s. to be payd in such paym^t as is before exp^rssed. or if they compound. it shall be according to the rule before exp^rssed.

Assemb: Joh Dwight: Tho: Wight: Fra: Chickering: Tymo Dwight and Eleazer Lusher

10 mo. 12 da:

Wheras the Town formerly vpon som reasons moueing them thervnto.

did pmise m^r Dalton som Lands ouer & besids his house Lott and ye appurtenances therof. & that the said m^r Dalton sold his Lott & all his Town Rights to m^r Powell. late of this Towne. vpon wch consideration the Town doth heerby Grante to the said m^r Michaell Powell. & to his hiers for euer. one pcell of vpland conteining 20 Acres. wch together wth tenn Acres formerly granted to the said Michaell Powell. vpon ye Great playne: is full satisfaction for that former pmise made to m^r Dalton. no more to be expected: in any respect therof. wch said pcell of twentie Acres. is to be layed out vpon the North side of Charles Riuer neere about that place wheras passage is vsually made ouer the said Riuer wth Canooes & it is to be layed out at discretion. & by ye direction of Joh Kingsbery & Joh: Haward

Granted to Richard Ellice libertie to fell & take for his owne vse vpon the Common Land of the Towne such timber as he shall from time to time stand in neede of for the vse of his trade & allso he hath heereby libertie Granted to him. to let his timber so felled. lye the space of one whole yeare after it is felled. pvided. that he marke euery such tree wth ye 2 first letters of his name. that it may be allwayes knowen whose it is

Granted to Richard Ellice & his hiers for euer one pcell of shruffie meadowe. lying at the north west corner of his former grant of vpland. Conteyning by estimation lesse then one Acre. and abutteth vpon the Land of Robt Crosseman toward the west. & vpon Charles Riuer towards the north

10 mo 19   Assemb: Joh: Kingsbery: Fra: Chickering: Joh: Dwight: : Tho: Wight: Will Bullard: Tymo Dwight & El. Lusher

Granted to Joh. Thurston & his hiers for euer. 2 Acres of swampe as it lyeth in that swampe adioyning to the southermost of his grant of vplande. that lyeth toward the south playne gate. this to be layed out to him by ye direction of Hen. Chickering & Tho Wight

1648   At a Genrall Meeting of the Towne

It is by genrall consent resolued to chuse 3 men for the ending of smale Cases. according to the Court in that case pvided

It is ordered that all such men as shall heereafter. by the select men for the time being. shall be chosen. ordered. or deputed. to doe any such seruice. as concerne the Town in Genrall. shall be reasonable satisfied for thier paynes therin. at the Townes charge

Joshua Fisher senio^r }
Tho: Battell: } ar admitted Townesmen
Tho. Bancroft   }

A schoole house & a watchouse. is resolued to be built this next yeare the care wherof is left to the select men

The choice of select men as followeth

Eleazer Lusher is chosen to keepe ye Towne Booke & to be one of ye select men

Henry Chickering: Thomas Wight   }
John Kingsbery: Joshua: Fisher: } ar chosen for ye select men
John: Dwight: Francis Chickering } for the yeare next ensueing

Eleazer Lusher   }
Henry. Chickering } ar chosen for the ending of smale cases according
John Kingsbery   } to the order of ye Court

Nathaniell Coaleburne: Daniell Fisher. & John Haward ar chosen surveyers

Joh: Gaye   John. Eaton   }
Josep. Kingsbery: John. Fraery   } ar chosen woodreeues

Eleazer Lusher. is discharged of his high waye worke for the yeare next ensueing. in regard of his many occasions for the publike

[*It is ordered that the Land now intended to be layed out shall be first surveyed at the Townes charge & layed out by the rules of psons & estates. each pson of the Towne w^t soeuer. to receaue so much as eight pound estate]

The disorderly feeding of Fields & meadowes lying in pprietie the select men now chosen ar desired to take care to p^{r}uent

Ordered that the Land now to be layed out in a genrall deuedent shall be first surveyed at the Townes charge. & deuided vnto psons & estates each pson in the Town w^t so euer. being an inhabitant shall receaue as much as eight pound estate

11 mo 15^d Assemb. Hen Chickering: Joh. Kingsbery: Joh: Dwight: Tho:
48   Wight: Fra Chickering: Lieft. Fisher: & El. Lusher.

Granted vnto James Allen one pcell of swampe not exceeding 2 Acres to be layed out neere the swampe formerly Granted to Henry Smith. at ye direction of Joh. Dwight & Fra: Chickering

Granted to George Fairebanke free libertie to fell and take for his own vse vpon the Comon Land of the Towne such timber as he shall from time to time neede for his trade pvided. that he neither sell nor trade a waye any such timber, vnwrought into vessels. & he hath allso libertie heereby to let his timber so felled. lye the space of one whole yeare it being sufficiently marked wth som knowen marke

Granted to serg^t. George Fairebanke. one smale pcell of Land. as it lye against the side of his own yard. for an enlargem^t to set a Barne vpon it to be layed out to him by the direction of Joh. Dwight & El. Lusher.

Wheras the disorderly feeding of pprieties is both a wrong & an offence. to the ppriators as well in Meadowes as allso in Corne fields that ar posessed & Impved by many owners. it is therfor. for ye p^{r}uenting of ye grieeuances aforesaid: ordered. That euery ppriator w^t so euer: that hold or Impue any Land in corne field or fields in our Towne. shall yearely & euery yeare. take in all his corne. w^t sort so sort it be of out of all such fields. before the 12th of the eight moneth vpon penaltie of beareing all damages w^t so euer may by neglect ther of before wch said daye. no man w^t so euer shall haue Libertie to put his cattell of any sort to feed in any such fielde vpon such penaltie as the Court hath all ready apointed. but after ye said 12 daye of the eight moneth. it shall be free for all ppriators. to feed thier cattell in such fields wher themselues posesse lands. as owners. or vpon rent. And no man w^t so euer shall put his cattell to feed in any Field. wher himself is no posessor. vpon pennaltie of forfieture of 5^s for euery such offence

Neither shall any keeper of any hearde of Cattell. w^t so euer. put the heard by him so kept. or any pt therof. into any Corne Field. to keepe them ther to feede. though the corne be all out vpon penaltye of payeing 5^s for euery offence against this order. neither shall he suffer them wittingly or willinglye. to continnue ther. if thorough deffect of the fence. they goe in of themselues. vpon the like penaltie as before said. or if ther be any damage done in corne the keeper by whose default it is. shall paye the damage besides the penaltie aforesaide. all wch pennalties shall be payed to whom so euer the greater part of the ppriators of the field. shall apoint. to receaue the same vpon demaunde

Vpon the demaund made by Daniell Fisher. of sattisfaction for the deffect of measure in his twelue acres of meadowe. due to him vpon his first grant we therfor in the consideration therof. doe now Grant to the said Daniell. & his hiers for euer. 3 acres & 3 roodes. of meadowe. to be layed out to him. or his assignes in such a place in Rosemary meadowe as the said Daniell shall chuse: that is at p^{r}sent free from all engagem^t. pvided. that he take it in full satisfaction for ye Clayme by him made to the high waye by Charles Riuer. in ye Broade Meadow

And for as much as vpon further consideration its adiudged pbable that the foresaid quantitie of meadow cannot be found in one place together we therfore doe further order heerein. that the said pcell shall be layed out at ye direction of Eleazer Lusher & Joshua Fisher who ar desired to take care so to laye it out. as it may giue satisfaction to the said Daniell so fare as they conceaue reasonable

12 of ye 8th mo 1649   Assemb: Hen Chickering: Tho. Wight: Joh. Dwight: Joh Kingsbery, Fra: Chickering: Lieft: Fisher & Elea: Lusher

Granted vnto Thomas Payne. & to his hiers for euer. 2 acres of swampe. to be layed out in the Comon swampe. neere ye south playne at ye direction of Thomas Wight

John Dwight. & Lieft. Fisher ar Deputed to treate & conclude wth Lambert Genery. for that smale parcell of his Land in his Lott wher Clay is to be had for Bricke. & to returne answer to the select men who returne answer that the said Lambert doe freely giue it to the Towne

1 of ye 11 mo: 1649
At a genrall meeting of the Towne

Joh. Haward
Joh: Thurston } ar requested & appointed to search out a place for ye feeding of a drye heard.
Geo. Barber

It is ordered that a platt shall be taken of ye bounds & lines of ye whole Towne and that it be made Capeable of a distinct platt of euery pprietie

Michaell Metcalf senio^r
Ensign. Phillips } ar apointed to take in ye accounts of ye select men. in such things as concerne the Towne for ye yeare last past:
Serg^t Fisher

Elea: Lusher
Lieft: Fisher
Ensig: Phillips } ar chosen and authorised to laye out the Grant made from this Towne to ye village. & to accomplish the same before the middle of ye 2 month next
Joh Dwight
Dan: Fisher

Those 3 men Chosen the last yeare to end smale cases. according to the Court order. ar againe chosen for the same worke for ye yeare next following

The select men Chosen as followeth

Eleazer Lusher is chosen to keepe the Booke & allso to be one of ye selectmen for ye year next ensueing

John. Kingsbery: Lieft Fisher
Henry: Chickering: Serg^t Fisher } ar allso chosen & haue ye same power put into thier hands y^t thier p^{r}decessors haue vsually had
John: Dwight: Tymo: Dwight

John Luson
Hen Smyth } ar chosen surveyors
John: Morse

Willm Bullard
Joh Thurston } ar chosen woodreeues
George Barber
Joh: Fraery

vpon consideration of the motion made & ye voate passed. for the giueing account to ye men deputed to audit the same. it is adiudged most meet & to informe them of the manner of our disbursem^{ts} by the Constable and referr them to his accounts

The 2 orders made the 31 of Decemb^r 1636 concerning felling trees ar heerby repealed as allso one orded made 16 of march 1640. concerning monethly meetings of ye select men is heereby repealed.

For as much as vpon experience it apeare. that som orders made in ye former yeares in ye beginning of our Towne ar not at p^{r}sent vsefull for ye p^{r}sent state therof. amongst wch. 2 orders. restrayneing the felling of trees. ar therfore heere aboue. repealed

It is therfor (for the pruenting disorderly & wastefull felling of trees. either for woode or timber) now ordered that it shall hence forth be in the Libertie. of any man that is admitted a Townesman heere wth vs. to fell any such fire woode as he shall for his owne vse stand in need of from time. to time. allwayes pvided that no oake trees be felled. but such as ar granted to such psons. according to ye order of the Towne. & that case pvided. and for euery offence comitted against ye true meaning. of this order. as is aboue exprssed. the offender shall paye vnto ye vse of the Towne such a pennaltie as shall be by the select men for the time being adiudged meete, so that no fine exceed 5^s for the felling of any one tree

Lieft: Fisher is deputed. & vndertaketh to take & make a true platt of ye out most Lines of the Towne

Granted vnto Ralph Daye free libertie to make vse of w^t Clay so euer he shall need for the vse of makeing Bricke in that parcell of Land late Lambert Generies & by him granted to the Towne to that end. allwayes pvided. that he secure the same by fence. from all hazard of damage. that may be by reason of the Clay pitts. Allso we doe heereby. grant to the said Ralph or his assignes libertie to fell & carry a way. (for the vse aforesaid). such wood vpon the Comon ground of the Towne from time to time as he needeth

7. of 11 mo 1649   Assembled at this meeteing last aboue mentioned the select men heere after named

Henry. Chickering, John: Dwight, Lieft: Fisher, Tymo: Dwight, Daniell: Fisher & Eleazer: Lusher

21 of 12 mo 1649   Hen: Chickering: Joh: Kingsbery: John: Dwight: Lieft: Fisher: Serg^t: Fisher: Tymo: Dwight & Eleaz: Lusher

Granted to Thomas Payne. & to his heyers for euer a supplye of swampe in that swampe formerly granted. to vse of burning Bricke if that grante so made hinder not this prsent grante. Joh Haward. Lieft Fisher ar to laye it out

Granted to Lieft Fisher: and to his heyers for euer. Tenn Acres of vpland to be layed out to him by the asistance and direction of Peter Woodward and Nathaniell Coaleburne. vpon the place called the planting fielde in full satisfaction for his right in the purchased vplands being one Cowe pastureing and one halfe. as allso in sattisfaction for his right that is or maye be in the next deuident of vpland. yet to be layed out pvided that if vpon the laying out of that deuedent it shall apeare that. 4 Acres according to his pportion is more then will com to his pt that he then shall sattisfie som other man for so much as the said Lieft haue too much we accounting that sixe Acres of this grant may be equally allowed for his right in the purchased Lands

John Bullard. and Henry Wilson. makeing request for supplye of meadowe ther is there vpon granted vnto the said John & Henry the free vse of the meadow. called the Church meadowe for the space of seauen yeares next ensueing. equally to deuide the same betwixt them. vpon this condition. that. they sufficiently stubb & cleere the same. allwayes pvided. that if the Town can other wise supply them wth meadowe: it shall be in the libertie of the Towne. to call it out of thier hands vpon alloweing them such recompence for thier cleereing the same as shall be Judged they haue deserued mor then the time they haue had the meadow. haue equally sattisfied for and further allso they ar enioyned by the entery of the said meadowe to mayntaine the fence belonging therto. & leaue the same In due repayre when so euer they shall leaue the meadowe

Eleazer Lusher. is deputed in behalfe of the Towne of Dedham to asist in laying out the Farme granted to Mr Edward Aleyne deceased wch is to be layd out at Bogastow. now called Medfield

15 of 4 mo 1650 Assemb: Hen Chickering: Joh Kingsbery: Joh: Dwight: Lieft Fisher, Serg^t: Fisher & Elea: Lusher

John Dwight: Lieft Josh: Fisher & Serg^t Daniell Fisher ar deputed to treat wth such of Cambridg men. as shall be by that Towne appointed and authorised to treat in refference to the sale of those Lands late in the posession of Dedham. or any pt of the same. now being desired to be purchased againe by the Inhabitants of Dedham. and vpon the tender of such ppositions as they Judg reasoneable. to returne answer to the select men. that the Towne may doe therein as they shall Judg meete

17 of 3 mo 1650 Assemb: John Kingsbery: Hen: Chickering: Lieft: Fisher: Tymo: Dwight: Serg^t. Fisher & Elea. Lusher

Vpon the demand of Joseph Kingsbery. made for the right he haue remayning due to him. in respect of his disbursement in the purchased Lands. at the begining of the Towne. ther is therfor granted to the said Joseph and his heyers for euer. foure Acres of vpland. if it be to be had on the north east side of Mr Greenes Farme

Vpon the request of Thomas Payne. ther is granted to the said Thomas and his heyers for euer: one smale pcell of vpland. lyeing adioyning to one pcell of the meadowe of the said Thomas. for the streightening of his Fence there. this is to be appointed & layed out to him by the direction of John Kingsbery

27 of 4 mo 1650 Assemb: John Kingsbery, Hen: Chickering, Lieft: Fisher, Joh: Dwight, Serg^t Fisher, & Eleaz: Lusher

The Rate for the purchasing of Ammunition according to the order of the Court made this day at the rate of penny farthing p £

Deputed. the men heereafter named. to treate wth Cambridg men about the purchase of half that Tract of Land that was formerly in the posession of Dedham and that they at thier discretion should in the best manner they can get the knowledg of w^t the price is like to be. and if they se vrgent reason they may offer fifty pounds or vpward. not exceeding sixtie £. except the select men first see reason to consent therto. they ar allso to endeavour to cleere vp: & put an end to all reckonings. at p^{r}sent betwixt Cambridg and Dedham.

men deputed therto John Dwight, Lieft: Fisher, Serg^t Fisher

Deputed the men heereafter named to treat with Roxbery men about the purchase of som pt of the Land in thier Town Bounds. that lye next our Towne. and returne answer to the select men. they ar Authorised to conclude if they can. & they see iust reason so to doe. so that they exceed not the price of sixtie pounds for one thousand acres Francis Chickering: John Dwight. Lieft Fisher & Elea Lusher

Granted vnto Joshua Fisher senior and to his heyers for euer sixe Acres of vpland to be layed out to him vpon that place called the planting fielde at the direction of Henry Chickering, Peter Woodward

Granted vnto Joshua Kent and to his heyers for euer sixe Acres of vpland to be layed out to him vpon the planting field at the direction of Henry Chickering, Nathaniell Coaleburne

31 of 6 mo: 1650 Assem: Joh: Kingsbery, Hen: Chickering. Lieft: Fisher, Joh. Dwight, Serg^t Fisher, Corporall Dwight & Elea Lusher.

The Countrey Rate this daye made

Vpon the request of John Littlfield. it is consented vnto. that libertie shall be allowed him. to hyer or purchase som habitation in our Town to dwell in. so long as his behauiour and carriag be honest industrious and peaceable

21 of 7 mo: 1650 Assemb: Hen: Chickering, Joh. Dwight, Lieft Fisher, Serg^t Fisher, Tymo: Dwight, & Elea. Lusher

Deputed to treat wth Roxbery men. and to conclude wth them about the setling of the waye yet vnsetled: & about the purchaseing of the Land in thier Towne that haue beene in pposall. Francis Chickering, Lieft: Fisher, Joh Dwight, Elea Lusher

Granted vnto Joseph Kingsbery and to his heyers for euer sixe Acres of Lande. to be layed out vpon the planting Fielde. next to Joshua Kent

[*Granted vnto Joshua Fisher senior and to his heyers for euer sixe Acres of Land. to be layed out vpon the planting Fielde next to Joseph Kingsberye.]

Granted to Robert Fuller and to his heyers for euer foure Acres of Land-to be layed out for his deuident. vpon the planting Field next to Joshua Fisher senior

 Henry Chickering } ar deputed to se these grants
Nathaniell: Coaleburne } layed out

 For as much as the satisfieing of the motion about the Accomadation of the village. to be erected for the Indians at Natick is a matter of great concernment. in many respects. it is thought meete. to nominate & depute the men whose names ar vnder written. to take a carefull and speciall viewe of the Lands in pposition to that end. who ar allso desired to make returne of thier app^rhensions therein to the select men. & to the Towne

 Eleazer Lusher, Lieft: Fisher, Joh. Dwight, Fra: Chickering, Antho: Fisher. seni, Joh: Haward, Serg^t: Fisher, Ensign Philips, Joh: Gaye, Tho Wight, Tymo Dwight

 12 of 10th mo: 1650 Assemb: Henry Chickering. Joh: Kingsbery. Lieft: Fisher, Joh: Dwight, Tymo: Dwight, Serg^t: Fisher, & Elea. Lusher

 Lieft: Fisher. & Eleazer Lusher ar deputed. in the behalf of the Towne to examine the accounts of the debt due from the Towne to Mr Haynes or in case they cannot be both p^rsent then either of them. & any one of the select men. besides for that time being. who shall determine the account. as they shall see Just. and they allso to compound for the sattisfaction of that debt. that then shall appeare due as they shall se most conueanient

 Whereas som doubtfullnes remayne about the setling of the southerly bounds wth in the Rocks of the house Lotts of Henry Chickering and Antho Fisher senio: the Town therfor doe tender them a refference & nominat and authorise John Kingsbery & Daniell Fisher in the behalf of the Towne. who together wth such other twoo men by the said Henry and Anthony Chosen shall haue full power to settle those bounds according to the grants

 Granted to Thomas Bancroft & to his heyers for euer one pcell of vpland to be layed out to him by the direction of William Bullard & Serg^t Fisher neere the land of Richard Ellice towards the place called the old Mille this pcell not exceeding three Acres pvided. that he empve the same. or the most pt therof. before the end of foure yeares next. otherwise it shall returne. againe to the Towne

 17 of 10th mo 1650 Assemb John Kingsbery, Hen: Chickering, Joh: Dwight, Lieft Fisher, Serg^t Fisher, Corporall Dwight & Eleazer Lusher

 The arbitrators Chosen by the Towne & by Henry Chickering & Anthony Fisher senior for the setling the southerly Bounds of the house Lotts of the said Henry & Anthony. make thier returne. & subscribe all thier names therto. wch settlment of thiers is confirmed by the Towne as followeth

We whose names ar heere mentioned namely John Kingsbery and Daniell Fisher. being chosen by the Towne of Dedham & William Bullard and John Gaye. chosen by Henry Chickering and Anthony Fisher senior being deputed. and Authorised. to issue a case depending as yet vnpfect. concerning the south limit of the Lotts of the fore named men. we doe now declare settle & determine.these head lotts as followeth.Anthony Fishers marke next Thomas Wight. to be at twoo white oakes. standing together. being marked. directing to Thomas Wights line. & so from thence towards the Lott of Henry Chickering to a maple aboue his lyne by a swamps side And the Line of the Lott of Henry Chickering. we settle and determine the bounds to be. according as his Fence there is now sett down. In wittnes that this is all our minds and resolutions we haue heere vnto set all our hands this p^{r}sent daye. being the 16th of ye 10th mo 1650

Joh: Kingsbery: Will Bullard
Dan: Fisher: Joh: Gaye

Granted vnto Thomas Bancroft liberty. to remoue his Fence that so he may haue such an enlargement on the back side of his Barne as maye necessary for the setting of a Leantoe against the said barne. this enlargm^t to be such as shall be according to the direction of William Bullard & Eleazer Lusher

pvided that the said Thomas doe alowe so much land on the other side of the way right against the foresaid place as may continue the waye ther at the due breadthe: & allso doe so much worke there in the waye. as the forenamed men shall Judg needfull to make the waye conueanient for passag there

20 of ye 10th mo 1650 Assemb: Henry: Chickering: John: Kingsbery: John: Dwight: Lieft Fisher: Tymo: Dwight: Daniell: Fisher: & Elea: Lusher

The Accounts of John Morse late Constable for the twoo Towne Rates by him gathered. ar this day taken

Granted. to Mr John Allen pastor. & to his heyers for euer one pcell of that swampe neere the middle playne. conteyning one acre and one half or there about. in exchang for the like pcell that he lay downe in the same swampe. neere thervnto. this is to be layd out by estimeation at the direction of Lieft Fisher and John Dwight. they to take care to p^{r}serue a waye there if they se cause

[*The Accounts of John Morse Late Constable. of that Rate made the 10th of ye 12 mo 1648: wherby was Levied of the Towne the sume of 33£ 13^s 4^d

Disbursements as followeth:

For Scales weights & measurs. together wth the siezeing sealing and Ironing of ye measures	03	04	00

Allowed ye Constable for his disbursements for his charges in his 2 yeares seruice	00	17	00
For the paym^t of diuers debts due from the Towne to seuerall men as apeare vpon the examination of thier accounts	08	08	11
For the Fence betwixt the high waye & James Allens Lott	01	08	00
To Joh Thurston for worke about the schoole house	11	00	03
For ye paym^t of other debts due from the Towne	00	19	10
more discounted out of this Rate vpon old debt	00	16	02
more p^d for mending the Carte Bridge	00	02	04
more p^d of old debt	00	04	00
	27	01	02
Remayne of this Rate aboue this account due to the Towne	06	12	01

out of this Rate ar debts yet to be payed.

To Mr Cooke of Cambridg by the assignm^t of Mr Haynes	01	04	00
To the Treasurer for the Court Orders	00	11	08

besides seuerall other debts that ar yet to be cleered vp.

The Accounts of Joh: Morse late Constable concerning the Rate made for & concerning the hunting of Wolues. wherby was Levied the sume of 5£ 6^s 5^d: dated ye 4th of ye 9th mo 1648

Disbursem^{ts}

p^d to an Indian for killing a wolfe	00	10	00
for 3 wolues killing in Towne	02	10	00
To Geo: Bearstoe for charge & time expended about the hounds	01	10	00
more discounted out of this Rate	00	00	04
	04	10	04
Remayne due to the Town of this Rate	00	16	01]

1 of ye 11 1650 At a genrall Meeteing of the Towne

It is ordered by Genrall consent. the select men that shalbe this daye chosen shall take care that such defects as ar in the Towne Bookes or any of them. be corrected and that such Tables. According to ye Alphabet be anexed to them as they shall iudge meete. for the better findeing of what so euer is recorded in them

    William Auery
    John Aldus } ar admitted Townsemen
    John Mason

It is now ordered. that whereas it apeare that seuerall pcels of Land that wer granted formerly by the Towne to sundry psons. many of which grants ar not yet recorded: All such grants wherof good euedence may apeare. shall be yet entered. wch grants so now entered shall now be good assurance. vnto the Grantee & his heyers for euer

The men heere after named. being formerly deputed to treate wth Roxbery men about the purchase of som of Roxbery Lands in pposition ar still intrusted with the same. and ar heereby further Authorised. in the behalfe of ye Towne. to conclude a firme Contract with whomesoeuer of Roxbery shall be enabled with the like power. vnto whose act or Contract. the Towne heereby engage to stand and make it good:

Joh Dwight, Fra: Chickering, Lieft Fisher, Elea: Lusher

It is by the Towne of Dedham. consented vnto. and. Ordered. that all the power. right. or p^{r}uelidg of Towne Gouerment. that hath hetherto. or yet is remayning in the Townshipe of Dedham or any thier Trustees or assignes wherby they haue & did act. in and on the behalf of ye Towne of Meadfield shall be heerby wholey & Totaly transmitted. & deliuerd in to the hands. power. & disposeing of the Townshipe in Genrall of Meadfield. & the select men there of. and to thier successors for euer: And doe allso further agree wth those of Meadfield that ar p^{r}sent that such care as is neccessary be taken. that due & seasonable payment be made. of that debt due from Medfield to this Towne. vpon reasonable demaund there of made. and further pmise as much forbeareance there of as the publike occasions. of ye Towne of Dedh may admitt of

The case in pposition concerning Dorchester bounds. is left to the care and discretion of ye select men for ye yeare ensueing. to doe therein as to thier iudgement shall seeme best for the good of ye Towne of Dedham.

Vpon the motion made demanding of the Towne that the vpland due to seuerall Inhabitants vpon the disbursments for the purchased Lands should be layed out to them to whome the same may apeare to belong. It is now Ordered that the same be forth wth referred to the Arbittrement of these 4 men heere vnder named to issue settle and determine w^t so euer is necessary for the resolution of this case & in case these 4 or any 3 of them cannot agree. then it shall be in thier power to chuse one man more to be a fifth man. to helpe to cast the said case

pvided that it shall not be in thier power to grante settle or laye out the same. in any of those places intended at p^{r}sent to be layed out in the next deuident

Henry Chickering
John Gaye } ar chosen by ye towne

John Dwight
Lieft: Fisher } chosen by ye ppriators

The care of pvideing for the sumer feede of the drye hearde is comitted

to the men whose names ar heerevnder written who are desired to enforme themselues of w^t so euer is needfull in that case for the due & seasonable ꝑvision of all things necessary in that case. and to act accordinglye
 Nathaniell: Coaleburne. William: Bullard. Francis Chickering.

Those men whose last deuision of Swampe is nowe taken away by Cambridg consent to wayt for w^t supplye may be attayned by the purchase of Roxbery Lands. where the Towne ꝑmise to make thier supplye. if ther it may be had other wise to take further care for thier sattisfaction in due time

Vpon consideration that the Transcript for som time past hath bene neglected. It is therfore for the ꝑfecting thereof now ordered. that Eleazer Lusher shall be heereby Deputed to that worke for the yeare ensueing to ꝑfect the same in w^t so euer is yet vndone therein. & so to carrye on that seruice to the end of the yeare ensueing. who shall haue for his paines therein w^t so euer the select men shall agree wth him for

The supplye of Meadowe. to those men whose. Meadow is now within Cambridge is left to the select men. to doe therein as they can agree wth those men.

Samuell Milles makeing request for one pcell of Meadowe. his motion is left to the discretion of ye select men. to doe therein as they shall judge meete.

Seuerall complaints being made of the insufficient ꝑformance of the worke of ye Mille Nathaniell Whiteing the Miller being p^{r}sent & tendering a refference to issue the grieuances. by twoo men to be chosen by the Towne. & twoo by himselfe. The towne accepting thereof make choice as followeth

Eleazer Lusher
Nathaniell Coalburne } chosen by ye Towne

John Kingsbery
Geo: Barber } chosen by Nath Whiteing

Elections   Eleazer: Lusher
    Henry: Chickering } ar chosen to end smale cases according to the order of Court in that case ꝑvided
    John: Kingsberye

Eleazer Lusher is chosen to keepe the Towne Booke
Joh: Kingsbery: Daniell Fisher
Joh: Dwight: Nathaniell Coalburne
Lieft: Fisher: Francis Chickering
} ar authorised to act in ye behalf of the Towne as thier p^{r}decessors were

Joh: Kingsbery is discharged. of watching for his own pson for the yeare ensueing

Joh: Gaye
Tho: Fuller } Surveyors:
Rich Euered

Jonath: Fayerbanke:
Josep: Kingsbery:
Willm: Bullard:
Joh: Haward:
} Woodreeues

 the request of Edward Hawes. concerning one pcell of Meadowe is left to the care of the select men

DEDHAM TOWN RECORDS. 135

At a Genrall Towne Meeteing 1651.

The question concerning the Right of Heyers. or purchasers. to all the Towne p^ruelidges. and right of voateing in all cases wth other Townesmen is refferred to ye Select men now to be chosen. that they may p^rpare and ripen the answer. and comend it to the townes Resolution

Tymo: Dwight Ju:	Ralph: Freeman	
Andr: Duein	Joh Rice	ar admitted Townesmen
Josep: Ellice	Danll Ponde	

It is resolued that a Schoole for ye education of youth in our Towne shall be continued & mayntayned for the whole tearme of Seauen yeares next. and that the settled mayntenance or wages of the Schoole m^r shall be 20£ p añn at ye leaste

A Towne stocke shall be raysed. to ye sume of 20£. at ye least

Elections

Eleazer Lusher	Joh: Kingsberey	
is chosen to keepe	Joh Dwight	
the Towne Booke.	Serg^t Danll Fisher	ar chosen select men
Lieft Joshua Fisher	Peter Woodward	
Fra: Chickering		

It is agreed that the Meetinghouse shall be couered wth shingle

The care concerning the drye heard is reffered to the select men for ye yeare ensueing

Antho: Fisher Ju:		Joh Morse	
Josep: Kingsberey	Surveyors:	Tho: Fuller	Woodreeues
Andr: Duein		Nath Coaleburn	
		Mich: Metcalf Ju	

The Accounts of ye Select men for ye yeare paste ar allowed of by ye Towne 1651

John Dwight. Francis Chickering. Lieft Fisher and Serg^t Fisher being deputed by the Towne to Joyne wth such of Watertown as should be in the like manner deputed by that Towne to laye out the Lyne that is not yet pfected betwixt the Townes aforenamed. who meeteing vpon the place with Srg^t Joh: Shearman and Srg^t Richard Bieers did accordingly settle & determine the said Line. begining at p[ticion] pointe and so the same is to runne from thence streight west. somthing enclineing towards the south so fare as the said twoo Towne bounds lye together there

about ye 14 of ye 3. mo: 1651

Lieft Fisher Joh Dwight & Francis Chickering. being deputed to meete wth such men of Roxbery as wer in the like manner by that Towne deputed. to Runne the Line. betwixt the Twoo Townes afore saide accordingly mett

vpon the Bounds aforesaid wth Surveyer Genrall Johnson Serg^t Crofts & John Ruggles. did together conclude & settle the said Line. begining at the Lott somtimes Lambert Generies at a marked oake vpon the toppe of a Ridge there. and so layed out that Line streight from thence to a farme somtimes the Land of Mr Samll Greene and from thence vpon a north easterly lyne adioyneing to the said Farme. takeing Two seuerall Angles therby & so concluding that Line at Cambrdg Bounds
ye 30 of ye 2 mo 1652

Lieft Fisher. Frances Chickering and Srg^t Fisher being deputed to meete wth such of Dorchester as should be in the like manner deputed by that Towne. did accordingly meete wth Srg^t Clarke & Srg^t Sumner vpon the Lowe playne according to apointment. who vpon treatie & discourse vpon the setling the Bounds could not agree. and therevpon concluded nothing but left the same as they founde it   28 of 2 mo 1652

This shall certifie whomso euer it may concerne. that we the Inhabitants of Dedham have chosen and Authorised our beloued bretheren. Lieft^t Joshua Fisher and Serg^t Daniell Fisher to treat and conclude wth the much Honourd Genrall Court now Assembled at Boston. or any Towne. pson. or psons. for and on the behalfe of o^r said Towne of Dedham. in any case. concerning the Accomadation of Naticke and the Indians the Inhabitants there. as allso the accepting & receaueing any Lands if any be tendered in exchange or any other thing that is necessary to be considered there in. according to thier best discretion   20 of 8 mo 1652

3 of 11 mo 1652
At a generall meeteing of the Towne
The acts and Accounts of the Select men for the yeare last past being giuen in to the Towne ar by voate alowed of and accepted
The question being pposed whether the foote Bridge vnto the Iland should be built againe or not. The answer by voate passed negatiue
The quest: concerning the Schoole being kept onely in winter being pposed for Resolution :—the answer is That the select men that shall be this daye chosen. shall attend to pcure a fitt schoole m^r. at the begining of the sumer and if it pue difficult or not to be attayned: they may ppose the case to the Towne for further resolution:
The case in question. concerning the Title that Dedham may yet haue to Foule meadowe. and any other Lands now accounted to belong to Dorchester. is referred to the three men heere vnder named. who haue full

power to treat and conclude the case. with whomso euer may be by Dorchester like wise empowered. either by Arbitration. composition or any other peaceable waye. as they by thier discretions shall judge most meete. and in case it shall not Issue wth out suite in Lawe. they ar desired to returne the case to the Towne

    Lieft. Josh. Fisher, Fra: Chickering, Serg^t Dan: Fisher

[^{1}The Coppie of the agreem^t concluded vpon betwixt the Townes of Dedham and Dorchester by the Comitte of each towne vizt

Whereas ther hath bene some difference betwene the Towne of Dorchester. and the Towne of Dedham. concerning som Land neere the Line betwene the said Townes. now both Townes. being willing of peace and loue to continue and that each might enjoye thier true right. haue chosen Three men of each Towne whose names are heere vnto subscribed to whome they haue giuen full power to conferre and determin the matter in difference. now we whose names are subscribed heerevnto doe agree as Followeth: first that the Line vpon the Lowe playne. that begin at the heape of Stones and so runne towards Mother brooke to a marked Maple neere the brooke shall be carried on vpon the Same streight Line towards Charles Riuer so fare as Dorchester bounds goe. And the Line from the aforesaid heape of Stones. into the Countrie to runne as formerly. both which Lines are the true bounds betwene Dorchester and Dedham:

Secondly. it is agreed that those psons of Dedham that bought some pprieties in the Foule Meadowe shall haue the Title of the Lande remayne sure to them and thier Assignes for euer: notwithstanding any pvisoe in any deed formerly made and further what Commons is in the abouesaid Foule Meadowe. shall be the pprietie of the Towne of Dedham. but still to be and remayne. within the Towneship of Dorchester To all which p^{r}mices we haue heere to set our hands. in the behalfe and power of both Townes. this 27 of ye 10th. mo. 1653:

                        John: Glouer
                        Humphrey: Atherton
                        Thomas: Jons
                        Wm: Clarke
                        Frances: Chickering
                        Daniell: Fisher
                        Joshua: Fisher]

    The former deputation and power giuen to Lieft Fisher and Serg^t Daniell Fisher in regard of settling the case concerning Naticke & the Indians ther is renewed and confirmed

    It is agreed that Libertie is giuen to builde another Mille wth in our Towne. & it is left to the discretion of the Select men now to be chosen for

---

^{1} Copied from a leaf now bound in Vol. 4.

the yeare next ensueing to conclude wth whom they se cause to pforme the same.

It is agreed and Resolued by voate that the one halfe of the charge occasioned by building the bridge intended to be made ouer Charles Riuer at the place where passage is vsually made wth Canooes or ther abouts shall be borne by such as shall haue Land in pprietie this next yeare ensueing wherby they may be occasioned to make vse of the said bridge. and the other halfe of the charge ariseing by makeing the said passage and the mayntaining thereof. shall be borne at the publike charge of the Towne by the comon Rule of Rateing. as other publike wayes are

Libertie is granted to cutt a Creeke or ditch thorough any Comon land of the Towne which shall be occasioned by the cutting the same thorough the broade meadowe from Riuer to Riuer:

Lieft: Fisher & Thomas Fuller[1] ar deputed to survey the length of the water course thorough the Broade meadow aforesaid. & the manner of the ground thorough which the same is to be cutt & the height of the water in the Lower Riuer. & make return to them concerned therein when they ar met together about that occasion

The select men ar desired to issue the case depending concerning the barrell of poulder deliuered to Ensign Phillips

Eleazer Lusher is chosen to keepe the Towne booke & to be one of the Select men for the yeare ensueing

Lieft. Fisher   Fra Chickering }
Joh. Kingsbery   Joh. Dwight   } are chosen select men
Dan: Fisher   Pet: Woodward   }

Joh Gaye   }
Antho. Fisher Ju   } are chosen Surveyors
Tho. Fuller   }

Jonath. Fayrbanke sen }
Antho. Fisher sen   } are chosen woodreeues
Joh. Haward   }
Joh. Morse   }

Mich: Metcalfe sen is chosen according to Court order to take in the voluntarie subscriptions referring to the Colledge

Isaac Bullard   }
Cornell: Fisher   } are admitted Townesmen
Joh Partridge   }

Deac. Chickering }
Antho. Fisher sen } are chosen to joyne wth the 4 select men to
Joh Gaye   }
giue instruction to.   Lieft Fisher
                        Fra Chickering
                        Danll. Fisher

---

[1] The Select men's Book includes John Haward as one of this committee.

At a generall meeteing of the Towne ye 2 of ye 11 mo 1653
the accounts of the Select men being read in publike wer accepted & passed
the rectifieing and equaling of the publike worke in the Mille creeke & the meeting house is comitted to the Select men this daye to be chosen

Elea. Lusher is desired to drawe vp. what he shall judge further needfull for the Legall assureance of Foule Meadowe. to be according to the agreem^t betwixt Dorchester & Dedham men deputed ther vnto

[*Eleazer Lusher is chosen to keepe the booke and to be one of the Select men for the yeare ensueing
the other Select men chosen are

Lieft Fisher Fra: Chickering
Joh: Kingsbery Joh: Dwight
Dan: Fisher Pet: Woodward

Joh Gaye ⎫
Antho: Fisher Ju ⎬ are chosen Surveyers
Tho: Fuller ⎭

Jonath Fayrbanke sen ⎫
Antho: Fisher sen ⎪
Joh Haward ⎬ are chosen woodreeues]
Joh. Morse ⎭

Eleazer Lusher is chosen to be one of the Select men for the yeare ensueing and to keepe the booke: and the other select men now so chosen are

Fra: Chickering Serg^t: Fisher
Lieft: Fisher Joh: Gaye
Joh: Kingsbery Joh: Dwight

Tho: Battely ⎫
Tho: Fuller ⎬ Surveyers
Nath: Coaleburn ⎭

Hen Wight ⎫
Ed Richards ⎪
Pet: Woodward ⎬ woodreeues
Joh: Haward ⎭

James Thorpe ⎫
James Draper ⎭ are admitted Townesmen

At a generall meeteing of the Towne ye 1 of ye 11: 1654
The acts and accounts of the Select men are read and accepted & allowed by the Towne

Joh Houghton ⎫
Jonath: Fayerbanke Ju. ⎬ are admitted Townesmen
James Vales ⎭

Elections as followeth

Eleazer Lusher is chosen to be one of the Select men and to keepe the booke the other Select men now chosen are

Lieft: Fisher Pet: Woodward
Fra: Chickering Joh: Haward
Joh: Kingsbery Nath: Coaleburne

Elea: Lusher ⎫
Hen: Chickering ⎬ Commissioners
Joh: Kingsbery ⎭

Joh: Gaye ⎫
Josep: Kingsbery ⎬ Surveyors
Rich: Euered ⎭

Michaell Mettcalfe ⎫
Ensign Phillips ⎬ woodreeues
Joh: Eaton
Antho: Fisher sen ⎭

At a generall meeteing of the Towne ye 1 of ye 11: 1655

Ellice Woode ⎫
Samll: Fisher ⎬ are admitted Townsemen
Benja: Bullard ⎭

Eleciions as followeth

Select men.

Eleazer Lusher is chosen to be one of the Select men for the yeare ensueing. and to keepe the booke. the other select men now chosen are

Fra: Chickering   Joh: Kingsbery
Lieft: Fisher   Serg^t Fisher
Pet: Woodward   Joh: Dwight

Nath: Coaleburne ⎫
Joh: Eaton   ⎬ Surveyors
Mich: Mettcalfe ⎭

Jonath: Fayerbanke sen ⎫
Joh: Gaye   ⎬ woodreeues
Joh: Haward
Josep: Kingsbery   ⎭

At a genarall meeting of the Towne the 5 of the 11 m^o 1656

The acts of the Select men in the yeare last past being read are by voate allowed and accepted

The Towne by voate giue a calle to Mich Meatcalfe to keep Schoole in our Towne and leaue it to the next Select men to agree with him therein

The Towne by voate resolue that the Swampe neere Meatfield shall be desposed of in propriatie

Granted to Daniell Morse two Seders to make Clabbord out in the aboue mentioned Swampe

Agreed that those that haue felled trees allready in that swampe shall be called to account to make sattisfaction according to Justice

Itt is ordered that the Swampe aboue mentioned shall bee disposed of by pteculur grante to each Towneseman according to the ordinarie rules by which Lands haue been devided provided that no other part thereof be layed out but only such as shall be vsefull for Ceder timber & shall be judged meete to be in propriatie by the men heere after deputed to order the same in that repect to whose Judgment in this case the Towne promise to submitt

Nath: Coalburne Sergt Fisher & Joshua Fisher are deputed & impowered therin

Libertie is granted to John Thurston of meatfild to set the fence about

the meadowe that he bought in our towne of Joshua Fisher and Ralph Daye
so as is necessarie to shorten that fence the pprietie of the Land so enclosed
yett remaineing pper to this Towne but the feed to be his while it is so
enclosed

Joshua Fisher[1] is chosen to be one of the Select men for the yeare ensueng and to keepe the towne booke the rest of the Select men nowe chosen are Capt Eleazer Lusher: Ensigne Fran: Chickering: Jo Haward Petter woodward John Dwight Sergt Daniell Fisher

Nath: Coalburne }
John Bacon } Surveyers
Robt Ware }

Thomas Fuller }
John Furington }
Edward Richards } woodreeues
Antho: Fisher Sen }

The Inhabatance of Dedham doe heerby renewe the former power giuin to any Commettie as in the 28 of the 8 m° 1651 so now to Issue the cause dependinge betwen Naticke and our towne of Dedham is left to the men heere after named Capt Eleazer Lusher Dea: Henry Chickeringe Ensi Fran: Chickeringe Sergt Daniell Fisher and Joshua Fisher

Thomas Metcalfe is admitted a Townesman

Att a Generall metting of the Inhabatance the 23 of the 11 m° 1656

Granted that the Comon rights of the Towne Concering feedinge and Devidents heerafter to be granted be settled and by some standinge: rule: be pportioned to the p^rsent Inhabitance being Townesmen to them and thier heyers for ever by the rule of persons and estats as lands haue ben formerly Devided

Itt beinge pposed to the Inhabatance to chuse a Commitie to settell the aboue mentioned grant

The Inhabatance by voate Commeted the Care & power of orderinge the aboue mentioned grant to the Select men for the time beinge

Granted to the widdowe Morse of Meatfild to take in sume smale parcell of vpland within the fence for the straytning of the lines to fence in the meadowe bought by Joseph Morse of Serg^t Avery neere Stope river

Itt beinge pposed to the Inhabatance the 6 of the 12 m° 1656 by the Select men whether thos that are removed out in towne & yett haue hovses & lands in the towne whether thay shall recaiue Comon rights for

---

[1] Fac-simile of Record, to show handwriting of Joshua Fisher.

142   DEDHAM TOWN RECORDS.

ther hovses & lands beinge in in towne it is Answered by the voat of the Inhabatance thay shall

2ly whether thay shall recaiue Comon rights for such catle as thay haue in Towne it is answerd by the voat of the Inhabatance thay shall not

The returne of the Commetie the 20 of the 12 mo

Whereas the Inhabitants of the Towne haueing generally had former notice were met the 23 of the 11 m⁰ 1656 and ther by thier voate then passed declared and acted thier resolution that all the Comon rights of the towne both of Comon feedinge for the home heards of cattell and all devisions of lands should be devided to the pʳsent Inhabitants by grants made to them being Townesmen & their heyres and assignes for ever by the rules of persons and estats as lands had been formerly devided and that this should be a standing rule for all Comon towne rights heerafter to be granted: and for further explication of thier mind therein did by voate allso resolue vpon the questan that such men as haue hovses or Lands in towne shall recaiue comon rights according to the pportion of thier estates though them selues liue att pʳsent out of towne and for the effecting heereof Cometted the care trust and power necessary there vnto into the hands of the Select men for the time being: who there vpon haue accordingly made the followeing devision and grants to the persons heere after named alloweinge each person as much as to 8£ estate and to estates being valued as formerly in devisions of lands and to towne and Cuntrie rates the whole account beinge putt to gether to every 18£ one Cowe or oxe or 5 sheepe with thier increase for one yeare or 5 goates the whole number of Cowe Comons aforesaid being thus granted being 477 and all brokin sumes or fractions that reach not to one Cowe Comon is pportioned to so many sheepe or goats as it will amount vnto and the rule of devison of Lands to be heereafter granted is pportioned to 532 acres according to which pportion & rule each devision is to be made heereafter. be the devident more or lesse

Where vpon is Granted to the men whose names are heere vnder written and to thier assignes for ever   To

The sumes of mens estats			Cowe Comons	Sheep comons	Devident: acres	parts of acres	Rodes
261	—	Mʳ Joh Allin	14	3	16	¼	28
149	19	Elder John Hunting	8	3	9	½	28
165	19	Capᵗ Eliazer Lusher	9	1	10	¼	16
141	15	Deac: Hery Chickering	8	3	9	0	36
69	4	Deac Nathan Aldis	3	4	4	¼	4
117	0	Mich: Metcalfe	6	2	7	0	32
117	3	Anthony Fisher: Sen:	6	3	7	¼	28
185	10	John Kingsbury	10	1	11	¼	36

DEDHAM TOWN RECORDS.   143

110	6	John Luson	6	1	6	$\frac{3}{4}$	38
143	9	John Haward	8	0	9	0	0
220	0	John Dwight	12	1	13	$\frac{1}{2}$	36
309	16	Ensigne Chickering	17	4	20	0	6
51	0	Henry Phillips	2	4	3	0	24
216	10	Joshua Fisher	12	0	13	$\frac{1}{2}$	0
108	2	Jonath: Fayrbank Sen	6	0	6	$\frac{3}{4}$	0
182	9	Petter Woodward	10	1	11	$\frac{1}{4}$	36
168	12	Joseph Kingsbury	9	2	10	$\frac{1}{2}$	12
31	0	Will Bullard	1	4	2	0	4
151	4	John Eaton	8	2	9	$\frac{1}{4}$	32
185	0	Rich: Evered	10	1	11	$\frac{1}{4}$	38
213	19	Nath: Coalburne	11	1	12	$\frac{1}{2}$	16
40	18	Robt Mason	2	2	2	$\frac{1}{2}$	34
203	12	John Gaye	11	2	12	$\frac{3}{4}$	12
24	10	Henry Smith	1	2	1	$\frac{1}{2}$	12
139	0	Sergt [Dan¹] Fisher	8	2	9	$\frac{1}{4}$	32
139	3	Sergt Fayrbanck	7	4	8	$\frac{3}{4}$	4
110	19	Sergt Avery	6	1	6	$\frac{3}{4}$	36
225	4	Edward Richards	12	2	13	$\frac{3}{4}$	32
57	15	Lambert Generey	3	1	3	$\frac{1}{2}$	16
165	4	Christo: Smith	9	1	10	$\frac{1}{4}$	16
161	19	Nath: Whitting	9	0	10	0	20
126	6	Theo: Frarey	7	0	7	$\frac{3}{4}$	20
96	12	John Fayrbanck	5	2	6	$\frac{1}{4}$	12
197	10	Samll Judson	11	0	12	$\frac{1}{4}$	20
108	11	Tho Hering	6	0	6	$\frac{3}{4}$	0
152	0	Rich: Wheeler	8	2	9	$\frac{1}{4}$	36
166	5	John Furington	9	1	10	$\frac{1}{4}$	16
104	0	John Aldis	5	4	6	$\frac{1}{2}$	4
167	7	Tho: Fuller	9	1	10	$\frac{1}{4}$	16
109	13	Tho Paine	6	0	6	$\frac{3}{4}$	0
126	15	Robt Ware	7	0	7	$\frac{3}{4}$	20
95	10	Antho: Fisher: Ju:	5	2	6	0	12
70	10	Thwayts Strickland	4	0	4	$\frac{1}{2}$	0
125	8	Robt Fuller	7	0	7	$\frac{3}{4}$	20
41	8	Thomas Metcalfe	2	2	2	$\frac{1}{2}$	32
76	14	Nath Fisher	4	1	4	$\frac{1}{2}$	36
136	8	Tho Batle	7	3	8	$\frac{1}{2}$	4
84	10	Tho Jurdin	4	3	5	0	28
91	19	John Guild	5	1	5	$\frac{3}{4}$	12
94	6	Andrew Duin	5	1	5	$\frac{3}{4}$	16

89	10	Samll Milles	5	0	5	½	20
9	10	Anthony Hubard	0	3	0	½	28
84	10	John Mason	4	3	4	½	32
96	1	Ralph Day	5	2	6	0	12
118	10	Henry Wilson	6	3	7	¼	28
136	7	John Bacon	7	3	8	½	8
110	12	Edward Hawes	6	1	6	¾	36
74	2	Joshua Kent	4	1	4	½	36
80	6	Rich Elice	4	2	4	¾	32
55	10	Robt Onyen	3	0	3	¼	20
171	1	Tino Dwight	9	3	10	¾	8
29	19	Joseph Elice	1	3	1	¾	8
42	0	Ralph Freeman	2	2	2	¼	32
41	0	John Rice	2	1	2	¼	36
80	0	Daniell Pond	4	2	4	¾	32
128	4	Henry Wight	7	1	8	0	16
76	4	Cornelias Fisher	4	1	4	½	36
68	10	Jonathan Fayrbank Ju	3	4	4	¼	4
42	16	James Vales	2	2	2	½	32
12	5	John Houghton	0	3	0	½	28
91	19	James Draper	5	0	5	½	20
21	0	James Thorpe	1	1	1	¼	16
96	6	Isack Bullard	5	2	6	0	12
33	10	Benja Bullard	1	4	2	0	4
20	15	Samll Fisher	1	1	1	¼	16
3	6	John Nevton	0	1	0	0	36
9	0	Tho Wight	0	3	0	½	28
10	0	Nath Bullard	0	3	0	½	28
5	0	Tho Fisher	0	1	0	0	36

 Vpon the complant of sume of the Inhabitance About the Comons be pportioned sume pertekuler persons bein straytned Richard Elice and Anthony Fisher Daniell Fisher & Joshua Fisher bein chosin by the persons greved & the select men to atend & heare the grevences of divers persons greved & to propose what might be done to the issueng ther of accordingly appointed a time when many did appeare & subcribed to this ingagment

 We whose names heerevnder written hauinge greuences in respect of being straytned by the rules giuinge to the Select men for the pportionenge of Devidents & stenting of Comons: hauinge declared our grevences vnto the two men chosin by the Select men & thos two chosin by the parties greued doe heereby ingage our selues to sitt downe as sattisfyed with thos things that shall be agreed vpon by thos four men viz Sergt Fisher Anthony Fisher Juner Richard Elice & Joshua Fisher to be propounded to the Towne in case

DEDHAM TOWN RECORDS. 145

the towne grant thos ppositions we ingage our selues to rest sattisfyed without makinge any further questan about the last act consering comons. In wittnes wherof we haue heere vnto sett our hands this 10 of the 1 m° 1656-7 Anthony Fisher Sen: Lambert Genarey, Robt Mason, Samll Milles, John Houghton, Nath: Fisher, Andrew Duin, John Mason, Tho: Paine, Benjamin Bullard, Joseph Elice, James Thorpe, Michell Metcalfe, Chisto Smith, Antho Fisher Juner, Richard Elice, John Bacon, Samll Fisher, Daniel

Itt is Agreed to propose to the Towne that there be granted 25 cowe comons more to be aded to thos allreddy granted to be setled vpon such persons as are straytned by the rules of pportion that wear giueng to the Select men for to devid & pportion comons by: as also the rights of Devident as is pportioned to Cowe Comons Agreed that this pposition & thes folloinge be pᵣposed by vs to the Towne for ther concurance as witnes our hands this 10 of the 1 m° 1656-7

Daniell Fisher, Antho Fisher, Rich Elice, Joshua Fisher.

This aboue mentioned pposition is granted by the towne only Sergt Fayrbancke desent by his voat

2ly Thomas Paine request that he may haue libertie to keep his stoke of goats for two or three yeare: over & aboue his cowe comons vpon the comon land: this is granted:

3 Decon Chickeringe desire he may haue comon rights for the person of his sone as persons are acounted in the proportioneng of comon rights this is granted by voat

4 That the woodlands aboute the Towne shall lye as thay doe in comon till the Towne see case to alter them; this is granted by voat

Itt is agreed in refference to the afore mentioned ppositiones that if a towne metinge be caled the aboue mentioned ppositiones shall only be pposed for the Townes Concurance and that men be then chosin to setle thos comons in case the Towne grant them vnto such persons as are greved being straytned by the former actt of the Towne: Subcribed by vs

Daniell Fisher, Antho Fisher, Rich Elice, Joshua Fisher

The former ppositions beinge Granted the men heerafter named are chosin by the Towne to setle the Comons that are granted by the persons greued

Antho Fisher: Juner, Richard Elice, Joshua Fisher

Granted to the persons heerafter named sume additions of comons & according to there proportion of addition of comons so is ther addition of Devidents

[¹memorand the whole Devisions with the two additions in the proportion of the Devident is 578 acres ¼]

---

¹Written in margin of Record.

	Cow Comons	Shep Comons
To Antho Fisher Sen: 2 sheep comons	0	2
To Lambt Genery 1 Cowe Comon 4 sheep comon	1	4
Robt mason 3 sheep Comons	0	3
Jo Houghton 2 Cowe Comons 2 sheep Comons	2	2
Eld Hunting	0	2
Nath Fisher	1	4
Benjamin Bullard	0	1
Isack Bullard for his father	1	1
James Thorpe	1	4
Joseph Elice	2	2
Sam Fisher	0	4
John Luson	0	4
James Vales	0	3
Ralph Freeman	0	3
Tho Metcalfe	0	3
Decon Aldis	1	1
Jo Aldis	0	1
Corneli Fisher	0	4
Rich Elice	0	3
Antho Fisher Juner	0	4
Jonathan Fayrbancke Sen	1	0
Anthony Hubard	2	2
Henry Smith	1	3

Subcribed by vs beinge chosin by the Towne to setle the 25 comons vpon such persons as were straytned by the rules formerly pportioned by to thes men aboue named we granted additiones as to ther names appeare

    Anthony Fisher Juner, Richard Elice, Joshua Fisher

    Att a Generall mettinge of the Inhabatance of the Towne of Dedham the 4 of the 11 m° 1657

Vpon a motion from diuers aboute the towne meadowe to know what prophett came to the Towne by it it is left to the next Select men to be chosin to inquire into & to doe what is right betwene the Towne & thos that haue or shall make improument therof

Conserninge the Grant of John Dwight vpon the Northsid of the Mill pond the Towne beinge not sattisfyed with it doe declare thay would haue the case Issued by way of refference or else by law consering the title of it; the Towne cometting the case to be managed on ther behalfe to the men heerafter named: Michell Mertcalfe Fran: Chickering Richard Elice

In refference to the proposition aboute the Iron workes the Towne resolue to make further triall whether there be provibibillitie of settinge vp an Iron worke in our Towne and to that end haue chosin the men heerafter named to make inquirie a bout the charge of such a worke and also what other things may be needfull to be done for the attaininge of the townes end & so to make there returne to the Towne by the first oppertunity the men chosin are Capt Lusher Ensigne Chickeringe & Joshua Fisher or any two of them

vpon the questan of the power of the Select mens power it is Answered by the voate of the Inhabitance that the same power that thay formerly haue had shall be from time to time continued ther former power beinge nowe read over

In refference to the proposition about the saw mill the Towne leue the answer till further considaration

The Towne declare them selues that thay will haue the mettinge hovse lathed vpon the studs & so dabed & whitted over workman like the care of gettinge this done att the Towne charge is left to the Select men now to be chosin

The Towne doe giue Michell Mertcalfe a call to keep the schoole the yeare insuinge & leue it to the next select men to agree with him for 20£ the yeare

Capt Lusher & Joshua Fisher are deputed to drawe vp an Instrument & p^rsent to the Inhabitance for Subcription about the Comons forthwith which is done & p^rsented

The Elections Joshua Fisher is chosin to keep the towne books for the yere insuinge & to be one of the Select men the rest of the Select men are Capt Lusher Elder Huntinge Ensigne Chickering Jonath Farb Jo: Haward Joseph Kingsbury: & invested with the same power that the Select men formerly had:

Rich: Elice		Thomas Fuller
Surveyers Tho: Fuller	woodreues	John Furington
Tho Battele		Edward Richards
		Anthony Fisher Sen.

The Towne declare by voat that in case the Indians & the Towne doe not com to composition a bout the land that the Indians make improument of att Naticke with in three months after the datt heerof that then there shall be a generall deuident layd out to the vse of the towne accordinge to the rules allready p^rposed 4 of the 11 m° 1657

The Isue of the case dependinge betwene Naticke and our Towne is left to thes men heereafter named to Isue accordinge to former derections from the Towne Ensigne Chickeringe: Sergt Fisher and Joshua Fisher

Itt is Agreed that there shall be but 3 days worke required from the Inhabatance for the yeare insuinge to worke in the highways:

At a generall meeteinge of the Towne 3: 11. 1658:

The towne declare thier minde to haue the case about the Iron worke psecuted further to see what encouragem^t the towne may haue to set vp an Iron worke. & the care heereof is left to the men heereafter named

Capt Lusher, Serg^t Averey, Antho Fisher Jun, & Joshua Fisher

Concerning the ordering of the assembly in the meeteinge house its left to our reuer^t Elder. & the Select men now to be chosen for the yeare ensueing

Vpon a motion of Anthony Fisher Ju: for to buye the land that Mrs Stoughton rent the answer is they will not sell it

Its agreed that Henery Willson shall paye to the Towne Twentie shillings for his former vse of the town meadow

Its agreed that Ralph Daye shall paye Twentie shillings for the vse of the Towne meadow formerly to the yeare 1657

It is agreed that Robert Onion shall haue his high waye worke set of: from yeare to year for his Seruice in Ringing the Bell forenoone and afternoone those dayes that are appointed for workeing in the high wayes

John Rice haue his defects in high waye worke remitted in the years: 57: 58

It is voated that the 2000 Acres granted to the Indians at Naticke shall be layed out at the westerly bounds of our Towne on the north side of Charles Riuer by the descretion of the men heere after named

Capt Lusher, Serg^t: Fisher, Joshua: Fisher

Further power is giuen to the Comittee. to jssue the case depending betwixt the Indians at Natick & our Towne pvided they doe not hinder the Town in layeing out a deuident

In refference to the setting vp of a Sawe Mille it is left to the men heereafter named to agree & conclude on the Townes behalfe with such psons as shall p^{r}sent them selues for the setting vp of a Sawe Mille & to giue them such encouragem^{ts}. as they shall Judge meete — these three men are chosen by the Towne & if any of the three apeere to pties. then the Elder is to be one of three & the first three are Serg^t. Fisher, Nath Coaleburne, Pet: Woodward

Robt Wares his motion about an exchange of Land in the Iland playne. its left to the next Select men that are now to be chosen to be further considered. & to act as they shall see cause

Elections as followeth

Eleazer Lusher is chosen to keepe the Town bookes & to be one of the select men. & further Select men chosen as followeth

| Eleder Hunting | Joh Haward | Ensi. Fisher |
| Lieft: Fisher | Pet Woodward | Nath Coaleburne |

Edw. Richards	} Surveyors:	Isaac Bullard	} woodreeues
Joh Aldus		Joh: Farington	
Rob. Wares		Andr Duein	
		Tymo Dwight	

Michaell Metcalfe is by voate called to keepe the Schoole againe another yeare. & its left to the select men to agree with him for that seruice for 20£

It is ordered that 3 dayes worke shall be pformed in the high wayes this yeare 1659

END OF VOLUME ONE.

PART SECOND.

SELECTMEN'S BOOK.

[First fourteen pages missing.]

[   ] they shall deliuer to [   ] for the time being who by those bills shall call the Constables to account for all such forfieters. the former order mad wherin the viewers of Fences. to viewe fences when they ar called. is yet in full force

all accounts that concern the 2 first Rats for the meeting house being taken in & put together ther remayn due to the Town   3£—10—[   ]

debts due yet from ye Town that arise to seuerall men for the [   ] of ye meeting house   3£—[   ]

12 mo 8 47   Assembled Joh Kingsbery, [   ], Tho Wight, Fra Ch[   ], Will Bullard, Tymo Dwight, El. Lusher.

things to be considered 1 the former order about viewing Fences — 2 concerning hunting wolues — 3 concerning Robt Crossemans satisfaction — 4 the Constables Rate to be accounted for — 5 the ppositions about minerals

the former order concerning viewing fences confirmed as it is ther drawen

Som liberty granted to Eleazer Lusher to cut ceadars in the comon swamp at the [   ] of his Lott of swamp to the valew of [   ]

that motion concerning minerals refered to [   ] meeting

Robt Crosseman [   ]

high [waye lay]ed out by Tho [   ] Sam. Morse being thervnto deputed by the Town. leading thorough one pcell of vpland of Daniell Morse to one pcell of the meadow of Joh Gaye adioyning vpon the west side of Charles Riuer

12 mo 18 47   Assemb: Joh. Dwight: Tho Wight. Tym: Dwight & El: Lusher

Resolued. to ppose to the Town. to know thir minde about the raising that tenn £ for the recompence of the Huntsman. whether therein they will exempt bullocks 4 yeare old & vpward. & horses & mares aboue that age. & how the same [   ] asessed. whether by the head [   ] the equall valuation of [   ] beast according to a generall [   ] & so raise the sum by ye pound [&] who shall make this rate

after Lectur these being pposed: all was left to the 7 men

12 mo 18 47   Joh Dwight & Francis Chickering giue notice of thier hopes of a myne neer certayn ponds. about 13 miles from the towne. so clayming the p^rvelidge of the town grant it is in or neer the south Lyne

12 mo 18 47   [   ] giue notice of his expectation of a myne on the north side of Charles Riuer. neer a sp[ ] ouer against m^r Cookes Farm or ther about

12 mo 29 47   Assembled. Joh Kingsbery Joh Dwight Fra Chickering Tho Wight Willm Bullard Tymoth Dwight & Ele Lusher

the Rate for the Charge of hunting wolues to be made

the passag of the water out of Christopher Smith his meadow: to make the water course 4 foote wide & a sufficient cart passag ouer it. is left to the care of Joh Kingsbery

4 mo: 16 48   Assemb. Joh Kingsbery Joh Dwight. Fra Chickering Tho Wight & El: Lusher

The Grant of ye trayned Company

the Consent to the p^rsent disposeall [   ]

the Grant to Lamb Genery

Deputed to laye out the breadth of the high way by the broad meadowe Joh Kingsbery. Tho Wight. Joh Dwight & El: Lusher

Dan: Fishers meadow abuttm^t next the riuer to be cleered

[   ] 23 48   Assemb: Joh Kingsbery Joh Dwight Fra Chickering Tho Wight Will Bullard Tymo Dwight & El Lusher

Rich Wheeler. & Joh Farington. haueing bought Will Bearstows grant of 8 acres request an adition therto from the town

Bro Woodward & br: Gaye. Constables brings thier accounts of the Town Rate for ye meeting house Charge   the Rate 3 —17— 1

Disbursed. In p^rs

to John Morse at the assignm^t of Robt Crosseman	1—19— 4
to Tho Wight	0—16-- 8 ob[1]
to Ed Kemp	0— 1— 0 ob
in Robt Goweings hand	0— 0— 4
[in] El. Lushers hand. of Aust Kalems rate	0— 0—11 ob
[ ] Crosseman from Jonath Fayrbank	0— 1— 6 ob
[ ] Tho Wight	0— 3— 0
	3— 3— 9
[*remayn yet to be accounted for	0—13— 8
p^d heerof by Peter Woodward	0— 0— 8
mor apeer pd by y^m]	

a motion made about the building a Schoole house. another about a bell to purchase

---

[1] Ob. abbreviation for obolus, meaning a half penny or two farthings; q. for quadrans was used for one farthing, and obq. for three farthings.

152 DEDHAM TOWN RECORDS.

5 mo 7: after Lectur p^rsent Joh Kingsbery: Fra Chickering Tho: Wight. El. Lusher

[× × × *Grant to Thos. Jordan, as on page* 121.]

1648: 7 mo 4   Assembled. Joh Kingsbery. Joh Dwight Tho Wight Willm Bullard Tymo Dwight Eleazer Lusher Fra Chickering

The Countrey Rate

Name	£—s—d	Name	£—s—d
Mr Allen Pastor	0—16— 1	Fra Chickering	0—16— 0
Elder Hunting	0— 6— 9	Ed Richards	0—18— 1
Elea Lusher	0—13— 4	Joh. Plimpton	0— 3— 8
Robt Mason	0—13— 6	Joh. Metcalf	0— 3—[ ]
Josep Kingsbery	0— 9— 0	Ed Kempe	0— 9— 3
Thwai Strickland	0— 5— 9	Joh Dwight	1— 0—10
Sam Foster	0— 3— 8	Tymo Dwight	0— 7— 9
Lamb Genery	0— 9— 8	Geo Fayerbanke	0— 7— 2
Joshua Fisher Seni	0— 2—11	Tho Hering	0— 5—10
Joseph Fisher Jun	0— 7— 9	Nath Whiteing	0— 4— 3
Nath Coalburne	0— 8—11	Rich Elice	0— 2—10
Hen Brock	0— 5— 5	Joh Kingsbery	0—13— 9
Hen Philips	0—14— 8	Joh Batchelor	0— 5—11
Nath Aldus	0— 7—[ ]	Joh Haward	0—10—10
Dan Morse	0— 6—[ ]	Sam Judson	0— 5— 1
Antho: Fisher Jun	0— 5—[ ]	Robt Ware	0— 5— 9
Sam Morse	0— 3—[ ]	Sam Bulleyn	0— 4— 5
Joh Morse	0— 4— 7	Aust Kalem	0— 4— 5
Geo. Barber	0— 6—11	Tho Alcock	0— 1— 7
Robt Onion	0— 3— 5	Tho Payne	0— 3—10
Hen Smith	0— 5— 0	Tho Fuller	0— 4— 7
Robt Gowing	0— 4— 3	Joh Ellice	0— 5— 0
Tho Bancroft	0— 3— 5	Joh Eaton	0— 8— 2
Ralph Daye	0— 3—11	Christo Smith	0— 3—10
Joh Guilde	0— 3— 6	Mich Bacon	0— 3— 5
Rich Euered	0— 3— 0	Antho. Hubbert	0— 4— 0
Pet Woodward	0—13—11	Joh Damant	0— 2— 6
Robt Fuller	0— 4— 0	Joh Bacon	0— 4—10
Rich. Wheeler	0—13— 1	Joh Kalem	0— 3—11
Joh. Frarey	0—14—10	And Duein	0— 4— 3
Mich Metcalf Seni	0— 8—11	Mrs Deengaine	
Mich Metcalf Juni	0— 3— 9	Jam Allen	0— 3— 5
Mich Powell	0— 5— 6	Jam Jordan	0— 2— 8
Joh Fayerbanke	0— 4— 5	Tho Jordan	0— 5— 2
Jonath. Fayerbanke	0— 8— 4	Hen Glouer	0— 3— 1
Geo Bearstoe	0— 3—10	Ed Hawes	0— 3—11

Joh Thurston	0— 5— 4		Will Bullard		0—12— 7
Hen Chickering	0— 8— 6		Robt Crosseman		0— 3— 2
Antho Fisher Seni	0—17— 8		Joh Bullard		0— 4—10
Tho Wight	1— 2— 1		Hen Willson		0— 4— 3
Joh Luson	0— 9— 8		[ ] Clarke		0— 7— 6
Tho Battaile	0— 2— 9		Robt Eames		0— 2— 6
Dan. Fisher	0— 9— 0		The Mill		0— 2—10
Nath Stearnes	0— 2—10		Joh Genery		0— 2— 6
Mt Wheelock	0— 5—10		Eliza: Fisher		0— 0— 6
Joh Gaye	0— 6— 8				
19 of 8	48				

Assembled. Joh Kingsbery Joh Dwight Tho Wight Elea: Lusher

that 10^s asessed vpon the houses that was abated by ye eight pt abated is left in the Constables hand for the Townes vse as an ouerplusse and so the Rate not altered

The seuerall Rates of the Townes in Suff.

Dorchester Rate	56— 6—0
Boston	125—10—0
Roxbery	35— 6—7
Dedham	30— 9—6
Brayntree	24— 9—9
Weymouth	22—19—6
Hingham & Hull apeere not	294—13—4

Elea Lusher is desired to speake Capt Atherton concerning the Laying out the Farme giuen by Mr Dudley

Fra Chickering & Tymo Dwight ar requested to viewe that place for direction in measuring som time the weeke next following

Joh Dwight & Tymo Dwight ar desired to asist the measurer in the laying it out. w^n Capt Atherton & Roxbery men shall be p^{r}sent together wth Eleazer Lusher

The valuation of the houses in Dedham as they wer estimated for the Country Rate 1648

	houses	£		
Mr Allen	45—36		Nath. Coaleburn	20—18
Eld^r Hunting	8—14		Hen. Brock	20—16
Elea Lusher	30—30		Nath. Aldus	20—16
Robt. Mason	14—20		Hen: Philips	28—28
Josep Kingsbery	18—15		Antho Fisher Juni	10— 8
Lamb. Genery	7— 6		Sam Morse	10— 8
Joshua Fisher	40—36		Geo Barber	20— 9
Thwai: Strickland	10— 8		Robt Onion	4

154   DEDHAM TOWN RECORDS.

Hen Smith	7— 6	Mrs Deengayne	6— 5
Robt Goweing	4	Sam Bulleyn	6
Ralph Daye	4— 5	Aust Kalem	6— 5
Joh Guilde	4	Tho. Alcock	
Rich Euered	4— 6: 10	Tho. Payne	5— 6
Pet Woodward	28—23	Tho: Fuller	5— 4
Robt Fuller	4— 5	[ ]h Elice	6— 5
Robt Hinsdell } Rich Wheeler }	16—13	[ ] Eaton	10— 8 [13]
		Christo Smith	4
Joh Fraery	12—10	Mich. Bacon	
Mich. Metcalf sen	25—20	Joh. Bacon	8—12
Mich. Metcalf Ju	8—	James Allen	2
Mich. Powell	16—13	Tho Jordan	5— 4
Joh Fayerbank	4	Ed Hawes	2
Jonat Fayerbank	28—23	Joh Thurston	14—12
Geo Bearstoe		Hen. Chickerin	32—24
Fra Chickering	30—24	Antho. Fisher seni	28—23
Ed Richards	13—11	Tho Wight	26—21
Joh Plimpton	5	Joh: Luson	30—24
Joh Metcalf	8— 7	Dan: Fisher	25—20
Ed Kempe	15— 5	Mr Wheelocke	12—10
Joh Dwight	33—	Joh. Gaye	6— 3
Geo Fayerbanke	4	Willm Bullard	25—20
Tho Leader		Joh: Bullard	5— 4
Tho Herring	16	Hen: Wilson	6— 5
Tymo Dwight	14—12	Josep. Clarke	5— 4
Nath. Whiteing	4— 3	Dan. Morse	20
Joh. Kingsbery	18—15	The. Mille	34—28
Joh Batchelor	3	Ed Allen	
Joh Haward	24—20	Thwai Strickland	
Sam Judson	all houses 10	Rich Wheeler	3— 5
Hen Aldridg	3	Joshua Kent	2—
Robt Ware	5— 4		

[× × × *Order concerning wolves, as on page* 122.]

voate   it is allso further ordered that the Rate formerly made for the raysing of tenn £ for the paying the hunts man in killing wooלues shall be forth wth be put in to the Constables hand who is heerby required speediely to gather the one half therof. that so he may haue in his hand to paye for the killing of wooלues according to the former order

8 of ye 9 ^{mo} 48.   Assemb: Joh. Kingsbery Joh. Dwight Tho. Wight
Tymo Dwight & El. Lusher Fra Chickering

voate Tho Wight is deputed to treat wth Ed Hawes about the doeing such daubing worke as is needfull about the meeting house. & vpon viewe to put that worke (if he can, to him to doe in conueanient time. & to see him p^d out of the Townes account. or in case Ed Hawes canot be attaynd. then to pcure som such other workeman to pforme the same as the case require wth all possible speed

a warrant to be mad wherby the Constable shall leauye of Theop Cushion 10^s 2^d for the meeting house rate. Tho Makepiece[1] 3. for that Rate allso. & Tho Makepiece & Joh Bearstoe 10^s for fine

ye 20 of 9 mo 48 Assembled. Joh. Kingsbery Joh Dwight Tho. Wight Fra: Chickering Will Bullard Tymo Dwight & El: Lusher

[✕ ✕ ✕ *Order concerning high way work, as on page* 122.]
the names of such as ar behind in the high [   ]

	ℐ	s.	d.				
Lamb Genery	0	2	0	Joh Plimpton to pay to El			
Robt. Goweing	0	4	0	Lusher	0	3	0
Antho Hubert	0	4	0	Joh Fayerbanke	0	5	0
Robt Wares	0	3	0	Hen Chickering	0	8	0
Sam Bulleyn	0	3	0	Antho Fisher senio	0	6	0
Sam. Judson	0	4	0	Ed Hawes	0	3	0
Tho Alcock	0	3	0	Joh. Gaye	0	4	0
Joh. Elice	0	1	0	Joh. Bullard	0	2	0
Robt: Fuller	0	1	0	Hen Wilson	0	2	0
Joh Fraery	0	2	0	Ralph Daye set of	0	5	
Joh Fayerbanke	0	5	0	Antho Fisher Juni	0		
Ed Richards	0	7	0				

to ppose at Genrall meeting

the choice of 3 men for smale cases

1 that a Feoffee for the schoole be chosen

2 by w^t rule men may be deputed to town seruice by ye select men wth out wrong to any

3 that care be taken about a drye hearde

4 that som order be made to p^{r}uent disorderly feeding comon fields. & foule meadowe

5 schoole house to be built & a watchouse

6 whether the reseruing of Land for sundry publike vses be still thought to conduce to the publike good of the Town: viz. the schoole Land &c

7 that its considerible whether it may not conduce to the publike good

---

[1] "Mr Thomas Makepeace, because of his novile disposition, was informed wee were weary of him vnlesse hee reforme."—March 13, 1638-9, Mass. Col. Rec. Vol. I., page 252.

of the town [*after all engagem^ts of Land be satisfied] that all [*other] vpland fitt for empuem^t w^thin a conueanient distance be layd out in a genrall deuident by rules of genrall pportion reserving land [   ] satisfie former engagem^ts

  Assembled: 10: mo 12 da / Joh Dwight. Fra Chickering Tho: Wight. Tymo Dwight & Eleazer Lusher
  m^r Wheelocks motion for aduice answerd
  [✕ ✕ ✕ *Three orders relating to Mr. Dalton and Richard Ellis, as on page* 122.]
  Eleazer Lusher is appointed to publish the body of Lawes vpon som Lectur dayes next. as the season and optunitie shall admitt

  10 mo 19. Assemb. Joh Kingsbery Joh Dwight Fra Chickering Tho: Wight Willm Bullard: Tymo Dwight & Elea Lusher
  A motion mad for the abateing the rent of the town meadow to John Bullard to 3^s 4^d and mayntayn the fence that belong therto. leaueing the fence in the same state he tooke it—consented to.
  Ed Hawes requesteth one smale pcell of meadow the vse therof is granted to him till a genrall deuident be made
  Joseph Kingsbery make a motion for the vpland due to him by his right of ye purchased Lands
  [✕ ✕ ✕ *Grant to Thurston, as on page* 123.]
  [*Reckoned wth Eleazer Lusher & the Town vndertake to paye the Countrey Rate 13^s 4^d & then remayn due to him at this daye—1^s 8^d
  the Land shall be surveyd at the Towns Charge. & be deuided by the rule of psons & estates: all psons to be valued at 8£ the pson. & to receaue as much as 8£ estate
  Recead by Eleazer Lusher from Tho Wight 1 bushell. ½. India
  due to Eleazer Lusher

for writeing the Town Rate	0	1	0
for one daye at laying out Farme	0	1	8
one daye in Dorchester bounds	0	1	8
one daye viewe & help to measur the deuident	0	1	]

  At a genrall meeting of the town 1648: 11 mo 1
  [✕ ✕ ✕ *Record of the meeting, as on page* 123.]
  resolued to send out a drye heard & the care & trust therof & power to pvide & couenant for the same is comitted to Antho Fisher sen, Tho Wight, Josep Kingsbery, Hen Philips, Joh Dwight, Pet Woodward
  [✕ ✕ ✕]
  11 mo 15 48 Assemb: Hen Chickering Joh. Kingsbery. Joh Dwight. Tho. Wight. Fra Chickering. Joshu. Fisher & Elea: Lusher
  A schoole house to be built as followeth. together wth a watch house

the length 18 foote being 14 foote beside the chimney. the widenes 15 foote. the studd 9 foote betwixt Joynts. one floore of Joyce: 2 conuenient windowes in the lower roome & one in the chamber. the plancher layed. the floore planked. the stayers made. the sides boarded. featheredged & rabbited. the doores made & hanged

the watch house. to be a leanto set at the back of the chimney sixe foote wide. the length therof 2 foote & one half mor then the house is wide. so placed that the end ther of may extend past the corner of the house so that the watch may haue an aspect 4 seuerall wayes. & open windowes therin suitable to a watch house & couered wth board. vp to those windowes. & vpon the roofe. & a mandle tree hewen & fitted for the Chimney

a motion by our pastor about a way to his meadow thorough the mead- of of m^r Joh. Newton to be layd out—consented vnto—

Hen Chickering Tho Wight & El. Lusher ar desired to viewe the same & return answer to the select men

[X X X *Grant and order, as on page* 124.]

12 mo 5 48 Assemb. Hen Chickering Joh Kingsbery. Joh Dwight Fra Chickering. Tho Wight Josh: Fisher: & Elea. Lusher

Joseph Clark & Hen: Wilson tender thier Rent 10^s in wheat for the Meadow assigned to be p^d to Lieft Fisher in pt of the debt due to him from the towne

granted to Joh Kingsbery ceader timber in the comon swamp to sup⁻ plye him in his finishing his house

& to Hen Wilson timber ther for 800 boards to sell

Will Bullard makeing demand of satisfaction for the way leading into the woods betwixt his Lott & John Bullards Lott. & vpon sc[ ] his title to that satisfaction. he is satisfied that ther was none due to him for the same

Foule meadow not to be Rated to this Towne

[X X X *Grant to Daniel Fisher, as on page* 125.]

11 of 12 mo 1648 Assemb: Hen Chickering Joh Kingsbery. Joh Dwight Tho Wight Josh: Fisher & Eleaz: Lusher. Fra Chickering

The Rate made for & towards the Charges of the Towne about a schoolehouse & watchehouse building paying for the Drum beating. the Charges at the genrall meeting. the purchase of weights & measurs & the fines sessed by the Court as followeth. asessed at 2^d p £

as allso for the charge of surveying & laying out the genrall deuidence

Deputed to view & help in laying out the genrall deuident Joh Dwight. Fra Chickering. Tho. Wight: Elea: Lusher. one of these 4 to be allwayes p^{r}sent allso Tymo. Dwight: Dan: Fisher Pet Woodward: Tho. Fuller or other wise in case such men as ar last named or any of them be not to be attayned. it shall be in the liberty of the other of the select men first named to pcure those they se fitt. all to be allowed out of this p^{r}sent Rate 1^s 8^d the daye

158 DEDHAM TOWN RECORDS.

the Town Rate	£	s	d				
Mr Allen	1	8	5	Tho Herring	0	7	8
Eld Hunting		8	3	0	Nath. Whiteing	0	3	2
Elea Lusher		15	10	0	Joh. Kingsbery	1	1	3
Ralph Daye		2	10	0	Joh Haward	0	17	6
Jose. Kingsbery		12	10	0	Joh. Eaton	0	14	1
Robt Mason		11	10	0	Sam Judson	0	7	1
Tho Bancroft		2	2	0	Robt Wares	0	5	4
Lamb Genery		10	4	0	Joh. Kalem	0	5	2
Josh. Fisher sen		0	10	0	Tho. Payne	0	2	7
Josh. Fisher Ju		10	0	0	Tho. Alcock	0	2	9
Hen. Brocke		8	7	0	Joh Ellice	0	5	4
Nath. Coaleburne		12	1	0	Tho. Fuller	0	5	8
Nath. Aldus		11	1	0	Christo. Smith	0	2	10
Hen Philips		13	4	0	Mich Bacon	0	6	11
Anth. Fisher Ju		5	1	0	And Duein	0	4	0
Joh: Morse		2	0	0	Anth Hubbert	0	3	9
Sam Morse		6	4	0	Dan: Morse	0	12	3
Thwa: Strickland		5	0	0	Ed Allen	0	1	6
Geo. Barber		8	10	0	Joh Bullard	0	5	1
Robt Onion		1	10	0	Jos. Clarke	0	5	2
Hen. Smith		6	10	0	Hen Willson	0	5	0
Jam. Jordan		0	5	0	Will Bullard	0	15	7
Joh. Bacon		0	1	4	Robt Crosseman	0	0	8
Joh Guild		1	3	0	Joh. Gaye	0	8	11
Rich Euered		6	8	0	Mr Wheelock	0	6	6
Pet Woodward		17	4	0	Dan Fisher	0	12	3
Rich. Wheeler		7	4	0	Joh Luson	0	11	0
Joh. Farington		10	9	0	Tho Wight	1	3	5
Robt Fuller		3	0	0	Antho Fisher sen	1	3	4
Joh. Fraery		15	9	0	Hen Chickering	0	18	4
Mich Mettcalfe sen		12	7	0	Ed Hawes	0	3	9
Mich Metcalf Ju		5	3	0	Tho Jordan	0	5	6
Mr Powell		3	4	0	Hen Glouer	0	1	9
Rich. Ellice		1	6	0	Jam. Allen	0	1	10
Joh. Fayerbank		4	4	0	Tho Battaile	0	5	4
Jonath. Fayerbank		13	5	0	Nath Stearnes	0	3	0
Fra Chickering		19	4	[ ]	Wide Fisher	0	1	0
Ed Richards		12	[ ]	[ ]	Joh. Thurston	0	8	10
Joh Plimpton		0	2	2	Joh. Newton	0	1	10
Joh. Mettcalfe		0	3	7	The Mill	0	5	8
Joh. Dwight		1	11	9	Mrs Deengaine	0	1	9
Geo. Fayerbanke		0	1	6	Ferd. Adam	0	2	1
Tymo Dwight		0	12	0				
[Rest of this page is torn off.]				totall	33	13	4

Fra Chickering and Joh: Dwight giue notice of thier expectation of a mine neer certain ponds. about 13 miles from the town. therby clayning the p^{r}uelidg of the town order: its in or neer the south line 2 of ye 3 mo 1649

20 of 2 mo: 1649

Mr John Allen Pastor and Eleazer Lusher giue notice of thier discouery of a mine of mettall or other minerall whervnto they lay clayme to them thier hiers executors or assignes for euer by vertue of the order of the Town in that case pvided wch lyeth betwixt Charles Riuer towards the south and the high Rocke neer the Great Playne towards the north, and in or neer about a smale stoney valley being encompased on the south. north and west sids with Rockey hills the east end of the sd valley opening towards a stoney brooke therby

notice heereof giuen to the men whose names ar subscribed being of the select men   Joh: | K Kingsbery   Joshua Fisher

Lieft Joshua Fisher and Sergeant Daniell Fisher giue notice of thier expectation of a Mine of Mettall clayming the benefit of the Town order to them and thier hiers. Lying on the north side of Charles Riuer and on the west side of a brooke that runnes in to the said Riuer ouer against the Farme late m^r Cookes, and on the south side of the great Playne   1 of 3 mo: 1649

Anthony Fisher senio: & Robt Crosseman giue notice of thier discouery of a mine of Mettall. Claymeing the p^{r}uelidg of ye Town order to them thier hiers and assignes. Lying aboue. or westerly of the place wher Naponcet Riuer deuide. part being on the south side of the greatest streame of the said Riuer. & in pt betwixt the deuision of the said streames. lying in seuerall places therabout.   26 of 3. mo. 1649

Assembled 4 mo. 8. 1649   Henry Chickering. Joh Kingsbery Joh Dwight: Fra Chickering & Elea: Lusher

ppositiones considerable

Joseph Kingsbery his sattisfaction in Land

the fines for neglect of high waye worke to be called for from the constable

those who ar entrusted to view fences. to be called to pform thier duties

George Bearstoe his bill to be considered

the stocks to be mended

[*the Iland field fence to be pportioned]

Cambridge Line to be new marked

voate   Joseph Kingsbery is to haue tendered to him a grant of 4 acres of vpland. adioyning to m^r Greenes Farme or else wher in pt of that Land due to him by vertue of his 5 rights in the purchased Lands. or else if he chuse to tarry for the whole sattisfac-

160   DEDHAM TOWN RECORDS.

    tion vntill the Land that pply the purchased Lands be measured and that all in the like interest be satisfied wth him

voate   Fra Chickering is deputed to call vpon the constable in the name of the select men. for the sums asessed vpon the Inhabitants for y^t neglected thier high way worke

voate   the Constable is assigned to paye vnto George Bearstoe or his assignes out of the Town Rate   1£ 10^s 0

voate   Hen Chickering is requested to speake to Joh Thurston to streighten the stocks so much as is needfull

  Eleazer Lusher & Daniell Fisher ar requested to meet wth Cambridge men to search the Record in respect of the lyne betwixt Cambridg & Dedham & then to apoint a time for to meet vpon that line to make a full issue of the case depending ther about

  Assemb: 6 mo 30 Joh. Kingsbery: Hen: Chickering Tho. Wight. Joh Dwight Fra: Chickering. Lieft Fisher Elea: Lusher to make the countrey Rate

      the Countrey Rate 1649

Mr Joh Allen	0	17	11	Joh Guilde	0	3	6
Joh: Hunting Eld:	0	4	6	Rich. Euered	0	4	9
Elea: Lusher	0	10	19	Pet Woodward	0	10	6
Robt: Mason	0	13	2	Robt Fuller	0	4	6
Ralph Daye	0	3	5	Joh. Farington	0	7	7
Josep: Kingsbery	0	9	1	Joh: Fraery	0	14	5
Lamb: Genry	0	7	9	Mich: Metcalf sen	0	8	11
Joshua Fisher sen:	0	2	11	Mich: Metcalf Ju	0	5	6
Josh: Fisher Juni:	0	7	3	Joh. Morse	0	4	11
Hen Brocke	0	4	7	Rich. Ellice	0	3	3
Nath. Coaleburne	0	9	0	Jonath. Fairbanke	0	9	1
Nath. Aldus	0	10	7	Joh. Fairebanke	0	3	11
Hen: Phillips	0	17	5	Fra Chickering	0	19	7
Anth. Fisher Jun	0	5	11	Ed: Richards	0	8	9
Sam: Morse	0	2	7	Joh. Plimpton	0	3	7
Thwaits Strickland	0	4	7	Joh: Metcalf	0	4	3
Geo. Barber	0	5	6	Joh. Dwight	1	5	2
Robt Onion	0	3	6	Geo: Fayerbanke	0	5	8
Hen Smith	0	7	8	Tymo. Dwight	0	8	8
Tho Battelye	0	5	5	Tho Herring	0	6	4
Robt Crossman	0	3	0	Nath. Whiteing	0	7	4
Jam Jordan				Joh. Damant	0	2	6
Joh Bacon				Joh. Leader	0	2	6
Rich Wheeler	0	6	1	Jonas Fayerbanke	0	2	6

DEDHAM TOWN RECORDS. 161

Joh. Kingsbery	0	13	3	Joh. Luson	0	8	5
Joh: Kalem	0	5	5	Tho Wight	1	2	11
Joh. Haward	0	10	8	Antho Fisher sen	0	17	7
Joh. Eaton	0	9	1	Hen. Chickering	0	8	11
And Duein	0	4	9	Joh. Thurston	0	10	8
Joh. Ellice	0	5	5	Tho. Jordan	0	5	3
Tho: Fuller	0	5	5	Hen Glouer	0	3	4
Tho. Payne	0	4	0	James Allen	0	0	6
Tho Alcocke	0	1	6	Nath. Stearnes	0	4	0
Sam. Judson	0	5	7	Ed: Hawes	0	5	10
Robt Wares	0	5	1	Eliza. Fisher vid.	0	0	6
Antho Hubbert	0	7	8	Tho. Bancroft	0	3	1
Sam: Mills	0	6	2	Tho. Makepiece	0	4	7
Christo. Smith	0	3	10	Joh. Parker	0	4	10
Dan: Morse	0	7	4	Tho Fisher	0	2	6
Josep: Clarke	0	5	3	Sam Bulleyn	0	4	0
Hen. Wilson	0	5	0	Ferd: Adams	0	0	9
Joh: Bullard	0	5	3	Mrs Deengaine	0	0	11
Will Bullard	0	15	2	Tho Ellice	0	2	6
Joh. Gaye	0	7	3	Joshua Kent	0	2	6
Mr Wheelock	0	5	9	Theop: Cushion	0	7	1
Dan: Fisher	0	9	1	Tho: Prentice	0	13	6
					28	19	00

12 of 8 mo: 49 Assemb Hen Chickering Tho Wight: Fra Chickering Joh. Dwight: Lieft: Fisher &: Eleaz: Lusher: &: Joh. Kingsbery

[X X X *Grant to Thomas Payne, as on page* 125.]

voate   for as much as by occasion: the dayes of working in the high wayes ar not yet all pformed. its therfor ordered that notwth- standing the former order limitting the surveyers to accomplish thier dayes of worke. befor the 20th of the 7 moneth. yet for this p^{r}sent yeare they ar allowed & ordered to appoint 2 dayes wthin 10 dayes after this p^{r}sent day. for ye pforming of that worke that is needfull yet to be done in the high wayes

Joh. Dwight is appointed to take care of this worke. if the surveyers be absent

voate   Elea. Lusher is requested to doe w^t he may. to pvide a workeman to build a watchouse

voate   The Countrey Rate is to be rectified & set at the due sum that is to be pd to the Countreye. by Lieft: Fisher & Elea: Lusher

voate   John Kingsbery & Tho Wight ar deputed to view Charles Riuer to see whether the Indians wares be a hinderance to the waters passag or not & Andrew Duein.

19 d of 10 mo. 49   Assembled Hen Chickering: Joh. Kingsbery Joh. Dwight: Lieft: Fisher Tho: Wight. Fra Chickering & Eleazer: Lusher
    the charge about the drye heard house & yard is vndertaken to sattisfie by pticular psons

    1. the vse therof by this Town. is to be pposed at the Genrall meeting to doe as the Town shall se cause

    2 to be pposed that the meeting house be allowed for the vse of a watchouse vntill the Town can pvide an house built for that end. or take other order therin its alowed so by voate

    3 that the ppriators in the Broad mead: may Joyne together for the encloseing the whole mead: and fitt it for further empvem^t as cause & optunitie may apeere—these to meet at the house of Eleaser Lusher 6 day fortnight

    4 whether the mead that is yet Comon in the town shall be deuided by rules of pportion. or granted to supplye those men that ar in most want
    this left as it is

    5 that Care be taken that the young hound doggs be in time taught to hunt
    this left to ye select men now to be chosen

    to be then Chosen select men: 3 men for smale cases. surveyers. woodreeues

    [× × × *Order relating to Clay, as on page* 125.]

    the names of such as ar behind in thier high worke. together wth the sum due for the same

Jos: Clarke	0	4	0	Rich: Ellice	0	1	0
Hen: Willson	0	6	0	[*Mich: Metcalf sen]	0	[*1]	0
Ralph Daye set off	0	5	0	Mich: Metcalf Ju	0	4	0
Robt [*Mason] to fetch 3				Joh: Fraery	0	6	0
loads of fence for Joh				Tho Bancroft	0	6	0
Bacon	0	[*9]	0	Joh: Farington	0	6	0
Nath Stearnes	0	4	0	Rich: Euered	0	2	0
Tho Battelle	0	2	0	Joh: Guild	0	4	0
[*Josep: Kingsbery]	0	[*1]	0	Joh: Kalem	0	4	0
Lamb. Genery	0	1	0	Rich. Wheeler	0	4	0
Robt Crosseman	0	4	0	Antho Hubbert	0	5	0
Thw Strickland	0	1	0	Robt Wares	0	5	0
Joh. Damat pd Lieft	0	3	4	Sam Judson	0	6	0
Edw Richards	0	[2]	6				
					5	5	0

    to ppose

    1 that an order be made that no Land or houses in Town be sold to any that is no Townesman. except the purchaser be apued of by ye Towne

    2 that a platt of ye Town be taken & the Town booke Corrected

    3 that men be deputed to laye out the grante made to ye village

1 of ye 11th mo. 1649   At a genrall meeteing of the Towne.

vpon a motion about building a newe Mill a complaint being made of the insufficient pformance of the p^rsent mill. ther wer deputed to treat wth Bro: Whiteing the p^rsent Miller. about the reforming that wronge. these men Henry Chickering, Joh: Thurston, Geo: Barber
[✕   ✕   ✕   *Other votes at this meeting, on page* 126.]

7 of 11: 49   Assemb. Hen Chickering: Joh Dwight: Tymo: Dwight: Lieft: Fisher, Serg^t Fisher & Eleazer Lusher
[✕   ✕   ✕   *Other orders, as recorded on page* 126.]
Lieft Fisher vndertakeing to take a true platt of the Lynes of the Towne John Dwight. or when he cannot his sonne Tymothie together wth Serg^t Daniell Fisher vpon request consent to help therin
[✕   ✕   ✕]

21 of 12 mo 49   Asemb: Hen Chickering, Joh Dwight, Serg^t Fisher, Joh Kingsbery, Lieft Fisher, Tymo Dwight &: El Lusher
a motion of Tho Payne for suply in that swampe formerly granted for buring bricke consented to if ye grante so mad hinder it not
to Ro Fullers desire of a pcell of Land by the lowe playne. its thought reasonable & br: Fraries motion to the contrary is desired to be fayerly diswaded

Hen. Willson & Tho Bancroft ar discharged of that 12^s due to the Town for thier deffect in high way worke vpon condicion that they pforme 2 sufficient dayes worke wth 6 cattell & a cart & a man in fetching fencing stuffe at ye Towns apointm^t for the encloseing the high way thorough Joh. Bacons Lott
[✕   ✕   ✕   *Grants, etc., as on page* 127.]

15—4 50   Assemb. Hen Chickering, Joh Kingsbery, Joh Dwight, Lieft Fisher, Serg^t Fisher, El. Lusher
Bro Lusons motion not consented vnto: except he fence his own Land leaueing the way free & open

voate   Lieft Fisher & Serg^t Fisher ar deputed to treat wth such men as ar Chosen by Eld: Froast about the purchase of his Farme and vpon pposition of the tearmes therof to take time to giue him a full answer. that the Town may take notice therof & resolue as they se cause
[✕   ✕   ✕   *Vote concerning treaty with Cambridge men, as on page* 128.]
[One whole leaf missing.]

[   ] 11 mo 1650   Assemb. Joh Kingsbery, Joh: Dwight, Lieft: Fisher, Fra Chickering, Serg^t Fisher, Nath Coaleburn & Elea. Lusher

voate   It is agreed that a quieere of paper be taken vpon the Townes account for the vse of ye select men for publike occasions

For the better ordering of our meeting [   ] the select men aboue named doe [   ] agree & engage our selues to attend the time of meeteings that shall from time to time be orderly apointed. and freely each of vs for our pticular pmise so to attend. both in timely apearance [   ] due staying till those meeteings shall be dissolued. or in case that any shall fayle in either of these pticulars. we shall tender the reasons of our actions in that case to be iudged by the major pt of ye select men which if they alowe not we each of vs for our selues doe engage to submitt to pforme w^t so euer censure or penaltie shall be by them imposed vpon any of ourselues

allwayes pvided that no censure or penaltie exceed 2^s 6^d

Deputed to treate wth Dorchester men about the Land in pposition adioyning to the Mill Creeke & vpon the search of the Court Records if they se cause so to doe. or the vse of any other meanes for light in the cause to conclude w^t euer is or may be needefull for the attayning the said Land to the vse & posession of our Towne according to the best discretion of the men heere vnder named   Eleazer Lusher, Lieft: Fisher, Serg^t Dan Fisher

wheras it apeere that [   ] a waye yet found to cert[   ] of Meadowe that lye neere [   ] Lands in the posession of Sam [   ] its therfor. for the supplye of th[   ] want. the men heere vnder named ar deputed & authorised to [search] for a conueanient Cart waye and if no other can be found. but that wch lye thorough the Land of Sam Mills then they ar to compound wth him or in case he agree not they shall tender him the liberty of the choice of 2 men together wth whome. they may conclud both for the waye & the sattisfaction for the same   Joh Kingsbery. Joh Dwight

a bill giuen to Joh Thurston [   ] of Joh Morse in full the sum of 0-7-0

Lieft Fisher is deputed to treate wth Joshua Kente & conclude wth him for the beateing the Drume: he is desired to put the Deacons in minde to put the worke that James Allen now [   ] into the hands of the said Joshua [   ] he may carefully attend the shutting the meeteing house doores & the keepeing out of the doggs. & further we apoint the said Joshua to be the graue maker for the occasions of ye Towne in genrall. and the keeper of the pound according to the order of ye Court

Eleaz. Lusher is requested to compose & enter a table to the booke of Records

[   ] mo 15 1650   Assemb. John Kingsbery, John Dwight, Lieft: Fisher, Fra: Chickering, Serg^t Fisher, & Elea: Lusher. Nath Coalburne cam late

Leift Fisher, Elea Lusher make their returne concerning Mr Haynes acco[   ] wch is accepted

DEDHAM TOWN RECORDS. 165

Fra: Chickering p^rsents an act of m^r Joh. Oliuer. concerning pt of Dorchester Line

Elea. Lusher is desired to write to such of Boston as haue giuen encouragem^t concerning a bell. for the publike vse of ye Towne that they may be still mindefull therof & know that we expect an answer

Lieft Fisher is requested to pcure whom he may best. to keep. out doggs from makeing disturbance in ye meeting house

for ye Correcting the Towne Bookes its concluded as followeth

1 that the Couen^t shall be transcribed & those names ther vnto subscribed to be anexed to the same

2: order about publike charges to be equally borne to be considered

3 order to keepe water free from ppritie transcribed

4. that 12 Acr Mead be grañ to 12 Acr vpland

5. that the Town in a genrall meeting & not ye select men shall admitt Townesmen to be considered transcribed

6. about due apearance at Town Meeteings to be considered

[*Br. Day coming. the reckoning being made. it apeere that ther remayn due to him   1—0—4
where vpon a Bill is giuen him to receaue of Robt Hinsdell   1—0—0
wth this condicion that if Br Wight can make pfe of his bill. that then so much as is so pued. shall be sattisfied to the Town by sd Br Daye: due to him still 4^d]

Ralph Day is agreed wth all to beate [   ] for th [   ]

Granted to Ralph Daye & to his heyers for euer. 4 Acres of vpland. to be layed out to him vpon the Planting. Field at the discretion of Henry Chickering, Natha: Coaleburne

John Ellice coming together wth Lambert Genery. the said Lambert Declareing that thier coming was to demaund sattisfactio for one pcell of Meadowe, formerly granted to Jo. Ellice the Towne. by ye select men. pmise & tender to sattisfie the grante. made to the said John & in conueanient season to giue him posession therof

return to the booke—

7: the grant of 4 Acr swampe to a 12 Acr Lott to be entred into the booke of recorde

8. the buriall place gra: to be entered in the Booke of record

9. less portions. Townsemen. transcribed

10. order concerning swine to considered

[*11 order concerning the survey of Lands to be considered]

12 order concerning the choice of select men to be transcribed

13 order to Certifie Alienat. to be transcribed after it be corected

14 Mr Stoughtons Couen^t to be recorded

15. extent of select mens power transcribed

16. Ladders the ordered to be contracted & transcribed

17. Woodreeues. an order necessary therin to be drawn.
18 Booke keepeing recompence transcribed
19: anoying high wayes wth trees. order transcribed. penaltie to pay according to the assignm^t of ye selectmen
20. that vpland be anexed to mead: adioyning transcribed
[* R. Hinsdells account
    Anno: 48. for y^e ½ year   1—0—0
          50: due   1—8—0
          51—due   2—0—0
                                  4—8—0
[   ]d by Joh Dwight [3]—13—4   ]

20 of 11: 1650 Assemb. Joh. Kingsbery, Joh Dwight, Fra. Chickering, Lieft. Fisher, Sergt. Fisher, Elea: Lusher, Nath Coalburne cam late

the notes concerning the great Playne ar deliuered to Fra. Chickering and John Dwight for the settling of the fence there. they being chosen by ye ppriators.

Eleazer Lusher for late apeareing this daye is fined   0—0—4

Elea. Lusher p^{r}sents the Table drawen to the Booke of record. wch is accepted

vpon the motion of Joseph Kingsbery concerning the supplye of the vpland due for the purchased Lands. its agreed to tender him these 3 ppositions. that he might take his choice in wch he please pvided that he giue in his resolution before our next meeteing

1 that he may hold his grant mad of Land vpon the planting field

voate   2 that he may haue the money repayed that he disbursed for those 4 rights he did purchase. & so much more lent him for so long time as he haue beene out of this disbursed for those rights

3. he may leaue it to the resolution of the Arbitrators who onely haue power to supplye these wants

Lieft Fisher is deputed to take care to tender these ppositions & bring his answer

Ed Hawes makeing motion concerning the pcell of Meadowe. is taken into consideration to be resolued at the next meeteing

Robt Hinsdell coming to make vp Mrs Stoughtons account for 4 yeares
    1647: 1 yeare is acknowledged to be due   2—0—0
      48—in the hand of Joh Dwight   1—0—0
         yet to be cleered for that yeare   1—0—0
    [*49—to Nath Aldus & Ralp Day each   1—0
      50 to Ralp: Daye   [   ]   [   ]]

for wch Debt yet behind Br. Hinsdell engage to sattisfie 4£—8—0

                                                         4—8—0

22 of 11 mo 1650   Joh: Kingsbery, Fra: Chickering, Lieft: Fisher, Joh. Dwight, Serg^t: Fisher, Nath. Coaleburne, & Eleaz: Lusher
    Lieft Fisher return answer from Joseph Kingsery that he accept not either of the former of ye 2 ppositions. but will waite the Issue of the act of ye 4 arbitrators. to doe therein as he se cause to accept thier act in his case or not
    grants not yet recorded
    M^r Ed Allen: 2 acr vpland
    Mary Morse her Meadow to be considered in respect of m^r Allens title. how it passed
    vpon consideration of the motion of Josep. Kingsbery. concerning his disbursments of paye for ye 4 rights in ye purchased Lands at the request of ye Towne it is agreed to aduise & desire him to rest sattisfied in expectatiō of the issue of the act of ye 4 Arbitrators wch if it shall fall out well we hope he will take sattisfaction in. if it pue otherwise then 'we desire it should. we conceaue it requesite. care be taken that be in no sort wronged in this case
    resoloued by voate that this answer be returned to Jos. Kingsbery. by Nath Coaleburne
    [*the Deacons coming to cleere the reckoning betwixt the Church & ye Towne concerning m^r Stoughtons reckoning vpon cleere accounts it a peere. that they receaued 20^s of that pay from her to the Towne before the end of the yeare 1646, wch is agreed to be left in thier hands vntill the select men in the behalf of ye Town. se further reason to call for it. wch if they doe. the Deacons pmise to make payem^t of and as for w^t so euer therof they haue receaued since they ar to pay to the Towne vpon reasonable damand—the sum to be payed is 2£—0—0]
    grants to be yet entered
    1 m^r Alleyns 2 acr. smooth Playne
    2. purchased Lands: to be recorded an Alienatiō
    3. grat. La gener: Ph. Dalton. Shephard Jos Morse
    4. mary morse her mead. pass fro. m^r Alleyn. howe. & her Fathers title to her. howe
    5. m^r Feeks farme
    6. Ralph Shephard. want 10 Acr. ½ mead. entreing
    7. the 18 Acres deuide amongst. 3. not cleere
    8. Joh Dwight 6. acr Mead. to enter
    9. moyese his gra, wig playne. to enter
    10. Bayes 6 acr gra 3 of mead to enter
    11. N. Philips 1 hill 1 pcell of mead to enter

12. Joh. Kingsbery fro. Genery: to enter
13. Sam. Morse. 2 ar ½ vpland. to enter
14. Ja herring. frō: huggin to enter
15. Timo Dwigh pcell mead. to enter
16. Mch. Metcalf 3: acr fro Jo Rogers. to enter
17. Tho. Jord. 1 acr swampe. to enter
18. M^r Ed Alleyns farme at medfield to enter
19. Joh. Kingsb. 1 pcell vpland to mead. to enter
20. Mich Metcalf. 1 pcell swampe. to enter
21. m^r Cooke 12 acr gra: to enter. 2 acr playn to enter
22. Jo Luson 2 Acr swamp Tho Wight 2 acr
23. m^r Wheelock dead swamp to enter
24. Joh Haward. 1 pcell vpland. to enter
25. m^r Wheelock. 4 acr gra:—to enter to be enterd wth refer to Anth: Fisher page 25
26. m^r Wheelock. 15. acr. gra. to enter   7
27. m^r Cookes woodland — to enter
28. Joh Guild frō: Jo. Rop. to enter
29. Tho Eanes 2 acr Il playne. to enter
    4 acres m^r Wheelocks gra. Alien to Anth Fisher seni. to consider
30. m^r Deengaiñ Sam̃ bulleyn &c. to enter
31 grants to Tymo Dwight Fra chickering &c to enter
32. Joh Haward pcell gra: to enter
33. Joh Eaton satisfie for brick ground. to enter
34. Willm Bearsto. 8 acr gra: to enter
35. Geor. Bearsto pcell swampe—to enter
36. shepheards Lott 2 acr gr playn. to enter
37. m^r Deeng. 8 acr mead. to enter
38. Aust Kalem 2. acr mead to enter
39. Josh Fisher 1 pcell. great playne. to enter
40. Joh Thurston 1 pcell mead — to enter
41. Josh Kent 2 pcells gra. to enter
42. m^r Joh Allen—exch at farme. to enter
43. m^r Joh Allin gra. pcell exchange at gre playne. to enter
44. Hen Chicke to short fence rock med. to enter
45. millitarie comp: 2 acr gra.—to enter
46. Crossman. to consider & Dan. Morse
[*47. Joh Dwight ½ acr gra: to consder]
48. Josep Clarke gra 3 acr. to enter
49. Hen Willson. 3 acr gra. to enter
50. Nath. Whiteing enlargem^t to enter
51. Ro. Crossem̃ 2 acr gra. to enter
52. Joh. Eaton smale pcell. to enter

53. Great playne waye deputation to enter
54. Pet Woodward 6 acre grat. to enter
55. Aust Kalem gra: not exceed 4 acr: to enter
56. Eames smale pcel vpland. to enter
57. Judsō. 4 Acr gra. to enter
58. Joh morse 2 Acr mead gra. to enter
59. Antho. Fisher. Wight. Luson. gra to enter
60. Clay groud gra to enter
61. Geo. Bearsto swamp. excha. gra to enter
62. Josep Kingsb. Lieft way refference. to consider
63. Dan. Fisher. pond to Town. to be entered
64. Wight. 2 acr swamp. gra. to enter
65. J luson 2 acr swamp gra. to enter
[*66. J batchelor smale pcell to consider]
67. Jo gaye high waye to enter
68. Compa: Millita: gra free vse to enter
69. Genery pcell great Playn. to enter
70 Da. Fisher. 3 acr ¾ gra. to enter
71. Dan morse 4 acr gra. to enter
72. Robt Crossem. 4 acr. gra to enter

voate   26: for ye p^{r}uenting of a negligent leaueing downe of Rayles or leaueing gates vnderset and open wherby damage haue bene oft times done in seuerall respects.

It is ordered that who so euer heere after. betwixt the 20th daye of ye first Month. and the 12 day of ye 8. mo: from yeare to yeare. shall offend in either of ye cases aboue said shall for euery such offence. that is either for takeing down & leaueing rayles or any rayle down in the fence of any field or Lott wher corne or other cropp. is groweing shall forfiet to the pson whose the fence is the sum of sixe pence. if no scath be done therby and the like sum for vndersetting any such gate & leaueing it vnderset open but if scath be done therby he shall allso pay & sattisfie the full value of the damage to the pson or psons so therby wronged. pvided all wayes. the offence be lawefully pued

25 of 11 mo: 1650   Assemb. John Kingsbery, Joh: Dwight, Fra. Chickering, Lieft: Fisher, Sergt: Fisher, Natha: Coalburne & Eleaz. Lusher

voate   Eleazer Lusher is deputed to enter the orders that ar agreed vpon. haueing Libertie to alter such words or phrases as may tend to giue the sence in more pp words or more full: or mor cleere: pvided the sence be in no sort changed

voate   its agreed that the order made at ye Genrall meeteing 1 of 11 mo. 1650: requireing the correcting of ye town booke. to be entered first of all in the new booke of orders.

170   DEDHAM TOWN RECORDS.

voate Joh Dwight is requested to buye a booke fitt for the entering of ye orders in to. in his first optunitie. at ye townes charge

[* A bill giuen to Antho Fisher Juni to receaue 2^s 6^d of John Morse for his days Journey to Capt Kayne & m^r Jaxton]

Bro Luson, his motion about fencing the mead belong to the Town, is answered: that he may let it stand & the Towne will alowe w^t is equall

it is agreed to alowe Eleazer Lusher for the makeing & entering the the table in the booke of recorde   0–12^s–0

Joseph Kingsbery making a motion about the waye to his Meadow thorough Natha Aldus to be considered

[*It is agreed that the recompence for entering Alienations shall be for each Alienation   0–0–6.]

John Haward: John Eaton. & Thomas Fuller ar requested and deputed to take care for the repayering of the foote Bridge. so much as may be. to be set of in high way worke. and the rest vpon the Townes charge. in equall sattisfaction

John Gaye & Richard Euered ar requested & deputed to take care of the repayering the Bridge ouer the little Riuer neere the house of John Dwight. and that Bridge ouer the Mille Creeke. to be done by high waye worke

in search of the court booke we finde that the order the coppie wherof is entered in our new towne booke is verbatum in the court booke dated 8 of ye 7 mo: 1636.   order 295[1]

further: at a Genrall Courte—its ordered that Mount Wollastone is to be bounded by the blue hills. & the rest is to be to Dorchester. to goe to the bounds of plimouth 1637: order. 367[1]

at a genrall court 1638. ye 17 of ye 3 mo: order 386[1] the return of m^r Alleyn. m^r Collicot. & m^r Oliver is entered. acording to the paper brought by bro: Chickering

4 of ye 12: 1650— searched out by Dan. Fisher: El. Lusher

1650   7 of ye 12 mo   Assemb: Joh. Kingsbery, Joh. Dwight, Fra Chickering, Lieft: Fisher, Serg^t Fisher, Nath Coalburne & Elea: Lusher

voate A Letter shall be sent to the select men of Dorchester. intreating. a resolution from them the line betwixt thier towne vs. that is now layed out. to hagins brooke.

vpon information concerning a bell. its agreed to send word to the select men of Boston to resolue them that we doe conclude a bargaine for the bell & engage paym^t. according therevnto

voate Eleazer Lusher is deputed to goe to Boston. to conclude for this bell, whose bargaine & couenant therein with the select men of Boston the Towne engage. to pforme

---
[1] Mass. Col. Rec., Vol. I, pp. 179-217-231.

a bill giuen to Joseph Kingsbery to receaue of Joh Morse 0—3—4 for 2 dayes seeking out the place for ye grant at Boggastowe

an order to be drawen vp that may settle the charge of rates ariseing vpon Lands & cattell vpon the posessors

10 of 12 mo 1650   Assemb. Joh Dwight, Lieft. Fisher, Dan: Fisher, Fra Chickering, Nath Coaleburne, Elea Lusher

† Elea. Lusher sell to Joh Fraery 2½ acres vpland. 2 of swampe lying together abutting east street east brooke in ye swampe west Pet. Woodward south Joh Fraery north

† Tymo Dwight 6 acres meadowe gra: in broade mead. abutting Charles Riuer east. Hen Phillips north Ed. Kempe. south. high way west

† Tymo Dwight. 2 acres swampe gra: abutting wigwam playne north east Turkey Iland southwest Joh Dwight south east. being a tryangle wth ye point west vpon ye wast land

† Tymo Dwight 4 Acres gr playne gra: abutting high way south. wast Land north. Aust Kalem east Hen Chickering west

† Rich Euered. 6 Acres mead. Rosemary mead. Abutting mr Allen south. wast mead. north. wast vp land. east & west

† Rich Euered. swampe 4 acres. gra: abutting. Rich Euered vpland. east Ja. Allen swampe west Elder Hunting north. Joh Morse soth

† Rich Euered 2 Acres swampe abutting Rich Euered vpland. easte wigwa plane west. Michael Mettcalfe. north. wast swampe south

† Joh Fraery 4 Acre swampe gra abutting vpon George Bestoe west Elea Lusher east. wigwam playne north. Antho Fisher south

† Pet Woodward 6 acres vpland gra abutting high way west. wast land east & south—Robt. Fuller North

Pet Woodward 4 Acr swampe abutting

† Serg^t Fayerbanke ½ an acre vpland. gra abutt. high way south. purchased lands north & east: mead. west

† Robt. Hinsdell. 2 acres swampe his home lott. abutting east. brooke in swampe west Elea. Lusher north. Michaell Metcalfe south

† Elea. Lusher 1 acre swampe. gra. abutting his home lott east. brooke in ye swampe west Joh Fraery. north. Robt. Hinsdell south

† Elea. Lusher 3 acres swampe. gra: abutting vpon Joh Fraery west. Tho. hering east wigwam playene. north. wast swampe south.

† Tho. Hering 2 acres of swampe. gra. abutting. Elea. Lusher west. Edw. Richards east. Jam. Allen. south. wigwam playne north

† Tho Hering 2 acres gra: swampe Abutting Iland west. vpland east. Nath Coalburne north. Ed Richards south

---

The paragraphs marked (†) are checked in the original, evidently to indicate that they have been entered elsewhere.

† Tho Hering 2 acres mead. gra. Abutting mill creeke north. his home lott south. high way west. his home lott east

† Tho Hering 4 acres mead. gra. Abutts Riuer north. Robt Hinsdell west Pet Woodward. south waste land. east

† Josep Kingsbery. 6 acre. mead. gra. abutt Riuer east. wast land west. Nath Coalburn north. Ferd Addams south

† Hen Smith 3 acres swampe exchange for high way at course swampe gra. Abutt Elder east waste land west Mr Cooke Ed Richards Tho Herring each of them in pt north Ja. Allen south

† Jos. Kingsbery 4 acres swampe gra Abutt great ponde east. wast land west Dan Fisher south Hen Brock north

† Nath Coaleburne 4 Acres swampe gra Abutts Tho Herring south Hen Philips north. an Iland. west. wast vpland east.

† Tho Bayes 2 acres swampe gra Abutts little pond south west, Robt Hinsdell south east. Ed. Kemp north west Iland north east

† Lamb. Genery. 2 acres swampe gra. Abutt Hen Philips south wast swampe north Geor Bearstow west vpland waste east

Hen: Brock 4 acres mead Broad Mead gra Abutt

† Hen Brock 2 Acres mead gra. abutts Riuer east. being a tryangle. Austen Kalem west. Joh Haward. North

† Nath Coaleburne 2 Acres mead gra Abutts Aust Kalem easte. Riuer south wast land north

† Ro. Mason 2 Acres swampe gra. Abutt wigwam playne north Iland south & east Lieft west

† Joh Morse 4 Acres mead gra: Abutts Riuer east. waste Land west Hen Smith south wast Mead North

Robt Mason 6 acres Mead. fro La Genery the pcell next belowe described

† Lamb Genry 6 acres. mead gra. abutts. an hill in ye mead south waste Mead north Joh Haward easte. waste Land west

† Lamb Genery 4 Acres ¼ gra. Abutt. Riuer east. & north. Ralph Shepheard south Jland playne. west

† Tho Bayes 3 acre meadow. gra Abutts Joh Ellice west. mich Bacon east. high waye south. Ed Kemp. Ed. Richards. north

† Lieft Fisher 2 Acres swampe gra: Abutts Tho Bayes Jland Ro Mason each in pt east. m^r Cooke west. wigwam playne north wast swampe west

† Gra: to Lieft Fisher in sattisfaction for land layed downe for enlargem^t to the high waye one pcell of woodland abutt high way east. wast Land south. Ed Hawes west Josh. Fisher aforesd north—as it is at p^rsent marked vpon sundery trees. the lyne varied accordingly

11 of ye 12 1650 Assemb Fra. Chickering, Joh Dwight, Lieft Fisher, Serg^t Fisher, Nath Coaleburne, & Elea: Lusher, Joh Kingsbery

† Willm Bullard 2 acres swamp gra: Abutts Jose Morse & little Riuer north. ponde south. Jose Morse easte. high way from pound west.

† Will. Bullard 2 acres swampe gra: Abutts Turkey Iland east. south playne west Joh Bacon North. Joh Gaye south

† Will. Bullard 4 acres mead gra: Abutting vpon Joh Gaye north. wast vpland: & mead on all other pts

† Joh. Gaye 3 acres ½ mead grat Abutts. Will Bullard south. & ye wast vpland & mead all pts else

† Joh. Gaye 1 acre mead gra: Abutt. his home lott west Riuer east. m^r Ed Alleyne north waste land south

† Joh Gaye 2 acres swampe gra Abutts Turkey Jland & William Bull each. in pt north m^r Wheelock south: south playne west Tymo. Dwight east.

† Joh Gaye 2. acres swampe gra: Abutts m^r Allen east. Joh. morse west a brooke in ye swampe south. vpland north

† Ed. Richards 1 acre mead gra: Abutting home lott east. little riuer west. Fra Chickering south. smiths Lott north

† Ed Richard 6 acres mead gra. Abutt m^r Dalton. north. Hen Smith south Riuer east. waste land west

† Ed. Richard 5 acres mead. gra. Abutts Riuer. east. wast land west. Fra Chickering south Ed Kempe north

† Ed Richards 2 acres swampe gra. abutts Tho Herring west. m^r Cooke east wigwam playne north. wast swampe south

† Ed Richards 2 Acre swampe. gra. abutts mich metcalfe south west. Tho Herring noreast: wast land: north west vpland southeast

† Hen Chickering 2 acres swampe gra. abutts Anth. Fisher north. wast swampe south. wast vpland west. Joh Fraery. east

† m^r Allen pastor 2 acre swampe gra: abutts vpland west. waste swampe east Tho Fisher south. wast vpland north

† Tho Fisher 2 Acre swampe gra. Abutts his home lott west. wast swampe easte Mr Allen past north. wast swampe south

† Rich Barber. 1 acre ½ swamp gra. Abutts Rich Barber east wast swampe west. Hen Smith south. wast swampe north

† Joh Luson. ¾ acre mead gra. Rosemary mead abutts Tho Wight north west. the wast vpland south east vpon waste mead. wast vpland. north east & south west

† Tho Wight ¾ mead gra Rosemary meadow Abutts. Joh Luson. south east. waste vpland all other pts

† Joh Luson 2 acres swampe gra. Abutts south playne west Tymo Dwight east. Tho Wight south. Dan Fisher north

† Joh Luson 3 acre ¾ mead. south mead gra. Abutts Antho Fisher north west Tho Wight north east. wast vpland all other pts

† Tho. Wight 3 acres ¾ mead. south mead abutts Joh Luson. south west. brooke in ye mead north west. wast vpland all other pts

† Antho. Fisher 3 acres. ¾ mead south mead. abutts wast vpland north west & north. brooke in ye mead. south & south east. wth a point stretching west to a m^rked white oake

† Dan Fisher 3 acres ¾ mead. south mead. Abutts. brooke in ye mead. north & norwest Joh Luson. south east wast vpland all other pts

† Jose Clarke 1 pcell vpland gra Abutt Josep Clark east. Hen Wilson south. & the wast vpland north & west

† m^r Wheelock 6 acres mead Broad mead gra. abutts. high way south. wast mead north. m^r Cooke. east. Ralph Shepheard west

† m^r Wheelock 6 acres mead gra Abutts ye Riuer. north. m^r Wheelocks vpland south Joseph Morse west. Church mead. east

† Mr Wheelock 1 pcell of vpland. gra. Abutts m^r Wheelocks mead. north. waste vpland south Church. Lands. east. wast lands west

† m^r Wheelock 2 acres swampe gra: Abutts Joh Gay swamp north. m^r Cooke south. south playne west. Joh. Dwight east

† Tho. Wight 2 acres swampe gra: Abutts Antho Fisher south. Joh Luson north: south playne west. Geo. Bearstoe east

† Tho. Jordan 4 acres mead at Bogastowe in one of the neerest places

† Martin Phillips. 2 Acre swampe gra. abutts Tho. Alcock east. Joh eaton west. high way south: in a trayangle wth ye point vpon a marked pine north

† Tho. Fuller 2 acres swampe gra abutts. Turkey Jland. east. south playne west. Joh Ellice north. Mich Bacon & Turkey Jland each south

† Joh. Batchelor 8 acres Mead Broad mead gra. abutts Joh. Rop east. Joh Haward & swampe each in pt west. hill in ye meadow south. Fra. Chickering Joh eaton each in pt north

† Joh Dwight 5 acres ½ Broad. Mead. gra: Abutts. Dan Fisher. south. in pt m^r Cooke south in pt. high way north. Hen Brock west wast vpland east

† Hen Brock 4 acres Broad mead. gra abutts Joh Dwights east. Elea: Lusher west. high way north. m^r wheelock south

† Joh Morse 2 acres mead Rose mary mead gra. abutts: brooke north east. Antho Fisher north west. wast vpland & meadow all pt ellse

† Antho Fisher ¾ mead gra. Rosemary mead gra. abutts brooke north-east Joh morse south east. wast lands all pts else

† Antho. Fisher 2 acres swampe. gra. Abutts south playne west. ye pond east. Dan Fisher north Joh Batchelor south

† Antho Fisher. 2 acres swampe gra: abutts. south playne west Joh Fraery east Tho. Wight north. Hen Chickering south

DEDHAM TOWN RECORDS. 175

† m^r Cooke 2 acres swampe gra: Abutts Dan Fisher: south. m^r wheelock north south playne west Joh Dwight east

† m^r Cooke 2 acres. swampe gra abutt Lieft Fisher east. Edw. Richards west wigwam playne north. wast swampe south

† Joh Ellice 7 acres ¾ Broad Mead gra abutts high way. south. Tho Bayes east. waste mead west. Joh. morse Jos morse Elder Rich. Euered each in pt north

† Joh. Ellice 2 acres swampe. gra. abutts south playne west. Turkey Jland east Tho Fuller south. Joh eaton north

† Joh Ellice. 2 acres swampe gra. abutts Tho Allcock. south west. Aust Kalem north east. Mr Deengane north west. high way. south east

† Joh Eaton 2 acres ½ swampe gra abutts Tho Fuller. east: Tho Payne west Joh Batchelor north. Aust Kalem in pt high waye in pt. south

† Joh Eaton 2 acres swampe gra. abutts south playne west. Turkey Jland east Joh. Ellice south. Joh Haward north

† Joh Eaton 4 acres ¾ mead gra. abutts high way. north wast mead. west. Joh Batchelor in pt wast land in pt. south Fra Chickering east

† Joh Rop 6 acres mead. gra. abutts wast land next the river. south an hill north. Ralph Shepherds east Joh Batchelor west

† Ralph Shepheard 6. acres gra. abutts Joh Rop west. m^r Wheelock east waest next riuer south. Elea. Lusher north

† Elea. Lusher 6 acres mead gra. abutts Ralph Shepheard south. high way north Fra. Chickering i n pt. an hill in pt west. Hen. Brock east

† Joh Haward. 1 pcell vpland: gra. abutts swampe east. waste land west. Jland playn north being a trayangle the point stretching south vpon Joh Haward

† Joh Haward. 6 acres mead. gra. abutts Jland playne east. m^r Carter west high way south. Robt hinsdell. Joh Frary. Ferd. Adams. each in pt north

† Joh Haward 6 acres mead. gra. abutts high way south. Joh Batchelor. martin philips. each in pt north. the hill east Lamb. Genery wast land each in pt. west

† Joh Haward. 3 acres swampe gra. abutt house lott south wast land north m^r Deengaine north east in a trayangle the point stretching south west vpon the waste land

† Joh Haward 1 acre swampe gra: abutts Joh Eaton south. m^r Deengaine north south playne west turkey Jland east

† Mr Deengaine 1 acre swampe gra. abutts Joh Haward south Joh Batchelor north south playne west turkey Iland east

† Joh Batchelor 2 acres. swampe abutts Mr Deengañe south Antho Fisher north south playne west turkey Jland east

† Chr. Smith 2 acres mead gra. abutts a long ridge west. ye ponde east Hen Brock south. waste swampe. north

† Hen Brock 2 acres gra. swampe. abutts Christo Smith north. Jos Kingsbery south a long ridge west ye pond easte

† henry philips 2 acres swampe. gra. abutts Joh. Eaton east. Mich Bacon west. waste vpland north & south

† Tho Alcock 2 acres swampe gra abutts. Tho Fuller south Joh Ellice north. high way east: a trayangle the point to a pine west

† Robt Ware 2 acres. gra: vpland abutts Tho Alcock. south. high waye. all other pts

† Dan Fisher swamp 2 acres gra. abutts Jose. Kingsbery North. Antho Fisher south great pond east. wast land west

† Dan Fisher 2 ac swampe gr abutt Mr Cooke nor Joh Luson south. Geo Bearsto east south playne west

voate Joh Haward is deputed to Joyne wth Joh Kingsbery. in asisting the measurer in laying out. the grant made to Mr Deengaine of 8 acres of meadow according to the grante Granted vnto Joh Kingsbery and his heyers for euer. 1 acre.

voate ¼ and 10 pole of meadowe. to be layed out in rosemary Meadowe. at the direction of Lieft Fisher & Joh Haward. this grant is to make a full supply of all defects in his meadowe due to him in that meadow wch he bought of Tho Wight it being wanting in measure

† Fra Chickering 6 acres mead. gra, abutt Joh Eaton west. Elea. lusher in pt an hill in pt east. high way north. Joh Batchelor & Joh Rop. each in pt south

† Ed Kempe 5 acres gra. vpland. vpon ye swampe playne. abutting vpon John Dwight northwest. waste vpland all other pts

˙ Tho. Fisher 4 acres. at Rosemary mead this grante to be entered. as it is abutted in Liefts deed to Joh Bacon

23. of 12 mo 1650 Assemb. Joh. Kingsbery, Fra Chickering, Lieft Fisher, Joh. Dwight, Serg^t Fisher, Nath. Coalburne & Eleazer Lusher

voate vpon the consideration of som questions concerning will. Bearstoes parcell of Mead of 3 acres. being pt of the 18 acres left for seuerall psons to whom it was granted its agreed that Robert Ware shall be aduised to rest quiet heerein vntill ther be further reasons to question will Bearstow. and allso that the 18. acres shall be carefully measured. and then taken into further consideration

Fra Chickering & Robert Ware Joh Haward ar requested & deputed to asist the Measurer in the measuring there of

voate vpon som question concerning the enlargem^t of John Gayes. in the rocks: it is agreed that Joh Luson & Eleazer Lusher who wer then deputed to laye out Lands shall view the that pcell and if they can call to minde how the lyne ther in question was layed out. to resolue the same. according therto. other wise to take knowledg of Br Gayes motion concerning water. & returne answer to the select men

voate   Joh Dwight. & Fra Chickering. ar deputed to asist & direct in laying out the 8 acres granted to Will Bearstoe and take notice of that vpland by south Meadow desired by Antho: Fisher & returne information to the select men

vpon the motion of Nathaniell whiteing in concernm^t to a floate or sluce to p^{r}uent damag by floods. Joh. Kingsbery & Lieft Fisher ar requested and deputed to resolue vpon viewe wher the said floate or sluce is most conueaint to be made

voate   the 2 men heere vnder named ar deputed to treate and conclude wth Carpenters. whom so euer they can finde to be fitt & willing to put in 2 windowes in the back side of the Meeting house. & make such necessary pvision for hanging vp the bell as shall be needfull for the vse of ye Towne. Lieft Fisher, Elea. Lusher

for the p^{r}uention of difficulties & mistakes in makeing & gathering of rates in our Towne. in or concerning lands or cattell that ar out of ye posession of the owners and ar posessed & empved by any such as haue them vpon hyer or rent by the yeare or other wise. It is ordered that all Towne Rates shall be asessed & leuied from time to time. in all cases as aforesaid. vpon the p^{r}sent posessor of houses. Lands & Cattell in our Towne

for the p^{r}uention of questions or mistakes in or concerning the recompence for entering and writing such things as concerne either the Towne in genrall or such pticulars therein as may concerne to the Towne to take care for by way of publike order. It is ordered that who so euer from time to time shall keepe our Towne Booke shall haue for the entering each Towne Order to be pd by the Towne 6^d. & for each grante pd by ye grantee 6. for euery ali. for one pcell 6. and if more then one pcell be put into one coppie or alienation. & be distinctly exp^{r}ssed by the seuerall abuttments therof shall haue for the first of these pcells 6^d. as before said. and for euery other pcell put into the same alien. & coppie shall be payd 1^d be they more or fewer be pd by the p^{r}sent posessor & the transcript shall be allso drawen according to Court order for the payment [   ] exp^{r}ssed. not expecting more

for ye p^{r}uention of ye waste of Tymber by any Jnhabitant that shall haue grante of Timber for his suplye. according to the order in y^t case pvided Ji is ordered that who so euer shall suffer any timber so granted to lye vnempued. more then six monethes except by speciall order or new grante after the same is felled. shall thereby forfiet the same to the Towne againe. who may dispose there of as they or any whome they shall depute therevnto, and it shall not be in ye liberty of any Inhabitant to make vse thereof wthout the consent or alowance of the Towne or thier trustees in that case

† mich Bacon 2 acres swampe turkey Jland easte. waste Land weste Tho Fuller north will Bullard south

† mich metcalf sen. 2 Acr swamp Abutt waste vpland south east. Rob Hinsdell south weste. Ed Richards north west. wast swampe northeaste

† gra to Joh Rogers. 4 acres mead abuts Cha riuer east. waste Lands west. Edward Kempe south. a trayangle the point stretch north

† this is sold by Jo Dwight to Joh Metcalfe deed to make

† gra. Nicho philips 2 acr swampe abutts. nath Colboñ south. Lam Genery north. wast land easte. Geo. Bearsto west
the grante of that swampe. now Mich metcalfes was granted to phel. Dalton

† Joh morse sell Henry Smith 4 acres mead as page 57.14
for m^r Alin

Tho Battell sell 1 acr $\frac{1}{2}$ swamp abutts Hen Smith south m^r Allin north. Tho battell east. wast swampe weste

fro Sam Foster. 6 acr vpland great plaine abutts. Ed Richards east. Mr Allin west high waye north. wast land south
gra. to Edward Kempe

† Joh Thurston sell Joh Fayerbanke those 2 grants to Joh Rogers as page 7—10 and 10 page. 6 section. and 1 acre of swampe that was Geo Bearstoes abutts littl riuer Joh Rogers mead aboue said on all other pts Jonath Fayerbanke south

† John Thurston sell Jonath Fayerbanke that 6 acres vpland as page 4. sect 4

† Joseph morse sell Rich Ellice 2 acres vpland. abuts high way east swampe west. Geo. Barber north Joseph morse south

† Joh Thurston sell Rich Ellice that 6 acres page 7. sect 4 and that acre of meadow betwixt the same & the little Riuer

† Ensigñ sell serg Fayerbanke $\frac{1}{2}$ acre mead abutts. Ensigne north little riuer west & south. serg^t Fayer easte and south

Serg^t Barber a coppie of the grante page 30 sect 8

† Dan Morse sell Josh Fisher sen 5 acr $\frac{1}{2}$ being as page 34. sect 6— being that his owne grant & 2 acres of michaell mettcalfes adioyneing the whole pcell at p^{r}sent abutts Tho wight. east Ro ware west

† Joh metcalfe sell dan Morse 2 acres y^t mich metcalfs Lott next Dan morse. abutts as page 34.5

† gra Daniell Morse 6 acr. in Rosemary Mead abutts Lieft east wast Land west. waste vpland south. brooke north

† and one other pcell of meadowe ther abutts Lieft in pt Dan morse in pt south east wast Land all other pts

† both these ar sold by Dan morse to Andrew Duein deed to make

† Ed Richards sell Joshua Fisher seni 5 acres mead. as page 58—13 deed to make

† henry Glouer sell Robt Fuller 6 acres vpland. as it lyeth Abutting

Joh Guild in pt. wast Land in pt. east. Joh Guild north pet woodward south. deed to make

† Ed. Richards sell Hen Glouer that 9 acres as page 30:6. deed to make

bill to make fro. Hen. Glouer to Ed Richards for ye paym^t for this purchas. whole price 10 £—payd 3 £ wheat. 1 £ Rye befor 25 of ye 10 mo. next. but befor that in Fenceing. 2 £ befor the end of ye 3 month next in moweing 1 £ at a weekes warning this next haye time & in Corn before 24. of ye 4 month next 1 £. and more 2 £ wheat befor. or about 29 of ye 7 mo 1652

† Jose: morse sell Tho payne. 2 acres his pt in that mead. as page 49.1. to be abutted by Tho. pains direction nath Aldus east trayangle pointe west. Riuer south waste Land north. deede

† Granted to Joseph Morse 3 acr great playne : in sattisfaction for 1 acr ½ mead abutts Josep. morse east. waste Land west. the wast Land. north. high way south

† Gra. to Samll. morse 1 acr. gr playne in sattisfaction for 1 acre. he wanted in his former deuidt abutts Joseph morse east. wast Land. west & north highwaye. south

† Gra to Joh Fayerbanke sixe acre abutts waste Land east & south Jonath Fairbank south geo. Beasto north. 23. of 4. mo 1640: onely to enter

† Nath Colburne sell Eld Hunting 3 acr vpland abutts Joh Aldus east. high way leading to ye pond west Sa. morse in part Geo. Barber in pt south. & nath Colburn in pt: Hen philips in pt north

mrd. that Eld Hunting is to mayntay that fence betwixt himselfe & this 2 acres aboue said deed to make

15 of ye 1 mo 1651 Assemb: Joh Kingsbery, Fra. Chickering, Joh. Dwight, Lieft. Fisher, Serg^t Fisher, Nath Colburne & Elea: Lusher

voate

† Granted vnto Willm. Auery Liberty to set his shoppe. in the high waye in the East Street. the west side thereof to stand in the p^{r}sent Line of his fence next his house puided that he lay downe so much land vpon the East side of the said waye as the same is streightened by his said shope. at such time as the Towne shall require the same and allso pvided that whensoeuer the said shopp shall be no longer vsed for a smithes shopp by the said William at any time heereafter. then it shall be remoued out of the high way if the Town shall require the same

voate

Joh. Dwight. Fra Chickering and Serg^t Daniell Fisher ar deputed to meet wth Watertown men. to renewe the markes of the Line betwixt watertown and Dedham according to the order of Courte

voate

ther vnto voate

Granted vnto Hen philips 1 acre of vpl. & 1 acr. swa. wch is due to vpon his right of an 8 acre Lott. wch is to be layed out to him together wth his purchased Lands by the men. chosen

Peter Woodward. in the behalfe of ye East Street. Nath. Fisher in the behalfe of the middle and smooth playne. & Antho Hubbert in the behalfe of ye Jland ar deputed to burne the Comon grounds so much as is needefull. to haue for each daye spent therein. the abatem^t of a daye worke of a man in the high waye worke this next sumer

voate

Whereas the hous Lott of Henery Chickering being in it selfe so deffectiue. that according to the grante made to other house Lotts in the same nature. ther is enlargem^t allowed in to the Rocks for wood and timber. and that vpon the exact layeing out of the same in reduceing the same to its true grante it falls out y^t he haue much lesse woode and timber for his aloweance then other his neighbours therby ther is therfor granted vnto the said Henery and to his heyers for euer that woode and Timber that stands within such a Line as may be drawen streight from the southeast corner of the wood land of Anthony Fisher that lyes adioyneing to his house Lott. vnto the southeast end or corner of the Rayles of the said Henery next Ed Hawes

Lieft Fisher & Serg. Fisher ar deputed to laye out that Line

† Eld Hunting sell N Colburne 3 acr: vpland. abutts nath. Colburn east. the high way to the pond west. Robt Croseman north Hen phillips in pt nath Colburne in pt south. deed to make

† Geo. Barber sell Eld 1 Roode vpland. abutts thwaits Strickland east ye high way to pond west & south. Geo Barber north—deed to make

† Tho Jordan: Tho. Herring & Nath whiteing Joyntely sell nath Coalburne sixe Acres great playne. abutts waste land south. high waye north. Eld Hunting easte Christo Smith weste. as page 33 sect 7–8–9– no deed. but coppie & enter

† m^r powell sell Tho wight 20 Acres vpland abutts Ch. Riuer south the high way. north the waste Land. easte & weste. coppie & enter

the grante heereof to be first to be entered to m^r powell

† Samuel Morse sell Tho Wight 2 Acres mead Abutts Ch. Riuer south waste Land north the Land of Tho. wight easte. and closeth in a point betwixt Ch Riuer & the waste Land towards the weste deed to make

Samll Mills hyer 8½ Acres of Joh. Dwight abutts Joh. Dwight east. Antho hubert west high way north. wast land south. for 6 yeares according as betwixt Jo. Dwight & Jo. Mason

Hen Willson hyer 7 acres of Joh Dwight. for 6 yeares. abutts El. Lusher: west. Dan morse easte &c as Joh Mason

Christo Smith hyer 3 acr. of Joh Dwight for 6 years. abutting Joh

Dwight east & west. high waye north. wast Land south as Joh masons—these 3 couen^{ts} to make

† Tymo. Dwight sell Joh Dwight 2 acr great playne. abutts Joh Dwight east m^r Allin. west: high way south wast land north and 9 Acres swampe playen
& 2 Acres lande abutts Geo. Bersto. east Tho. Herring west. mill creek. north. Fra Chick. in pt will Auerey in pt south
& on pcell mead. abutts high way easte little Riuer west Geo. Fayerb. north tryangle forme the point stretche south deed to conteyn all these

† Nath Fisher sell Dan. Pond. 2 acres vpl abutts Thw. Strickland easte: Nath Fisher west. high way to pond north swamp. south
& 2 acrs swampe. abutts Thwa Strickland east. Nath˙ Fisher west the forsed pcell north. waste swampe south deed to make

mrd the 2 acrs vpland. is to mayntaye fence rond. about: & nath Fisher is to haue the refussall. if Dan. pond sell

bill fro. Dan pond to Na Fisher. 8£ 4£ p^{r}sent paye. 3£ mor 1 month after 29: 7. mo. next 1£ more befor ye end of 7. mo. 1652

Joh Thurston sell Antho Fisher Jun. 4 Acr. mead at Foule meadowe abutts. the Riuer weste. high waye in the mead easte. Lieft. north. Tho. wight south

mrd that Joh Thurston pmise and binde himselfe in a sum to Antho Fisher Ju: that if he the said Antho. doe paye & sattisfie 2£ 10^s to Edward Richards. Anno 53 according to the bargaine betwixt the said Joh. & Edward that then the said John shall [   ] the said Antho such a [   ] of 3 Acres of Foule mead now in the hand of ye said Edward as himselfe receaued or shall receae of Edward Kempe

Granted vnto Michaell Bacon 2 Acres Swampe abutts ye Causey waye leading to great Playne west Robt Ware south. & south east. Thomas Payne east Sam Judson North this to enter. & Coppie to drawe for Ro: Ware

Tho Eames sell Robt Ware 3 acres. vpland Jland playne abutts Tho Alcock. east. wast Land north high way. south. Sam Bulleyne west—this Alien: to record & copie to drawe for Ro ware

Deed to make to Robert Ware of that pcell mead. as page 57 sect 12

deed to make for Joh Dwight fro Tymo Dwight for 4 Acres mead at Foule mead—to haue Lieft^s deed to Tymo. Dwight

† deed to make fro. for Tho Herring Tymo Dwight one house Lott 6 acres more or lesse vpland & all houses &c. abutts mill Creeke East. Joh. Dwight & Rich Ellice. west. Tho. Hering north Joh Dwight south. reserueing a Cart waye foreuer to Joh Dwight & his heyers adioyneing to ye East end of the house Lott of ye said John together wth the purchased Lands & woodeland & w^t so euer other Lands Tymo Dwight haue now in Dedham vnsold to be dated July. 1. 51

Bill to make to Tymo: Dwight fro Tho Herring 16£ 10^s to be payd: 6£.

10£ ye 10 of ye 9 mo 1651: merchantible Corne in dedham at ye Currant price there to the sattisfaction of Tymo afforesaid. & ye other 10£. vpon ye 10 of ye 9 mo: 1652 in the like paye as ye former

   30 of ye 6 mo 1651 Assemb: Joh. Kingsbery, Joh. Dwight, Fra: Chickering, Lieft: Fisher, Sergt Fisher, Nath: Coalburne, & Eleazer Lusher
ye Countrey Rate made
  quest. whether broken Land lyeing yet vnfenced shall paye Countrey Rates. voated that it must paye
  quest: who ar ye men that ar exempted from ye Countrey Rate by ye polle. in regard of sicknes. lamenes &c. resolued as followeth
  Mich. Metcalfe seni, Joh. Kingsberey, Josh. Fisher seni, Sam: Morse, Rich Euered, Jonath Fayerbank, Nath. Aldus, Lamb. Genery, Joh. Eaton, Hen: Chickeren, Jam: Jordan, Ed Hawes, Christo: Smyth, Henerey Brock
  A motion made by seuerall Inhabitants for ye hasteing the Layeing out of the generall deuident formerly Intended

   1 of ye 7 mo 1651 Assemb: Joh: Kingsberey, Joh: Dwight, Fra: Chickering, Lieft: Fisher, Sergt Fisher, Nath. Coaleburn. & Eleazer Lusher
ye Countrey Rate finished
  the Rate of Dedh for Countrey Charges is 39£ 18s 0 psons in Dedham that paye to ye Rate. 80: the value of houses 730£. Reserued at home 15s 11d
  Br Dwight is requested to treat & conclude wth a workeman for ye shingling ye schoolehouse
  Sergt Fisher & Eleazer Lusher ar requested to treate & conclude wth a workeman or workemen for ye building of a chimney in ye schoole house
  vpon consideration that more Land then is yet taken into the prsent measure may be fitt for empuemt in the deuident next to be layed out. these men vndernamed ar therfor deputed to assist the measurer in searching vieweing & measureing wt Land they shall finde & Judge fitt for yt vse. Joh: Dwight: Nath. Coalburne Joh. Haward: Andr. Dewein together wth Lieft: Fisher
  & Sergt Fisher in case Nath Coaleburne cannot attend it

   20 of 7. 1651 Assemb: Joh. Kingsberey, Fra Chickering, Joh: Dwight, Lieft: Fisher, Nath: Coaleburne, & Elea: Lusher
  mett to newe make the Countrey Rate after ye Shire meeteing
  Whereas the shire Comissioners did determine & settle our Towne Rate for Countrey charges should be abated by exempting all that Land that was broken this prsent yeare. & som thing in ye valuation of houses. it is therfor

resolued to make that abatem^t by takeing out of this p^{r}sent Rate all the said newe broken Land. & to drawe a new valuation of houses. to ease the owners for time to com. & so to gather the whole Rate as it is in all other respects. & to [   ] the ouer plusse for Town charges

mrd that the Countrey Rate 1651 doth gather of ye Towne 42£ 0—6^d where of 39£ being due to ye Countrey ther remayne ouer plusse due to the Towne in that Rate 3£—0—6

Br. Kingsberey is desired to treate wth Tho: Fuller concerning the worke of a gager to know whether he haue any considerable reason to refuse that worke. if he be chosen thereto. & returne answer to ye select men

Granted vnto Thomas Jordan & to his heyers for euer one pcell of swampe as it lyeth adioyning vnto the house Lott of ye said Thomas. not exceeding 3 acres by estimation to be layed out at the discretion of Lieft Fisher & Daniell Fisher

The Rates of Joshua Fisher senior. Nathan Aldus & Lieft Fisher. in ye Countrey Rate being in ye ouer plusse: is assigned vnto Lieft Fisher—Sum –1–12–9

an order to be drawen to restrayne the taking away cannooes. wthout ye owners Leaue pennaltie of 2^s to ye owner

an order to be drawen to restrayne anoying high wayes. or drawen wayes. in the Towne or in ye woodes—but to cleere the said wayes forth wth before the feller goe from the said tree. vpon penalties of 1^s for euery tree to be pd to ye first informer to ye select men

[*Serg^t Fisher fined 1^s 6^d for not seasonable apearance at meeting this daye]

A valuation of houses taken 1651

Name	£			A new valuation 1655	£	Name				£
Mr Joh. Allin	31					Ralph Daye	07	07	00	£
Eld Hunting	12	10	10		15	Joh. Guilde	04	04	00	10
Elea: Lusher	26	23	00			Rich. Euered	09	09	00	15
Robt Mason	17	15	00			Rich. Wheeler	06	05	10	10
Josep: Kingsberey	13	16	00			Pet: Woodward	20	22	00	
Lamb: Genery	05	04	10			Robt Fuller	07	07	00	10
Lieft: Fisher	31	27	00			Joh: Farington	16	20	00	
Thwa: Strickland	07	06	00			Joh. Fraerey	09	08	00	6
Nath. Coaleburne	16	14	00		15	Mich: Metcalfe sen	17	15	00	
Hen. Brock	14					Mich: Metcalf Ju	03			
Nath: Aldus	14	10				Jonath. Fayerbanke	20	17		
Hen. Phillips	26	20	00			Joh. Fayerbanke	04	08	00	
Antho: Fisher Ju	11	10	00			Fra. Chickering	23	20	00	
Sam: Morse	07	08	00			Will Auerey	16	14	00	£
Nath: Fisher	12	10	10			Joh. Metcalfe	06	05	10	6
Robt Onion	04	03				Rich. Ellice	05	05	00	
Hen. Smyth	08	07	00			Joh Dwight	26	23	00	20

Geo: Fayerbanke	04	06	00		Joh: Gaye	08	10	00
Tho: Hering	14	12	10	15	Will Bullard	18	14	00
Nath. Whiteing	12	14	00		Sam Mills	04	01	00
Joh: Kingsberey	18	16	00	£	Hen. Wilson	05	06	00
Joh: Haward	17	15	00	16	Tho. Bancroft	04		
Sam: Judson	09	08	00	12	Ed. Richards	18	$\frac{27}{16}$	00
Robt. Ware	04	04	00	8	Josh. Kent	02	02	00
Mrs Deengaine	04				Joh Aldus	15	15	00
Tho Payne	05	07	10		The Mille			
Tho Fuller	04	03	10		Robt Crosseman	02		
Joh. Eaton	10	12	00		Joh Plimpton		3	
Christo Smyth	04	06	00		Lambert ginery			
Joh. Bacon	16	14	00		Joh Morse			
James Allen	02				The Mill	50	100	
Tho Jordan	09	08	00		Tymo Dwight	16	14	00
Ed: Hawes	04	03	10		Antho: Hubert	2	03	00
Tho Battell	18	16	00		Cor Fisher	3	02	00
Hen Chickering	23	20	00		James Draper	0	3	
Antho: Fisher seni	20	17	10		Joh Houghton	0	4	
Tho. Wight	19	17	00		Ralph Freman	2		
John. Luson	21	16	10		Tho: Meatcalfe	5		
Dani: Fisher	17	15	00		Joh. Littlefield	1		
m^r Wheelock	09	07	00					

For as much as diuers men that haue Canoes for thier necessary vse and occasions. haue complayned of great wrong done to them by seuerall psons by takeing away thier said Canoes wthout thier Leaue or knowledg. which haue bene much to the trouble & damage of ye sayd owners. therfor. in consideratiō & for ye p^{r}uention thereof. It is ordered that if any pson w^t so euer shall after the daye of the publication heere of. take awaye or Remoue any Canoe or Canoes wthin our Towne from the place wher the owner or his assignes haue from time to time fastened or left the same. wthout leaue or consent from the owner thereof or his assignes first had & attaynd shall for euerey such offence forfiet to the owner therof or his assignes the sume of one shilling or if the said Canoe be so taken away or Remoued that the owner is disapointed of the vse thereof the space of one whole daye or more then the pson or psons that did remoue the same shall paye to the owner or thier assignes double the damage w^{t}so euer may be made apeere. to be recouered in both cases aforesaid by legall pceedings as other debts in case the same be not payed quietly other wise

It is ordered that if any pson wthin our Town. w^{t}so euer shall. after the publication heere of. encumber Anoye or Interrupt any high waye or drawen Waye. in our Town. or in the woods. by felling trees or any tree crosse the same. either by the Body or topp. or any pt thereof & shall not forth with before he or they depart from the same. fully & sufficiently. take the same awaye & cleere the said way. he shall paye & sattisfie for euery such tree so felled to the Anoyeance of any such waye as aforesd the sume of 2 shillings to him or them that shall first giue information there of to ye select men of our Towne for ye time being or any twoo of them and if the pson that haue so felled the sayd trees shall not vpon demand of the said 2^s p tree by the Informer forth with remoue the said tree or trees as before said. then the said pson so felling those trees shall for euerey weeke that they lye vncleered out of the waye. paye to the Towne & ye vse thereof. 5^s p tree in to the hand of ye Constable for the time being

† deed to make to Anthoney Hubbert from Joh Kalem of that pcell page 39. 8. Edwa. Richards East Tho Bancroft west

† deed to make from Fra Chicker to Ed Kempe of 5 acres on ye great playne abutts Fra Chickering. east Joh Dwight west. high way north. wast land south

17 of ye 9 mo 1651. Assemb Joh Kingsberey, Joh Dwight, Fra Chickering, Lieft: Fisher, Serg^t Fisher, Nath Coaleburne & Elea: Lusher

Granted to Edward Kempe & his heyers foreuer Three Acres of Meadowe in Broade Mead: Abutting Charles Riuer East: waste Meadow west. Ed Richards south & Tymo. Dwight North

& Three Acres mead Abutts Charles Riuer East. the waste vpland west Joh Rogers North. Will Bearstow south

Joh Dwight is requested to certifie Joh: Ellice that we cannot forbeare any pt of the paymt now due from Medfield. but in regard of that meadowe due to him from ye Towne that the Towne will doe w^t is. & may apeere to be iuste therein wn he shall com & demand the same: it being in conueanient time

The Account of ye Surveyors as followeth:
:psons yet behinde in thier highwaye worke

	1651						
	£	s	d				
Joh Guilde	0	2	0	Joh: Metcalfe	0	1	0
Rich Wheeler	0	0	0	Nath Whiteing assigned			
Pet. Woodward				to Jo Dwight	0	4	0
Joh. Farrington	bushell wheat assigned to Jo Dwight			Joh. Aldus	0	2	0
				Sam Morse	0	2	0
Robt Fuller	0	8	0	Thwa Strickland	0	1	0
Joh: Fraery	0	2	0	Robt. Mason	0	2	0
Mich Metcalf Ju	˙0	4	0	Joh. Mason	0	8	0
Jona. Fayerbanke	0	9	0	Josep Kingsbery	0	6	0
Fra: Chickering	0	6	0	James Jordan	0	2	0

Tho. Jordan	0	4	0	Tho. Bancroft	0	6	0
Hen Glouer	0	4	0	Joh. Bullard	0	4	0
Tho. Battell	0	5	0	Edw: Richards	0	6	0
Tho: Wight				Joh Haward	0	3	0
Joh Luson	0	8	0	Antho: Hubbert	0	0	0
Mr Wheelock	0	4	0	Tho. Payne	0	0	0
Hen Wilson	0	8	0				

[*Serg^t Fisher vndertake to pay 4^s for Joh Bullard]

4 of ye 10 Mo: 1651 Assemb Fra: Chickering, Joh. Dwight, Lieft: Fisher, Serg^t. Fisher. Nath Coaleburn & Elea: Lusher

[*Eleazer Lusher is requested to referr those grants. in ye Record. that ar entered vnbutteled to those enteries y^t ar abutted to p^{r}uent questions & mistakes in time to com

Elea: Lusher p^{r}sent his accounts by Bill the Sum   2—19—9
that Bill vpon examination was alowed & passed by voate
he had receaued   0— 9—2
Remayn due to him from ye Town   2—10—7

Fra Chickering Tender his Bill of accounts the Sume 11^s 3^d vpon examination it was allowed of & passed by voate   0—11—3

Joh: Dwight Tender his bill of accounts Sum 1£. 14^s. 4^d. vpon examination of ye pticulars it was allowed of & passed by voate   1£—14^s—4^d

Serg^t Daniell Fisher p^{r}sent his Bill. Sum 1—13—6. alowed vpon examination & passed by voate   1—13—6

Recd vpon this account by ye said Daniell. from Danll Morse 18^s. & from Joseph Morse 5^s. the sum of receits   1— 3—0

Remayn due still   0—10—6

Tho: Fullers account p^{r}sented sum 9^s allowed & passed by voate 0—9^s—0

Antho Fisher senio: his account p^{r}sented and alowed of & passed by voate 5^s—recd. heereof from Joh Bullard   0—1—0

Remayn due still   0—4—0]

† James Alin sell to Joh. Morse 3 acres ¾ vpland on south playne Abutt: as page 56. sect 3: deed to make to Joh. Morse

20 of ye 10th mo. 1651.

mrd that Lieft Fisher & Eleazer Lusher in the behalfe of ye Town being ther vnto deputed agree wth Daniell Ponde Carp^{tr} as foloweth. the sd Daniell doth vndertake to frame & set vp 2 windowes vpon the back side of ye meetinghouse at ye direction of ye Towne. of each side of ye officers seate one. that shall be like in all respects to those girth windowes in ye newe meeting house so fare as the places ar capeable of. & allso frame & set vp a sufficient frame vpon the north end of ye meeting house for ye hanging of ye Bell and doe all ye Carpenters worke therevnto necessary. the shingling of the penthouse ouer ye Bell excepted. & to make & set vp one conueanient & sufficient payer of flewe boards at the said end of ye meeting house. the Towne vndertakeing onely all the necessary cariage of the timber therevnto necessary. & puide the boards for ye flew boards

this frame for ye hanging ye Bell is to be made according to ye forme & pportion then betwixt ye pties exp^rsed. all this worke is to be done wth ye first optunc & fitt season

For & in Consideration whereof the said Joshua & Eleazer in the behalfe of ye Town engag to sattisfie to the sd Daniell the sume of 3£ & in case the sd Daniell when the worke be done shall ap^rhend he loose by the worke & shall make it reasonably apeere he is to haue Ten shillings more. the whole to be p^d. halfe in wheat & halfe in Jndian corne. the Jndian when the sd Daniell shall demaund vpon reaso[   ] warning & the wheat when the worke is done

vnto which Couenant as is all ready expressed on the other side of this Leafe the pties engaged subscribe thier names

    Eleazer Lusher, Joshua Fisher in ye behalfe of ye Towne
    Daniel Pond in ye behalfe of himselfe
    Robt Onion sell Nath Coaleburn 5 Acres 2 acres one halfe meadow in ye purchased mead. abutts Nah Coalebor north. Robt Onion is to in form the other abuttm^ts. & 2 acres ½ vpland yet to be layd out

[*26 of ye 10th mo. 1651. Robt Hinsdels account in refference to m^rs Stoughtons Anuall Rent

Anno 1647: due for ye whole yeare—	2— 0—0	
1648: due for ye half yeare—	1— 0—0	
1650: due—	1— 8—0	
1651 due—	2— 0—0	
	6— 8—0	
heere of p^d by Joh Dwight	2—13—4	
Assigned to receaue of Joh. Plimpton wheate		1— 0—0
of Antho: Fisher Juni: 5 bushels Indian Corne		0—15—0
		4— 8—4
Joseph Morse assigned to pay		2— 0—0
		6— 8—4]

18 of ye 10 mo 1651   Assemb Joh Kingsbury, Joh Dwight, Fra. Chickering, Lieft: Fisher, Serg^t Fisher, Nath: Coalburne

Joshua Fisher is deputed to take a note of w^t is passed vpon this daye by ye select men

It is agreed to ppound the supply of fireing at ye Generall meeting

It is agreed that Francis Chickering shall take 40^s of Joseph Morse. wch is due to ye Towne: from m^rs Stoughton for ye yeare 1651

Fra: Chickering doe engage to pay 5 £ 12^s due to Boston for ye Bell.[1] and to deliuer the Cp^ts Bill to the Capt wherein he is engaged for ye Towne 5 £ 12^s

It is agreed that Capt Lusher, Joh. Dwight & Joshua Fisher or any Twoo of them ar apointed to take in ye Carpenters account that did groundcell the Meetinghouse to see w^t is due to him when he shalt p^rsent his account

[*Reckoned wth Joshua Fisher & ther is due from the Town to him 2-16-10]

Reced. of Robt Hinsdell by Joh Dwight 2 £ -13^s-4^d-wch was due to y^e-Town from m^rs Stoughton. wch John Dwight haue sattisfied to ye Towne in Corn. to ye Carpenter and by a Bill wch he p^rsented. wch was examined & alowed by the select men so ther remaynes due still from Robt Hinsdell to the Towne 1-14-8 of that which was due from m^rs Stoughton. Anno 1650

---

[1] See previous records relating to this bell on pp. 165, 170, 177, 187.

It seems pretty clear that this was one of the six bells given to Boston by Capt. Thomas Cromwell in his will dated Aug. 26, 1649 and proved two months later. He seems to have taken a liking to Boston. His will contains this bequest: —

"I giue my six bells being in the Custody of Henry Walton vnto the towne of Boston." The Records of Boston show that "The 9th mo., 1650. At a Generall towne meting upon warning, it was agreed that the Bells Capt. Crumwell gave the Towne should be by the Select men disposed of to the Best Advantage, and the produce Laid out for one Bell for a Clocke." *Boston Rec. Com.* 2^d *Report*, page 102. Another of Cromwell's bells may have gone to Castle Island, 1655. See *Memorial History of Boston*, *I*, 509.

Capt. Thomas Cromwell was one of the earliest of the famous buccaneers. In 1646 he was in command of three fast-sailing brigantines under commission of High-admiral (Earl of) Warwick, and having captured in the West Indies several richly laden Spanish vessels was driven by a gale about the middle of May into Plymouth harbor. "He had abord his vessels aboute 80. lustie men, (but very unruly,) who, after they came ashore, did so distemper them selues with drinke as they became like madd-men; and though some of them were punished & imprisoned, yet could they hardly be restrained; yet in ye ende they became more moderate & orderly. They continued here aboute a month or 6. weeks, and then went to ye Massachusets." *Bradford's Plymouth IV Mass, Hist. Soc. Coll., iii,* 441. After a short stay in Boston, he set forth on another voyage to the West Indies, was gone about three years, and returned to Massachusetts with many rich prizes, and "ther dyed the same somere, having gott a fall from his horse, in which fall he fell on his rapeir hilts, and so brused his body as he shortly after dyed therof." Two chapters are devoted to this bold Buccaneer by Jane G. Austin in *Betty Alden,* one of her stories of the Pilgrims.

It is agreed that the Grante of enlargement in ye Rocks made to John Gaye & Layed out by ye Capt & John Luson. shall be entered in the Town booke according to the grante

Joh. Gaye. Serg^t Fisher & Joshua Fisher. ar apointed to newe marke the Line at the west end of John Newtons Lott. according to the grante that the Towne may know thier owne Land

[*Nath Coaleburn is assigned to receaue of Joseph Clarke. 15^s wch is due to the Towne from Meadfield. in pt of paye for that 4 bushels of wheate wch the said Nathaneell did lende to ye Town to pay for the Bell

Remayn due to Mathaneell Coaleburn one bushell of wheate & 5^s that he payed to Edward Hawes]

30 of ye 10th. 1651 Assemb. Joh: Kingsbery, Joh: Dwight, Lieft: Fisher, Serg^t: Fisher, Nath: Coaleburn & Elea. Lusher

voate whereas Thomas Wight haue bene deputed to laye out to Thomas Jordan that 4 Acres of Meadowe Granted to the said Thomas at Bogastowe & that the same is not yet done It is now ordered that those men that wer formerly deputed to lay out the Line betwixt Meadfield & dedh they or any 3 of them ar deputed to appoint the layeing out of that grante. & Thomas wight is discharged

[*Joh Morse p^{r}sent his accounts in refference to that 7£-8^s-3^d due the last yeare. as allso for accounts due to the Town by seuerall defects in highway worke wch the sd John was assigned to gather 1649. remayn still due of those accounts-18^s-Totall.-8-6-3

Recd heereof by the Town	6—	2—8
Remayn still due from John Morse to ye Town	2—	3—7
In this account of John Morse—he haue p^d to Serg^t Daniell Fisher	0—	10—0
Remayne still due to Serg^t Fisher	0—	0—6
Recd more of John Morse his account 100 Ceader boarde	0—	4—0
Remayn still due from Joh Morse vpon ye Ballancing the accounts	1—	19—7
	1—	19—7
The Deacons coming to cleere thier accounts ther apeare to be in thier hands yet due to ye Town	2—	0—0
this 2£ the Deacons ar assigned to pay to Eleazer Lusher	2—	0—0
Assigned to be p^d more to Eleazer Lusher by bill out of Meadfield Rate by the glouer of Boston	0—	9—0
remayn due to Elea. Lusher	0—	1—7

ye Deacons vndertake to paye that 20^s to Joh Kingsberey at the Towns assignm^t wch Joh Dwight stand Debtor to the Town in as is entered before in this booke 1— 0—0

Joh Dwight is discharged thereof

Discounted wth Joh Morse in regard of 2^s—6^d lost in ye Countrey Rate by Robt Eames & 5^s—3^d by ye Treasurers account 0— 7— 9]

Remayn due in Totall from Joh Morse 1—11—10

vot Granted vnto Eleazer Lusher & to his heyers for euer that pcell of Swamp wch was layed down to the Town by m^r John Allen Pastor conteyneing one Acre & one halfe or there about lyeing adioyneing to that house Lott somtimes Ralph Shepheards. or neer there vnto

vote: Granted vnto Nath: Coaleburne & to his heyers for euer one pcell of vpland conteyneing halfe an Acre more or lesse as it lyeth adioyneing to that Land somtimes Lambert Generys & the mill Creeke. Reseruing such a passage thorough the same in all respects as shall be needfull for the vse of those that ar ppriators in the purchased meadowe there. Joh Dwight & Lieft Fisher ar deputed to lay it out

Sergt Daniell Fisher is deputed to call the Rolle of the Townsemens names. at ye Genrall Meeting

A Bill of the names of those Townsemen that ar to be called at the genrall Town meeteing

Mr Allen Pastor, Eld^r Joh: Hunting, Mr Ralph Wheelock, Captaine Lusher, Deacon Hen: Chickering, Deacō Nath Aldus, Joh: Kingsberey, Mich. Metcalf. senio, Josh: Fisher senio, Samll Morse, Joh: Luson, Hen: Brock, Antho Fisher seni, Joh Dwight, Joh: Haward, Fra: Chickering, Tho. Wight, Lieft Josh: Fisher, Ensign Hen. Phillips, Jonath. Fayerbank, Peter Woodward, Joh Fraerey, Joseph Kingsberey, Willm Bullard, Joh. Eaton, Rich. Euered, Nath: Coaleburne, Robt Mason, Joh. Gaye, Henry Smyth, Serg^t. Dan: Fisher, Serg^t George Fayerbank, Joh: Morse, Edw: Richards, Willm Auerey, Lamb: Generey, Christo: Smyth, James Jordan, Nath. Whiteing, Mich: Metcalf Juni, Joh: Fayerbank, Samll Judson, Tho: Hering, Rich. Wheeler, Joh. Farington, Joh. Aldus, Tho: Fuller, Tho: Payne, Robt Ware, Antho: Fisher Junio, Thwa: Strickland, Robt Fuller, Nath. Fisher, Tho. Batteley, Tho Jordan, Joh Metcalfe, Joh. Guilde, Andrew Duein, Antho: Hubert, Joh. Mason, Joh. Plimpton, Ralph Daye, Hen. Willson, Tho: Bancroft, Joh. Bacon, Edw. Hawes, Henry Glouer, Josh. Kent, Rich. Ellice, Robt Onion, Samll Milles, Timo. Dwight, [*Andr Duein] Josep. Ellice, Ralp Freeman, Joh. Rice, Dan: Ponde, Hen Wight, Cornll Fisher, [*Robert Crossman], Jonath Farba: Ju, Ja. Vales, Joh Houghton, Ja Draper, Ja Thorpe, Jsa. Bullard

Considerations to be pposed at the genrall Meeteing

1. consideration w^t supply of firewood may be safe for ye Town. whether to lay out wood Lotts. or giue larger Libertie of felling wood

DEDHAM TOWN RECORDS. 191

 2. that the time of Couen^t in ye schoole keepeing. being expired. w^t may be the resolution of ye Town therein.
 3. w^t may be done for the supply of swampe to those Inhabitants whose deuision lay in that wch Cambridg now posesse & those whose Lotts. being drawen & the Rate being the rule of thier pportion is lost allso
 4. whether no meanes can be found to p^{r}uent damage by horses. &c: in ye Great playne most especially. & other comon fields allso
 5. w^t the select men may doe. wn they cannot attayne paye suitable to defray the necessary charges of ye Town
 6. a Motion about ye drye heard
 7. whether the Meetinghouse shall be couered wth shingle or not
 8. whether we shall call for pay from Meadfield or how much & when
 9. whether it be not Just & reasonable to allow the select men thier diet vpon the Just occasions of the Townes seruice in Town meeting Dayes & allso allow equall recompence for the time our Deputies shall expend in ye countrey seruice heere after

 Accounts to be p^{r}sented at ye genrall Meeting

Recd from Meadfield in pt of ye 20£ demanded from thence	10— 1— 0
from Mrs Stoughton	9— 8— 0
fro Joh Morse	6—15— 7
Recd by an ouerplusse in ye Countrey Rate	3— 0— 6
	29— 5— 1
Disbursm^{ts}. for ye Bell & the cariage of ye corne for ye paym^t	6— 0— 0
for building the schoole house chimney	3— 0— 0
to m^r Haynes	1— 4— 0
for Boarde. nayles schoole house &c:	1— 8— 0
to Lieft Fisher for measuering & seuerall Journeyes at ye Townes apointm^t	2—14— 7
charges at ye last genrall meeting	1— 2—[ ]
more for diet for ye select men & for the Arbitrators chosen to settle the purchased Lands & about the question concerning ye mille & the constable in makeing the Countrey Rate. and other disbursements for the Towne as apeere by his bill	3— 4— 8
[*To Eleazer Lusher for composeing & entering the table in the booke of Record. & new draweing & entering the Towne orders. & for seuerall Journeyes at the Townes assignm^t	2—19— 9
To Serg^t Dan: Fisher for diuers dayes Journeyes & other occasions of attending at ye townes assignm^t	1—13— 6]
To Joh Dwight for seuerall Journeyes: draweing timber & disbursem^{ts} for ye towne	1—14— 4

192   DEDHAM TOWN RECORDS.

 To Fra Chickering for nayles & Journeys   0—16— 3
 Besids these. p^d to seuerall other men for Journeyes. & other publike occasions we haue allowed. as vpon thier Bills to vs haue apeered Just & reasonable
vncertaine sume   25—12— 9
[*m^rd that Ralph Daye owe mor in ye Countrey Rate then is therin assessed   0— 1— 4]
 seuerall other Accounts by Reckoning will be due to seuerall men who haueing notice of our meeteing yet not apeereing it must be left to the care of ye next men chosen

 [*whereas ther remayne tenn shillings yet due to Joh. Kingsberey for that wheat he lent ye towne the Constable is assigned to sattisfie him that Tenn shillings out of ye ouerplusse of the Countrey Rate]

 Due to Willm Auerey for nayles for ye Schoole house as apeere by his Bill: 0—17—3

 Joh. Plimpton is assigned to pay to Lieft Fisher for Robt Hinsdell   1— 0—0

 Thwaits Strickland & Nath: Fisher ar assigned to pay that 1£—16^s that is in thier hand from meadfield Rate vnto Lieft Fisher   1—16—0

 all these assignm^ts to Lieft Fisher being p^d. he is debtor to ye Town   0—10—0

 more questions to pposed
 10. whether succession in Lands by purchase make the purchasers to be Townsemen or not
 11. w^t way the questions by Meadfield men in refference to the charge of purchaseing Amunition for a Town stock shall be issued

 At a Genrall Meeteing 1651 ye first of the eleuenth mo: called Januarie

voate   The question concerning the right of heyers or purchasers to all Town p^ruelidges. & Right of voateing in all cases together wth other Townsemen is referred to ye Selectmen now to be chosen. that they may p^rpare & ripen the answer & comend it to the Townes resolution

 Tymo: Dwight, Andr: Duein, Josep. Ellice, Ralph. Freeman, John: Rice, Dan: Ponde ar admitted Townesmen

voate   It is resolued not to deuide woodland into ppriaties for firewood. and the care of ordering the cutting of firewood is left to ye select men for ye yeare ensueing

voate   Its Resolued that a Schoole for the education of youth shall be continued & mayntayned in our Towne

DEDHAM TOWN RECORDS. 193

voate   its resolued that som settled way of the maintenance of the Schoole shall be agreed vpon.

voate   its ordered that 20£ a yeare at the least shall be the settled recompence of the schoolem^r for 7 yeares next ensueing

the 5 men heerevnder named ar chosen to ripen this case of rayseing 20£ p añ for the schoolem^r. and ppose thier thoughts to ye Towne Elder Joh. Hunting, Fra: Chickering, Joh Dwight, Lieft Fisher, Nath Coaleburne

the sattisfaction of those men that ar disapointed of swampe in Cambridg swampe is left to ye care of ye selectmen for ye yeare ensueing to be made either in vpland in the next deuident or in swampe as they can best agree wth the psons and can best make supplye

the damage done by horses & other vnruely cattell in Comon Fields is left to be recouered in a due course of Lawe

It is resolued to raise a Town stock of 20£ by that paym^t due from Meadfield & so to vphold this stock by suppies in our Towne. from time to time. the publike stock to be raised this yeare

the care of a drye heard is left to the select men for ye yeare ensueing

the meeteinghouse shall be couered wth shingle

its concluded that meadfield can make no iust clayme to any pt of the stock of Amuniton

its ordered that the select mens dyet vpon the Town meeteing dayes shall be payed for by the Town from time to time heereafter

Its ordered that those that shalbe heerafter chosen deputies for the genrall court shall be alowed for thier time. the sum & the manner is left to the select men to resolue & settle

Elections.

{ Eleazer Lusher is chosen to keepe the booke
  Lieft Fisher, Fra Chickering, Joh. Kingsbery, Joh. Dwight. Serg^t
  Fisher, Pet. Woodward, ar chosen select men for the yeare ensueing

Antho. Fisher Ju, Joseph Kingsbery, Andr Duein, Surveyors

Joh Morse, Tho: Fuller, Nath. Coaleburne, Mich. Metcalf Ju, Woodreeues

The Accounts of ye Select men for the yeare last past ar alowed of by the Towne

5 of ye 11: mo. 1651 Assemb: Joh Kingsberey, Lieft. Fisher, Fra. Chickering, Joh. Dwight, Serg^t. Fisher, & Eleazer Lusher

vpon examination of ye Surveyers Bill for ye yeare 1650. ther apeere yet to be due to the Towne for defect of the high way worke of that yeare from the psons heere vnder named as followeth

Robt Mason	0 6 8	Sergt Barber	0 5 0
Lamb Generey	0 [ ] 0	Robt Onion	0 1 6
Deacon Aldus	0 3 8	Josep. Clarke	0 3 8

194   DEDHAM TOWN RECORDS.

Mr Wheelock		0	3	8	Edw Richards	0 3 4
Tho. Bately		0	3	8	Joh Haward	0 5 0
Joh. Fraerey		0	[ ]	[ ]	Sam: Judson	0 1 8
Mich: Metcalfe senjor		0	1	8	Joh. Bacon	0 1 8
						3 0 10

A bill to be drawn to send to Joh Bullard to demand 10^s for ye vse of halfe the Meadowe called the Church Meadow one yeare — he haueing pformed. none of ye condicions wherevpon he entered the said meadowe

vvate: Joh. Dwight, Fra: Chickering & Elea. Lusher ar Deputed to settle the way leading vnto the wigwam playne & thorough the same vnto the swampe as pticular ppryaties may necessarily require. & to sattisfie for the land layed out for ye waye by land vpon the said playne. as they shall iudge equall & most conueanient

Granted vnto John Rice and to his heyers for euer. one pcell of vpland lyeing neere the ponde. as it shall be layed out to him by the direction of Serg^t Fisher & Eleazer Lusher

6. of ye 11 mo. 1651. Assemb. Joh. Kingsberey, Joh. Dwight, Fra: Chickering, Lieft: Fisher, Pet Woodward, Serg^t Fisher & Elea: Lusher

20£ p añ for ye schoole for ye schoole

The rule of rayseing 20£ p añn this day considered and resolued

Elnathan Dunkely & Matthewe Edwards being sumoned apeere this daye befor ye select men

Robt Mason & Joh. Mason for former defect in thier high way worke vndertake to paye in shingling ye meeteinghouse when the Town call for it

0—16—8

Antho: Fisher Juni. being assigned by Robt Hinsdell to pay vpon his account for m^r Stoughtons Rent. 15^s he vndertakes to paye it & is assigned to paye this 15^s & 9^s mor for gdm Rockwood of Meadfield wch is to pay for him. to Ralph Daye. 1—4—9

12 of ye 11 mo. 1651 Assemb: Joh Dwight, Lieft Fisher, Pet: Woodward, Serg^t Fisher, Joh. Kingsberey, & Elea: Lusher

Tho. Payne. coming to cleere vp that he haue pformed 3 daye worke in the high waye the last yeare. its resolued that if he can make it apeere to the Surveyers. that they may testifie it to any of ye Select men. that then except he heare from ye select men further demaund of worke he shall take himselfe discharged therof

Nath Whiteing is to paye for not apearing at the generall Towne Meeteing 0—1—6

assigned to pay it to Joh Dwight

Joh Haward is assigned to paye to Lieft Fisher for defect in high way worke 0—13—0

Henry Smyth is assigned to pay out of Meadfield Rate vnto Tho: Batteley in pt for shingling ye Schoolehouse   1—18—7

vpon information that our Bretheren of Meadfield haue declared themselues grieued that our Town haue haue resolued to call for 20£ from thence. & that they haue declared a purpose not to paye till it be cleered whether any be oweing to Dedh or not its therfor concluded to write a letter to send to the Inhabitants & Select men of Meadfield to desire a loueing treatie wth som of them such as the Towne or select men shall send. Eleazer Lusher is desired to drawe vp this letter

Samll Judson is assigned to paye to Lieft Fisher for his defect in high waye worke 1650   0—1—8

Lieft Fisher is deputed together wth Nathan Aldus & Joseph Kingsbery to agree about a Leading waye to the Meadow of Joseph Kingsbery thorough the vpland of Nathan Aldus: & to return answer to ye Select men

Joseph Kingsberey inform that Lambert Generey hath taken shingle Timber & oakeing Timber. wthout leaue from the Towne. its resolued that Br Generey shall be called to the next Town meeteing. by warneing by Lieft Fisher

Tho. Batteley haueing taken building & shingle timber wthout Leaue. its to be considered of heereafter. he answers he thought building Timber had bene at libertie in comon

Elnathan Dunckley is according to ye Court order in that case provided. placed in seruice for one whole yeare next ensueing to dwell wth Anthoney Fisher senior. and the said Anthoney Fisher doth couenant & agree to pay to the said Elnathan or his assignes the sum of 9£ for ye yeares seruice. vizt 2£. 5^s each quarter of ye yeare

John Bullard is assigned to paye to Joh: Dwight that debt due to the Towne by his rate in Meadfield & that due for the yeares rent for the meadowe. the whole   1£—0—0

Joseph Clarke is assigned to paye to Danll Ponde 12^s due from him selfe in pt for defect in high waye worke. & in pt from meadfield Rate   0—12—0

13 of 11. 1651 Assemb. Joh: Dwight, Lieft Fisher, Pet: Woodward, Serg^t. Fisher, & Elea: Lusher, Joh: Kingsbery

voate Whereas it apeare vpon experience that such firewood as hath hetherto bene alowed to be made vse of as in comon libertie to each of our Inhabitants is now much spent and therefor for ye more conueanient supply of the Towne more libertie is found necessarie. and that allso such care be taken to p^{r}serue such oake trees as at p^{r}sent ar: or hereafter ar like to be vsefull timber for supply of building fencing &c:

It is therfor ordered. that it shall be henceforth in ye libertie of euerey

Inhabitant in our Towne. from time to time. to take. fell & carry away any such firewood of the comon Land of the Towne as he or they shall neede from time for his own burning

pvided all wayes that they be such as by reason of the rottennes crookednes or other defect ar vnfitt for timber but if any man shall fell any such oake tree. or young oake stand or plant. as in a reasonable ap^{r}hension & Judgm^t. may apeere by this order. is truely & really intended to be p^{r}serued & that is not burnt at the bottom or stubb. or very crooked or defective as aboue said. shall forfiet 2^s. 6^d. for euery such tree so felled contrary to the true intent of this order except they haue leaue fre wood. the offence to be Judged of by thee woodreeues. the forfiet or penaltie to be the one halfe due to the informer & the other halfe to ye towne. and any order or clause or pvisoe in any former order to the contrary. is heereby repealed

pvided allso that if any Inhabitant shall fell firewood & suffer it to lye vncutt or vnsett vp 14 dayes after it be felled it shall be in the libertie of any other Inhabitant to take it & cary it away

17 of ye 11 mo 1651. Assemb. Joh Kingsberey, Joh. Dwight, Fra: Chickering, Lieft Fisher, Pet. Woodward, Serg^t Fisher & Elea: Lusher

We conceaue it safe that all such Inhabitants in our Towne from time to time. as doe not subscribe to ye Towne Booke and thereby declare his engagement to subiect to ye gouerm^t of ye Towne & beare pportionable charges therein &c: according to the Couenant whervnto we haue genrally subscribed shall be debarred all Libertie of cutting firewood or hearding Cattell in ye Comon Land of ye Towne. except such as shall by inheritance posesse any one house Lott all ready built whose p^{r}decessors haue formerly subscribed pvided that the libertie & power of ye Towne exp^{r}ssed in ye 2 Article of ye Couenant be not heereby p^{r}iudiced but remayne in full force

pvided allso that the select men for ye time being shall haue power to alowe libertie. to make vse of the Comon p^{r}uelidges before exp^{r}ssed to any Inhabitant vntill he haue an optunitie to subscribe & is by the Towne admitted there vnto

vpon ye motion from ye Selectmen of Dorchester desireing a meeteing to consider a way to take wolues Lieft Fisher & Elea: Lusher ar deputed to attend therevpon

Joh. Fraerey is allowed 6^s for that charge he was occasioned to be at concerning the woman & childeren that cam thorough the Towne & stayed diuers dayes in the Towne at his house he being Constable: & went to Seaconque. this 6^s is discounted in his defect of high way worke 1650

Agreed wth Lieft Fisher. that he shall shingle the meetinghouse and doe all the worke & beare all the charge thereof that is the takeing of of the old couereing & make the spares feite & set them on. lay on the board shingle &

flewe boards at one end & one pyramedy at ye south end and shingle the penthouse ouer the Bell the Town onely to beare the charge of all the Iron nayles therein necessary and all this to be pformed sufficiently before ye 24 of ye 4 mo: next. 1652

for all which he is to receaue of the Towne in such paye as by Rate will arise. the sum of 15£—0—0

30 of 11 1651 Assemb. Joh. Kingsbery, Joh: Dwight, Fra: Chickering, Lieft Fisher, Pet: Woodward, Danll Fisher & Eleazer. Lusher in answer to our former letter to Meadfield S^{r}g^t Geo: Barber & Serg^t Hen: Adams ar sent by the Towne of Meadfield to treate.

the grieuances of Meadfield ar

1 that the voate of grant of ye 3 pt of ye meadow ptly by sale & pt by gift is so altered that those y^t would giue thier pts now cannot

2 that ther is not so much loue from Dedh as they expected apeere in demanding 20£ at this time

3 in that it is demanded for ye raysing a towne stock. it being pmised to be for borne as long as the occasions of Dedh could admitt

vnto all wch pticulars this answer is giuen

1 the Town of Dedh will make good any regular voate passed to that end. & to that end desire that in the first conueanient time: consideration may be had to giue a full issue therein wherein if it cannot be sattisfactorily composed betwixt our Bretheren of meadfield & our selues we shall yeld to a free & indifferent refference. & engage to make thier conclusion good

2 we shall willingly attend w^t reasons and desires of forbeareance may by our Bretheren of meadfield be pposed. & p^{r}sent them to our Town & pmote them to attayne forbeareance in thier behalfe. so fare as the weight of thier reasons may extend

3 this 20£ is reffered to the vse of a Town stock rather then for p^{r}sent vse meerely out of respect to meadfield to ease them both in matter & time of paym^t

wth wch answers the foresaid Bretheren declare them selues in the name of the Town of meadfield. to rest sattisfied.

3 of 12 51: Assemb. Joh. Kingsbery, Joh. Dwight, Fra: Chickering, Lieft: Fisher, Pet: Woodward, Serg^t. Fisher, & Elea: Lusher

voate Antho: Fisher Ju., Joh Fayerbanke, Rich. Ellice, Jonath. Fayerbank ar by the Towne deputed to attend vpon the worke of takeing wolues & ar apointed to receaue tenn shillings for each wolfe they shall kill. aboue w^t the Court order doe apoint & pvide. pvided that the said wolues may be made apeare to be killed wthin 3 miles of the meetinghouse of Dorchester Roxbery. Dedham or Braintree

the Town Rate

Mr Joh. Allen	01	09	02	Mich Metcalfe Ju	00	06	10
Eld Joh Hunting	00	07	06	Joh. Fayerbanke	00	03	04
Elea: Lusher	00	18	06	Sam Judson	00	06	06
Deac. Chickering	00	18	10	Tho. Hering	00	09	04
Deac Aldus	00	08	02	Rich Wheeler	00	10	01
Joh Kingsbery	00	19	06	Joh Farington	00	11	04
Mich Metcalf seni	00	13	10	Tho: Fuller	00	12	01
Josh. Fisher seni	00	04	00	Joh Aldus	00	07	10
Sam Morse	00	05	04	Tho Payne	00	05	08
Joh. Luson	00	11	04	Robt Ware	00	11	06
Hen. Brocke	00	10	07	Antho. Fisher Ju	00	04	10
Antho. Fisher seni	01	01	04	Thw Strickland	00	06	07
Joh Dwight	01	06	10	Robt Fuller	00	07	01
Fra. Chickering	00	17	03	Nath. Fisher	00	08	10
Joh Haward	00	15	00	Tho. Battelly	00	08	04
Tho. Wight	00	12	02	Tho Jordan	00	07	06
Lieft Fisher	00	15	07	Joh. Metcalfe	00	06	00
Ens. Philips	00	16	04	Joh. Guilde	00	02	02
Jonath Fayerbanke	00	15	00	Andr Duein	00	08	04
Pet. Woodward	00	19	04	Antho. Hubert	00	06	08
Joh. Fraery	00	05	08	Joh. Mason	00	03	10
Josep. Kingsbery	00	18	06	Joh. Plimpton	00	02	08
Willm Bullard	01	00	00	Ralp Daye	00	03	07
Joh. Eaton	00	15	00	Hen: Willson	00	06	08
Rich Euerel	00	10	00	Tho. Bancroft	00	06[5]	04[7]
Nath Coaleburn	00	16	04	Joh. Bacon	00	07	00
Robt Mason	00	10	07	Ed. Hawes	00	04	10
Joh. Gaye	00	12	00	Hen Glouer	00	03	06
Hen. Smyth	00	06	02	Josh. Kent	00	02	04
Serg^t Fisher	00	11	09	Rich Ellice	00	02	06
Serg^t Fayerbanke	00	02	05	Robt Onion	00	01	10
Joh. Morse	00	07	00	Sam: Milles	00	09	04
Edward Richards	00	16	08	Ralp Freeman	00	01	07
Willm Auery	00	05	06	Josep Ellice	00	00	04
Lamb. Genery	00	12	10	Tho Ellice	00	01	03
Christo. Smyth	00	06	00	Robt Crosseman	00	01	01
Jam. Jordan	00	00	10	Dan Ponde	00	03	04
Nath. Whiteing	00	11	02		35—04—00		

· It is agreed that the charge of pvideing a habitation for the heards man. & the fenceing of ye yard for the drye heard. and such other publike charges thereabout as ar of the like publike concernm^t. shall be defrayed & borne by the Towne Rate

Antho Fisher seni. Ensign Phillips and John Gaye ar appointed and deputed to take care for and pforme all such things as ar yet necessary for the furthering of the drye heard vizt to pvide & agree wth a heardsman and make som habitation for the heards man. & fence in a conueanient yarde for the heard. the charge wherof is to be borne by the Town as is before pvided

Tho. Battely is appointed to pay 8^s to the vse of ye Towne for that breach of order in felling ceader & oake timber wthout Leaue from ye Town or ye woudieeues

16 of ye 12 51 Assemb. Joh. Kingsbery, Joh. Dwight, Lieft. Fisher, Pet: Woodward, Serg^t Fisher, & Elea. Lusher, Fra: Chickering

voate Fra: Chickerg is fined one quart of saick for late coming this daye

meadfield giuing notice that they haue chosen 3 men to attend our Towne for resolution of ye sum of debt yet behinde due to this Towne: its taken into consideration

Resolued that all the Inhabitants of this Towne shall haue notice giuen them forth wth before the next Lecture daye that they may then attend to declare w^t day they will meet to Resolue wth meadfield men or w^t way they shall chuse to Issue that case

The State of ye question

1 we conclude that the first voate of the Towne in puting the question. who would giue thier pt of ye 3 part of ye meadowe to Meadfield is direcly null by reason the voat of the Town declareing that they would not giue thier pt was equall in number and power. whence we resolue. no man is bound to giue his pt or any pt thereof by vertue of that voate

2 we conceaue that the voate of the Town being the onely voate in force was that Meadfield should haue that Land ptly by gift. & ptly by sale. the Town is therby engaged as a Town to giue som pt (lesse or more) of that 100£ wch was the price of the meadowe in question

3 we conceaue it yet to be in the libertie of any Inhabitant of our Towne. to giue w^t he please to Meadfield (puided it be out of his own estate) wherein we ar vnwilling any man should be hindered

4 we conceaue vpon all the p^{r}mises being considered that if the Town should demand & receaue of Meadfield 60£ in 3 yeares next ensueing. or 50£ to be payed in merchantible paym^t wthin the space of one whole yeare next. the Town of Dedh shall at full make good any Regular voate passed in this case & shewe our Loveing respect to our Br^t of Meadfield

5 we conceaue it necessary that the Town should resolue & declare whether they will Joyntly attend at some day apointed to answer such as

shall be sent from Meadfield or leaue it to som pticular psons whom they shall entrust & Authorise there vnto

Granted to Francis Chickering and his heyers for euer 12 Acres of vpland w[ch] he accepts in full sattisfaction for that 6 acres of meadowe wherof he was disposessed by Cambridge bounds. this 12 acres is to be layed out vpon that playne wher Jonath Fayerbanke haue Land layed out at the direction of Lieft Fisher, Joh. Dwight, Pet. Woodward

Lieft Fisher is deputed to asist in the reneweing the Lines & marks of the swampe of Tho: Batteley & Eleaz. Lusher. according to the grants

Lieft Fisher is deputed to treat and conclude wth som workeman for y[e] repayring the pounde

the Clerke of y[e] writts is requested to newe drawe the Regester & place each pticular in the yeare whervnto the same pply belonge. for w[ch] he is to receaue of y[e] Town 2[s]—6[d] y[e] daye for the whole time he is in y[e] pformance there of

26 of y[e] 12 mo. 1651. Assemb: Joh: Kingsbery, Joh. Dwight, Fra: Chickering, Lieft: Fisher, Pet: Woodward, Serg[t]: Fisher, & Elea: Lusher

Ed Coluer pmise to passe that pcell beyond Serg[t] Danll Fisher (that was somtimes vpon purchase. posessed by Jos. Kent) to Danll Fisher aforesaid & subscribe a deed thereof to him. & Josh: Kent allso consent therto & pmise to subscribe the said deed as wittnes

Elea. Lusher vndertakes to doe w[t] is yet more to be done to compleat the hanging of the bell & the mending the hanging of y[e] 3 doores & help one day about the hanging the bell higher

[*A Bill is deliuered to Lieft Fisher to receaue 20£ of the Constables out of the p[r]sent Town Rate]

the Inhabitants of Meadfield haueing chosen 3 of thier freemen to attend a treatie w[th] y[e] Select men of Dedham. for the resolueing w[t] was necessary concerning the debt due from Meadfield to Dedh [*Twoo of] the said 3 men apeereing [*and engageing themselues that thier Town shall confirme w[t] so euer themselues shall conclud w[th] our selues in the case p[r]mised] that case is taken into consideration

The psons sent ar Robt Hinsdell, Hen: Adams, Geo: Barber w[th] whome it is concluded vpon thier earnest request in consideration of thier many and great Charges lyeing vpon thier Towne and other like considerations. that they shall paye or cause to payed to our Town or thier Assignes the whole & full summ of fiftie poundes besids the first Twentie. that is to saye Twentie pounds w[th]in the space of one whole yeare next after this daye and Thirtye pounds more within the space of Twoo years after this p[r]sent daye. & both these sums ar pmised to be payed in such paym[t] as much as may be. as may suite our Towns occasion so 30£. of y[e] 100£ is remitted which payments being made as before saide the Towne of Meadfield is fully and for euer discharged of that 100£ agreed to be p^d to Dedham from thence for the third pt of the Meadowe wch was granted being intended by som to be freely giuen & by others. to be sold

Its ordered that euery deputie who euer shall henceforth be chosen to attend the seruice of ye Genrall Courte shall haue 3£ for that seruice. ꝓvided that he attend the whole seruice of the Court so that another be not occasioned to be chosen to supplye his deffect in any pt of that yeare. to be p^d out of the Towne Rate

Deputed to burne the woods for ye lland Tho: Fuller, for ye East street Rich: Ellice and Mich: Metcalf Ju, for ye midle & smooth playnes Joh. Rice Ed. Hawes

Joh. Dwight. Lieft Fisher. Ensign Phillips and Serg^t Fisher. ar deputed and Authorised. to ioyne wth Elea: Lusher. to settle and laye out the grant of a Farme at or neere Bogastowe. made to m^r Ed Aleyn by the Towne of Dedh as by the Record in that Towne book may more fully apeare. wch grante is to be layed out. as to ye major pt of those men aboue named shall apeare most meete

Willm Bullard is assigned to pay to Danll Ponde 2 bushels of wheat out of his Town Rate

Fra: Chickering & Serg^t Fisher ar deputed to take care to call in pay & satisfie the Carpenter of Boston. they to take 20^s—7^d of Joh Morse. of old debt

Granted to Rich. Wheeler one parcell of vpland. being about 1 acre more or lesse as it lyeth vpon the south & west side of his house Lott a high way to the swampe reserued

Joh Kingsbery, Lieft Fisher, Joh Haward, Joh Gaye, or any 3 of them ar deputed and authorised to laye out a waye as shall apeere to them most fitt and necessary that may leade from this Towne toward Sudbury the dry hearde place or Rosemary meadowes

Granted to Francis Chickering and his heyers libertie to take in so much of the waste Land as shall be necessary for the shorteing. or streighteing his fence at the Rock meadowe

Lieft Fisher is chosen. deputed and Authorised to keepe the pounde. to receaue detayne. and deliuer all cattell impounded according to ye Lawe in that case ꝓvided

17 of 3 mo: 1652 Assemb. Fra: Chickering, Lieft Fisher, Pet: Woodward, Serg^t. Fisher, & Elea: Lusher

Granted vnto Antho: Fisher senio: 4 Acres of vpland as pt of his deuident in the next deuident now forth wth to be layed out ꝓvided that his ꝑportion com to so much: if not then so much is to be abated in the deuident due to Daniell Fisher according to pportion. this is to be layed out vpon the north side of the great playne. at the discretion of Lieft Fisher & Josep. Kingsbery.

Sergean^t Daniell Fisher demanding satisfac͞ for the pt of the ponde by him layed down to the vse of the Towne. vpon Composition and 2 Indifferent men according to that agreem^t being to resolue the quantitie. Joseph Kingsbery is chosen in the behalfe of the Towne & Lieft Fisher is chosen by Dan. Fisher to laye out the same according to what they shall Judge equall at the north side of the great playne

Tho Bancroft is abated 9^d. in ye Town rate. it being so much mistaken

Concerning the Schoole. these ppositions ar to be tendered to the consideration of the Towne for the mayntayning therof for 7 yeares

1 that all such Inhabitants in our Towne as haue Male children or seruants in thier families betwixt the age of 4. and 14 yeares. shall paye for each such to the Schoolem^r. for the time being or to his vse at his assignment in Towne in Currant payement the sum͞e of 5^s yearely pvided that such children be then liueing and abideing in our Towne

2 And w^t so euer these sum͞es fall short of the sum͞e of Twentie £ shall be raised by waye of Rateing vpon estates. according to the vsuall manner

3 that these sum͞es shall be payed in 2 equall sum͞es at the end of each half yeare for the space of 7 yeares next ensueing.

to be pposed whether the Town require that girls should be taught in this Schoole or not:

Lieft Fisher & Serg^t Fisher ar deputed to take in the accounts of the Meadfield Rate of Henery Smith. that w^t so euer is yet due from thence may be called for Town vse

Bills sent to the Constable to paye out of the Towne Rate

[*To Antho: Fisher seni   3— 9—6
    Joh. Gaye   1— 6—6
    Ens. Philips   0—19—0
    to them that killed one wolfe   1—10—0
                                           7— 5—0
more
    to be p^d to Danll Ponde   3— 0—0
    to the Carpenter of Boston   3—10—0]

Lieft Fisher & Fra: Chickering vpon request vndertake to pcure nayles for ye meeteinghouse vse

John Haward: Serg^t Fisher & Henry Wight ar deputed in the behalfe of our Towne to asist in the layeing out of the waye to Sudbury the first daye of ye 4 mo: or w^t day else shall be agreed vpon by them that shall be concerned ther in

John Dwight. Fra: Chickering & Serg^t Fisher ar deputed to Joyne wth

such men of Roxbury. Cambridg & Watertowne as shall be apointed to laye out the waye betwixt watertown. & Dedham

Pet: Woodward. Rich Euered. & Rich Wheeler ar deputed to Joyne wth such as ar concerned therein. to laye out the waye from Dedham to Brayntree vpon the Request of Joh. Gaye. Libertie is granted to him to enclose and empue the Land left for a waye to the Lott som times Granted to m^r Edward Alleyne pvided that if wthin the tearme of seauen yeares the said Lott be built & dwelt vpon at that vpper end that then vpon demaunde made by the select men for the time being a conueanient passage to the said Lott be then layed out neere there about agayne. wher the Town shall require it this way is that wch passe by Joh Gayes Barne doore. & to be enclosed the breadth of his own house Lott if he se cause and no further

3 of ye 7 mo: 1652 Assemb. Joh. Kingsbery, Joh. Dwight, Fra: Chickering, Lieft: Fisher, Pet: Woodward, Serg^t Fisher, & Elea: Lusher

Rich. Euerd & Ed Richards Constables thier account. Disbursed by them out of ye Town Rate of 35: 4^s as followeth, by bill from ye selectmen

pd to ther Carpenter of Boston	0	7	6	to Dan Pond by W Bullard	1	0	0
to them that killed the wolfe	1	10	0	to the treasurer for the }			
to ens. Phillips	0	6	0	Court orders 1650 }	0	6	8
to Joh. Gaye	1	6	6	to Serg^t Fisher	2	12	0
to Elea. Lusher	0	18	6	more discounted by mistake		1	8
to Anth Fisher sen	3	9	6				
to Leift Fisher	20	0	0		33	1	6
to treas: for Country orders	0	10	4	more to HenryChickerng 2^s }			
to Joh Kingsbery. being borrowed	0	10	0	more to Henry Phillips 10^s }	4		
to the vse of ye Town by Na Coaleburne	0	12	0		£ 34:	s 2	–0

Joseph Kingsbery & Antho: Fisher Jun being Surveyors. thier account: psons deffectiue in thier high way worke. 1652

	s		
Ralph. Daye	8	Nath. Whiteing	2
Robt Crosseman		Tho. Jordan	0
Josh. Kent		Ralph Freeman	0
Hen Smyth	4	Robt Onion	2
Micha: Metcalfe		Robert Fuller	4
Tho. Hering	4	Antho: Hubbert payed 4^s	8

the Surveyors vndertake to call these to doe worke in the high worke according to order. & giue account to the select men vpon demande

mrd that in the Countrey Rate remayne due to ye Town   0—5—0

27 of ye 10. 1652 Assemb. Joh. Kingsberye, Joh. Dwight, Lieft: Fisher, Fra. Chickering, Pet. Woodward, Serg^t Fisher, & Elea: Lusher

Nath Coaleburne coming & demanding sattisfaction for that meadowe at Balepate that he is disposessed of. its agreed that it be Reffered to 2 men chosen one by the Towne and another chosen by the said Nathaneell to whose determination the Towne & he pmise to stand satisfied

Joh Dwight chosen by the Towne
Serg^t Fisher chosen by Nath. Coaleburne
this meadow to be allowed in sattisfaction is to be layed out neere Meadfield

Joh Partridg com to demande 5^s disbursed by him for board for the heardhouse & 2^s for 1 daye for burning the ground wch account is alowed of & paym^t pmised   0—7—0

A full discharge is this day giuen to John Morse of all accounts debts & reckonings formerly depending betwixt the Towne & himselfe wherein he haue bene any way debter to the Towne

vott   vpon the request of John Dwight for sattisfaction for the swamp belongine to Tho: Ledors lott that was takin a way by Cambridge it is granted that he shall be sattisfyed vpon the swamp plaine as it shall be layed out by Jonath: Fayrb: sen & Petter Wodward

vott   vpon the request of Fran: Chickring for sattisfaction of the swamp du to hime that was takin a way by Cambridge it is granted that he shall bee sattisfyed for the same vpon the plaine called will Bastows plaine his sattisfaction to be left to the descretion of Petter Woodward & Joshua Fisher

28 of ye 10 mo 1652 Assemb. Lieft Fisher, Fra. Chickering, Joh Dwight, Pet. Woodward, Serg^t Fisher, & Elea: Lusher, Joh Kingsbery

being mett to make the Towne Rate

† Deed to make frō Tho Wight to Hen Wight of 2 acres on smooth playne abutts Antho Fisher sen east Tho Wight west & north the high way south

† & of ye pcell 30. 5... and of 6 acres 20 pole great playne: abutts Eli Lusher east Tho Wight West highway north waste Land south.

† Deed to make frō Tho Wight to Joh Wight of 3 acrs 60 pole great plaine. abutts Hen Wight east Joh eaton west high way north. waste Land south

† Deed to make frō Hen Brock to Robt Crosseman of 2 acr vpland more or lesse. abutts Na. Colburne southeast. high street north. high way leading to ye pond. west. lyeing trayanglewise the point stretching east

† Deed to make frō Ro. Crossem̄ to Josh Kent half acre vpland more

DEDHAM TOWN RECORDS. 205

or lesse. abutts Na. Coalburne south east. high street north Ro Crossem west. trayanglewise ye point stretching east
   † Deed to make to Joh Aldus of that pcell page 71.6. fro Hen Glouer Deed to make fro Tho Bancroft to Hen Wilson of 4 Acr ½ mead page 32.5 and 3 Acr ½ mead 58. 7. and that 3 acr vpl. 52. 1—and 6 acr vpland 18—7. and that 32. 7. and that vpland 59. 13.

The Towne Rate at 1^d y^e [ ] com to 17£—2—3

m^r Joh. Allen	00	14	11	Sam: Judson	00 05 03	
Eld^r Joh Hunting	00	06	06	Tho. Herring	00 05 00	
Elea: Lusher	00	09	09	Rich Wheeler	00 04 05	
Deac. Hen Chickering	00	09	01	Joh. Farrington.	00 06 01	
Deac. Nath Aldus	00	03	11	Joh. Aldus	00 04 01	
Joh Kingsbery	00	09	03	Tho. Fuller	00 05 01	
Mich Metcalfe sen	00	06	08	Tho. Payne	00 02 10	
Sam: Morse	00	01	10	Robt Ware	00 04 0	
Joh: Luson	00	05	09	Antho. Fisher Ju	00 03	
Anth: Fisher sen	00	09	10	Josh Fisher seni	00 02 01	
Joh. Dwight	00	14	06	Thwai Strickland	00 02 04	
Fra: Chickering	00	08	01	Robt Fuller	00 03 11	
Joh. Haward	00	06	06	Nath. Fisher	00 03 03	
Lieft Josh Fisher	00	08	00	Tho: Battaille	00 05 10	
Ens: Hen. Phillips	00	07	10	Tho Jordan	00 03 10	
Jonath Fayerbanke	00	06	09	Joh. Guilde	00 01 06	
Pet. Woodward	00	08	04	Andr. Duein	00 04 03	
Joh. Fraerey	00	06	03	Antho Hubert	00 04 11	
Josep. Kingsberey	00	08	00	Joh. Mason	00 07 11	
Joh. Eaton	00	05	08	Ralph. Daye	00 02 00	
Rich. Euered	00	06	09	Hen Wilson	00 04 05	
Nath. Coaleburne	00	07	00	Hen. Wight	00 07 09	
Robt Mason				Joh. Bacon	00 04 07	
Joh. Gaye	00	05	10	Isaac. Bullard	00 08 05	
Hen. Smyth	00	03	09	Edw. Hawes	00 02 08	
Srg^t Dan: Fisher	00	06	02	Josh Kent	00 01 02	
Srg^t Geo Fayerbanke	00	01	09	Robert Onyon	00 00 11	
Joh. Morse	00	03	01	Sam. Milles	00 03 08	
Edw. Richards	00	07	02	Robt Crosseman	00 01 05	
Willm Auerey	00	03	06	Dan: Ponde	00 01 06	
Lamb: Generey	00	03	03	Rich Ellice	00 01 08	
Christo Smyth	00	03	09	Ralp. Freeman	00 00 05	
Jam Jordan				Cornelius Fisher	00 00 03	
Nath. Whiteing	00	06	00	Vid. Maplehead	00 00 05	
Mich. Metcalfe Ju	00	03	02	Joh. Metcalf	00 01 04	
Joh. Fayerbanke	00	01	06			

Brother Generey being called to make answer for takeing Timber contrary to towne order. he apeereing is respited till the select men call for him this to be informed to the select men the next yeare

Lieft Fisher & Serg^t Fisher ar deputed to joyne wth Eleazer Lusher to resolue w^t ought to be transcribed out of the daye booke into the booke of Recorde

[*Ralph Daye p^{r}sents a bill of 3^s—4 for makeing the chimney stocke at the heard house]

the Rate heere aboue written is deliuered to Richard Euered Constable p^d to Ensigne Phillips out of the Rates for Towne charges 18^s—2^d—being 10^s 4^d. out of the first Rate & 7^s—10^d out of the last Rate. so remayne due to him for his charge about the drye heard house & yard 10^d onely

more 6 was payd out of the first Rate so both the whole Rates ar discounted wth him

vpon reckoning wth John Dwight we finde due to him 13—6— for wch a bill is giuen him to receaue the same of the constable out of the last Rate

Eleazer Lusher p^{r}senting a bill of account whereby the Towne was indebted to him the sum of 4—13—7

Willm Auereys bill being by the Constable p^{r}sented of 1— 1—8
and another bill from the Secretary. of 1— 5—4
and another for killing 4 wolues. of 4— 0—0
and Frances Chickering p^{r}sents a bill of 1—19—4
and Joh. Dwight p^{r}sents a bill of 0—13—6
and Joh. Kingsbery p^{r}sents a bill of 1— 2—4

a bill to the Constable heerof. deliuered to Jo Kingsb:

all these bills are allowed of by the select men according as they wer p^{r}sented

14—15—9

14—15—9

[*Due from Thomas Battell vpon agrem^t for meadowe of the Townes this yeare 10^s

Thomas Battelly is assigned to pay that 18^s due from him to the Towne into the hand of Richard Euered Constable]

Reckoned wth Rich Euered Constable 30 of ye 10. mo. 1652 and vpon account remayne due to the Towne out of the 35£—4^s Rate

1£—9^s—6^d
more p^d 0 —7 —6
remayne due still 1 —2 —0
m^{rs} Stoughtons Rent demanded

Br.Woodward is desired to make damaunde of Joseph Morse of the Rent due to the Towne frō m^{rs} Stoughton for ye yeare 1652 2£—0 —0

[*a bill deliuered to Joh Gaye to receaue of the Constable 0 —6^s—0]

DEDHAM TOWN RECORDS. 207

The Accounts of the Rate made ye 3 of ye 12. mo. 1651: whereby was Leuied the sume of 35£ 2^s 4^d

Disbursem^ts

vnto the Carpenter of Boston in remaynder of payeing for the groundcelling the meetinghouse	00—07—06
It for the killing one wolfe	01—10—00
It to Ensig: Phillips in pt of his charge about the heard house	00—06—00
It. to Joh. Gaye for charge about the heard house	01—06—06
It. to Elea. Lusher for hanging the bell. writeing & seuerall Journeys at the Townes asignm^t	00—18—06
It to Antho Fisher sen: for charges about the heard yard & house &c.	03—09—06
It to Lieft Fisher. for couering the Meeteinghouse. nayles & other charges	20—00—00
It to the Treasurer for Countrey orders	00—10—04
It. to Joh. Kingsbery. being by him lent to the Towne [*a bill heereof to the Constable deliuered to him]	00—10—00
It. by Nath. Coaleburne for the Townes vse	00—12—00
It to Danll Ponde for worke at the meeteinghouse	01—00—00
It to the Treasurer for more court orders	00—06—08
It. to Serg^t Fisher in pt for the carp^tr & for seuerall Journeyes vpon the Townes assignm^t	02—02—00
It to Hen. Chickering being due	00—02—00
It more to Ens. Phillips for charge about ye heard yard	00—10—04
	34—02—[ ]
remayne of this Rate	01—00—[ ]
Debts due at p^rsent from the Towne as followeth	
Inp^rm^s to Joh Dwight for seuerall Journeyes &c:	00—13—06
It. to Elea: Lusher for the deputies Alowance & for seuerall Journeyes & writing	03—15—01
It. to Willm Auerey for nayles and other worke	01—01—08
It for Court orders due to the Treasurer	01—05—04
It for the killing 4 wolues	04—00—00
It to Francis Chickering for nayles &c:	01—19—04
It to Joh Kingsbery lent to the Towne for the purchaseing & carying corne for brick	01—02—02
a bill heere of to the constable deliuered to him	
It. to Josh. Fisher sen for Irons about the bell & som about the schoole house	01— 4— 2

It to Antho Fisher sen for helping to take a plott of the riuer 00—02—00
                                                                 ———————
                                                                  15— 1— 3
besides som other debts the accounts where of ar not yet p^rsented

[✕ ✕ ✕ *General Meeting of* 3: 11: 1652, *as recorded on page* 136.]

6. of ye 11. 1652. Assemb: Lieft Fisher, Joh. Dwight, Fra. Chickering, Pet: Woodward, Serg^t Fisher, & Elea. Lusher

the Case respecting the Ens. motions concerning the poulder. taken into consideration.

its answered thus that the Ensigne not auouching and signing his bill, doth disable all men except him selfe to gather vp the account & though we be vnwilling to put the ensign to so meane an employm^t yet we conceaue we haue no other way at all. but that he must gather it or else it must be lost and therfor we aduise that he will vse the best meanes & all lawefull meanes that he can to gather all the bill and then wn that is done if he please to make returne of the state of the case to the select men. they shall be ready to take it into further consideration: and giue w^t content to the said Ens: as they shall conceaue they may giue a good reason of

Hen. Chickering Antho Fisher sen & John Gaye this daye p^rsent themselues according to the choice & deputation of the Towne to Joyne wth the select men to consider & resolue of Instructions meet to be giuen to those 3 bretheren chosen & Authorised to attend the case depending betwixt vs & Dorchester doe wth them agree as followeth vizt:

1 in case Dorchester men shall consent to a loveing & free treatie betwixt them selues & you: you shall to them & in our name & behalfe declare & so fare as you may. & according to your best abillatie make cleerely apeere to them. the right & title our Town had granted them by the genrall Court the coppies of which you shall haue p^rsent at hand to make vse of as occasion may require.

2 such obiections as shall be by them made you shall answer according to the nature of the foresaid grants. & the iust reasons of our Towne in regard of our need. & thier sufficient supplye w^thout that land

In case they shall not send any answer or send a refusall of such a treatie

1 you shall vse the best meanes you can to attayne the knowledg of the time & place of the meeteing of the select men there. at w^t time and place you shall attend & desire audience. which being attayned you shall doe as before said. wherein you shall doe as much as in you lye vpon the cleereing of our Title to attayne the w^thdraweing of thier clayme of any Title there namely in the Lands in question

2 in case you cannot attayne the whole then you may offer composition [*so that Foule Meadowes & such other necessarie Lands adjacient. may be disclaimed by them & left to vs the Towne of Dedh as our Right] according to your best discretion for the best good of our Towne in whole or in pt

3 in case neither of these issue as aforsd but they sattisfie you that the title is truely & legally thiers then you shall forbeare makeing further claime there of

4. in case none of the former issues shall succeed. you shall offer them a refference to Arbitration to such men & so many men chosen for & on the behalfe of each Town as you shall see & judg meet & safe to whose arbitration you shall & may engage the towne.

Lastly in all these treaties. adgetations & conclusions. you shall by all your care and dilligence waue & auoide so much as in you lye. all occasions w^t so euer may tend to pvocation or breach of peace & shall from time to time as occasion is offered p^{r}sent them wth the loveing respect our Town in genrall beare towards them

in all these cases p^{r}mised you shall doe according to these instructions or vse your best skill and abillatie to attayne the end the Towne aymes at. not goeing directly contrary to any of them

It is agreed wth Robt Crosseman & granted to him libertie to erect a water mill vpon Charles Riuer at the place where a mill was formerly began to be built and a pmise is allso made to him of such Land adjacient as may conueaniently Accomodate the building & supplye of the mill aforesd pvided alwayes that the mill be fully p^{r}pared in all respects to grinde sufficiently befor the 29th daye of ye 7. month next. or in case the mill aforesd be not by that time p^{r}pared as afore said then all Lands so granted as aforesaid shall be returned to the towne againe otherwise to remaine to the sd Robt & his heyers for euer

10 of 11 mo 1652 Assemb. Joh. Kingsbery, Lieft Fisher, Joh. Dwight, Fra: Chickering, Serg^t. Fisher, Pet. Woodward. & Elea: Lusher

Robt Crosseman hath Libertie to accept or refuse the building of a mill according to the grante to him made. vntill Lectur day comseuennight

Joh Kingsbery & Joh. Dwight ar at the request of Ens Phillips deputed to attend the heareing of those his priuate reasons that cause him to decline the gathering of the poulder bill & and to returne to the other select men thier Judgm^t in the case vpon those his Reasons

Joh Fraerey who was Constable 1650 p^{r}sents the account of the Rate made that yeare for the purchaseing of Amunition ye sum of the Rate 22—13—1—

that whole Rate of 22—13—1— is assigned to be p^d by the said Constable to Lieft Fisher. whose bill of Receit thereof by the sd Lieft shall be the discharge of the sd constable

A warrant is deliuered to Joh Fraery to leuie that Rate

Joh. Morse vpon request from yᵉ Select men vndertakes. to gather in the bill of debt for poulder pʳsented by the Ensigne for which he is ρmised equall sattisfaction for that his paynes. the bill is to be assigned to him by such as by the court order is authorised therto Ens: Phillips onely engageing to take to himselfe the accounts of such as shall not vpon demaund acknowledge the bill. or refuse to make due pay[   ] all the sum̃s so gathered ar assig[   ] to be payed to Ens Phillips who engages to ρcure the Towne an other Barrell of Merchantible poulder for the same paye for the price of eight pounde

Joh. Gaye & Tho: Fuller ar deputed to order. & require highway worke for the layeing a newe floore of clifts wher need is sufficientlye vpon the great Cart Bridge. in due season

Antho Fisher Ju: Rich. Ellice & Elea: Lusher ar deputed vpon viewe to resolue of som fitt waye to repayer the Cart Bridge neere Joh. Dwights: & the worke is left to be effected by the guideance of the said Antho & Richard according to the former agreemᵗ of all the three abouesaid. this to be pformed by high waye worke as much as may be

Joh Morse haue a bill deliuered to him of the assignmᵗ of the poulder bill. at 2ˢ p lb in yᵉ name of yᵉ selectmen:

               84 lb poulder by bill.

21. of 11. 1652. Assemb. Joh. Kingsbery, Joh. Dwight, Lieft. Fisher, Fra: Chickering, Pet: Woodward, Sergᵗ. Fisher, & Elea: Lusher

Robt Crosseman lay down that grant of libertie made to him to build a water mill at or about the place called the old mille

Lieft Fisher. Joh Gaye & Sergᵗ Fisher ar deputed to Joyne wᵗʰ such of meadfield as shall be like wise by that Town deputed to lay out a cart way from Dedham to Medfield

28. of 11. 1652 Assemb. Joh. Kingsberey, Fra: Chickering, Lieft. Fisher, Joh: Dwight, Pet: Woodward, Sergᵗ. Fisher, & Elea: Lusher

ρpositions about the buyeing the mill

the things tendered to be sold as followeth

the mill itselfe. the mill house. the burze bought to make a new millstone. the pulleyes & Rope and all other the Appurttenances to the said mill belonging. what so euer

Item the dwelling house. the Barne. the Land as well vpland as meadowe and the Appurttenances. Fences. and empuemᵗˢ there vpon wᵗ euer. except the young apple trees. all the lands. houses town Rights &c: that ar the ρp estate of Nathaneell Whiteing lyeing & being in Dedh   £

the price of all the pʳmises is   250—0—0

the time of paym^{ts}. at the deliuery of the foresaid p^{r}mises
being demanded. by the Towne. being not before midsumer next 100—0—0
that time twelue month 100—0—0
that time 2 yeare after the 1 paym^t 50—0—0
matter of paym^t
the one halfe being 20£ in money the rest in wheate
the other [*halfe] in Jndian corne & Rye in equall portions
or in merchantible Cattell at price Currant
all deliuered in Dedham at the assignm^t of Natha Whiteing

Libertie is granted to Thomas Wight to take timber in the bounds of Dedham for the fenceing in one pcell of Meadowe Lyeing in Meadfield wch meadowe was formerly granted to Thomas Jordan & purchased of him by Thomas Wight aforesaid

Joh. Dwight. Lieft Fisher & Fra: Chickering, ar deputed to take care for the pcureing a heards man & pvideing a yard for the drye heard and all such things that shall be necessarie there in

7 of ye 1 m^o 1652 Assemb. Joh. Kingsbery, Lieft. Josh. Fisher, Joh. Dwight, Fra: Chickering, Pet: Woodward, Serg^t Danll Fisher, & Elea: Lusher to consider pportioning deuident

quest 1 whether such psons as ar entered townesmen in other Townes & there vpon take Town p^{r}uelidges ther. be not therby disengaged in any such Town as from whence they remoue

2 whether the Inhabitants of meadfield being by genrall consent exempt frō takeing deuident heere by reason of thier accomadation ther. riseing from Dedh be exempt from this deuident though thier psons be yet resident heere at p^{r}sent. & pt of thier estats but yet entered townesmen at Meadfield & act thier Town power & take Town p^{r}uelidges there

ye 7 of ye 1. Mo. 1652
The deuision of the deuident of 500 Acres to the Inhabitants vpon the rule of psons & estats;

	number of place	acres	roods	poles					
Mr Joh Allen	27	17	1	28	Mich. Metcalfe sen	14	9	0	34
Eld Joh: Hunting	25	8	1	5	Joh. Luson		7	1	28
Elea. Lusher	24	11	2	11	Antho: Fisher sen	50	10	2	0
Deac Hen: Chickering	58	12	0	22	Joh. Dwight	5	15	1	5
Deac Nath Aldus	44	4	2	00	Fra. Chickering	36	16	1	28
Joh. Kingsberey	38	12	¼	05	Joh. Haward		7	0	11

212   DEDHAM TOWN RECORDS.

Name					Name			
Lieft. Josh: Fisher	49	15	3	5	Thwa. Strickland	4	6	0 34
Ens. Hen. Phillips	52	12	1	5	Robt Fuller	3	7	2 11
Jonath. Fayerbanke sen	43	9	0	11	Nath. Fisher	48	4	2 11
Pet. Woodward	46	11	3	28	Tho. Battelle	1	8	0 23
Joh. Fraery	51	4	1	28	Tho. Jordan	57	4	3 5
Josep. Kingsbery	54	12	1	16	Joh. Guilde	39	4	2 34
Joh. Eaton	35	8	2	0	Andr. Duein	6	0	0
Rich. Euered		10	1	16	[*Antho. Fisher]			
Nath. Coaleburne	28	11	3	17	Antho Hubert	45	4	2 22
Robt Mason	21	4	0	22	Joh. Mason	34	3	1 16
Joh. Gaye		10	1	28	Ralph. Daye	63	4	0 11
Hen: Smyth	61	3	0	22	Hen: Willson	18	7	0 22
Serg^t Danll Fisher	41	8	0	34	Hen. Wight	22	8	0 11
Serg^t Geo: Fayerbanke		5	1	28	Joh. Bacon	17	5	2 22
Joh. Morse	53	8	2	0	William Bullard	31	8	0 11
Edw. Richards	6	10	3	32	Edw Hawes	32	5	2 0
Will Averey		5	3	18	Josh. Kent		4	0 11
Lamb. Genery	26	4	3	5	Robt Onion	2	3	0 11
Christo Smyth	23	5	0	34	Samll Mills		7	2 22
Jam. Jordan	47	1	2	22	Robt. Crosseman	37	3	2 0
Nath Whiteing	19	5	3	28	Danll Ponde	7	4	2 22
Mich. Metcalfe Ju	16	6	3	28	Rich. Ellice	9	4	0 33
Joh. Fayerbanke	20	4	3	18	Ralfe Freeman	15	2	0 11
Samll Judson	42	8	0	11	Cornell Fisher	59	1	3 5
Tho. Hering	10	7	0	22	Video. Maplehead	11	2	0 11
Rich Wheeler	29	8	0	11	Joh. Rice		1	3 5
Joh. Farington	30	8	3	28	Joh. Partridge	12	0	2 11
Joh. Aldus	60	4	2	11	Mrs Deengaine	40	0	2 33
Tho. Fuller		8	½	17	Joh. Newton	8	0	2 34
Tho. Payne	62	6	2	0	Tho. Wight		1	1 17
Robt Ware		6	3	5	Samll & Tho. Fisher		0	2 22
Antho. Fisher Ju	13	6			Tymo. Dwight	55	5	1 5

11 of ye 1 mo 1652. 53. Assemb. Joh. Kingsberye, Joh. Dwight, Lieft. Fisher, Fra: Chickering, Pet Woodward, Serg^t Fisher, & Eleaz. Lusher

for the settling of the forme & scituation of each pticular Lott in the seuerall tracts of land now to be layed out. its agreed and before any lotts ar drawen it is ordered that this order be obserued in the layeing out the same. that is heere after declared

its ordered that any man that shall at any time after the draweing the Lotts finde out any place to take any pt of his deuident: (pvided it be not in a place of such p^{r}iudice that the select men shall not alowe of it.) shall haue liberty so to doe. & he shall take the remaynder wherso euer his Lott shall cast his deuision pvided allso that this place so chosen be measured befor any pt of the deuident be measured in pticular deuision

a bill of 1£ 4ˢ 2ᵈ—ob[1] is giuen to Josh: Fisher seni to receaue of Meadfield Constable

the lotts in this deuident ar this daye drawen. by the seuerall Inhabitants after Lecture

18 of yᵉ 1 mo Assemb Joh Kingsbery, Fra. Chickering, Lieft. Fisher, Joh. Dwight, Sergᵗ Fisher, & Elea: Lusher, Pet. Woodward

agreed wᵗʰ Jacob Farrow to keep the Schoole to begin 28 of 1 mo. 1653 to haue 20£ p añ to be payed in towne paye being merchantible at the end of each halfe yeare the one halfe of the said sume he vndertakes to teach. to read English & the Accidence & to write & the knowledg & art of Arithmeticke & the rules & practice therof: this to be pposed to the towne

Its agreed that the Towne Amunition should be layed vp in a place to be made safe for it in the Roofe of the new Meetinghouse ouer the east gallerie

Granted to Edw Richards that smale pcell of Land formerly reserued for other vse as it abutts vpon his own Land east & north. & the way leading in to the woods. towards the southwest

The aboue written agreemᵗ wᵗʰ a schoole mʳ was this daye pposed to the towne after Lecture & consented vnto

a bill giuen to Tho Fuller to receaue of yᵉ Constable 7ˢ.
a bill giuen to John Partridg to receaue of the Constable— 7ˢ:
a bill giuen to Robt Crosseman to receaue 20ˢ of yᵉ Constable 20ˢ.

29 of 6 mo: 1653 Assemb Joh Kingsberie. Joh. Dwight, Lieft Fisher, Fra Chickering, Pet. Woodward, Srgᵗ Fisher, & Elea: Lusher

the Countrey Rate made

mʳ Joh. Allin	2	7	4	Joh. Haward	1	3	8
Eld Joh. Hunting	0	16	7	Fra Chickering	2	11	8
Elea. Lusher	1	9	9	Lieft. Jo. Fisher	1	9	10
Dea. Hen Chickering	1	8	10	Tho. Wight	0	3	4
Dea: Nath. Aldus	0	13	4	Ens. Hen Phillips	1	10	4
Joh Kingsbery	1	17	2	Jonath: Fayerbanke sen	1	3	10
Mich metcafe sen	1	3	1	Pet Woodward	1	7	8
Joh. Luson	1	7	4	Josep: Kingsbery	1	1	3
Antho. Fisher sen	1	11	3	Joh: Eaton	0	19	1
Joh. Dwight	1	12	6	Rich: Euered	1	5	3

[1] See Note, page 151.

Nath. Coaleburn	1	0	6	Ralp: Daye	0	10	2
Robt Mason	0	5	0	Hen Willson	0	12	4
Joh: Gaye	0	15	3	Joh. Bacon	0	14	6
Serg^t Dan: Fisher	0	16	7	Edw. Hawes	0	5	3
Serg^t Geo: Fayerbanke	0	13	6	Josh. Kent	0	6	8
Serg^t Willm Avery	0	16	10	Rich: Ellice			
Serg^t Nath. Stearnes	0	8	10	Robt Onion	0	6	10
Joh Morse	0	11	4	Samll. Mills	0	15	11
Edw: Richards	1	3	2	Jam. Thorpe	0	5	10
Lamb: Generie	0	6	8	Theo. Fraery	0	14	4
Christo. Smyth	0	16	11	Hen. Smyth	0	3	6
Jam: Jordan	0	0	10	Jam. Draper			
Nath Whiteing	1	1	11	Rich. Hartely			
Mich. Metcalfe Ju	0	11	[ ]	Joh Houghton	0	5	0
Joh: Fayerbanke	0	8	[ ]	Samll Dane	0	5	0
Samll Judson	1	1	[ ]	Joh. Littlefield	0	5	0
Tho: Hering	1	1	8	Joh. Rice	\	5	2
Rich. Wheeler	0	19	08	Joh. Kent	0	5	6
Hen Wight	1	5	0	Ralp. Freeman	0	6	9
Tho. Battell	1	3	9	Elnath. Dunckely	0	5	0
Joh. Farington	1	2	10	Willm Bullard	0	13	10
Joh. Aldus	0	14	0	Joh Newton	0	1	8
Tho Fuller	1	0	0	Isaac Bullard	0	13	8
Tho. Payne	0	11	3	Danll Ponde	0	14	0
Robt Ware	0	12	5	Josh. Fisher sen	0	0	10
Antho. Fisher Ju	0	16	5	Rich Hartely ⎱	0	12	3
Thwa: Stricklaud	0	10	10	Jam Draper ⎰			
Robt Fuller	0	12	8	Rich Ellice	0	7	11
Nath. Fisher	0	11	6	Tymo Dwight	0	13	10
Tho: Jordan	0	12	5	Joh. Fraery	0	1	2
Joh. Guilde	0	8	4	Math Edwards	0	5	0
Andr: Duein	0	17	3	Tho Saluadge	0	5	0
Joh. Mason	0	18	2	Joh Generie	0	5	0
Antho: Hubert	0	7	0	Jonas Fayerbanke	0	5	0
Jonath. Fayerbank Ju	0	5	2	Christo: Webb	0	5	0

5 of 7 mo 1653 Assemb. Joh Kingsbery, Joh. Dwight, Lieft: Fisher, Pet: Woodward, Serg^t: Fisher, & Eleaz: Lusher

Rich Euered Constable p^{r}sent to giue account of Towne Rates one made 17 of 10 mo. 1652. the sume 17£. 2^s. 3^d.

a bill of 2£. 3^s deliuered to Fra Chickering

vpon the Request and motion of Jacob. Farrow its consented vnto that himselfe or his Brother shall attend the keepeing the Schoole according to the Couen^t formerly made wth the said Jacob & the Couen^t to remaine in force as its

leaue is granted to Jacob Farrow to fell 2 or 3 oakes for his vse vpon the Comon Lands of the Town

[*vpon the Constables account of the Rate aforesaid he p^rsenting bills of Disbursm^ts &c ther remayne due of that Rate— 2—12—4]
p^d to Serg^t Danll Fisher for his own. & Nathaneell Fishers & Ralp: Dayes Rates the sum of 1£ 14^s. sixten shillings & 6^d p^d in boarde. & 17^s—6. p^d by bill deliuered to the Constable. p^d—1£—14^s—0
this paym^t is for seuerall dayes worke of them all being reckoned amounting to that sum of. 1£—14
[*this was reckoned befor the account last from the constables]

Granted vnto Willm Averey & his heyers for euer one pcell of Meadowe conteyning about 4 or 5 acres. abutting vpon and adjoyneing vnto Stopp. Riuer neere Meadfield & in pt vpon Nath Coalburns Meadowe & vpon Meadfield Line & the wast vpland

a bill deliuered to Joh Gaye to receaue of the constable   0—6— 0
p^d Lieft. Fisher out of the Town Rate of 17—2—3—   1—6—10
[*Remaine due of the last Town Rate   3—2— 5
after all the accounts made aboue said]

16 of ye 7. mo 1653   Assemb: Joh Kingsbery, Joh Dwight, Fra: Chickering, Lieft Fisher, Pet: Woodward, Serg^t Fisher, & Elea. Lusher

The men heere vnder named ar deputed vpon viewe to settle the line of an enlargem^t vpon the west side of Ensign Phillips his Farme not exceeding 20 Acres and make report of that thier act to the select men: who shall settle the Title of that Land to the Ensig vpon what account they shall Judg meete & equall   Lieft Fisher, Serg^t Fisher

Whereas Lambert Generey did formerly giue one smale pcell of Land in his Lott beyond the Mill Creeke for the vse of the Towne in publike the Towne vpon experience findeing that it is not like to be vsefull doe disclaime and giue vp all that right & Title that the Towne haue there vnto. seing the clay is not vsefull as was expected

to be pposed after the Lecture this day to the Towne that whereas it is ap^rhended needfull that the meeteinghouse should be better enclosed by daubeing the walles, and that workemen fitt to accomplish the same vpon our experience ar hard to attayne and paye to thier content is scarce at p^rsent: its therfor thought meet if a better way cannot by the Towne be pposed. that the Towne should com joyntely together to doe that worke a true account to be kept what euery man doe. that equall alloweance may be made accordingly.

the Account of the Surveyors taken those whose names ar vnderwritten ar behind in thier worke as followeth

216   DEDHAM TOWN RECORDS.

Ralph Daye	4 dayes	Dea Aldus	½	Joh Smyth	4
Jam Thorpe	4	Ens. Phillips	1	Fra Chickering	½
Lieft Fisher	2	Cornell. Fisher	2		

The Schoole Rate—24 of 7 mo. 1653

Mr Joh Allen	0 10 7	Joh. Farington	0 8 3
Eld Joh. Hunting	0 7 11	Joh. Aldus	0 7 3
Elea. Lusher	0 9 11 ob[1]	Tho. Fuller	0 9 0 ob
Deac Hen. Chickering	0 4 8 ob	Tho. Payne	0 11 7
Deac Nath Aldus	0 2 1	Robt Ware	0 11 10 ob
Joh Kingsberie	0 5 6 ob	Antho. Fisher Ju	0 1 6 ob
Joh Luson	0 3 1	Robt Fuller	0 6 11 ob
Mich: Metcalfe sen	0 3 3 ob	Nath. Fisher	0 1 7 ob
Antho: Fisher sen	0 5 4	Tho. Jordan	0 1 10 ob
Joh. Dwight	0 6 3 ob	Joh. Guilde	0 5 10
Joh Haward	0 9 8	Andr. Duein	0 1 10
Fra Chickering	0 6 8	Joh. Mason	0 3 3 ob
Lieft Josh Fisher	0 5 0	Ralp. Daye	0 1 3 ob
Ens. Hen Phillips	0 9 8	Hen. Wilson	0 6 10
Tho. Wight	0 0 10	Joh. Bacon	0 1 10 ob
Johath: Fayerba:	0 3 5 ob	Tymo. Dwight	0 2 2 ob
Pet. Woodward	0 4 5	Theop: Fraerie	0 2 4
Josep. Kingsbery	0 19 1	Will Bullard	0 3 5 ob
Joh. Eaton	0 3 6 ob	Isaac Bullard	0 0 11
Rich Euered	0 8 10	Samll Milles	0 2 9
Nath. Coaleburn	0 13 10 ob	Rich. Ellice	0 0 9
Serg^t Dan: Fisher	0 2 5	Edw. Hawes	0 1 4
Serg^t Geo: Fayerba:	0 0 10 ob	Danll Ponde	0 1 0
Serg^t Will Avery	0 6 8 ob	Robt Onion	0 0 5 ob
Serg^t Nath. Stearnes	0 1 0	Jam: Thorpe	0 0 2 ob
Joh. Morse	1 1 7	Ric. Hartley ⎱	0 0 7
Edw. Richards	0 14 6 ob	Ja: Draper ⎰	
Joh Gaye	0 12 7	Joh. Newton	0 0 5
Lamb. Generie	0 1 8	Ralp: Freeman	0 0 5 ob
Christo. Smyth	0 1 9	Joh Fraery	0 0 3 ob
Nath Whiteing	0 14 3	Hen. Smyth	0 0 10 ob
Mich. Metcalf Ju	0 6 7 ob	Josh. Kent	0 0 5
Joh. Fayerbank	0 15 10 ob	Thwa Strickland	0 6 5 ob
Samll Judson	0 12 9 ob	Antho. Hubert	0 0 6
Tho. Hering	0 2 11		
Rich. Wheeler	0 7 5		19 5 7
Hen Wight	0 3 9		[*12]
Tho. Battell	0 3 5 ob		
			19 4 0 ob

[1] See Note, page 151.

this sume com short of the schoole m^{rs} due payem^t 19^s—5^d which we Judge may be payd out of the ouerplusse of the Countrey Rate mrd that Tho. Fullers Rate was abated 6^s—2^d. being mistaken so much

29 of ye 10. 1653 Assemb: Joh. Kingsberie, Joh. Dwight, Lieft: Fisher, Fra: Chickering, Serg^t. Fisher, & Elea. Lusher, Pet. Woodward

Granted to Ralph Freeman and to his heyers for euer one pcell of vpland conteyneing about 2 acres which is to be layed out at the discretion of Peter Woodward & Richard Euered beyond the south end of the east streete. betwixt the drawen waye there & the swampe pvided that if the said Ralph Freeman doe not build & in habit vpon the said pcell wthin the space of one whole yeare after this daye: then this p^{r}sent grant shall be voide & one of none effect. pvide allso that if the said Ralph his heyers or assignes shall purpose to sell the said pcell wthin the space of 7 yeares after the grante. then the said pcell & the appurtenances therof shall first be tendered to the Towne or the Select men therof for the time being at such a price as another would realy giue which if the said select men refuse it shall be at libertie to sell to any other

[*A bill giuen to Joh Dwight of 1£—11^s 3^d being due for diuers Journeyes & otherwise

A bill giuen to Eleazer Lusher of 1£—5^s—8^d for worke about the Amunition place & diuers Journeys for the Towne 16^s—10^d. due of the last year 2£ of this debt is assigned to be p^d from Joseph morse: rest due 2^s—6^d]

A bill giuen to Thomas Herring of 6^s—8^d for his pt in the killing of a woolfe

A bill giuen to Isaac Bullard of 20^s for killing one wolfe to be payed by the Constable

Josh. Kent a bill of 2^s for one daye worke for the Towne

p^d by the Constable to Joh Kingsberie in debt from the Towne to him 6^s remayne due from Joh Kingsberie to the Towne 0—0—4^d

Fra Chickering p^{r}sents a bill of 4£—2^s. whereof 3£ is due for his deputies. aloweance the other for nayles & Journeyes. and other disbursem^{ts}. this bill is allowed

the acc^t of that Twentie pounds. due from Meadfield ye 26 of ye 12 mo: 1652

Rec^d by Lieft Fisher	10£	8^s	4^d
recd by Pet. Woodward	4	2	0
in board to the Towne	1	5	0
p^d for killing of wooluees wthin Dedham Bounds	1	13	4
p^d to Josh Fisher seni for Iron worke for the bell—&c	1	4	2
p^d to Danll Ponde for work about the meeteing house	0	12	0
p^d to Dan. Fisher for worke	0	5	[ ]
	19£	9^s	10^d

A bill giuen to Joh Dwight of 1£—10ˢ—3ᵈ due for diuers Journeyes &: 11 bushels of Lime brought to Towne & for money disbursed

A bill giuen to Ensigne Phillips of 5ˢ due for 2 Journeyes to Meadfield

A Bill giuen to Fra Chickering of 1£—6—3—to receaue of yᵉ Constable out of the 17£—2ˢ—3ᵈ in pt of paymᵗ of the 4£—2ˢ rate due to him

Disbursed by Pet Woodward out of that wᶜʰ he receaued of Meadfield

for Court orders   1—10—0
for glasse for the meeteinghouse   1— 0—0
for the payeing of seuerall workemen in the Townes worke 1—10—0
rest due. 2ˢ this 2ˢ is assigned to be pᵈ to Richard Ellice

[*due to Daniell Fisher for 2 Journies to Dorchester   0—5—0]

whereas Thomas Battelie was apointed to paye 10ˢ for the rent of the meadowe that he did mowe the yeare 1652 wᶜʰ was the Townes and at pʳsent it apeere that the grasse was nothing so good as it was then judged we doe now. abate 5ˢ to him wᶜʰ is to be set of in the next yeares high waye worke:

of which bills ther remayne in all yet vnpayed more then is yet in hand to paye wᵗʰ all the sume of   4—18—6

mʳᵈ that the publike worke at the mille Creeke & the meeteing house be pposed to be comitted

Lieft Fisher his account
he receaud of medfield Rate   10— 8— 4
in nayles from meadfield former paye   2— 0— 0
in wheat for debt [*for] the Townes [*medowe]   0— 7— 6
vpon a bill of highway worke of old account   0— 9— 0
                   13— 4—10
disburse for the Town as apeere by his bill   12—13— 9
remaine due from him to the Towne   0—11— 1

At a generall meeteing of the Towne 2 of yᵉ 11 1653

[✕ ✕ ✕ *Record of the Meeting, as page* 139.]

Lieft Fisher Fra. Chickering & Danll Fisher ar further entrusted & empowered to make a finall settling of that case respecting foule meadowe.

the disposeall of the comon in foule meadow at reasonable rates according to the goodnes of the meadowe for the supplye of them that ar in most want. is left to the descretion of the select men this day to be chosen

the whole case concerning Natick is still left to the 5 men last deputed therevnto. according to the first deputation giuen to Lieft Fisher & Sergent Fisher haueing the same power then giuen to those 2 men

the bridges ouer Charles Riuer before in adgetation ar resolued to be both forborne building for this pʳsent yeare

[✕ ✕ ✕ *Elections, as page* 139.]

Elea Lusher, Deac Chickering, Joh Kingsbery, Comissioners

11 mo 3 53

the returne of them that measured the length of the great playne Fence from gate to gate on the south side is 27 score rodd on the north side 24 score rodd & 4 rodd & 6 foote

Joh Gaye desire his deuident to be layed out in a place on the north side of Charles Riuer neere Naticke. vpon the south side of a playne there that abutts vpon the Riuer towards the East. south. & west & a swampe towards the north. he desire his pt should lye. wthin the elbowe or turne of the Riuer by a smale swampie place by the Riuer side. & so to haue his pcell runne east & west by. or on both sides of a long hill. ther. or there abouts 9 of ye 1st mo: 1653.

Andrew Duein desire his deuident should lye on the fore said playne. & John Haward desire his deuident may lye there also. if it be there to be had. 9 of ye 1 mo. 1653

Henry Chicering hath sold his deuident to Hen. Wight. acknowledged by himself

Tho. Battell Rich Ellice & Ralp Daye chuse pt of thier deuedent ouer against Rock meadowe on the left hand of meadfield waye adioyneing to ye pastors Farme or neere therto 7 of ye 1st mo 53-54: Tho Battell desire som ther vpon the grant of Ed Hawes. and mor 1 acre ½ by the side of Rocke Field on the south side. neere Ralp Dayes Lande

Ralp Daye & Rich Ellice desire to take all thier pts in the fore named place if they may

Rich Euered desires his deuident & the remaynder of his purchased land at the southerly end of south playne as it abutts vpon that brooke that runnes into south meadowe. or if not all there. then w^t he may wth conueaniencie 15 of 1st mo 53-54

Tho Battell: desires his deudent beyond strawbery hill being pt of his own Jonath Fayerbanks Dan. Pondes Joh Rices.

Joh Luson desires to haue his layed out there. & allso Cor: Fisher

Deed to make fro my selfe to Robt Ware 2 acre mead. abutts Charles Riuer east vpland west Ro. Ware north Mrs Deengan south

a grant to make entery of to Joh Ellice of a pcell of meadowe 3 acres. neere medfield bounds wth such conueaniencie of vpland as may be needfull to shorten the fence abutts wast vpland round about a smale brooke runing thorough it

A Band to make from Daniell Antho. Natha: & Cornell: Fisher to thier mother to paye tenn £. p añn: at 2£ 10^s the quarter of the yeare in paym^t to her iust content. dureing her naturall life. after thier Fathers decease

[1]Whereas the Towne haue hetherto bene content to leaue the common

---

[1] This paragraph is written on the same page as the preceding, but with the book reversed.

fe[ ] at libertie to all Townesmen which we conceaue may in time pue inconueanient in seuerall respects &c: its therfore ꝓposed to consideration for the settling of euery mans libertie & right in comon feed that for as much as to our obseruation it apeers that the cattell at p^{r}sent in Towne are competently sufficient for the comon feed therein or very neere there vnto that it is necessary to com to som equall waye of stinting or limitting euery mans number of cattell to be kept in comon feede according to p^{r}sent rules. being the same that lands in generall deuident are deuided by & no inhabitant in our Towne to haue libertie vpon any p^{r}tence heere after to put more cattell to comon. feede then according to the same ꝓportion vpon penaltie and allso for the more full settling of comon rights that all deuidents in lands be deuided & layed out according to the p^{r}sent rules as mens estats shall be at p^{r}sent founde and by no other what changes so euer may come heereafter

DON GLEASON HILL, Esq.,

DEAR SIR:—

In accordance with your suggestion I herewith submit a list of the original papers from which the autograph signatures were reproduced, which appear on pages 221—225 of the third volume of Dedham Records, just published by the Town and edited by you.

Thomas Alcock, from the Compact in Medfield Records, furnished by James Hewins; *John Aldis*, administrator's bond on the estate of Deacon Nathan Aldis, April, 1676; *Edward Alleyn*, page 42 of the third volume of Dedham Records; *John Allin*, page XI, of the Introduction to the second volume of Dedham Records; *William Avery*, will of John Dwight, June 16, 1658; *John Bacon*, inventory of Serg. Ralph Day's estate, Jan. 10, 1677-78; *George Barbor*, will of John Frairy, of Medfield, March 27, 1670; *Thomas Battelle*, inventory of Mary Lusher's estate, Feb. 4, 1672-73; *Isaac Bullard*, same as John Aldis, above; *Francis Chickering*, inventory of the estate of John Morse, of Boston, June 9, 1657; *Henry Chickering*, page 89 of third volume of Dedham Records; *Nathaniel Colburn*, inventory of Dea. Aldis, April, 1676; *James Draper*, petition of Nath¹ Colburn, and others, May 7, 1662, Mass. Archives, Vol. CXII, p. 142; *Timothy Dwight*, inventory of John Pepper's estate, March 22, 1669-70; *John Eaton*, inventory of Michael Bacon's estate, April 20, 1649; *Richard Ellis*, administrator's bond on the estate of Joseph Ellis, Aug. 2, 1672; *James Fales*, same as James Draper, above; *John Farrington*, in private hands; *Jonathan Fairbanks*, petition of the Dedham Selectmen, Aug. 30, 1658, Mass. Archives, Vol. CXI, p. 29; *Anthony Fisher* will of Nathaniel Fisher, Jan. 26, 1660-61; *Cornelius Fisher*, same as James Draper, above; *Daniel Fisher*, will of Michael Bacon, April 14, 1648; *Samuel Fisher*, same as James Draper, above; *Thomas Fuller*, inventory of Samuel Judson's estate, July 24, 1657; *John Gay*, inventory of John Kingsbury's estate, Oct. 9, 1660; *John Guild*, his will, Oct. 3, 1682; *John Haward*, same as Thomas Fuller, above; *Edward Haws*, same as John Farrington, above; *Thomas Herring* will of Joseph Kingsbury, Senʳ, May 22, 1675; *Robert Hinsdell*, inventory of estate . John Wight, of Medfield, Oct. 3, 1653; *Ezekiel Holliman*, furnished by Edward Field, Record Commissioner of Providence, R. I.; *John Huntting*, same as Jonathan Fairbanks, above; *Samuel Judson*, his will, June 7, 1657; *Joseph Kingsbury*, same as Jonathan Fairbanks, above; *Robert Mason*, same as Thomas Alcock, above; *Michael Metcalf*, in the DEDHAM HISTORICAL REGISTER, Vol. III, p. 142; *Thomas Metcalf*, administrator's bond on the estate of Robert Onion, Jan. 30, 1673; *John Morse*, same as Richard Ellis, above; *John Partridge*, from an old document; *Thomas Payne*, same as John Farrington, above; *Henry Phillips*, will of Richard Barbor, May 27, 1644; *John Plympton*, same as Thomas Alcock, above; *Daniel Pond*, account book of the First Parish of Dedham, May 21, 1687, p. 28; *Nathaniel Stearns*, same as Timothy Dwight, above; *James Thorpe*, same as James Draper, above; *John Thurston*, sen'r, same as John Farrington, above; *Robert Ware*, same; *Ralph Wheelock*, same as Thomas Alcock, above; *Henry Wight*, same as Thomas Herring, above; *Peter Woodward*, inventory of Anthony Fisher, of Dorchester, April 7, 1670.

These signatures all appeared to be original.

Yours very truly,

JULIUS H. TUTTLE.

Dedham, Jan. 2, 1893.

FAC-SIMILES OF SIGNATURES.

Thomas Alcock
about 1655

John Ledis
1676

Edward Alleyn
1638

Jo: Allin
about 1640

William Avery
1658

John Bacon:
1678

George Barbur
1670

Tho: Battelle
1673

Isaac Bullard
1676

Ffrancis Chickering
1657

Henry Chickering
1642

Nathaniel Colbarn
1676

James Draper
1662

Timothy Dwight
1670

John Eaton
1649

Richard Elline
1672

James Fales
1662

FAC-SIMILES OF SIGNATURES.   223

John Fivington
1673

John Guild
1682

Jonathan ffayerbanck
1658

John Harvard
1657

Anthony ffitzã
1661

Edward Haws
1673

Cornelius ffisher
1662

Thomas Herring
1675

Daniel fisher
1648

Robert Hempsted
1653

Samuell fisher
1662

Ezkiell Hollyman
1639-59

Tho ffuller
1657

John Huntting
1658

John Gaye
1660

Samuel Hudson
1657

FAC-SIMILES OF SIGNATURES.

Joseph Kingsbury
1658

Daniel Pond
1687

Robt Mason
about 1655

Nathanoll Stearnes
1670

Michael Metcalfe
senior
about 1618

James Thorpe
1662

Thomas Metcalfe
1673

John Thurstan sen^r
1673

John Morse
1672

Robert Abarre
1673

John partridge
1672

Thomas: payne
1673

Ralph Wheelocke:
about 1655

Henry Phillips
1644

Henry Wight
1675

John Plympton
about 1655

Peter Woodward
1670

INDEX OF NAMES.

ADAMS—Ferdinando, 3, 32, 38, 39, 40, 41, 45, 46, 47, 51, 53, 66, 94, 96, 106, 107, 110, 158, 161, 172, 175; Henry, 197, 200.
ALDIS and ALDUS—John, 3, 132, 143,146, 148, 179, 184, 185, 190, 198, 205, 212, 214, 216, 221; Nathan (*see Deacon*), 3, 67, 75, 76, 77, 78, 79, 80, 81, 82, 83, 84, 85, 86, 89, 90, 91, 92, 94, 95, 97, 100, 101, 102, 104, 106, 107, 108, 109, 111, 113, 142, 152, 153, 158, 160, 166, 170, 179, 182, 183, 190, 195, 205, 211, 213, 216; Deacon, 146, 193, 198, 216.
ALDRIDGE—Henry, 81, 92, 104, 106, 109, 154.
ALCOCKE — Thomas, 3, 42, 74, 92, 95, 100, 109, 152, 154, 155, 158, 161, 174, 175, 176, 181, 221; Mr., 23.
ALLEN and ALLIN—Ed., 154, 158, 167; James, 3, 42,49, 59,74,76, 95, 111, 113, 124, 132, 152, 154, 158, 161, 164, 171, 172, 184, 186; John, 3, 32, 35, 38, 39. 40, 41, 43, 44, 45, 46, 47, 48, 49, 51, 53, 55, 56, 58, 67, 71, 72, 75, 78, 92, 95, 98, 100, 102, 104, 107, 109, 113, 131, 142, 152, 153, 157, 158, 159, 160, 168, 173, 183, 190, 198, 205, 211, 213, 216, 221; Mr., 171, 173, 178, 181.
ALLEYN—Edward, 3, 20, 21, 22, 23, 25, 26, 27, 28, 29, 30, 31, 32, 35, 36, 38, 40, 41, 42, 43, 44, 45, 47, 48, 49, 51, 52, 53, 54, 55, 57, 59, 60, 61, 66, 67, 68, 70, 71, 73, 75, 76, 77, 78, 79, 80, 81, 82, 83, 84, 85, 86, 87, 88, 89, 94, 95, 101, 115, 128, 154, 168, 173, 201, 203, 221; Mr., 167, 170.
ATHERTON—Humphrey, 137; Capt.,153.
AUSTEN—Francis, 3, 20, 21, 22, 26, 27, 28, 29, 30, 31, 32, 33, 35, 38, 41, 45, 47, 71, 94; Jane G., 188.
AVERY—William, 3, 132, 141, 143, 148, 179, 181, 183, 190, 192, 198, 205, 206, 207, 212, 214, 215, 216, 221.

BACHELER—John, 3, 33, 35, 40, 44, 45, 46, 48, 49, 51, 53, 57, 59, 60, 61, 62, 63, 64, 66, 67, 68, 69, 70, 71, 72, 74, 75, 80, 81. 86, 92, 95, 96, 97, 100, 107, 110, 113, 117, 152, 154, 169, 174, 175, 176.
BACON—John, 19, 107, 141, 144, 145, 152, 154, 158, 160, 162, 163, 173, 176, 184, 190, 194, 198, 205, 212, 214, 216, 221; Michael, 3, 73, 95, 100, 101, 102, 103, 106, 107, 109, 113, 152, 154, 158, 172, 174, 176, 177, 181; Mr., 68; Mrs., 69.
BANCROFT—Thomas, 123, 130, 131, 152, 158, 161, 162, 163, 184, 185, 186, 190. 198, 202, 205.
BARBER—George (*see Sergeant*), 3, 74, 87, 91, 92, 100, 111, 113, 114, 126. 134. 152, 153, 158, 160, 163, 178, 179, 180, 197, 200, 221; Richard, 3, 50, 52, 57, 75, 95, 100, 173; Sergeant, 178, 193.
BARTLET—Thomas, 3, 20, 22, 23, 25, 27, 28, 36, 50.
BATTELEY, BATTLE and BATTELLE— Thomas, 123, 139, 143, 147, 153, 158, 160, 162, 178, 184, 186, 190, 194, 195, 198, 199, 200, 205, 206, 212, 214, 216, 218. 219, 221.
BAYES—Thomas, 3, 42, 44, 45, 47, 49, 50, 92, 96, 111, 167, 172, 175.
BEARSTOE and BEARSTOWE — George, 3, 34, 66, 92, 93, 96, 104, 110, 112, 113, 132, 152, 154, 159, 160, 168, 169, 171, 172, 174, 176, 178, 179, 181; Joh., 155; William, 3, 21, 22, 25, 26, 28, 29, 30, 31, 32, 33, 34, 38, 40, 45, 46, 48, 58, 60, 62, 79, 86, 92, 96, 106, 110, 151, 168, 176, 177, 185.
BIERRS—Richard, 135.
BRADSTREET—Mr., 1.
BROCKE—Henry, 3, 48, 49, 51, 53, 95, 100, 107, 108, 109, 152, 153, 158, 160, 172, 174, 175, 176, 182, 183, 190, 198, 204.
BULLARD—Benjamin, 3, 140,144,145,146; Isaac, 3, 138, 144, 146, 148, 190. 205, 214, 216, 217, 221; John, 3, 45, 51, 75, 84, 88, 91, 92, 95, 98, 100, 102, 104, 110, 113, 127, 153, 154, 155, 156, 157, 158, 161, 186, 194, 195; Nathaniel, 144; William, 3, 45, 47, 48, 49, 51,53, 66,71,72,75, 91, 92, 94, 95, 97, 98, 99, 100, 101, 102, 103, 104, 107, 109, 112, 113, 114, 117, 118, 119, 121, 122, 123, 126,130,131,134,143, 150, 151, 152, 153, 154, 155, 156, 157, 158, 161, 173, 177, 184, 190, 198, 201, 203, 212, 214, 216.
BULLEN—Samuel, 3, 68, 71. 72, 75, 82. 92, 96, 103, 106, 109, 111, 113, 152, 154, 155, 161, 168, 181.

CAKEBREAD—Thomas, 3, 30, 32, 42.
CARTER—Thomas, 3, 29, 31, 32, 35, 40, 41, 43, 44, 47, 48, 49, 51, 53, 55; Mr., 36, 42, 47, 48, 60, 175.
CHENERY—(*see Genery.*)
CHICKERING — Francis (*see Ensign*), 3, 42, 44, 46, 47, 48, 51, 53, 54, 59, 60, 66, 70,

71, 72, 75, 76, 77, 78, 79, 80, 81, 82, 83, 84, 85. 86, 87, 90, 91, 92, 93, 94, 96, 97, 98, 99, 100, 104, 105, 106, 107, 108, 110, 113, 114, 115, 116, 117, 118, 119, 121, 122, 123, 124, 125, 129, 130, 133, 134, 135, 136, 137, 138, 139, 140, 141, 146, 150, 151, 152, 153, 154, 155, 156, 157, 158, 159, 160, 161, 162, 163, 164, 165, 166, 167, 168, 169, 170, 171, 173, 174, 175, 176, 177, 179, 181, 182, 183, 185, 186, 188, 190, 192, 193, 194, 196, 197, 198, 199, 200, 201, 202, 203, 204, 205, 206, 207, 208, 209, 210, 211, 212, 213, 214, 215, 216, 217, 218, 221; Henry (*see Deacon*), 78, 79, 80, 83, 84, 85, 86, 87, 88, 89, 90, 91, 92, 93, 94, 95, 96, 97, 98, 99, 100, 102, 104, 107, 108, 110, 111, 112, 113, 114, 115, 116, 123, 124, 125, 126, 127, 128, 129, 130, 131, 133, 134, 140, 141, 142, 153, 154, 155, 156, 157, 158, 159, 160, 161, 162, 163, 165, 168, 171, 173, 174, 180, 182, 184, 190, 203, 205, 207, 208, 211, 213, 216, 219; Deacon, 138, 145, 198, 218; Ensign, 143, 147;——, 170.

CLARKE—Joseph, 3, 71, 77, 99, 103, 106, 109, 112, 113, 153, 154, 157, 158, 161, 162, 168, 174, 189, 193, 195; Rowland, 34, 38, 84, 85; William, 137; Sergeant, 136;——, 153.

COBB—J. H., 88.

COALEBURNE and COLBURN—Nathaniel, 3, 34, 40, 41, 44, 45, 46, 49, 51, 53, 79, 81, 84, 92, 93, 95, 97, 99, 100, 101, 104, 105, 106, 107, 111, 113, 118, 124, 127, 129, 130, 134, 135, 139, 140, 141, 143, 148, 152, 153, 158, 160, 163, 164, 165, 166, 167, 169, 170, 171, 172, 173, 176, 178, 179, 180, 182, 183, 185, 186, 187, 188, 189, 190, 193, 198, 203, 204, 205, 207, 212, 214, 215, 216, 221.

COLLICOT—Mr., 170.

COLVER—Edward, 3, 37, 57, 95, 96, 98, 100, 104, 110, 112, 200.

COOKE—Samuel, 68, 69, 77, 82, 95, 109; Mr., 89, 99, 107, 121, 132, 151, 159, 168, 172, 173, 174, 175, 176.

COOLIDGE—John, 3, 20, 21, 22, 23, 25, 26, 27, 32, 33, 40, 47, 48.

CROFTS—Serg', 136.

CROMWELL—Capt. Thomas, 188.

CROSSMAN—Robert, 3, 93, 97, 98, 102, 103, 104, 108, 111, 113, 123, 150, 151, 153, 158, 159, 160, 162, 168, 169, 180, 184, 190, 198, 203, 204, 205, 209, 210, 212, 213.

CUSHION—Theop., 155, 161.

DALTON—Philemon, 3, 20, 21, 22, 23, 25, 26, 27, 28, 29, 30, 31, 32, 34, 35, 38, 39, 40, 41, 43, 44, 45, 47, 48, 49, 51, 53, 54, 84, 85, 167, 178; Timothy, 3, 32, 35, 36, 38, 40, 41, 43, 44, 45, 47, 48, 49, 51, 53, 59, 94; Mr., 32, 36, 48, 52, 62, 123, 156, 173.

DAMANT—John, 152, 160, 162.

DANE—Samuel, 214.

DANFORTH—Mr., 23.

DAYE—Ralph, 105, 106, 112, 113, 127, 141, 144, 148, 152, 154, 155, 158, 160, 162, 165,

166, 183, 190, 192, 194, 198, 203, 205, 206, 212, 214, 215, 216, 219.

DEENGAYNE—Henry, 3, 48, 60, 68, 71, 75, 82, 96, 109, 168, 175, 176; Mrs., 152, 154, 158, 161, 184, 212, 219.

DEWING and DUEIN—Andrew, 3, 135, 143, 145, 148, 152, 158, 161, 178, 182, 190, 192, 193, 198, 205, 212, 214, 216, 219.

DRAPER—James, 3, 139, 144, 184, 190, 214, 216, 221.

DUDLEY—Samuel, 26; Mr., 41, 153.

DUNKLEY—Elnathan, 194, 195, 214.

DWIGHT—John, 3, 20, 21, 22, 23, 25, 26, 27, 28, 29, 30, 31, 32, 33, 35, 36, 37, 38, 39, 40, 41, 43, 44, 45, 46, 47, 48, 49, 51, 52, 53, 54, 57, 58, 59, 60, 62, 63, 64, 66, 67, 68, 69, 70, 71, 72, 74, 75, 76, 79, 80, 81, 82, 83, 84, 85, 86, 87, 89, 90, 91, 92, 93, 94, 96, 97, 98, 99, 100, 101, 102, 103, 104, 105, 106, 107, 109, 111, 112, 113, 114, 115, 116, 117, 118, 119, 121, 122, 123, 124, 125, 126, 127, 128, 129, 130, 131, 133, 134, 135, 138, 139, 140, 141, 143, 146, 150, 151, 152, 153, 154, 155, 156, 157, 158, 159, 160, 161, 162, 163, 164, 166, 167, 168, 169, 170, 171, 173, 174, 175, 176, 177, 178, 179, 180, 181, 182, 183, 185, 186, 187, 188, 189, 190, 191, 193, 194, 195, 196, 197, 198, 199, 200, 201, 202, 203, 204, 205, 206, 207, 208, 209, 210, 211, 212, 213, 214, 215, 216, 217, 218; Timothy (*see Corporal*), 3, 47, 49, 51, 57, 72, 75, 79, 92, 96, 99, 100, 101, 102, 107, 109, 113, 117, 118, 119, 121, 122, 123, 126, 127, 128, 129, 130, 131, 135, 144, 148, 150, 151, 152, 153, 154, 155, 156, 157, 158, 160, 163, 168, 171, 173, 181, 182, 184, 185, 190, 192, 212, 214, 216, 221; Corporal, 129, 130.

EAMES—Robert, 153, 190; Thomas, 3, 71, 74, 80, 81, 82, 91, 95, 98, 106, 108, 109, 168, 181; ——, 169.

EATON—John, 3, 31, 35, 37, 39, 40, 41, 43, 48, 49, 51, 53, 60, 72, 73, 75, 80, 92, 93, 95, 96, 97, 100, 103, 106, 107, 110, 113, 114, 110, 118, 124, 140, 143, 152, 154, 158, 161, 168, 170, 174, 175, 176, 182, 184, 190, 198, 204, 205, 212, 213, 216, 221; ——, 154.

EDWARDS—Matthew, 194, 214.

ELDERKIN—John, 3, 83, 94.

ELLICE and ELLIS—John, 3. 20, 27, 33, 45, 49, 50, 70, 75, 79, 82, 87, 88, 95, 100, 107, 109, 113, 152, 155, 158, 161, 165, 172, 174, 175, 176, 185, 219; Joseph, 3, 135, 144, 145, 146, 190, 192, 198; Richard, 3, 18, 19, 85, 93, 95, 107, 109, 113, 123, 130, 144, 145, 146, 147, 152, 156, 158, 160, 162, 178, 181, 183, 190, 197, 198, 201, 205, 210, 212, 214, 216, 218, 219, 221; Tho., 161, 198; ——, 154.

EVERETT—Richard, 3, 20, 22, 25, 27, 40, 47, 49, 51, 75, 92, 96, 98, 100, 105, 106, 108, 109, 113, 114, 134, 140, 143, 152, 154, 158, 160, 162, 170, 171, 175, 182, 183, 190, 198, 203, 205, 206, 212, 213, 214, 216, 217, 219, 221.

INDEX OF NAMES. 229

FAIRBANK and FAYERBANKE—George, (see *Sergeant*), 3, 124, 152, 154, 158, 160, 181, 184, 190, 205, 212, 214, 216; John. 3, 63, 68, 83, 96, 110, 113, 143, 152, 154, 155, 158, 160, 178, 179, 183, 190, 197, 198, 205, 212, 214, 216; Jonas, 160; Jonathan, 3, 28, 29, 30, 31, 32, 35, 38, 40, 41, 43, 44, 45, 46, 47, 48, 49, 51, 53, 58, 75, 79, 80, 86, 92, 96, 103, 104, 110. 112, 113, 114, 116, 118, 134, 138, 139. 140, 143, 144, 146, 147, 151, 152, 154, 158, 160, 178, 179, 182, 183, 185, 190, 197, 198, 200, 204, 205, 212, 213, 214, 216, 219, 223; Sergeant, 143, 145, 171, 178, 198.

FALES (see *Vales*).

FARRINGTON — John, 114, 141, 143, 146, 148, 151, 158, 160, 162, 183, 185, 190, 198, 205, 212, 214, 216, 223.

FARROW—Jacob, 213, 214, 215.

FEKE—Robert, 3, 21, 22, 23, 25, 26, 35, 49, 50, 55, 57, 69, 167.

FISHER — Anthony, 3. 32, 35, 38, 40, 41, 43, 44, 45, 46, 47, 48, 49, 53, 66, 72, 73, 76, 78, 81, 84, 90, 92, 95, 104, 107, 108, 109, 110, 111, 112, 113, 114, 115, 116, 130, 131, 135, 138, 139, 140, 141, 142, 143, 144, 145, 146, 147, 148, 152, 153, 154, 155, 156, 158, 159, 160, 161, 168, 169, 170, 171, 173, 174, 175, 176, 177, 180, 181, 183, 184, 186, 187, 190, 193, 194, 195, 197, 198, 199, 201, 202, 203, 204, 205, 207, 208, 210, 211, 212, 213, 214, 216, 219, 223; Cornelius, 3, 138, 144, 146, 184, 190, 205, 212, 216, 219, 223; Daniel (see *Sergeant*),53, 66, 75, 79,89,90, 91, 92, 93, 100, 104, 108, 110, 113, 116, 124, 125, 126, 127, 128, 130, 131, 134, 135, 136, 137, 138, 139, 141, 143, 144, 145, 151, 153, 154, 157, 158, 159, 160, 161, 163, 164, 169, 170, 171, 172, 173, 174, 175, 176, 179, 183, 184, 186, 189, 190, 191, 197, 200, 202, 205, 211, 212, 214, 215, 216, 217, 218. 219, 223; Elizabeth (see *Widow*), 95, 106, 107, 110, 153, 161; John, 3, 32, 46; Joseph, 152; Joshua (see *Lieut*.), 3. 38, 65, 75, 87, 89, 98, 100, 104, 106, 109, 113, 114, 115, 116, 123, 124, 125, 128, 129, 130, 135, 136, 137, 140, 141, 143, 144, 145, 146, 147, 148, 152, 153, 156, 157, 158, 159, 160. 168, 172, 178,182,183,187,188, 189, 190, 198, 204, 205, 207, 211, 212, 213, 214, 216, 217; Nathaniel. 143, 145, 146, 180, 181, 183, 190, 192, 198, 205, 212, 214, 215, 216, 219; Samuel, 3, 140, 144. 145, 146, 212, 223; Thomas, 3, 32, 33, 38, 40, 41, 43, 44, 45, 46, 49, 51, 144, 161, 173, 176, 212; Ensign, 148; Lieut. (see *Joshua*), 124, 125, 126, 127, 128, 129, 130, 131, 133, 134, 135, 136, 137, 138, 139, 140, 148, 157, 160, 161, 162, 163, 164, 165, 166, 167, 169, 170, 171, 172, 173, 175, 176, 177, 179, 180, 182, 183, 185, 186, 188, 189, 190, 191, 192, 193, 194, 195, 196, 197, 198, 199, 200, 201, 202, 203, 204, 206, 207, 208, 209, 210, 211, 212, 213, 214, 215, 216, 217, 218; Serg^t (see *Daniel*), 126, 127, 128, 129, 130, 135, 136, 139, 140, 143, 144, 147, 148, 163, 164, 166, 167, 169, 170, 173, 176, 179, 180, 182, 183, 185, 186, 188, 189, 193, 194, 195, 196, 197, 198, 199, 200, 201, 202, 203, 204, 206, 207, 208, 209, 210, 212, 213, 214, 215, 217, 218; Widow,59, 65, 158.

FOLGER—John, 48.

FOSTER—Samuel, 152, 178.

FRARY—John, 3, 37, 40, 41, 43, 45, 46, 47, 48, 49, 51, 53, 75, 80, 86, 92, 96, 100, 105, 106, 110, 113, 115, 124, 126, 152, 154, 155, 158, 160, 162, 163, 171, 173, 174, 175, 183, 185, 190, 194, 196, 198, 205, 209, 210, 212, 214, 216; Theo. 143, 214, 216.

FREEMAN—Ralph, 3, 135, 144, 146, 184, 190, 192, 198, 203, 205, 212, 214, 216, 217.

FROST—Elder, 163.

FULLER—Giles, 50, 94; Robert, 113, 120, 143, 152, 154, 155, 158, 160, 163, 171, 178, 183, 185, 190, 198, 203, 205, 212. 214, 216; Thomas, 3, 91, 110, 113, 134, 135, 138, 139, 141, 143, 147, 152, 154, 157, 158, 161, 170, 174, 175, 176, 177, 183, 184, 186, 190, 193, 198, 201, 205, 210, 212, 213, 214, 216, 217, 223.

GAYE—John, 3, 20, 21, 22, 25, 26, 28, 29, 30, 31, 32, 35, 38, 40, 41, 43, 45, 48, 51, 75, 89, 91, 92, 95, 104, 105, 110, 113, 115, 118, 124, 130, 131, 133, 134, 138, 139, 140, 143, 150, 151, 153, 154, 155, 158, 161, 169, 170, 173, 174, 176, 177, 184, 189, 190, 199, 201, 202, 203, 205, 206, 207, 208, 210, 212, 214, 215, 216. 219, 223.

GENERE. GENERY and CHENERY — John, 153, 214; Lambert, 3, 20. 21, 22, 23, 26, 27, 28, 29, 30, 31, 32, 38, 40, 41, 43, 44. 45. 46, 47, 49, 51, 53, 54, 56, 61, 72, 92, 96, 104, 107, 110, 113, 114, 115, 121, 125, 127, 136, 143, 145, 146, 151, 152, 153, 155, 158, 160, 162, 165, 167, 168, 169, 172, 175, 178, 182, 183, 184, 190, 193, 195, 198, 205, 206, 212, 214, 215, 216.

GLOVER—Henry, 3, 93, 97, 110, 152, 158, 161, 178, 179, 186, 190, 198, 205; John, 137.

GOWEN and GOWING—Robert, 3, 75, 87, 91, 95, 105, 110, 113, 151, 152. 154, 155.

GREENE—Samuel, 136; Mr., 41, 106, 128. 159.

GUILD and GUILE—John, 3, 79, 92, 96, 97, 105, 110, 113, 143, 152, 154. 158, 160, 162, 168, 179, 183, 185, 190, 198, 205, 212, 214, 216, 223.

HARTLEY—Rich. 214, 216.

HASTINGS—Thomas, 3, 20, 21, 22, 23, 25, 26, 27, 31, 40, 46, 54, 55, 61.

HAWARD and HAYWARD—John, 3, 22, 23, 25, 26, 27, 29, 31, 32, 35, 36, 38, 40, 43, 44, 47, 48, 49, 50, 54, 61, 62, 63, 64, 66, 67, 68, 69, 70, 71, 72, 74, 75, 76, 77, 80, 81, 84, 86, 92, 93, 94, 95, 96, 98, 100, 101, 102, 103, 104, 105, 106, 108, 110, 111, 112, 113, 123, 124, 126, 127, 130, 134, 138, 139, 140,

141, 143, 147, 148, 152, 154, 158, 161, 168, 170, 172, 174, 175, 176, 182, 184, 186, 190, 194, 198, 201, 202, 205, 211, 213, 216, 219, 223.

HAWES—Edward, 134, 144, 152, 154, 155, 156, 158, 161, 168, 172, 180, 182, 184, 189, 190, 198, 201, 205, 212, 214, 216, 219, 223.
HAYNES—Mr., 23, 29, 130, 132, 164, 191.
HERRING—James, 3, 56, 94, 96, 168; Thomas, 3, 101, 111, 143, 152, 154, 158, 160, 171, 172, 173, 180, 181, 184, 190, 198, 203, 205, 212, 214, 216, 217, 223.
HINSDELL—Robert, 3, 32, 33, 35, 38, 40, 44,45,46,47, 49, 51, 53, 54, 59, 60, 61, 62, 63, 64, 66, 67, 68, 69, 70, 71, 72, 73, 74, 75, 79, 92, 97, 100, 104, 105, 106, 108, 110, 113, 114, 154, 165, 166, 167, 171, 172, 175, 178, 187, 188, 192, 194, 200, 223.
HOLLIMAN—Ezechiell, 3, 21, 22, 23, 25, 26, 27, 28, 32, 223.
HOUGHTON—John, 3, 139, 144, 145, 146, 184, 190, 214.
HUBBERT and HUBARD—Anthony, 144, 146, 152, 155, 158, 161, 162, 180, 184, 185, 186, 190, 198, 203, 205, 212, 214, 216.
HUDSON—William, 60, 62.
HUGGIN—John, 3, 20, 22, 23, 25, 26, 27, 28, 29, 38, 40, 41, 44, 45, 46, 48, 49, 51, 53, 56, 168.
HUMFREY and HUMPHREY—Jonas, 3, 42, 50, 67, 74.
HUNTING—John, 3, 48, 49, 51, 53, 75, 79, 84, 86, 90, 92, 95, 100, 104, 105, 106, 107, 111, 113, 142, 146, 147, 148, 152, 153, 158, 160, 171, 172, 179, 180, 183, 190, 193, 198, 205, 211, 213, 216, 223.

JAXTON—Mr., 170.
JOHNSON—Surveyor General, 136.
JONS—Thomas, 137.
JORDAN—James, 3, 74, 88, 95, 100, 102, 109, 152, 158, 160, 182, 185, 190, 198, 205, 212, 214; Thomas, 3, 60, 61, 79, 95, 106, 110, 113, 121, 143, 152, 154, 158, 161, 168, 174, 180, 183, 184, 186, 189, 190, 198, 203, 205, 211, 212, 214, 216.
JUDSON—Samuel, 105, 107, 108, 113, 143, 152, 154, 155, 158, 161, 162, 169, 181, 184, 190, 194, 195, 198, 205, 212, 214, 216, 223.

KALEM—Austen, 3, 76, 82, 92, 95, 96, 97, 99, 100, 104, 107, 109, 113, 151, 152, 154, 168, 169, 171, 172, 175; John, 152, 158, 161, 162, 185.
KAYNE—Capt., 170.
KEMPE—Edward, 3, 47, 48, 49, 51, 53, 66, 84, 92, 93, 96, 98, 100, 104, 106, 107, 110, 113, 151, 152, 154, 171, 172, 173, 176, 178, 181, 185.
KENT—John, 214; Joshua, 98, 100, 113, 129, 144, 154, 161, 164, 168, 184, 190, 198, 200, 203. 204, 205, 212, 214, 216, 217.
KINGSBURY—Henry, 23; John, 3, 20, 21, 22, 25, 26, 27, 29, 31, 32, 35, 36, 41, 42, 43, 44,47,48, 49, 50, 51, 52, 53, 54, 57, 59, 60, 61,

62, 63, 64, 66, 67, 68, 69, 70, 71, 72, 73, 74, 75, 76, 77, 79, 80, 81, 82, 84, 92, 95, 96, 97, 99, 100, 101, 103, 106, 107, 109, 110, 113, 114, 115, 116, 117, 118, 119, 121, 122, 123, 124, 125, 126, 127, 128, 129, 130, 131, 134, 135, 138, 139, 140, 142, 150, 151, 152, 153, 154, 155, 156, 157, 158, 159, 160, 161, 162, 163, 164, 166, 167, 168, 169, 170, 173, 176, 177, 179, 182, 184, 185, 188, 189, 190, 192, 193,194,195,196,197, 198, 199, 200, 201, 203, 201,205,206,207,209, 210, 211, 212, 213, 214, 215, 216, 217, 218; Joseph, 3, 32, 33, 35, 38, 39, 40, 41, 42, 43, 44, 45, 46, 49, 51, 53, 55, 56, 75, 78, 90, 92, 95, 97, 99, 100, 104, 105, 107, 108, 109, 113, 114, 115, 118, 124, 128, 129, 134, 135, 140, 143, 147, 152, 153, 156, 158, 159, 160, 162, 166, 167, 169, 170, 171, 172, 176, 183, 185, 190, 193, 195, 198, 202, 203, 205, 212, 213, 216, 225.

LEADER—John, 160; Thomas, 3, 48, 49, 51, 53, 59, 92, 96, 104. 109, 113, 154, 204.
LITTLEFIELD—John, 129, 184, 214.
LOWER—Mr., 72.
LUSHER—Eleazer, 3, 32, 35, 36, 37, 38, 40, 41, 44, 45, 46, 47, 49, 51, 52, 53, 54, 57, 59, 61, 62, 63, 64, 66, 67, 68, 69, 70, 71, 72, 74, 75, 76, 77, 78, 79, 80, 81, 82, 84, 88, 89, 90, 91, 92, 93, 94, 96, 97, 98, 99, 100, 101, 103, 105, 106, 107, 108, 110, 111, 112, 113, 114, 115, 116, 117, 118, 119. 121, 122, 123, 124, 125,126,127,128,129, 130, 131, 133, 134, 135, 138, 139, 140, 141, 142, 147, 148, 150, 151, 152, 153, 155, 156, 157, 158, 159, 160, 161, 162, 163, 164, 165, 166, 167, 169, 170, 171, 173, 174, 175, 176, 177, 179, 180, 182, 183, 185, 186, 187, 188, 189, 190, 191, 193, 194, 195, 196, 197, 198, 199, 200, 201, 203, 204, 205, 206, 207, 208, 209, 210, 211, 212, 213, 214, 215, 216, 217, 218.
LUSON—John, 3, 32, 35, 38, 40, 41,43,44,45, 46,47,48,49, 51, 52, 53, 54, 57, 59, 60, 61, 62, 63, 64, 66, 67, 68, 69, 70, 71, 72, 73, 74, 75, 77, 80, 87, 91, 92,97, 98,99,100,101,104,108, 110, 113, 117, 126, 143, 146, 153. 154, 158, 161, 163, 168, 169, 170, 173, 174, 176, 184, 186, 189, 190, 198, 205, 211, 213, 216, 219.

MAKEPIECE—Tho., 155, 161.
MAPLEHEAD—Widow, 205, 212.
MASON—John, 3, 132, 144, 145, 180, 181, 185, 190, 194, 198, 205. 212, 214, 216; Robert, 61, 75,92,94,95, 100, 107, 111, 113, 143, 145, 146, 152, 153, 158, 160, 162, 172, 183, 185, 190, 193, 194, 198,205,212,214,225.
METCALF—John, 104, 152. 154. 158, 160, 178, 183, 185, 190, 198, 205; Michael, 3, 32, 35, 38, 40, 41, 43, 44, 45, 46, 47, 49, 51, 53, 58, 63, 69, 70, 75, 76, 77, 78, 79, 80, 81, 82, 92, 96, 103, 104. 106. 107, 109, 110, 113, 114, 115, 126, 135, 138, 140, 142, 145, 146, 147, 149, 152, 154, 158, 160, 162, 168, 171,173.178,182,183. 185, 190, 193, 194, 198, 201, 203. 205, 211, 212, 213, 214, 216, 225; Thomas, 3, 141, 143, 146, 184, 225.

INDEX OF NAMES. 231

MILLS—Samuel, 3, 105, 112, 113, 134, 144, 145, 161, 164, 180, 184, 190, 198, 205, 212, 214, 216.

MORSE and MOYSE—Daniel, 3, 20, 22, 23, 28, 29, 30, 31, 32, 33, 35, 38, 40, 41, 43, 45, 46, 48, 49, 51, 53, 75, 83, 85, 92, 93, 96, 97, 100, 104, 105, 106, 107, 110, 113, 118, 140, 150, 152, 154, 158, 161, 168, 169, 178, 180, 186; John, 3, 32, 33, 35, 38, 39, 40, 44, 45, 47, 51, 53, 69, 75, 92, 95, 100, 104, 109, 110, 113, 126, 131, 132, 135, 138, 139, 151, 152, 158, 160, 164, 169, 170, 171, 172, 173, 174,175,178,184,186, 189, 190, 191, 193, 198, 201, 204, 205, 210, 212, 214, 216, 225; Joseph, 3, 20, 29, 30, 31, 33, 35, 38, 40,41,43, 45, 46, 48, 49, 75, 93, 94, 95, 98, 99, 100, 107, 109, 110, 113, 141, 167, 173, 174, 175, 178, 179, 186, 187, 188, 206, 217; Mary, 167; Samuel, 3, 20, 21, 22, 23, 25, 26, 27, 28, 29, 30, 31, 32, 35, 38, 39, 40, 41, 43, 44, 45, 46, 47, 48, 49, 51, 53, 55, 70, 71, 73, 75, 76, 77, 78, 79, 80, 81, 82, 83, 84, 85, 86, 89, 90, 95, 97, 101, 104, 106, 108, 110, 113, 114, 116, 118, 150, 152, 153, 158, 160, 168, 179, 180, 182, 183, 185, 190, 198, 205; Widow, 141; ——, 167.

MYNGEY—Jeffery, 3, 34, 42, 49, 59, 60.

NEWTON—John, 86, 93, 94, 95, 100, 104, 106, 109, 144, 157, 158, 189, 212, 214, 216.

OLIVER—John, 44, 61, 79, 165, 170.
ONION—Robert, 3, 105, 110, 113, 144, 148, 152, 153, 158, 160, 183, 187, 190, 193, 198, 203, 205, 212, 214, 216.

PARKER—John, 161; Mr., 94.
PARKES— ——, 59, 62.
PARTRIDGE—John, 3, 138, 204, 212, 213, 225.
PAYNE—Thomas, 3, 73, 92, 95, 98, 107, 111, 113, 125, 127, 128, 143, 145, 152, 154, 158, 161, 163, 175, 179, 181, 184, 186, 190, 194, 198, 205, 212, 214, 216, 225.
PHILLIPS—Henry (see Ensign), 3, 32, 33, 35, 38, 40, 41, 42, 44, 45, 48, 49, 51, 75, 84, 85, 91, 92, 93, 95, 100, 104, 105, 106, 108, 111, 113, 143, 152, 153, 156, 158, 160, 171, 172, 176, 179, 180, 183, 190, 203, 205, 208, 212, 213, 216, 225; Martin, 3, 33, 35, 38, 40, 41, 44, 47, 48, 49, 51, 53, 91, 174, 175; Nicholas, 3, 20, 21, 22, 25, 28, 29, 30, 31, 32, 33, 34, 35, 38, 39, 40, 41, 42, 43, 44, 45, 47, 48, 49, 50, 51, 53, 84, 167, 178; Ensign (see Henry). 126, 130, 138, 140, 198, 199, 201, 202, 203, 206, 207, 208, 209, 210, 215, 216, 218; Mr., 48, 88.
PLIMPTON—John, 3, 97, 110, 113, 152, 154, 155, 158, 160, 184, 187, 190, 192, 198, 225.
POND—Daniel, 3, 135, 144, 181, 186, 187, 190, 192, 195, 198, 201, 202, 203, 205, 207, 212, 214, 216, 217, 219, 225.
POPE—John, 52.
POWELL—Michael, 3, 62, 66, 80, 92, 93, 94, 96, 97, 98, 99, 100, 101, 102, 103, 104, 105, 106, 107, 108, 109, 111, 112, 123, 152, 154, 158, 180.

PRENTICE—Tho., 161.
PRUDDEN—Peter, 33; Mr., 35.

RICE—John, 3, 135, 144, 148, 190, 192, 194, 201, 212, 214, 219.
RICHARDS—Edward, 3, 50, 54, 61, 72, 75, 82, 87, 91, 92, 96, 97, 104, 107, 110, 111, 112, 113, 139, 141, 143, 147, 148, 152, 154, 155, 158, 160, 162, 171, 172, 173, 175, 178, 179, 181, 184, 185, 186, 190, 194, 198, 203, 205, 212, 213, 214, 216.
ROCKWOOD— ——, 194.
ROGERS—John, 3, 20, 21, 22, 27, 28, 29,30, 31, 32, 35, 38, 40, 44, 45, 46, 47, 48, 49, 51, 58, 168, 178, 185.
ROPER—John, 3, 33, 35, 38, 40, 41, 44, 45, 47, 49, 51, 53, 75, 83, 92, 95, 98, 103, 109, 168, 174, 175, 176.
RUGGLES—John, 136.

SALUADGE—Tho., 214.
SHAWE—Abraham, 3, 20, 21, 22, 23, 25, 26, 27, 28, 29, 30, 31, 32, 35, 36, 38, 40, 41, 43, 44, 45, 47, 48, 49, 51, 52, 115; John, 61; Joseph, 3, 21, 22, 26, 28, 30, 31, 32, 35, 38, 40, 45, 46, 48, 51, 61; Mr., 35.
SHEPARD—Ralph, 3, 20, 21, 22, 23, 27, 28, 29, 30, 31, 32, 33, 35, 37, 38, 39, 40, 41, 43, 45, 46, 47, 49, 51, 53, 58, 72, 94, 167, 168, 172, 174, 175, 190.
SHERMAN—John, 135.
SMITH and SMYTH—Benjamin, 3, 87, 89, 109, 113; Christopher, 3, 67, 74, 92, 96, 100, 106, 107, 110, 113, 143, 145, 151, 152, 154, 158, 161, 175, 176, 180, 182, 184, 190, 198, 205, 212, 214, 216; Henry, 3, 34, 37, 38, 40, 41, 44, 45, 47, 49, 51, 53, 57, 79, 83, 92, 95, 104, 107, 110, 113, 124, 126, 143, 146, 152, 154, 158, 160, 172, 173, 178, 183, 190, 195, 198, 202, 203, 205, 212, 214, 216; John, 216; Mr., 68; Mrs., 69.
STACEY—Hugh, 3, 73.
STEARNES—Nathaniel, 153, 158, 161, 162, 214, 216, 225.
STOUGHTON—Israel, 58, 59, 60, 61, 74, 80, 91, 104, 105, 167, 194; Mrs., 114, 148, 166, 187, 188, 191, 206.
STRICKLAND—Thwaits, 3, 72, 75, 78, 95, 110, 113, 143, 152, 153, 154, 158, 160, 162, 180, 181, 183, 185, 190, 192, 198, 205, 212, 214, 216.
SUMNER—Sergeant, 136.

THORP—James, 3, 139, 144, 145, 146, 190, 214, 216, 225.
THURSTON—John, 3, 88, 92, 95, 99, 100, 102, 104, 110, 113, 115, 123, 126, 132, 140, 153, 154, 156, 158, 160, 161, 163, 164, 168, 178, 181, 225.
TING—Mr., 94.
TRUMBLE— ——, 50.
TYLER— ——, 114.

VALES and FALES—James, 3, 139, 144, 146, 190, 221.
WALTON—Henry, 188.
WARD—Thomas, 50, 94.
WARE—Robert, 3, 91, 95, 107, 110, 113, 141, 143, 148, 152, 154, 155, 158, 161, 162, 176, 178, 181, 184, 190, 198, 205, 212, 214, 216, 219, 225.
WARWICK—Earl of, 188.
WEBB—Christo., 214.
WEEDEN— ——,48.
WHEELER—Richard, 114, 143, 151, 152, 154, 158, 160, 162, 183, 185, 190, 198, 201, 203, 205, 212, 214, 216.
WHEELOCK—Ralph, 3. 32, 34, 35, 38, 40, 41, 43, 44, 45, 47, 48, 49, 51, 53, 60, 62, 63, 64, 66, 67, 68, 69, 70, 71, 72, 74, 75, 77, 79, 80, 81, 82, 87, 90, 92, 94, 97, 100, 104, 110, 113, 114, 115, 153, 154, 156, 158, 161, 168, 173, 174, 175, 184, 186, 190, 194, 225.
WHITING — Nathaniel, 3, 92, 96, 103, 109, 134, 143, 152, 154, 158, 160, 163, 168, 177, 180, 184, 185, 190, 194, 198, 203, 205, 210, 211, 212, 214, 216.
WHITMORE—Robt., 27.
WIGHT—Henry, 139, 144, 190, 202, 204, 205, 212, 214, 216, 219, 225; John, 204; Thomas, 3, 32, 35, 38, 39, 40, 44, 45, 46, 48, 49, 51, 53, 54, 60, 66, 69, 72, 73, 75, 76, 77, 78, 79, 80, 81, 82, 83, 84, 85, 86, 87, 88, 89, 90, 91, 92, 93, 94, 95, 96, 97, 98, 99, 100, 101, 102, 103, 104, 106, 107, 108, 109, 112, 113, 114, 115, 116, 117, 118, 119, 121, 122, 123, 124, 125, 130, 131, 144, 150, 151, 152, 153, 154, 155, 156, 157, 158, 160, 161, 162, 168, 173, 174, 176, 178, 180, 181, 184, 186, 189, 190, 198, 204, 211, 212, 213, 216; ——, 165, 169.
WILLIAMS—Robert, 37, 40, 41.
WILSON—Henry, 68, 71, 76, 77, 96, 103, 104, 107, 109, 112, 113, 127, 144, 148, 153, 154, 155, 157, 158, 161, 162, 163, 168, 174, 180, 184, 186, 190, 198, 205, 212, 214, 216.
WINTHROP—John, 23.
WOODE—Ellice, 3, 140.
WOODWARD—Peter, 3, 71, 74, 80, 92, 93, 94, 96, 97, 98, 99, 100, 101, 103, 104, 105, 107, 110, 112, 113, 114, 116, 118, 127, 129, 135, 138, 139, 140, 141, 143, 148, 151, 152, 154, 156, 157, 158, 160, 169, 171, 172, 180, 183, 185, 190, 193, 194, 195, 196, 197, 198, 199, 200, 201, 203, 204, 205, 206, 208, 209, 210, 211, 212, 213, 214, 215, 216, 217, 218, 225.

YONGS—Richard, 48.

INDEX OF SUBJECTS.

AMMUNITION—31, 128, 138, 192, 193, 208, 209, 210, 213, 217.
ARBITRATION—2, 11, 77, 116, 120, 133, 134, 137, 144, 166, 167, 191, 202, 204, 209.
AUTOGRAPHS—42, 76, 89, 100, 141, 221, 223, 225.

BALDPATE—Hill, 86, 87, 90; Meadow, 99, 204.
BARREN HILLS—29.
BAY (Boston?)—83.
BELFRY—187,197; Bell, 148, 151, 165, 170, 177, 187, 188, 189, 191, 197, 200, 207, 217.
BIRDS—19.
BIRTHS, Reg. of—66, 96.
BLACKSMITH—47.
BLUE HILLS—170.
BOARDS, for Apparel—88; for Corn, 83; for Pay, 113, 115, 215.
BOATS—49, 98; Boating Place, 29.
BOGASTOW—67, 68, 121, 128, 171, 174, 189, 201.
BOSTON—22, 61, 136, 153, 165, 170, 188, 189, 201, 203, 207.
BOUNDARY LINE—12, 79, 126; Boston, 61; Dorchester, 58, 59, 81, 133, 136, 137, 139, 156, 164, 165, 170, 208; Cambridge, 128, 136, 159, 160, 200, 204; Medfield, 189, 219; Roxbury, 23, 135; Watertown, 30, 135, 179.
BRAINTREE—153, 197, 203.
BRICK—74, 75, 80, 106, 125, 127, 163, 207; Ground, 168; Kill, 73, 98, 106; Maker, 74, 106; Strieker, 48.
BRIDGE—21, 73; At the Canoes, 138; Footbridge, 36, 60, 71, 72, 73, 136, 170; Little Bridge, 111; Little River, 23, 35, 170; Mill Creek, 170, (see also Cart Bridge).
BROAD MEADOW—125, 138, 151, 162, 171, 172, 174, 175, 185.
BUILDING—15, 24, 83, 34, 55.
BURIAL PLACE—42, 57, 165.

CAMBRIDGE—128, 129, 132, 134, 136, 159, 160, 163, 191, 193, 200, 203, 204.
CANOES—12, 37, 49, 123, 138, 183, 184.
CARPENTERS—39, 124, 177, 186, 187, 188, 201, 202, 203, 207.
CART BRIDGE—71, 102, 132, 210.

CARTS—8, 112, 113, 163; Cart Ways (see Ways.)
CATTLE—10, 11, 16, 27, 47, 53, 70, 74, 81, 119, 122, 124, 125, 142, 193, 196, 211; Dry Herd, 19, 126, 133, 135, 155, 156, 162, 191, 193, 198, 199, 211; Home Herd, 19, Stover for, 47.
CAUSEWAY—35, 49, 71, 181.
CHARGES—Public or Country, 1, 2, 4, 22, 43, 165 (see also Rates).
CHARLES RIVER—1, 2, 22, 35, 36, 48, 56, 58, 69, 72, 81, 82, 93, 94, 102, 103, 104, 118, 123, 125, 137, 138, 148, 150, 151, 159, 161, 171, 178, 180, 185, 209, 218, 219.
CHILDREN—16, 202.
CHIMNEY STOCK—206.
CHURCH—24, 56, 92, 167; Lands, 92, 114, 128, 174, 194.
CLAPBOARDS—25, 30, 32, 36, 45, 140.
CLAY—112, 113, 125, 127,162,215; Ground, 112, 169; Pits, 35, 50, 80, 84, 127.
CLERK—(see Town); of the Trained Band, 30; of the Writs, 200.
CLIFF—The, 21.
CLIFTS—210.
COLLECTOR—23, 25, 26, 31, 34, 36, 49, 53, 55, 64, 75, 78, 81, 83, 93, 101.
COMMISSIONERS—140, 218.
COMMON—80, 112, 218.
COMMONS—144, 145, 146, 147; Com Land, 7, 9, 15, 16, 77, 90, 91, 117, 118, 121, 123, 124, 125, 145, 150, 155, 157, 162, 180, 193, 196, 215; Com. Rights, 141, 142, 144, 145.
CONCORD—2.
CONSTABLE—1, 4, 6, 7, 8, 15, 18, 101, 111, 118, 121, 122, 126, 131, 132, 150, 151, 153, 154, 155, 159, 160, 185, 192, 196, 200, 202, 203, 206, 207, 209, 210, 213, 214, 215, 217, 218.
CONTENTMENT—1, 20, 21.
CORN—11, 12, 83, 84, 115, 122, 124, 125, 169, 182, 188, 207; fields, 5, 11, 124, 125; mill, 27, 28, 29, 51; for Bell, 191; for Fines, 8; for Pay, 8, 179; for voting, 18.
COURSE—Meadow, 70, 88; Swamp, 172.
COURT—Quarter, 57; (see also General Court.)
COVENANT—2, 4, 16, 20, 165, 196; Breaker, 20.
Cow—Common, 142, 145, 146; pasturing, 127.

CREEK—98, 138.
CROPS—12, 169.

DEACONS—164, 167, 189.
DEAD SWAMP—168.
DEATHS—Reg. of, 66, 96.
DEBTS—7, 52, 132, 201.
DEED—58, 178, 179, 180, 181.
DEPUTIES AND GENERAL COURT—15, 16, 30, 44, 191, 193, 201.
DISTRESS—4, 7, 8, 53, 55, 85.
DITCH—50, 51, 60, 65, 98, 138, 151.
DIVIDEND—5, 13, 92, 93, 99, 100, 124, 127, 130, 133, 140, 141, 142, 144, 145, 147, 148, 156, 157, 162, 182, 193, 201, 211.
DIVISION OF LAND—142.
DOGS—162, 164, 165; Hounds, 132. 162.
DORCHESTER—58, 59, 60, 81, 133, 136, 137, 139, 153, 156, 164, 165, 170, 196, 197, 208, 218.
DRAWN WAY—14, 78, 183, 184, 217; (see *Highway.*)
DRUMS—Beating, 30, 113, 157, 164.

EAR MARKS—52.
EAST BROOK—51, 70.
EAST PLAIN—33, 74, 79, 97.
EAST STREET—13, 18, 76, 82, 84, 91, 93, 97, 111, 171, 179, 180, 201, 217.
EDUCATION—15, 16, 105, 135.

FALLS—1, 26.
FARM—Alleyn, 67, 128, 168, 201; Allin, 71, 72, 102, 219; Cooke, 69, 82, 151, 159; Dudley, 153; Feke, 21, 35, 50, 55, 69, 167; Frost, 163; Greene, 159; Haynes, 23; Lower, 72; Parker, 94; Phillips, 215; Stoughton, 59; Tyng, 94.
FARMS—Granting of, 5, 80, 156.
FEEDING OF CATTLE—11, 16, 124, 133, 141. 155, 219, 220.
FEES—75, 196; for Poundage, 6; Swine Keeper, 19; Town Clerk, 13, 177.
FENCES—5, 9, 11, 12, 17, 19, 28, 37, 41, 65, 67, 76, 77. 81, 82, 84, 96, 97, 101, 104, 106, 107, 108, 115, 117, 118, 120, 125, 150, 159, 169; Viewers and Viewing, 5, 6, 9, 19, 97, 118, 150.
FEOFFEES—105, 108, 155.
FINES—4–9, 11, 12, 14, 15, 17–20, 25–28, 30, 31, 36. 61–65, 78, 85. 125, 127, ·157, 159, 164, 166, 183, 184. 185, 194, 196, 199.
FIRE—7, 19, 64; Firewood, 12, 15, 16, 127, 190, 192, 195, 196.
FISHING FREE—4, 20.
FLUE BOARDS—187, 197.
FOOT-PATHS—34, 79, 84.
FOWL MEADOW—136, 137, 139, 155, 157, 181, 209, 218.

GATES—12, 84, 107, 169; South Plain, 123.
GAUGER—183.
GENERAL COURT—Petition to, 1; Dedham Plantation, 2; Confirmation of Grant, 22, 170.
GENT—67, 69, 73, 77, 88.
GIRLS—202.
GLASS—218.
GOATS—52, 142, 145.
GRANT—to Town, 112. 116; to Village, 126; Grants, 1, 2, 4, 5, 9, 10, 12. 13, 14, 16, 20, 21, 24, 28, 36, 40. 42, 43, 47, 52. 55, 69, 77, 85, 86, 92, 93, 97, 109, 110, 111, 119, 125, 126, 127, 133. 140. 142, 162, 167, 186, 211; Relinquished, 87, 93.
GRASS—57, 108.
GRATIFICATION LOT—33, 34, 37, 45, 46, 47, 74.
GRAVE DIGGER—164.
GREAT ISLAND—28, 35, 55, 71, 73, 74, 82, 83, 85.
GREAT MEADOW—45.
GREAT PLAIN—13, 76, 94, 98, 99, 102, 103, 104, 106, 107, 113. 114, 121, 123, 159, 166, 168, 169, 171, 178, 179, 180, 181, 185, 191, 202. 204. 219.
GREAT POND—46, 81, 172, 176.
GREAT RIVER—36.

HARVARD COLLEGE—138.
HAY—102.
HEIRS—Rights, 135, 192.
HERD—House, 204, 206, 207; Keeper, 11, 125; Yard, 207; Herdsman, 19, 198, 199, 211; Place, 201.
HIGH STREET—72, 204, 205.
HIGHWAYS—6, 9, 14, 36, 37, 46, 58, 66, 67, 71, 73. 76, 77, 78, 80, 82, 86, 88, 89, 96, 97, 98. 100, 101, 102, 103, 105, 112, 114, 115, 118, 121, 125, 150, 151, 163, 166, 169, 171–176, 179, 180, 181, 183, 184, 185, 201, 204; Surveyors, 8, 9, 13, 75, 112, 116, 122, 161, 162, 185; Work, 8, 13, 23, 112, 116, 122, 124, 147, 148, 149, 155, 159–163, 170, 180, 189, 193–196, 203, 210, 218.
HILLS—21, 35, 45, 46, 50, 51, 87.
HINGHAM—153.
HOGS—Park, 50; Yard, 28.
HOME LOTS—9, 51, 74, 90, 121, 171, 173.
HOOP POLES—104, 112.
HORSES—17, 150, 191, 193; Horseway, 34.
HOUSES—6, 7, 17, 19, 25, 33, 34, 38, 39, 41, 45, 47, 50, 56, 57, 60, 64, 71, 83, 106, 108, 112, 116, 117, 141, 142, 153, 157, 162. 170, 177, 196; Valuation, 153, 154, 182, 183; House Lots, 5, 10, 16, 21, 33, 35, 30, 45, 52, 55, 68, 71, 77, 82, 86, 87, 89, 91, 92, 96, 98, 99, 100, 103, 112, 114, 117, 119, 123, 130, 180, 181, 183, 190, 201, 203.
HUGGINS BROOK—170.
HULL—153.
HUNTING—150, 162; Huntsman, 150, 154.
HUSBANDMAN—92.

INDEX TO RECORDS—132. 164, 166, 170.
INDIAN CORN—19, 115, 156.
INDIANS—31; at Natick, 130, 136, 137, 141, 147, 148; Weirs, 161.

INDEX OF SUBJECTS.   235

INFORMER—15, 17, 183, 185, 196.
IRELAND—68, 69.
IRON MINE—9, 10, 119; Work, 146, 147, 148.
ISLAND—13, 31. 37, 42, 76. 80, 81, 84, 93, 96, 97, 98, 99, 103, 105, 106, 108, 111, 136, 172, 180, 201.
ISLAND FIELD—159.
ISLAND PLAIN—97, 103, 108, 148, 168, 172, 175, 181.

JOINER—48.

KEY—The, 42.

LABORERS—10, 112, 120, 155, 161, 200, 218.
LADDERS—6, 7, 19, 64, 67, 76, 84, 97, 101, 117, 118, 165.
LANDING PLACE -115.
LAWS—Body of, 156.
LEAD- -119.
LEANTO—131, 157.
LECTURE—56, 150, 152, 156, 199, 209, 213, 215.
LICENSE—25, 48, 49, 50, 55, 71, 83.
LIME—218.
LITTLE BRIDGE—13, 111.
LITTLE BROOK—35.
LITTLE POND—172.
LITTLE RIVER—23, 27, 31, 35, 36, 41, 45, 46, 49, 57, 58, 112, 113. 170, 173. 178, 181.
LOTS—2, 4, 5, 12, 16, 20-24, 26, 33, 34, 36, 40, 43, 45, 51, 54, 55, 61, 67, 72, 79, 92, 93, 212, 213; 8-Acre Lots, 21, 23, 26, 31, 93, 180; 12-Acre Lots. 23, 26, 30, 31, 165; Alienation of, 7, 13, 24, 50, 52, 54, 85, 162, 165, 170, 177; Forfeited, 54, 55; Improvement of, 33; Returned, 31, 32, 37, 49, 50, 55, 57, 58.
LOW PLAIN—58, 80, 91, 98, 136, 137, 163.

MAGISTRATES—to end small Cases,123, 126, 134, 155. 162.
MARRIAGES—Reg. of, 66, 96.
MEADOW—5, 11, 13, 21, 44, 46, 54, 146, 148, 156, 170, 206, 218.
MEAL—84.
MEASURER—28, 36, 40, 43, 44, 66, 108.
MEASURES—131, 157.
MEDFIELD—12, 13, 128. 133, 140, 141, 168, 185, 189, 191-195, 197, 199, 200, 201, 204, 210, 211, 213, 215, 217, 218, 219.
MEETING HOUSE—18, 19, 26, 29, 38, 39, 44, 45, 48, 49, 51, 53, 55, 78, 94, 104, 108, 113, 115, 116, 122, 135, 139, 147, 148, 150, 151, 155, 162, 164, 165, 177, 186, 187, 188, 191, 193, 194, 196, 197, 202. 207, 213, 215, 217, 218; Deacons' Seat, 186; Seats, 115.
METALS—9, 119, 159.
MIDDLE PLAIN—13, 18. 33, 76, 78, 84, 97, 108, 111, 114, 131, 180, 201.
MILITARY—Company, 102, 121, 151, 168, 169; Exercises, 1.
MILL—28, 29, 51, 58, 79, 103, 130, 134, 137, 153, 154, 158, 163, 177, 184, 209, 210; Dorchester, 58, 59, 60; Miller, 134, 163.
MILL BROOK, or CREEK—71, 83, 114, 139, 164, 170, 172, 181, 190, 215, 218.
MILLPOND—83, 146.
MINE—9, 10, 11, 119, 120, 151, 159; Minerals, 9, 119, 120, 150, 159.
MONEY—151; English. 31; Marks, 50, 55, 69; Corn for, 8, 211; Rye for, 179, 211; Wheat for, 157, 211.
MOTHER BROOK—51, 137; (see also Mill Brook.)
MOUNT WOLLASTON, 170.

NATICK, 130, 136, 137, 141, 147, 148, 218, 219.
NEPONSET RIVER—58, 159; Neponset Swamp, 86.
NEWTOWN SWAMP—34.

OAK HILL—80.
OBOLUS—151, 213, 216.
OLD MILL—130, 210; Field, 102, 103.
ORDERS—4-19, 126, 169, 170.
OXEN—19, 81, 142, 163.

PALES—5, 28, 77, 117.
PAPER—164.
PASTOR—45, 56, 67, 71, 72, 78, 92, 102, 131, 157, 159, 190.
PASTURE—27, 79. 81, 97, 113.
PENTHOUSE—197.
PEQUOT WARS—51.
PETITION—1, 22.
PITS, THE—39.
PLAINS—37, 73, 89, 91, 219.
PLANCHER—157.
PLANTING FIELD—121, 127, 129, 130, 165, 166; Ground, 71, 72, 74, 79; Lot, 100, 102, 103.
PLAT—of the River, 208; of the Town, 126, 127, 162, 163.
PLOWING—Ground, 44, 78, 92; Plain, 81.
PLYMOUTH—170, 188.
PONDS—34, 46, 116, 175, 180; Free, 4, 20.
POUND—57, 86, 164, 173, 200, 201.
POWDER—(see Ammunition.)
PRAYER OF THANKSGIVING—for "success at yᵉ Courte Gen'rall." 22.
PROPRIETORS—106, 111, 125, 126, 133, 142, 144, 166, 192.
PRUDENTIAL AFFAIRS—88, 93, 100.
PUBLIC SERVICE—155.
PURCHASED LANDS—13, 26, 27, 40, 41, 50, 51. 59, 61, 101, 111, 127, 128, 133, 134, 156, 159, 160, 166, 167, 171, 180, 181, 187, 190, 191, 192, 219.
PURCHASER'S RIGHTS—135, 166.
PYRAMEDY—197.

QUADRANS—151.

RAILS—5, 12, 17, 28, 77, 117, 169.
RANK—92.

RATES—2, 5, 7, 8, 16, 19, 23, 24, 52, 53, 56, 64, 66, 103, 111, 114, 131, 132, 153, 156, 157, 158, 160, 171, 177, 191, 197, 198, 199, 200, 202, 203, 207, 214; Abatement of, 7, 111, 153; for Ammunition, 128, 209; for Constable, 150; Country Rate, 7, 114, 142, 152, 153, 156, 160, 161, 182, 183, 190, 191, 192, 203, 213, 217; for Debts, 52; for Huntsmen, 150; for Meetinghouse, 44, 53, 94, 113, 116, 150, 151; for School, 16, 105, 216; for School-house, 157; for Suffolk Co., 153; for Surveys, 43; for Watch-house, 157; for Ways, 138; for Wolves, 132, 151, 154.
RECOMPENSE GROUND—67, 71, 84, 85, 90, 121.
RECORDS—Approval, 23, *et seq.*
RECORD BOOK—85, 94, 206.
REGISTER OF BIRTHS, MARRIAGES, AND DEATHS—66, 96, 200.
REMOVAL OF TOWNSMEN—18, 141.
REPRESENTATIVES (*see Deputies.*)
RIVER POND—57.
RIVERS—Free, 4, 20.
ROCK FIELD—100, 219.
ROCK MEADOW—99, 102, 168, 201, 219.
ROCKS—The, 28, 35, 40, 56, 65, 69, 70, 106, 180, 189.
ROLL CALL—190.
ROSEMARY MEADOW—96, 102, 108, 109, 125, 171, 173, 174, 176, 178, 201.
ROXBURY—23, 114, 129, 133, 134, 135, 153, 197, 203.
RULE—for dividing lands, 142; of Persons and Estates, 141, 142, 156, 211.

SACK—fined a quart of, 199.
SAW MILL—147, 148.
SCALES—131.
SCANTLING—25, 39, 63.
SCHOOL—15, 16, 92, 105, 108, 135, 136, 155, 192, 202, 213; Feoffees, 105, 108, 155; House, 123, 132, 151, 156, 157, 182, 191, 192, 195, 207; Lands, 92, 105, 108, 155; Master, 15, 16, 105, 135, 136, 140, 147, 149, 193, 194, 202, 213, 214, 217; Rate, 16; Studies, 213.
SEEKONK—196.
SELECTMEN—4-12,15-19, 53, 62, 78, 88, 92, 101, 123, 126, 183, 188, 191, 194, 195, 200, 203, 206, 218; Selectmen's Day-Book, 150, 206; Diet, 15. 191, 193.
SERGEANT AT ARMS—29, 30.
SERVANTS—16, 20, 23, 77, 92, 195, 202.
SHEEP—31, 142; Commons—146.
SHINGLES—135, 182, 191, 193, 195, 196, 197.
SHIRE — Commissioners, 182; Meeting, 182; Town, 114.
SHOEMAKER—50.
SHOP—179.
SINGLE MEN—21.
SLUICE—177.
SMALL CASES—(*see Magistrates.*)
SMITH—The, 38, 47, 50.

SMOOTH PLAIN—21, 29, 40, 73, 76, 84, 97, 108, 111, 167, 180, 201, 204.
SNOW—38, 41.
SOCIETY—1, 2, 20, 22, 23.
SOUTH HILL—89, 91.
SOUTH MEADOW—87, 174, 177, 219.
SOUTH PLAIN—78, 79, 80, 81, 84, 85, 88, 101, 102, 123, 125, 173, 174, 175, 176, 186, 219.
SPARS, 196.
STOCKS—The, 159, 160.
STOP RIVER—141, 215.
STORE-HOUSE—60, 66; (*see Warehouse*)
STOUGHTON'S RAILS—74, 104.
STRANGERS—2, 10, 196.
STRAWBERRY HILL—219.
SUDBURY—201, 202.
SUFFOLK CO. RATES—153.
SURVEYS—43, 60, 85, 92, 124, 156, 157, 165; Surveyors, 52, 53, 54, 57; Surveying, 13, 157.
SWAMP PLAIN—82, 98, 176, 181, 204.
SWAMPS—4, 22, 26, 29, 30, 31, 33, 36, 41, 93, 125, 150, 165.
SWINE—6, 17, 18, 28, 31, 37, 43, 47, 50, 52, 65, 85, 165.

TAXES—(*see Rates*).
TEAMS—9, 113. 122.
TEN ROD TURN—58.
THATCH FOR MEETINGHOUSE—48.
TIMBER—6, 10, 14, 15, 17, 25, 28, 36, 37, 38, 39, 41, 57, 63, 65, 66, 83, 90. 119, 123, 124, 127, 157, 177, 180, 187, 195, 199, 211; Cedar—63, 88, 104, 113, 115, 140, 150, 189, 199; Oak—10, 12, 38, 39, 195, 199, 215; Pine—26, 36, 37, 38, 39, 83, 104, 113.
TITLE TO LAND IN DORCHESTER—136.
TOWN—Clerk, 10, 75, 93, 100, 105, 111, 112, 114, 115, 124. 126; Grant, 94; Land, 92, 105: Meadow. 146, 148, 170; Meetings and Attendance at, 4, 5, 13. 30, 145, 165, 166, 183; Stock, 135; Service, 155; Townsmen, 4, 5, 9, 10, 12, 16, 18, 20, 23, 24, 32, 43, 52, 71, 90, 120, 127, 135, 141, 142, 162, 165, 192, 211, 220; List of Townsmen, 190.
TRADES—92, 123, 124.
TRAINED—Band, 30; Company, 121; Training Ground, 73, 102, 108. 121.
TREASURER—132, 190, 203, 207; (*See also Collector.*)
TREES—14, 15, 25, 26, 29, 36, 60, 62, 63, 66, 78, 96, 126, 127, 140, 184, 196; Cedar, 63, 88, 150; Oak, 12, 15, 39, 119, 195; Pine, 26, 39, 62, 104.
TURKEY ISLAND—171, 173, 174, 175, 177.

UPLAND—5, 13, 29, 56, 94, 127, 133, 166.

VILLAGE GRANTS—126, 162.
VINE BROOK, 71, 81.
VOTERS—List of, 190; Voting, Wheat and Indian Corn, 18; Right of, 135.

INDEX OF SUBJECTS. 237

WAGES—115, 157.
WARDS TO BE SET—29, 31.
WAREHOUSE—59; (*See Storehouse.*)
WARRANT— Concerning License, 48; by Selectmen, 4, 6, 7, 8, 18, 155.
WATCH—29, 31; Watchmen, 134; Watchhouse, 123, 155, 156, 157, 161, 162.
WATER MILLS—29, 51, 79.
WATERS FREE—4, 20, 165.
WATERTOWN—23, 29, 30, 57, 61, 66, 135, 179, 203.
WAYS—51, 57, 85, 112, 114, 131, 138, 157, 163, 164, 169, 170, 194, 201, 202, 203, 213; Cartways, 34, 79, 88, 100, 112, 114, 151, 164, 181, 210; Leading, 79, 195.
WEIGHTS AND MEASURES—131, 157.
WEIRS—Indian, 161.
WEST FIELD—103, 112.

WEST HILL—98, 100.
WEYMOUTH—153.
WHEAT—115; for Bell, 189; and Corn, 18, 115, 187; as Money, 157. 179, 189, 211, 218; for Highway Work, 185; for Town Rate, 201.
WHEELBARROW—22.
WHEELWRIGHT—37, 47.
WIGWAM PLAIN—33, 34, 38, 48, 59, 82, 87, 94, 99, 103, 167, 171, 172, 173, 175, 194.
WILL BEARSTOW'S PLAIN—204.
WOLVES—60, 122, 132, 150, 151, 154, 196, 197, 202, 206, 207, 217.
WOOD—10, 11, 12, 15, 57, 120, 127, 183; Woodlands, 109, 145, 181; Woodreeves, 5, 9, 14, 15, 17, 19, 66, 83, 117, 162, 100, 199.
WOODY HILL—21.

DEDHAM HISTORICAL SOCIETY BUILDING.

CORRECTIONS.

Page 158. Last 5 lines, first column, beginning with Joh Plimpton, with the whole of the second column, were entered on a new page in the original. The numbers against these names represent £, s. and d., and should not have been printed as s. d. q.

Page 189. 10th line. Read Nathaneell, instead of Mathaneell.

www.ingramcontent.com/pod-product-compliance
Lightning Source LLC
Chambersburg PA
CBHW061954180426
43198CB00036B/914